# Single by Chance, Mothers by Choice

# Single by Chance, Mothers by Choice

### How Women Are Choosing Parenthood Without Marriage and Creating the New American Family

ROSANNA HERTZ

OXFORD
UNIVERSITY PRESS
2006

# OXFORD
UNIVERSITY PRESS

Oxford University Press, Inc., publishes works that further
Oxford University's objective of excellence
in research, scholarship, and education.

Oxford   New York
Auckland   Cape Town   Dar es Salaam   Hong Kong   Karachi
Kuala Lumpur   Madrid   Melbourne   Mexico City   Nairobi
New Delhi   Shanghai   Taipei   Toronto

With offices in
Argentina   Austria   Brazil   Chile   Czech Republic   France   Greece
Guatemala   Hungary   Italy   Japan   Poland   Portugal   Singapore
South Korea   Switzerland   Thailand   Turkey   Ukraine   Vietnam

Published by Oxford University Press, Inc.
198 Madison Avenue, New York, New York 10016
www.oup.com

Oxford is a registered trademark of Oxford University Press

Library of Congress Cataloging-in-Publication Data
Hertz, Rosanna.
Single by chance, mothers by choice : how women are choosing
parenthood without marriage and creating the new American
family / Rosanna Hertz.
p.  cm.
ISBN-13: 978-0-19-517990-3
ISBN-10: 0-19-517990-0
1. Family—United States.
2. Single mothers—United States.
3. Middle class women—United States.   I. Title.
HQ536.H48   2006
306.874'3208622—dc22
2006000897

A version of chapter 4 originally appeared in *Symbolic Interaction* 25, 1 (2002): 1–31.

1 3 5 7 9 8 6 4 2
Printed in the United States of America
on acid-free paper

This book is dedicated to Alyssa Raven Hertz Thomas,
who will inherit a world that will still include families.
I will support her decisions, whatever they may be.

# CONTENTS

# PROLOGUE

## Joy McFadden*

I was stuck. By night I dreamt of a grassy yard to romp in with my dogs and blooming trees to lie under. By day I patrolled the gray halls of an aging Boston hospital. Skyrocketing property taxes and a demanding job conspired to keep me pale, cramped, and stuck. And, of course, there was the dull ache that throbbed every time I considered my prospects for marrying and having a family. "Stuck" didn't even begin to describe that. Try "nailed to the floor." I finally understood

---

* All women quoted in the text of the book are identified by pseudonym, and I have changed certain details for some women to protect their identity, such as sex of child, exact occupation, and community of residence. However, income, level of education, race, age, and routes to motherhood are unchanged. Demographic information about each woman, listed alphabetically by first name, can be found in appendix 1.

The first-person vignettes that open the prologue and various chapters are not verbatim accounts from the women's interview transcripts. I wrote these vignettes drawing upon the information and stories the women told me. Two of the opening vignettes are composites of several women with similar stories; they resembled each other closely enough that I merged them to create one story. Further, without blurring stories in this way, these particular women would have been too easily identified.

Apart from the opening vignettes, all of the quotes in the body of each chapter are taken directly from the interview transcripts of a single woman, the one whose pseudonym accompanies the quotation.

something I'd heard my father mumble after an especially trying day: "You're damned if you do and damned if you don't."

In the spring of 1995, I finally mustered the strength to pry myself loose. I bought a house with a yard and trees twenty minutes from the hospital. What more could I ask for? Even before I unpacked, I remember seeing a small crowd of people two doors down the street. They were clustered around tables decorated with colorful streamers and balloons. The smoking barbecues told me it was a block party. I wandered over. Adults introduced themselves while I snacked on chips and salsa. Before long I gave up trying to figure out who lived where and with whom and whether the kids being pointed out were their children or their stepchildren, from the first marriage or the second, and who was straight, gay, or whatever. What I really remember was the surprise I felt as that stuck feeling snuck up again and grabbed me as I walked back to my own house alone.

I began to think about single motherhood seriously in my mid-thirties. My friends would tell me what a terrific parent I would make, and I guess I agreed. But the missing ingredient was a relationship. I didn't have prospects of getting married. Dates became more infrequent as my girlfriends ran out of men to introduce me to—that was the way I used to meet men. The last of my friends seemed to be getting married just to have children. It wasn't clear to me that these relationships were going to be long-lasting ones because the goal didn't necessarily seem to be to find a soul mate—someone to be happy with for the rest of your life. But instead it was "My biological clock is ticking and I need to have a child" and "I can't do it without having somebody." I felt that wasn't the right decision for me. To look for a man to father a child, as opposed to looking for someone who would be right for me, wasn't the same decision. A new crop of men appeared on the dating scene: divorced with children. They were looking for companions, but they didn't want more children. I couldn't make these kinds of marriage compromises.

I realized that if I didn't do something soon, I would remain everybody's favorite aunt. I would always regret never having tried to have children. Whereas if I took the plunge and tried to do it myself, however hard that would turn out to be, I couldn't imagine regretting becoming a mom. Work had never been enough. But I wondered: could I have a career and a child without a man?

I chose the occasion of a Sunday dinner to reveal my plan to my parents. It was important to me to have my parents' approval. My mom is a good sounding board, and she always makes me feel okay about my decisions. She'd stopped asking me about my social life years ago. Every once in a while I told her that I wondered if I would ever meet a man to marry, and even though she didn't have to say it to me, I knew she was concerned that I would never be a mom. As the quintessential homemaker, her kids were her whole life.

That particular evening I approached my mom with a career situation because it seemed easier than blurting out what was really on my mind. I wasn't sure how my mom would react to my secret. We started our usual kitchen talk with the job offer I'd received that week. We were talking about "Should I do it?

Shouldn't I?" and I said, "Well, the money is a little better, the hours aren't quite as good, I'd be more in demand," and then I added, "You know, I guess one piece of the decision has to do with whether I have decided for sure that I will never have kids."

She put up her hand and said, "Well, I hope you haven't decided that."

I blanched. I had to sit down and set aside the vegetable peeler. I calmed down and said, "Well, as a matter of fact, I've been thinking about having a baby. I can't wait for a man anymore."

Surprisingly to me, because my mother is really rather conservative, especially in terms of social issues, she was very supportive of the idea. At first my mom looked startled by her own words of support, but then she smiled. She said, "I really think you'll be a terrific mother. And I want you to have a child. I don't want you to miss out on the best part of life and the most important part of being a woman." I bit my lip at the last part. This was not the time to debate generational differences. Moreover, I felt terrific that she took what I was saying so well. While I stood there a bit dumbfounded, she refilled our wineglasses. We toasted my future.

My mom told the news to my dad that evening after I had gone home. Even though I'd always talked to him about work, this was not something I felt I could tell him directly. She called me later and reported, "Your father was really shocked."

"Well," I said, "frankly, I'm less surprised about that than I am that you weren't."

And then my mom said, "He walked out of the room, and then walked back two minutes later and said, 'I could be a grandfather again.'" That was that. He was fully behind the idea after that point. And I began to feel more settled with the idea of becoming a mom on my own. I passed up the job offer.

I'd decided early on that I wanted the pleasure of actually going through a pregnancy. But I knew I needed to think carefully about whether I should try to know who was going to be the father. I asked a couple of male friends to be sperm donors, and when two agreed, I was inclined to have a known donor. My cousin, however, pointed out the possible legal risks a known donor could present, and I have to admit that chilled me. But I was not willing to totally reject the idea. I came up with an interesting alternative: a quasi-known donor. Since two male friends had volunteered, I would mix their sperm together—not unlike what I'd heard infertile couples sometimes do when the husband has a fertility problem. As a medical professional, I knew that a DNA test could ultimately tell who the genetic father was, but at least for a while I would have the benefit of knowing who the men were without involving them beyond their obvious contributions.

Still, my cousin's legal caution haunted me. And in the end, I could not imagine having a known donor who was not also a dad to my child. So I decided upon an anonymous donor. The only place for me to find an anonymous donor and be inseminated at the same time was an infertility clinic. I felt slightly out of place among the infertile couples, because while I did not have a man to become pregnant by, there was no indication that I had fertility problems. After three tries, a miscarriage, and then another try, I became pregnant.

Six weeks after the birth of my daughter I had the first thoughts of having a second child. I was taking a walk, it was a lovely summer day, I was pushing her along in her stroller. And I was thinking to myself, looking down at this absolutely gorgeous baby: "This was supposed to be the be-all and end-all event. This was supposed to complete my life. Whatever else happened, it was going to be perfect to have been blessed to have had this one child." And I looked down and I said, "You know, I adore you, but if the world were a different place, I would have many more of you." It was clear to me that I would obviously never do this again, unless this time I happened to meet somebody and marry before the time frame ran out when I could do it physically.

I actually had never particularly put aside the idea of finding somebody, my thought being that without a time pressure there was more likelihood. And of course, anyone that I would meet would have to love kids anyway, so what difference would it make that there was already a child? So I said, "Well, of course, I can't do this again by myself." And that's the end of that.

Just before my fortieth birthday I returned to the infertility clinic. Finding a man to marry had still not happened. I knew I had the energy for a second child. So why not? I wanted my daughter to have a brother or a sister to give her more family.

The infertility clinic told me that they usually advise couples to put away additional sperm from the original donor for a second child. But because I was a single woman no one had thought to recommend this. The original donor was unavailable and for a few fleeting moments I thought, "Gee, they will only be half siblings," but then I said to myself, "It doesn't make any difference. I will only try for six months. Not very likely." Well, this time I became pregnant on the first try.

When I brought the baby home from the hospital my daughter, then almost four years old, came over and said, "Can I give you a hug?" And I said sure. And she said, "How about a family hug?" So she hugged both of us and she said, "You know, Mom, now we're a family." So for her, it was somehow the addition of a second child that really made a big difference. I, too, felt my family was now complete.

### Claudia D'Angelo

I couldn't commit or the men I dated couldn't commit to me. I could have married at age twenty-three. I was in a very serious relationship in college and had a boyfriend and we talked about getting married. He lived in Minneapolis and wanted me to move there, but I was terrified. I just wasn't ready to make this commitment. Besides, I wasn't ready to follow a man anywhere. I watched my mom follow my dad around throughout my whole childhood. The way my mom coped was to have another kid with every move. By the time we moved to Idaho I was eight years old and Mom was pregnant for the fourth time. We were there five years. Everything was going to be gravy. We kids all had close friends. My two older brothers were playing high school football. We never missed a game. My youngest sister had just gotten into grade school, staying until three in the afternoon, and my mother went back to teach at the grade school, which was close to our house. Our house was paid off. And then my father was restless and asked his company to transfer him to Arizona. When the transfer came through he told us at dinner. He didn't even ask her or think about us kids; he just did it. I remember my mother being very upset. She did not want to move again, and neither did any of us. I was really angry with my father. It was the only time I ever saw my mother cry. So one summer we were just gone.

And that's just it about men and commitment. I think there were certain things about my parents' marriage that bugged me, that I was sort of turned off by. Which is that even though my father and my mother really have a lot of respect for each other, my father is obviously the power. Not that I understood male privilege at the time—I just remember seeing my mother so upset and not understanding why there was nothing she could do about it. And I lost a lot of friends with each move. No one cared that this was really tough for me, to have to start all over. Even though there was a silver lining in that these moves probably made me closer to my brothers and sisters, I remember really disliking my father at that time.

So when I think about why I'm not married, sometimes I wonder if this isn't part of the reason. Maybe part of it was growing up in the beginning of feminism in the 1960s and early 1970s, so by time I was in college I was hearing a lot of feminist messages. To a certain extent what a lot of those messages distilled down to was "Don't get married."

But that message didn't stop me from dating. I had a series of relationships with men that didn't work out for one reason or the other. I kept hoping the next relationship would be different. At thirty-six I began to think seriously about the pulls that seemed to dominate my life: I felt equal pulls to be in a relationship and to be a mother. So if I was in a relationship that felt satisfying, it was hard to extricate myself and say, "Okay, now I'm going to be sensible and break up sooner rather than later because I already know that this relationship isn't going to last. And since I've had this other desire, I'm going to go and have a child." And as I got older, the men already had children or clearly didn't want them. I was trying to run two races and I was winning neither.

At that time, my mother started having health problems, major heart issues. I think she was really concerned that she wasn't going to make it after almost dying on the operating table. Still groggy and in intensive care, I can almost remember her exact words because her frankness startled me so much. She said, "I just want to tell you something. Your father would kill me if he knew I was saying this, but my having children meant so much to me that I don't care if you don't get married. You may not want to be married. But you should have a kid." I tucked my mother's confession away. Maybe I should have told her then how much I wanted a child. But the scene at the hospital just choked me up too much. No words came out to comfort her on this subject. . . .

It took me nine years to finally put in the adoption paperwork. And the reason I did it then was because I had reached an age deadline, a cutoff point where the local agencies wouldn't consider me anymore. When I told my parents I had finished the paperwork, they were very nervous about it. When my mom revealed how much she wanted me to be a mom, I don't think she had adoption in mind—for her, the biological thing was really deep.

A few weeks after putting the paperwork in, I met Carl. I told him on the first date I had with him that I really was attracted to him. And I remember thinking to myself, "If I tell him I'm planning to adopt, that will be it." And then I thought, "I have to tell him. Have to tell him right away. This is me." So I did. And he was interested in me. So he stayed with me. But he made it clear that he did not want to be a father to another child. He was divorced and raising his two children and that was enough for him. He stayed with me and we fell in love.

At that time, a baby was just a possibility. Who knew how long it would take or if I'd ever get one. However, a few months later I got a letter saying that I would be getting this toddler in six months! I asked a close friend to travel with me to bring home my son. For all my parents' concern, they absolutely fell in love with him.

That was six years ago. Carl and I don't live together, although we're very committed to each other. Still, I don't feel like I've found my perfect mate. And maybe I'm screwed up because I'm looking for a perfect mate. You know?

The first year I had my son, William, it was almost like the relationship with Carl was on hold. It was still there even though the logistics of being together was hard; we'd manage to find a weekend night to ourselves or Carl might stop over to have dinner with William and me. But I needed that intense time for William, and Carl was busy with teenage kids of his own. Carl has always been a part of William's life. He didn't say he didn't want anything to do with the child. He just didn't want to be a father to him. . . .

Now we're in contact every day. We may go a week without seeing each other, but we see each other on the weekend. I feel like I have two lives. In one I'm very much a single mother. And then when I'm with Carl, at times I feel like I'm really part of a couple.

# INTRODUCTION

First comes love. Then comes marriage. Then comes baby in a baby carriage. Or maybe not. Suppose love falters or a marriage dissolves or a careerist lifts her head momentarily in the mad dash to professional success only to notice that she's all alone. What then? What about baby? Does the progression halt, leaving a woman (or a man, for that matter) stuck forever in a liminal state, alone and childless with no clear prospects for a baby, a family?

Apparently not: in 2005, single moms head a fast-growing category of family. And they are the subject of constant public debate. One out of every three children today is born to an unmarried mother.[1] While popular belief paints these single mothers as young and poor, not all are in their teens and on welfare. In fact, only 25 percent of all nonmarital births occur to teenagers.[2] Moreover, the percentage of births to unmarried women over thirty years old *doubled* between 1970 and 1993, declining slightly to 12 percent as of 2004.[3] And these statistics do not include single-mother families created through adoption.

This book is about women are who single by chance and mothers by choice.[4] They are among the growing segment of women with jobs, often high-paying professional ones, who have elected to bypass the storied progression from love to marriage to motherhood. They have taken matters into their own hands, as it were, to fulfill a familiar dream in an unfamiliar way.

Just who are these single moms? Why did they reverse the traditional order of love, marriage, and children? Where are the partners in their lives? Are the families they're forming transient phenomena—detours, as it were, around temporary roadblocks to a more conventional arrangement? Or is the mother-child pair a finished family?

To answer these questions, I interviewed sixty-five women in depth, asking them about motherhood, men, and how they manage their lives and families as single mothers. I deliberately sought out women who had taken a range of paths to motherhood because I was well aware that there are other ways to have children besides accidental pregnancy. Thus I talked with women who bought anonymous sperm from fertility banks and others who had called upon men they knew to donate sperm. I discussed becoming a mother with women who adopted from all over the world, as well as those who chanced pregnancy, sometimes calling motherhood an accident. Finally, because I wondered just how durable their improvised families were, I called them back years later, in winter 2005, for an update.[5] I asked them how their lives had changed. The surprising things I learned are recounted in this book, where I explore single moms and their families sequentially: from their prehistories as unattached women through the critical factors they incorporate into their decision making, their routes to motherhood, and building a family. Suffice it to say here that these women give us a unique window on the future of family.

As interesting as it is to learn who these women are, it's surprising to find out who they are not. Given that they matured in an era of dramatic change—feminist struggle, rapid advances in reproductive technology, accessible labor markets—it might be reasonable to expect that the kind of woman who chose pregnancy without a marital partner would be at the leading edge of a women's movement. Indeed, as I began the research I suspected that I would find women actively involved in creating new work relationships, publicly announcing their decisions without a lick of defensiveness, and advocating a new language of family roles and relationships.

What I found, however, was something quite different. Instead of ideologists, I found women who blend easily into their communities and who, because they are self-supporting, do not get—and do not seek—the attention of government agencies. They are neither the older woman who missed motherhood to have a career nor the teenager who happened upon it too soon.[6] While they might have more in common with the former than the latter, they are not regretful careerists lamenting the lack of children. These women did not forget about motherhood, and neither did they let it slip away. These women cover a wide range in age, from older ones who waited for their last moments of fertility and sometimes even the end of their eligibility as adoptive mothers to younger women who did not put motherhood off and took advantage of sperm banks, turkey basters, and other reproductive technologies as well as chanced pregnancy.

They are our neighbors and co-workers, literally the girl next door, a sister or a sister-in-law, and we may have listened as they struggled with what they should do. Or they may be ourselves, either having already embarked upon single motherhood or seriously contemplating it. Instead of mothers who wore their singlehood as a badge of honor, I found a category of women who denied that they were at the leading edge of anything and who assiduously shunned the spotlight. They aspired to acceptance in a middle-class milieu and alignment with conventional definitions of mother, child, and family. At the same time, they often concealed the decisions they made, except to the closest of kin and friends. Most preferred anonymity precisely because their decisions bent gender norms to the breaking point. Some chose routes to motherhood, such as adoption, that concealed their agency in a shroud of altruism—for example, taking on an "unwanted" child is an unselfish act in the eyes of society. Others chanced pregnancy, often telling their partners they were doing so. And then there is the group that selected donor-assisted routes to motherhood. Yet regardless of the route they chose, these women all wanted children. They may have been silent, but they were hardly passive actors.

These women are both straightforward and paradoxical. Having tossed out the rulebook in order to become mothers, they nonetheless adhere to time-honored rules about child rearing, ones that are rooted in dominant notions of the nuclear family. For example, once children arrive, women strive to reconcile the route they took to pregnancy with myth and folklore about the role of genetics in child development and family life. Women who use sperm from an unknown donor often start out assuming that nurture will trump nature, but over years of watching their children, many end up building a case for the power of genetics. Because all they know about the donor is what he jotted down on a form at the sperm bank, single moms end up crafting speculative biographies in order to explain the origins of a child's temperament and talents. Similarly, women simultaneously protect themselves and their children from claims of the father (or birth parents) and seek out functional substitutes for the father—such as strong relationships with the men in their families (including grandfathers, uncles, and cousins), male teachers, coaches, and close family friends—in order to conform to middle-class notions of the "right" family environment for a child.

Part I focuses on how women move from contemplation to action. How does a woman decide to become a single mother? How do personal story and social history intersect to enable these women to pursue their dream for motherhood without marriage? Facing alternative routes to pregnancy, how do women decide which one to choose? This section of the book demonstrates that choosing motherhood alone is a complicated process, one in which women engineer ways to counter existing laws and use medical technology, neither of which was meant to address their circumstances.

Part II explores how fathers fit into these families and how the families fit into the world around them. It still takes a man to make a child. So, once children arrive, what becomes of these men? Are they lost and forgotten, or do they have a place in these families? How do women who settle on using donor sperm involve the genetic father of their child, whether he is physically present or not? For women who chance pregnancy, how do they monitor men and negotiate the law's expectations of fathers? How do women who adopt negotiate identity and geographic location as they fit children and birth parents into their families? In Part II, women confront the borders and boundaries of family, wading through the confusion surrounding genetic and social kinship in America, unable to ignore either.

Part III examines how these mother-child families navigate daily life. What does it mean to be single in terms of romance and parenting? How do women juggle earning a paycheck and parenting their children? What creative ways have women devised to shore up these families? Finally, beyond fathers, how do women incorporate men and gender into their child-centered families? In this part we learn how the mother-child pair centers itself in a constellation of connections to others, finding love, providing other sets of hands for help, and creating chosen family.

The bottom line of this book is clear: we can no longer deny that the core of family life is the mother and her children. Marriage was once the only socially sanctioned way to have a child, just as sex was once coupled with procreation. Even though it still takes both sexes to create a baby, only the availability of both sets of gametes is essential. This sea change is rendering sexual intimacy between husbands and wives obsolete as *the* critical familial bond. One story from many in this book captures the essence of the changes taking place: Heather Johnson and her lover, Mike, enjoyed a caring and satisfying physical relationship. She, however, wanted children, and he was adamantly opposed. She deemed his reluctance unfair but had little hope of changing his mind. After months of talking, he agreed to donate his sperm but forswore any interest in being a dad if Heather conceived. For both Heather and Mike, the child was an entirely separate matter. To take another example, Nadine Margolis created a donor-assisted family, but only she is the caring and loving parent to the child. While this begs the question of where men fit in, it is the reality of the new family, built on the assumption that romantic ties are no longer the foundation of family life. Caregiving and nurturing, which have always long been the responsibility of women, are at the center of U.S. family life in the twenty-first century. This book explores the intricacies of middle-class single motherhood and the reconstruction of the family, with or without men.

\* \* \*

I am grateful to Wellesley College for its commitment to a world-class student body. This project has benefited from Wellesley's undergraduates who worked on parts of this research in various capacities. Wellesley College's generous research award, the Luella LaMer Chair Funds, and the National Science Foundation under grant number SES-0353604 have been critical in my ability to hire these (now former) students. I especially thank Christina Lapointe-Nelson, Jennifer M. Silva, Nina Botto, Lyle Cates Pannell, Emma Sydenham, and Kara Gooding, who worked on different parts of this book in varying capacities. I also thank the women in my seminar in 2004 and 2005 for reading parts of the manuscript, especially for their thought-provoking political views on single motherhood. Any opinions, findings, conclusions, or recommendations expressed in this material are mine and do not necessarily reflect the views of Wellesley College, NSF, my former students or my colleagues.

Jennifer O'Donnell deserves special mention. Her organization, enthusiasm, and creative input in reworking the manuscript during this last year pushed me to finally complete this project. When I began this project, Faith I. T. Ferguson, then a graduate student (also a Wellesley alum), interviewed half of the initial group of women. She wrote her dissertation on part of these interviews. She is an outstanding interviewer whose colleagueship shaped the first years of this project.

I have benefited enormously from a small group of sociologists who have made up a virtual scholarly community. I thank Kathy Charmaz, Jane Hood, Peter K. Manning, Jane Attanucci, Robert Alford, Marjorie DeVault, Naomi Gerstel, and Kathleen Gerson for reading various chapters and parts of this work along the way. I am especially grateful to Anita Garey and Karen Hansen, who read several drafts of parts of the final manuscript and whose colleagueship over these last years has been invaluable. I thank Susan Reverby, my women's studies colleagues, and the members of the Feminist Inquiry reading group, who have listened to bits of research talk wedged between other college agendas. Wellesley College professor Dennis Smith clarified my futurist biology questions. The expertise of colleagues Esther Iwanaga and Jessica Irish in the final stages of manuscript work was invaluable. Cherie Potts has been a key player in my interview studies. She expertly transcribed the audiotapes on each woman. Pierre Chiha took the author photo.

My friends and family can't wait for this project to be over. They have passed along media articles, listened to me talk about why these women's stories should be told, and even suggested women they'd met in the course of their lives and thought I might want to interview. As some of their own family members decided to become single moms, the subject of single moms became part of the dinner conversation in a way that was not simply an exercise in our usual work banter. I thank them for cheering me on from the sidelines, and I apologize in print for my need to say, "I can't go out—I have to finish this book."

I approached Dedi Felman, my editor at Oxford, with this project. I wanted to work with her again, as she is the only editor at several presses that I have worked with who actually reads, comments on, and critiques what I write. She does so with great energy numerous times over multiple drafts. Dedi's sage advice, copious notes, and ideas have made this a clearer, richer, and more engaging book. I also thank the first-rate production team at Oxford, including Michele Bové, Sue Warga, Lelia Mander, and Betsy DeJesu.

Finally, my family is the cornerstone of my life's work. Alyssa Raven Thomas, my daughter, was in kindergarten when this project began. She has grown up with this project as background to her own life. Her insight and questions to me about this study have always given me pause. Alyssa has become an incredible writer, helping me make editorial decisions including finding just the right word.

Bob Thomas is the best sociologist I know. His gift to see clearly the main points of an argument is in every chapter in this book. He has always shared his insights freely, caring more about how to make a project reach its best presentation than about reserving credit. This is the mark of a great colleague. Bob also continues to believe in the old adage that hard work pays off. He pushed me to work hard and to persevere. I thank him especially for telling me the truth on each chapter. Despite his own work schedule and book writing, he always takes the time from his work life for our life together. We made a perfect decision some twenty-two years ago!

Finally, I thank the women who told me their stories. They wanted me to get it right, and several who wish to remain anonymous read parts to make sure that I understood. I was most encouraged by their generosity when out of the blue last January I called the women I had interviewed and asked for updates on their lives. They can't wait to celebrate this publication. I appreciate all that they have shared with me, from their most personal soul-searching to great laughter over the twists and turns in all our lives.

# *Part I*
# The Big Decision

# 1

## "WHY CAN'T I HAVE
## WHAT I WANT?"

*Stuck*. Virtually every woman I interviewed expressed the feeling. Something conspired to disrupt the trajectory of love to marriage to children. Joy, whose story opened the prologue, pointed the finger at her demanding job and a shortage of candidates in the marriage market. She declared herself unwilling to settle for her girlfriends' compromises: a marriage arrived at to serve other ends. Claudia, also featured in the prologue, acknowledged her tug-of-war between independence and intimacy and the difficulties it caused her in her relationships with men. She worried about marriage transforming her independence into narrowed opportunities, as it had for her mother. And when she did become involved with a man, he didn't share her desire for children.

In some instances, being stuck meant being mired hip deep in a bog of commitments and bereft of energy or time to search for alternatives. For the vast majority of women I interviewed, however, being stuck was a dynamic thing, like Claudia's tug-of-war. That is, there was a great deal of energy expended by opposing forces—some internal and deeply personal, many external and broadly observable—but the net effect was no movement. It might appear to outsiders as motionlessness, passivity, or even resignation. But, listening to women such as Claudia and Joy, I clearly got the sense that although it may have been enervating, it was rarely passive.

What are the opposing forces that keep women stuck? Middle-class women, I found, are caught between a battered but resilient ideology of marriage-then-motherhood and the experience of independence and self-fulfillment in a workplace that poses fewer barriers to women than previously. In the late 1970s, when at least half the women I interviewed reached the age of majority, women stopped sporting engagement rings at college graduation and started brandishing their degrees, which galvanized them as agents of change. As they took to heart the expectation for equality in the workplace, middle-class women no longer had to strike a risky bargain with men to achieve economic stability in their adult lives.[1] Marriage receded in importance as women had other options and a greater range of opportunities for defining themselves in the world. While women did not stop seeking marriage, simply the fact that it no longer was an immediate mandate changed its meaning in these women's lives. Their expectations for the institution were transformed as the need for a man for economic security and social stability fell away, leaving only the idealized image of marriage for love.[2]

Unlike generations of middle-class women before them who believed their fate was either marriage and motherhood or spinsterhood and career, these women always expected they would have both.[3] Second-wave feminism had great impact. Women willingly took their places alongside men in graduate school and the workplace. However, entering the workforce was not a decision to give up motherhood or marriage—quite the contrary. Most women heard messages like the one Susan did:

> I felt like everyone was saying to me hurry up and get married—my parents in particular. As proud as they were of my work accomplishments, they would call me up and say, "So, how is the *male* situation?" and I would say, "There is no *mail* strike in Chicago. Is there one at home?" It was my way of dancing around the question. What they really wanted was to become grandparents. And clearly a man and marriage was the only route.

As much as this quote captured a clever way of answering her parents, the play with words was a sticking point. Though she was expected to marry and become a mother, there was no man. She knew that employment, even for a professional woman, was not a substitute for family. In short, middle-class women still clung to the belief that marriage was an essential credential for motherhood.

While some scholars suggested that it would be difficult to have children and continue to be employed simultaneously, and some early second-wave feminists argued that family obligations to nurture children would make competing equally with male peers difficult, neither scholars nor activists urged women to give up children entirely. Ironically, feminism never seemed to need to reject motherhood, focusing instead on women's achievement outside the home. Academics, by contrast, argued that it was possible to have it all, but maybe it would be easier to have baby and career sequentially; marriage and heterosexuality were taken for granted.

Despite social change, compulsory motherhood—the taken-for-granted belief that all women aspire to having children as part of deep biological programming—remains a critical part of women's value to society.[4] Compulsory motherhood is a truly hegemonic concept, so deeply ingrained by cultural beliefs that it is rarely challenged. The belief that all women must want to become mothers as a fundamental part of being a woman is also a powerful form of social control.[5] But the social component of motherhood, as much as biology, is often the driving force behind the decision to have kids. Susan, quoted above, knew that her parents wanted to be grandparents in order to continue kinship into the next generation. This kind of pressure to become a mother from either one's parents or society at large is not unusual. For middle-class women, the concept of compulsory motherhood reinforces marriage as the prerequisite for becoming a mother.[6]

As women's achievements render them ever more independent, this ideology of compulsory motherhood continues to be reinforced, both by women who never renounced motherhood and by the broader culture that continues to reinforce motherhood as primary to defining women. In short, womanhood remains defined not by workplace achievement but by parenthood: real womanhood is not defined by being a surgeon, but it is questioned if one is not a mother.[7]

Compulsory motherhood has strengthened its hold as new reproductive technologies and the globalization of adoption have put children within every woman's reach. Further, children transform women's lives, not only making them mothers but also bestowing upon them a new kind of status. Motherhood has always been a critical status worthy of achievement. In preindustrial times, children were necessary family laborers. Now they are "economically worthless but emotionally priceless."[8] The combination of priceless children and the tenacity of compulsory motherhood's hold on women is the driving force behind many women's intense desire for children, a desire that collides with the reality of their independent lives. In order to defuse this conflict, women must form a new kind of family, of which mother and child form the core, as they try to make sense of the gradual dissolution of the nuclear family.

## The Tacit Agreement That Fell Apart: Marriage Post-Employment

Joy and Claudia represent the two-thirds of women in this study who are middle-class. These women grew up imagining white picket fences and perfect children. They worked hard in school with the goal of going to college, even though they did not necessarily anticipate lifelong careers. Everyone assumed they would settle down and raise a family. In their families, men would be the providers.

However, Joy and Claudia found themselves in a time of enormous flux when they graduated from college in the mid- to late 1970s. As young women in their early twenties, they were in the midst of a rapid expansion of employment opportunities and an influential women's liberation movement. Most parents—even conservative ones—encouraged their daughters to be "whatever they wanted to be." Family and marriage were put on hold as exciting job opportunities arose and young women started to bring home a paycheck. Joy and Claudia were genuinely surprised by how much they enjoyed their independence. They liked making decisions about how to spend the money they earned, and they reveled in the many different ways they could shape their lives as self-sufficient women.

The irony, they discovered, was that although they had been raised to follow in the footsteps of their mothers, they were actually imitating their fathers. Dads were pivotal and yet problematic influences in their lives.[9] Mothers were typically subjected to husbands who were authority figures in the family and whose work lives determined the mother's (and children's) home life. Yet daughters remember dads as encouraging them to follow their dreams, including finding satisfaction and status through employment. In their daughter's memories, dads were both liberators and oppressors: they opened the doors of opportunity for their daughters, but their work lives depended upon wives' subordination to their needs.

By contrast, women with working-class origins usually came from dual-earner families. Working-class moms rarely left the labor force except when their children were babies, and even then some were employed. Even though their parents may have only completed high school, these daughters were likely to have some college education. Unlike the middle-class pattern in which the wives stayed home and raised their families until the youngest child was entering high school, working-class daughters watched their mothers bring home a paycheck even if the hours they worked made it appear that they were waiting at home for the school bus.[10]

For example, when Abby was growing up, her dad, upon returning home from his construction job, would sit in the living room watching TV, his reward for a long day. Her mom, on the other hand, rushed back from her nursing shift to prepare dinner while Abby and her preteen sister peppered her with questions about carpool arrangements, weekend plans with friends, and math homework. Dinner was always on the table on time, but as Abby grew older she noted that her mom also had worked all day. Abby loved her mother but never could stand how her mother allowed her father to sit and not help every night. The women in this study witnessed their mothers' resigned acceptance of a seemingly immutable status quo; more than one shook her head in disbelief at the signs of exhaustion their mothers often displayed. Women who came from working-class backgrounds were at one and the same time proud of their mothers' employment achievements and sad that it was their mothers who were doubly burdened with keeping family life together.

Women, regardless of social class origins, admired and appreciated the loving home that their parents created; however, they did not want this same gendered arrangement for themselves in the future.[11] They could not sustain a charade in which they minimized their outside employment in order to perpetuate the ideal of the husband as the primary provider. Often, women found that the men they dated voiced the rhetoric of equality but did not follow it in practice. These women worried that unless they redefined marriage, their husband's employment would slowly overshadow their own and they would become their mothers. Women in this study were too committed to pursuing their employment and independence to let that happen.

## A PAYCHECK OF ONE'S OWN

The surge of importance employment took on for the women in this study is not without context. Second-wave feminism, emerging in the 1960s and 1970s, emphasized the struggle for equal opportunity. Focusing on the transformation of social structures, including law, education, and employment, second-wave feminism sought to change and expand all aspects of women's and men's lives. By integrating both workplaces and educational institutions across the social spectrum, women could achieve parity with men in the economic sphere.[12] Supported by legislation and enforced by subsequent legal battles, women made their way into the workforce in numbers unknown to previous generations. As a result of the expanding economy, the labor force was able to accommodate the influx of these new employees. A few of the oldest women in this study, who had been the first to achieve in the workplace, spoke of a strong attachment to feminism. Mostly, however, these women were free riders, reaping the benefits of feminist activism without feeling part of the movement themselves. They attended college and established their careers in a time of economic expansion when equality was already mandated and enforced. In essence, they no longer had to settle for good-enough opportunities.

Although higher education and workplace norms have changed to reflect new legislation, the social revolution initiated by women's entry into the economy seems to have stalled at the threshold of the home.[13] Husbands have continued serving as main providers and wives as primary caretakers, even if breadwinning is an increasingly shared endeavor.[14] While division of labor in the workplace can be resolved through government regulation, the politics of family life have remained outside the realm of government intervention.

The majority of the women I interviewed described themselves as having been strongly committed to work prior to motherhood.[15] They have occupations as diverse as lawyers, managers, consultants, waitresses, and aerobics instructors. Many work in the service sector in feminized occupations (such as nurses, secretaries, social workers, and elementary school teachers). Others work in major corporate, university, and nonprofit settings as managers, professors, and lawyers. A smaller group is self-employed, including small-business owners, writers, Web designers, and contract workers for corporations and hospitals. Annette, a senior manager with a local high-tech firm, described with pride her rapid rise in the company's ranks in the early to mid-1980s after completing her MBA:

> I was working for a company that I had been with for six years, that I had grown up with, that I had gone from being an entry-level programmer to a senior programmer, a project leader and a manager, a director. My career developed

there and my identity was my work. I kept getting promoted and with each promotion I continued my pace. I reached a pretty lofty position and then the company was bought.

Likewise, Abby, who has master's degrees in both educational administration and educational psychology, threw herself into her work as an elementary school teacher, winning awards for her innovative style. Abby dreamed of moving up the ladder, too:

> I teach gifted and talented children and I love working with young children, particularly troubled kids. I put in extra time developing a new curriculum. I was always working on making myself as a teacher more child-friendly. . . . Still, I saw that in the schools where I worked, there was a good chance that both of the principalships were going to turn over. I was interested in it. I wanted to move up. So I went back to get certified to be a principal.

Both Annette and Abby received great personal satisfaction from their workplace accomplishments, but they, like Leigh, a journalist groomed for the national stage, marveled at how they had gotten so ensnared in the rush to status that they lost track of their plans for motherhood. Leigh explained:

> It was an era where we were constantly reading about the first woman lawyer to do this, the first woman to become senior VP at that. And there was very little discussion about motherhood. Now, when I got into my late thirties and began looking back even then and thinking, "Why didn't I do some of these things? Why didn't I think more about having children?" Then of course you get into that thinking, "Well, was the message right?" But motherhood just wasn't on my radar screen. It just wasn't.

Akin to the factory workers whom sociologist Michael Burawoy studied in his 1979 book *Manufacturing Consent*, these women got so caught up in the intricate game—being first, being fastest, making out—that they unconsciously embraced, at least in the first few years after college, the male model of careerism before they felt the pressure to either get out or rebel.

Besides employment, the living arrangements of women I interviewed represented a significant departure from the past—a departure made possible by the combination of economic and legislative changes. For example, nearly half of the women in this study owned property, and the vast majority of that group received income from renting space. Joy rented alone, close to her job, and then bought a house in the suburbs. After college Claudia moved into a triple-decker (three-family house) with her girlfriends. When Claudia's landlord decided to sell, her father encouraged her to buy the property, financing it through the rent she collected from the other two units. As important as the condition of the real estate market was at that time, Claudia benefited from the fact that banks had begun extending credit to women to buy houses on their own. This, by itself, separated Claudia from the women of her mother's generation, who rarely had established credit histories of their own.

## The Baby or the Bathwater: Tossing Out Marriage but Keeping Motherhood

These women still considered marriage as essential to motherhood. Thus before considering motherhood, they had to confront marriage. The belief that it takes a partner to have a child was a cultural mandate that even these successful women were unable to ignore. Most busied themselves with work, hoping the right partner would materialize and start the sequence. But as marriage was transformed by women's employment, women no longer depended on husbands for economic survival. As marriage became less of a risky exchange of economic security for homemaking, women sought marriage in its idealized form—two people joined by love, forsaking the pragmatic arrangements that formerly characterized the institution. Put simply, women raised the bar for marriage. It started on the first date—women no longer let men pick up the dinner check, and they expected good conversation and respect to escalate to intimacy. As a result of women's diminishing need for marriage, they were more fully able to invest in the romanticized vision of the institution, in which the magic of love overshadows more practical considerations.[16]

Claudia, who shared similar experiences with many of the other single moms in this study, talked about how she wanted to experience life before settling down. She wanted to take things on her own terms. She couldn't fathom moving out of her college dorm to follow a boyfriend who had entered graduate school. In her words, "the relationship had potential but the timing was off." Timing, I was told repeatedly, was critical to forming intimate and lasting relationships. Timing was not simply a matter of finding the right person. Both people had to be ready to commit, and not just to a relationship but also to a future that included marriage and children. Lily, age thirty-nine and with a one-year-old conceived through anonymous donor insemination, described succinctly what for her turned out to be nearly two decades of bad timing and weak commitments:

> The way I look at it in a nutshell is that in my twenties, I wasn't ready. In my thirties I was. I dated three men in my thirties. The first one wasn't ready to get married; I would have married him, wise or unwise. The second one I would have married, but he said, "You're the most wonderful woman I've ever dated, but I'm not in love with you." And the third one I definitely expected to marry. I was like, "Oh, I'm glad the other two didn't work because this is the one for me." And he wasn't ready. He said he was, and then once I got on board, that totally changed things for him, and he couldn't take it.

Like Claudia, Lily felt she had time on her side. She was convinced that a much better prospect was just around the corner. Her optimism was buttressed by the fact that her search did not have to be confined to a small community such as her hometown or fraternity/sorority house on a college campus; now the possibilities seemed to extend infinitely (including the Internet). This is not to say that these women, heterosexual or lesbian, lacked in relationships. The overwhelming majority described long-lasting and, in many instances, very fulfilling commitments. But in every instance, whether the relationship was simply romantic or included cohabitation, marriage, or partnership, circumstances conspired to stop things short of the full package—commitment with children. Nearly a quarter of the women had been married, but their relationships, on average, lasted just over a year, and only two children in this study were born from those marriages. Another quarter of the women, including both gay and straight women, had cohabited; though the partners' split may not have been solely about having children together, these breakups often occurred when talk of children turned serious.[17]

Men's ambivalence about commitment loomed large in women's accounts, and a man's waffling often derailed plans for moving forward. Over coffee, Charlotte gave me the abridged version of the men she had dated:

> The guys I meet are either married or gay. The married ones I'm not interested in. The guys that are straight—well, they've just broken up with the most fabulous woman on earth. Or they've just broken up with a bitch who happens to look just like me. Or they're in transition from marriage and they need more space. If they don't need space, they just can't commit. Or they can commit but they are afraid to get close. There are men who want to get close, but those are the men I don't want to get near.

Nicole, forty-five years old with two adopted young teens, claimed that after twenty-plus years of continuous dating she could tell in the first fifteen minutes of a date if there was even a slim chance that there would be a second date. She explained how incompatible she was with a man who responded through a dating service shortly after her long-term relationship ended.

> I went out with a guy who pulled out a list as I was reading the menu and said, "I have questions." I said, "Okay"; I thought he was joking. And he said, "When you go shopping and you come home, what do you do?" I said, "I [put] the groceries away, get a cold drink, put my feet up, and say, 'Thank God that's over.'" I said, "What do you do?" He said, "Well, I line up all the peas." And I'm listening to this and I'm thinking, "This is a joke." So then he goes, "Where do you squeeze the tube of toothpaste?" I said, "Wherever my hand lands. I don't give it a lot of thought." And he said, "Oh, no, I always squeeze from the bottom to the top front." Now I started to figure out that he was serious. This was not joking. I said, "You know, we're not compatible. Why don't we just have a nice dinner and we won't see each other again." And he said, "Okay." It turned out he is a prison guard and he would line up his prisoners from the shortest to the tallest! So this was the kind of experience I was having.

As humorous as these two accounts are, they point to the frustration with the lack of eligible potential partners that women met in their attempts to find love and intimacy. The men Charlotte met could not commit. By contrast, Nicole's date knew exactly what he wanted, and she was not it, immediately disqualified by the way she squeezed her toothpaste. Women grew tired of these men who were not good matches either in their expectations for a relationship or in their compatibility as future partners.

Frequently, but not unanimously, a woman would succumb to moments of self-blame for not finding a marriage partner. The pressure to find suitable partners is not limited to straight women—gay women in this study also felt a sense of failure to find someone with whom they could both spend their life and have a child. At some level, self-doubt and self-criticism insinuated themselves into every woman's story: "Is there something wrong with me? Am I to blame? Did I refuse to compromise? Am I naive?"

The painful irony is that women would blame themselves for not marrying at a moment in history when the institution of marriage is itself changing, perhaps even failing.[18] For heterosexual women and men, the postponement of first marriage is at an all-time high.[19] The phenomenon that Lily described as "not ready yet" has resulted in the age of first marriage stretching into the late twenties for both women and men. Divorce rates—that is, failed marriages—have declined in recent years but remain extraordinarily high. The percentage of couples cohabiting steadily increases.[20]

The women I interviewed looked toward marriage and found themselves depressed by the dwindling odds of finding love that would lead to children. They were hardened through horrible dates, failed relationships, and bad timing, and marriage took on an elusive quality that had been previously reserved for motherhood. As they believed marriage to be slipping further and further out of their reach, motherhood, on the other hand, moved closer, drawn in by their desire for children. As Claudia put it, women were "running two races and losing at both." Faced with the decision to choose one or the other in order to win, women found themselves making a difficult life decision. While social norms would dictate throwing the baby out with the bathwater—that is, discarding motherhood because marriage seemed unattainable—women salvaged the baby. Women shed the burden of marriage, determined to win the race to motherhood alone. Taking stock of the road ahead, women saw a course very different from that of women in generations before.

### The Changing Social Climate: The Backdrop to Severing the Link Between Marriage and Motherhood

In earlier generations, this sense of being stuck most likely would have resulted in spinsterhood—in becoming the "favorite aunt," to use Joy's words.[21] Both Joy and Claudia believed that marriage and children would happen naturally and effortlessly. Joy was caught up in enormous professional demands that limited her social life. Claudia framed her story around ambivalent relationships, even though she also had a demanding career as a clinical psychologist. Joy would accept nothing less from a man than both marriage and children. Even after she had her first child, she thought it would take a man to make her family feel complete. Claudia met Carl at a propitious moment: having already filed the paperwork to adopt, she did not feel she had to choose between a hypothetical baby and a relationship. In both Joy's and Claudia's cases, it is possible to sense each woman's dogged resolve to have a child and a family, even if it meant reordering the conventional sequence of events. Neither woman rejected marriage as a social institution; indeed, both honored it by exhausting virtually every route to marriage before electing to have a child as a single mom. Similarly, the lesbian women in this study embraced the idea of a stable partnership with the same fervor as the straight women; they, too, clung tenaciously to the ideal of motherhood even when the possibility of having a partner was remote.

As with many changing social forces, the idea that marriage is a prerequisite to having children remains dominant even as men and women put off marriage until later and later in their lives. Women are aware that the climate is changing and that their choices are quite different from the ones available to women in earlier generations. Ellen, thirty-one years old and with a toddler conceived through "benign neglect" of birth control use, made the point emphatically:

> One of my very good friends who is ten years older than I am said to me, "You did what I could never have done, because the times weren't right for me." And it's true. And I don't think I would have done it ten years before that [in 1987] either. The time just wasn't right. So it opened up the world to do things a little bit differently.

Ellen, like the other women I talked with, knew that her place on the generational timeline was important to her decision to become a single mother, yet women do not see themselves as part of a large shift spurred either by feminism or the times. In other words, single motherhood was not to the 1980s what bra burning was to the 1960s. Rather, single motherhood is a product of a historical patchwork of legal decisions in the beginning of the nineteenth century that changed the tightly woven and highly male-dominated fabric of family life. These decisions shook husbands' unchallenged authority within marriage over their wives and the children they bore, yet also slowly bolstered men's responsibility to children born outside of marriage. Initially, children born outside of marriage were not the responsibility of the father or his heirs. Without the status granted by marriage, these children were the children of no one. In an effort to evade responsibility, the state established the mother as the custodian, passing on the financial burden to her alone. However, by the twentieth century, laws governing illegitimate children, once meant to protect men's property and kin lineage from claims by out-of-wedlock children, were amended to protect children from the circumstance of their birth.[22]

Illegitimate children became eligible to collect survivor's benefits, receive child support, and inherit.[23] The civil rights movement, political scientist Mary Shanley argues in her 2001 book *Making Babies, Making Families,* abolished all legal disabilities of illegitimacy, no longer distinguishing between children born in or out of wedlock.[24] These legal enactments reshaped marriage by eroding patriarchal control—a system of rights and power that gave men familial control over women and children—and redefining parental responsibility to children as no longer dependent upon marital status. As a result, the legal stigma of illegitimacy was all but removed.

The legalization of birth control was another turning point as it altered women's ability to decide when they had children. In Massachusetts, unmarried women were finally allowed access to birth control in 1972 with the Supreme Court decision of *Eisenstadt v. Baird.* Reproductive control removed much of the moral burden of single motherhood; women could now actively choose when to become mothers, and children born out of wedlock were no longer symbolic of a moral transgression that would make either the woman or child a pariah. The changes in family law that dissolved the concept of illegitimacy and granted birth control rights to women thus removed the pressure for women to have a child only within marriage. In short, a series of individual-rights-based legal decisions and social movements paved the way for middle-class women to have a child outside of marriage.

While the legal context for single motherhood may have been established by this time, the social reality did not catch up until two decades later. By trumpeting an intimate link between unmarried motherhood and poverty, social policy makers and the media stigmatized single motherhood just as it was gaining legal acceptability.[25] A related backlash against unwed teenage mothers further slowed the erosion of the stigma attached to middle-class single motherhood. But for middle-class women who could distance themselves from unwed teen mothers by remaining financially independent, the moral boundaries surrounding motherhood changed. A contributing factor was the rise in the divorce rate, particularly among white middle-class women, which meant that more middle-class children were no longer living with two parents. Because they had once been married to their children's fathers, divorced women were not seen as immoral mothers, and they opened the doors for other women to follow. The overall rise in the number of children raised outside of marriage kindled the possibility for middle-class women to have children without partners and still be accepted in their communities. Instead of branding single women who had children with scarlet letters, the broader community judged these middle-class women by their ability to support themselves.[26] Maeve, a thirty-year-old woman with an eight-year-old and a recently adopted six-month-old, conceived the older child while changing birth control pills. She explained how her presence was accepted in a way that it wouldn't have been in the past:

> Well, if it weren't for feminism I wouldn't be hired by a predominantly male institution. My landlord wouldn't have rented me this apartment because it would have made his apartment complex look cheaper because I would have been stigmatized as white trash. I think that still exists, but not really. There are laws that protect me, and people at my job are wonderful. They would never dream of giving a shit that I am a single parent. It allows me to feel confident in the fact that I am a single parent and gives me the perspective to see it from that angle, even though most people don't.

Maeve credited feminism with paving the way for her to have a good-paying job that enabled her to pay her rent. Yet she realized that the social norms surrounding motherhood had also changed; if they hadn't, her landlord might not have been so willing to rent her an apartment, particularly if other tenants complained about her lifestyle.

### Did Social Change Movements Matter?

Social movements are usually started by ordinary people intent on changing institutions they find intolerable. Ironically, subsequent generations often appear to be free riders, enjoying the benefits of earlier struggles and unconsciously or (to the dismay of the pioneers) consciously downplaying the relevance of struggle in the first place. Did the achievements of the civil rights and women's liberation movements influence the choices made by the single mothers I studied? From their perspective, what were the critical events or markers that encouraged them to act? Most women in this study could not articulate the societal changes that made single motherhood possible for them. Even though they stood on the shoulder of feminist activists and in the wake of many social movements, they struggled to explain the sociopolitical context in which they became mothers. More often than not, these women described their lives within the shifting ground of the politics of family, a culture war over family structure, and the place of women.[27] However, these women rarely detected feminism's involvement, for example, in that battle. In general, individuals credit their own agency, their internal world, for the decisions they make, often blind to the broader context in which they operate. Consistent with this, the women in this study were reluctant to credit feminism as anything more than a vague mandate "to be whatever you want to be." Abby, thirty-eight years old with a two-year-old, noted:

> I guess feminism gives me some strength to be who I want to be and try to be as much as I can be. Feminism allows you to be nontraditional, to go against traditional gender roles and have a child as a single person. It gives you some backing and some support to do that. . . . So it opened up the possibility to do things a little bit differently.

Said Penny, age thirty-nine with a preschooler she adopted after mourning the death of an infant son:

> Everyone in my life knew what I was up to [trying to become pregnant]. And I wouldn't have been able to do that, I think, without a pretty strong feminist base that I *could* do stuff like that . . . to be able to express my feelings about how I live my life and to be able to assert myself.

In Penny's mind, feminism enables women to think outside of imposed restrictions. The ability to become a mother outside of marriage could be embraced as part of an altered consciousness, a new identity. Motherhood, a cultural mandate these women do not defy, does not have to be shelved for lack of a partner. It can be pursued on different terms.

At the same time, these single mothers did not view themselves as trailblazers, much less as revolutionaries. Rebecca, age forty-five with a four-year-old, put it this way:

> I feel tremendously fortunate in that I am not a groundbreaking kind of person, and I didn't have to do this thing that even ten years ago would have been a lot harder, or fifteen years certainly.

For the youngest women in this sample, feminism was like fluoride in the water: it was just there. They did not think much about its contribution to their lives; neither did they fret about a backlash limiting their opportunities and rights (to abortion, for instance). As Naomi, who was in her early thirties, explained:

> I don't know how it has affected me. I grew up in an era in which it was already out there. My youngest and oldest sisters say they are not feminists, but of course they live a very feminist life.

Despite the varied understanding of the context of single motherhood, there is an absence of feminist discussion about motherhood in general. This means that what is considered "appropriate" mothering remains limited in important ways by social and cultural norms, many of them unspoken and unexamined. Trish, forty-eight years old with a child almost twelve, felt as if motherhood itself is a taboo topic, not politically palatable to discuss. She commented that as much as things have changed, motherhood itself remains unaltered and unscrutinized. Women who wish to adopt alternative models of parenthood, such as part-time parenting, face significant barriers. Trish, who shared a child with two dads in an arrangement that worked well for her, felt that her engineering of motherhood was greeted by skepticism even among women with the best intentions:

> At the beginning I really felt very alone about that. People were really skeptical; they couldn't believe it was going to work. I felt like people were waiting for the

shoe to drop, that kind of thing. Like the only person you could have a kid with was a romantic person, or to do it as a single person. You couldn't construct another arrangement that would be as assured to work as the other two.

Prior attempts to change social policy that would have altered our present ideals of "good middle-class mothering" have failed, and the care of children remains an issue that is hotly contested. In 1971 a coalition of feminists and child care activists did try to pass national legislation that would have provided child care to all women, but this became a politically untouchable subject when universal child care was tarnished as a communist movement that would "lead to the Sovietization of American children."[28] In the time since then, motherhood has only intensified in its importance, exacerbating the tensions between work and family.[29]

Further, feminism is a moot point, according to women in this study. Feminism is the background, not the catalyst, for beliefs about having children outside of marriage. That is, it creates a context allowing these women to see themselves and to be seen by others as economically and socially capable. Children become something that women want to achieve once they have the means to achieve this goal without support, such as government assistance with child care costs. Women's desire to parent has moved to the forefront of their lives unaccompanied by the ideology of a social movement. This is how second-wave feminism trickled down—as a silent contributor to the rise of a new motherhood.

Women of color tell a different story, more readily crediting the civil rights movement as a critical force—more responsible than feminism for the context that shaped them. Single motherhood is a reality with harsh economic consequences that these families know from their church communities, though as solid middle-class citizens they have rarely experienced it themselves. When Althea, an African American woman, gave birth to a child when she was in her late thirties, it was greeted differently:

> My mom is older, she was about seventy-four at this point—and many of her friends were her age and even older. And their opinion was, "Althea's finished her education, she has a stable job, she has a good head on her shoulders, let her do this. If she made this decision, it is clear that she must have thought long and hard about it, so it was a good idea." Nobody had any trouble with it. My church community has been very supportive. You know, in the black community, it's teen pregnancy that still riles people. But when you're older, it's generally accepted.

For women of color, particularly African American women, the legacy of a male-headed household is not something they have to set aside.[30] They all know single mothers who are their relatives and neighbors and church members. What middle-class women of color do worry about is the prospect of career stagnation due to raising a child. Althea, forty years old with a three-year-old at the time of the interview, shared the difference:

I knew lots of women who were single parents. God knows, there are a lot of African American women who are single parents. I did not know black women who were professionals and then made the decision. I did know many black women who were single parents and then later became professionals. But it seemed as though—I mean, one of the things I was kind of concerned about was would this derail my career? And I didn't know anybody who was struggling with that issue.

When she became a mother over sixteen years ago, Janica, a contemporary of Althea's, saw the right to adopt as a civil right. She credited the civil rights movement primarily and the feminist movement secondarily for the opportunity to challenge state and private adoption agencies for healthy children, even if single women remained second-choice parents. State agencies have become more open to helping unmarried women adopt children, as Janica pointed out:

> We had a voice. It grew out of the civil rights movement and then the women's movement. Before then you had to take what you could get. As Black women, the informality of adoption used to happen anyway. But as women entered the labor force permanently and as marriage did not have to be the ultimate goal—that afforded us to say " I don't have a husband. Why should that keep me from having a baby? And if I don't want to physically have one or can't physically, why should this keep me from adopting a healthy one?" The stigma was in my head when I signed those papers with my older child; I thought, "I just became an unwed mother." But two years later when I adopted my second child I never thought about that. As the movement grows and as we grow we have become stronger and more defiant and we have made them make some changes.

Janica's assertion of her right to become a single mother echoes the language of civil rights. Changes in adoption are another example of how social movements have made cracks in the status quo, opening up inroads for single mothers.

For the 17 percent of women in this study who identified as lesbian or bisexual, the social movement they credited for shaping their motherhood is the gay rights movement. This movement has very recently been evolving the relationship between lesbian women and motherhood. While straight single women having children challenged the link between marriage and motherhood, lesbian women had to dismantle the view of lesbians as sexual but not procreative women. Anthropologist Kath Weston explains in her 1991 book *Families We Choose* how "the term 'lesbian mother' presents an oxymoron insofar as it joins a procreative identity (mother) to a sexual one (lesbian) that is frequently represented as the antithesis of procreative sexuality" (p. 169). However, as the gay and lesbian movement shifts from a countercultural movement toward a more mainstream lifestyle, so do these women's lives. Baby boom lesbians, "the decisive generation who remade lesbian life," were influenced by the cultural and political shifts during the 1960s and 1970s.[31] The American conception of the lesbian identity is moving from a narrow focus on sexuality into a normative identity—which includes partners, families, and careers. For example, the older lesbians I interviewed assumed that when they came out they forsook any possibility of mothering a child as a single mom. Veronica, forty-two years old with an adopted five-year-old, explained it succinctly:

> It just wasn't part of the culture, and I just have a lot of concerns about raising a child where other people would see our family as not healthy, and I didn't want to raise a child in that kind of environment. But as it became more and more of a popular thing to do within the gay and lesbian community, it just seemed like it was an okay option.

Though the dividing line is blurry, it is safe to say that lesbian women who came out in the 1980s or prior experienced a very different level of social acceptance than those who have gone public with their sexual identity more recently. Enormous changes in the level of comfort and the extent of alternative community institutions separate these two groups of women.

The "lesbian baby boom" came about as women from two distinct generations, with qualitatively different experiences, began becoming mothers at about the same time. For women who are part of the historical baby boom generation, becoming a mother was the next stage of the movement. The alternative families they created grew out of the alternative health, legal, and social services lesbian women of this generation founded (and which often remain their employment). By contrast, younger women, under forty years old, always knew that coming out would not deter them from having children. While the gay rights movement has substantially shifted lesbian women's path to motherhood, the assumption that they will be accompanied by a partner still holds fast.

For many women in this study, the influence of these different social movements was about intersecting identities. Barbara, who held several advanced degrees, discussed the multiple timelines that intersected to make her path possible:

> My girlfriend and I often talk about what a remarkable time we live in! We talk often about how we would have lived in other times. Because I'm African American, I could have been a slave. My dad grew up during segregation and he went to segregated schools and so many racial barriers made for these really important stories in people's lives. As a gay woman, it's an exciting time. We have gay marriage in Massachusetts. I always think about which part of me—my being black or gay or a single mother—will surface in every place I enter in ways that people aren't really conscious of. It plays out in different ways.

Barbara's experience is also that of many other women, whose lives are partially products of their place in history. While women usually identify with one social movement, if any, that they as individuals stand upon, the reality for most is that their choices exist in the wake of multiple movements.

In the following chapters, women tell incredibly personal stories, often unsure of how their individual story intersects with the larger epic. Both a context and a structure, the backdrop of their stories is as important in the shaping of their choices as the women themselves. It is impossible to do any more than summarize the social forces (made visible through changes in the legal and political structure and in social norms) that constitute the foundation on which these women walk. Far from crusaders themselves, these women are undeniably part of the momentum of the feminist, civil rights, and gay rights movements. While a difficult force to measure, the presence of these movements and the legacy of accompanying legal decisions are visible in the lives of these sixty-five women. The agency that each woman exhibits, very real to her when faced with this decision, does not exist in a vacuum—it is the flyaway spark of the social explosions in the late twentieth century, an unanticipated but traceable end to marriage and motherhood as we know it.

## Hungry for Motherhood: The New Mother

Being "stuck" has a vivid meaning in the context of a traditional, mainstream life sequence in which marriage is a prerequisite for motherhood. Stymied in their efforts to give and get commitment, many women have abandoned the belief that marriage is an essential part of the family equation. The women in this study set marriage aside, fully realizing that as they aged motherhood could slip out of their grasp.[32] These particular women refused to be driven to the altar by their desire for children. Reserving marriage only for love, they no longer reserved motherhood for marriage.

To become a single mother is not an inherently selfish act, because what drives parenthood is neither wholly altruistic nor completely self-absorbed. These women's decisions to become a mother reflect the broader mandates of American culture that tie motherhood to womanhood, parenthood to adulthood. Their decision is akin to that made by their partnered heterosexual peers, although it is not sheltered by social norms. Parenthood in the context of single mothers is regarded with needling suspicion by much of the rest of society, as it is a threat of the unthinkable—families without dads, the ultimate displacement.[33]

These women are hesitant in their decision. Without a precedent, middle-class women have the heavy burden of setting one.[34] No longer constrained by social pressures in the same ways as before, women are still kept static and stuck by the fear that two parents (even same-sex parents) are inherently better than one. However, at some point motherhood becomes a more compelling force than fear. Compulsory motherhood, painted as a biological urge to emphasize its necessity, overtakes these women. As Susan, forty-eight with a nine-year-old, described it:

> Time was running out and I began to start wrestling with the idea that I might not meet someone in time. And so I knew that by this time I really had a *very*

strong desire to have a child. And it didn't abate. It got increasingly larger. I knew that I would be really unhappy if I didn't have a child. I'd made a decision that come hell or high water, I was gonna have a child. But I hadn't decided how even though my first choice was not to be a single parent. My first choice was to have a partner.[35]

Many women suddenly and overwhelmingly become hungry for the motherhood they have put on the back burner up until this point.[36] As their desire for a child overtakes them, other considerations such as work, success, and the search for a suitable partner pale. Single motherhood can be the solution to the dilemma for these women.

However, the decision to go it alone is not made overnight. Joy elected an anonymous donor after deciding against the possibility of complications that might occur with a known donor. Claudia delayed applying for adoption until her age nearly disqualified her. The paths to single motherhood, as we'll see in later chapters, are diverse and involve complex decisions about timing, insemination or adoption, and racial, ethnic, religious, and ideological considerations.

How did these women I interviewed for this study get "unstuck"? What nudged (or shook) them free? These are the questions I take up in the next chapter, when I explore the liminal stage—the time between socially sanctioned statuses, the period during which new alternatives are possible. There we stand to gain deep insights into the mechanisms of social change by examining the thoughts and behaviors of people at the leading edge of change.

# 2

---

## LIMINALITY AND
## THE COURAGE TO CHANGE

### Making the Decision to Become a Single Mother

**Gina Schecter**

James was my first really true love relationship. But it just wasn't meant to be. We shared quirky amusements—like who could do the Sunday crossword puzzle faster—and I admired his artistic talents. He would wake me up in the morning by playing music at the foot of our bed; he wrote love songs to me that made me melt. We shared a connection that is really beyond words, a soul mate. He loved my "flashes of insight," his exact words, which still remain with me. I just remember that he would listen to me—I would entertain him every night with my embellished stories of things that happened. He was so sweet. I still carry him with me—in a box in my head—and every once in a while I untie the satin bow on it and I slowly replay the most wonderful memories. He just elevated my life.

So, what was wrong, you ask? I met him after his divorce [after] fifteen years [of marriage] and two children. From the very beginning he told me that he did not want more children. This was the time for him to develop himself and things he wanted to do. I thought he might change his mind. I became a kind of grown-up friend, not a stepmother, to his daughters, who I still see every once in a while.

James and I took a turn for the worse when I started to snap at him. I just couldn't help but bring my bitterness home after each girlfriend's baby shower. I would say nasty things to him. I couldn't keep myself from these outbursts of yelling. I wanted him to hear my pain since he ignored the deep longing in my eyes. And I began to resent weekends when his teenage daughters would be around. They made me all the more hungry to raise a baby from the start. I went so far as to offer to do most of the work if he agreed to have a child with me. Fortunately, he had some sense and he stuck by his decision. He would have liked to get married, but he was not going to mislead me that he was going to change his mind. I was deeply in love, and I had to force myself to acknowledge that as long as I remained satisfied with the way things were—that I could only have a piece of him—I was tacitly consenting to forgo motherhood. I finally packed up my things and left him because I could not rule out having a child of my own.

I met Luke in an unlikely place. On a humid Sunday evening in August, the line in the organic food store was long. The guy in front of me was sweaty and in running clothes, and I was fumbling with the magazines on the rank. We struck up a conversation when I noticed the college logo on his T-shirt. I must have waited half an hour in that line. And to cut to the chase, we'd gone to the same college but didn't overlap. Luke waited while I paid for my groceries, and we continued to talk in the parking lot as a summer shower turned to a downpour. I called my best friend as soon as I got home because I couldn't believe I stood in the rain with a strange man as my hair became wet and frizzy, my shirt sticking to me, until finally we made a date for that week. What can I say—I loved his sweat. The chemistry between us overwhelmed me.

But he was troubled. He would go from being very up to deep depression, and I hated the mood swings. He started to feel like a yoke around my neck in that he became very needy with the darkness of his depression. He knew this about himself. And at some point whatever was good about that relationship faded, and where I was in my mid-thirties, I thought, "I want to nurture a *real* child." Unlike James, Luke might have been willing to have children, but I couldn't see him as a co-parent because of his own needs. And in terms of shared values and where we are heading in our lives, it really wasn't in sync. Let's just say that the organic food turned out to be the only common ground. I chose the possibility of a good father over passion, and I left him.

I was on the sidelines of my own life, and this place was making me miserable. I knew I needed to take action and consciously force myself to actively change my thoughts in order to allow me to think outside the box about becoming a mom. My friends had become busy discovering the many places in Boston which they could enjoy with their children. I felt left out, preferring to read a book at home than join them in their adventures. The quiet and the stillness, which I once relished after a full day at work, echoed as I tried to read. I became a hermit, alone more than I wished to be.

I kept having these painful but transformative thoughts about what I wanted in my future. What I became conscious of when I thought about not becoming a parent was what my life would be without kids. What I envisioned was having a good job, living in a nice place, and being involved in my friends' lives with their children, including celebrating holidays and continuing to take group vacations, and I came up feeling that it won't work. In ten years I will be so depressed, I will be ready to jump. It felt extremely depressing being the good friend, the good aunt, having the good job, the nice house, having all the time in the world to go to the ballet and theater—all things I love. When I envisioned that, it was scary. And when I envisioned my life without a child, it was not the idea that I would be depressed or ready to jump that scared me, but the idea that I did not know what else would be in my life. I needed something to shake up my life.

So I envisioned trying to find a job that would afford me the ability to travel a couple of months a year. More, maybe, in salary. And I envisioned moving away from my friends and my sister in this fantasy. But with hindsight this jetsetting scenario was a survival strategy. I couldn't just keep going the way I was. I exhausted imagining a life without a child. I knew that a baby would shake up my life positively. And in a way, I stayed closer to the friends I value and love because I became a parent. It felt like I would have had to distance myself from the people I love to survive if I didn't become a parent. . . .

I was now thirty-six years old and still not a parent. That year I felt like I was slipping backward, and the way to move forward was to find a way to finally become a mom. Other parts of my life were beginning to come apart. I lost a job, but I wasn't worried, as I always landed good jobs. I had just redone my resumé with a new twist on my skills and I was about to send it out when my dad called. My mom was very ill, he couldn't reduce his work hours, and my mom needed someone to be with her. My dad offered emotional support, but I became my mom's companion.

I knew I was going to have to do the daughter thing and take care of my mom. And I wasn't really happy about that and I didn't want to be *only* a single middle-aged woman taking care of my mother. I just wanted more out of my life.

\* \* \*

Gina's story has the key ingredients that lead up to a decision to become a single mother. She found herself in a series of relationships that were going nowhere if she wanted a child. Her account represents the experiences of many women in this study who were stuck without a partner willing to co-parent. Tracing Gina's and other women's stories reveals the progression of how women go from being stuck to being mothers. To complete this passage, I have found, all women must imagine a child in a new context, test this idea on friends, experience a catalytic event, and disclose their decision. Women progress in different orders, shifting between stages, concerned about an uncertain future. Even though this chapter is presented in a linear way, the real-life experiences are often more nebulous and less neat. The parts of the process that occur before women act on becoming mothers depend on how they go about their mission of becoming unstuck, the starting point of the liminal state. The difficult and confusing process of tearing down internal barriers against families headed by women and created through their agency constitutes liminality, a key concept discussed in the next section. Liminality creates a new context, riskily embraced by middle-class women who seek to establish a new family life.

## Liminality

A generation or two earlier, Gina might reasonably have assumed that the men she was dating were both potential partners *and* potential fathers. However, when her latest relationship ended, she concluded that she faced two pursuits: one for a child and the other for a partner. In her case, as in most of the women I interviewed, baby came first. Time would run out on having a child, they reasoned, but not on finding a mate. And having a child would not impede finding a mate. Thus, women stepped forward into what I call a liminal state: a period of uncertainty that can last for months, even years, during which a woman's identity is suspended between the person she was and the person she wants to be: between being childless (but determined) and being a single mom.

The term *liminality* is derived from the Latin word for "threshold" and is used by anthropologists to refer to the transitory phase in a rite of passage between two concrete and socially accepted roles (see, for example, Van Gennep 1960; Turner 1967). For example, in Judaism a bat mitzvah is a well-known public ritual with set stages. When a girl reads from the Torah on this occasion, she is at the threshold between adolescence and adulthood. Once she completes her portion, she is recognized as a full-fledged adult member of the community and is subject to new but established rights and obligations.[1] At one level, this concept describes nicely the situation facing Gina, Joy, Claudia, and the other women I interviewed. However, unlike initiates to a sorority or adolescents on the brink of full membership in a community of adults, these women were entering unfamiliar territory. They knew where they wanted to be, but they didn't know how to get there or whether they would be welcomed once they'd arrived. In other words, single motherhood was not then a socially accepted destination.

Rather than treat liminality as merely an interlude, I believe it's a profoundly important time in which individuals—unmarried women in this case—actively entertain alternative realities. Certainly it begins as an individual venture, but it can also be a seed for social change, particularly when other people notice the decisions these women make, see that alternatives can be pursued successfully, and thus find it easier to imagine a similar destination for themselves.[2]

Without romanticizing the situation of women who want a child but can't find a partner, it is important to recognize the courage that's required to sustain a positive self-image in the liminal state. Even the simple act of imagining carries risks. For example, the women I interviewed risked their identities as "good girls" with parents, friends, and communities that mattered to them when they began to verbalize their innermost desire to become mothers on their own. Facing the unknown consequences of breaking deep tradition (though they would still fulfill another—the cultural obligation for women to reproduce) required the "real courage" novelist Tom Robbins once described in *Another Roadside Attraction*: "Real courage is risking something that you have to keep on living with, real courage is risking something that might force you to rethink your thoughts and suffer change and stretch consciousness. Real courage is risking one's clichés" (p. 251).

What are the common events that trigger a redirection? What makes single women realize that they have to take control of their lives and stop waiting for men to carry them across the threshold? The process in almost every case begins with imagining a child in a new context and testing the idea on important people in one's life.

## Imagining

Single motherhood begins with a conviction and a secret. The conviction is to become a mother. The secret is the possibility of becoming a single mom. The secret comforts the conviction: it is there on dates, in relationships, in the workplace, and when single women see mothers with their children. Knowing they have the option and that they could exercise it if need be eases the pain of not yet having what they want.

Imagining single motherhood, women challenge themselves and test their readiness to become single mothers by setting progressively higher hurdles. Each hurdle is higher until they convince themselves that they can handle anything— even motherhood without a co-parent. Lily, for example, who talked about timing and weak relationship commitments in chapter 1, unthinkingly accepted the propriety of marriage as the first in the order of events. But in her late thirties, Lily dreamed of being a single mom—all the while marveling at her own defiance of convention:

> Daring to consider getting pregnant on my own just seemed like such an outrageous thing to do. And from that point of thinking about it, to doing it, was the longest stretch because I was kind of shocked that I would think that way, and I wasn't sure if that's what I really wanted to do.

Like Joy and Claudia, she talked of being stuck, but each time she considered the option of single motherhood, the stuckness gave way a little more. Lily thought she could overcome the remaining obstacles to her decision to move ahead if she received approval from the various key leaders in the communities that were central in her life. She told me, "My faith is a really big part of my life, and I started really praying about what to do. I thought if I start talking to people about it, and explain that I really care about doing this, then I would have an answer." She remained alone with her thoughts until she felt comfortable enough with single motherhood that it didn't feel so much against everything she believed and valued. Only then could she speak these thoughts aloud to important people in her life.

Women often weigh their decisions to postpone motherhood against fears about diminishing fertility. At several points Nadine rethought the choice to have children alone, balancing it against continuing her education and enhancing her engineering career. A biography she had read years earlier about a female scientist who elected to have a child on her own in her early thirties steeled Nadine's conviction that she too could have children and stay successful at work, even if she did not find a man to marry. Nadine felt an affinity with the female scientist whose life she admired. The scientist, who studied migration patterns of sea turtles, led an adventurous and comical life, overcoming all sorts of obstacles. Nadine, whose own work was confined to an office, vicariously enjoyed the experiences of this scientist, whose decision to have a baby followed a pattern of thinking outside the box. It fueled her imagination to think that she also could follow the example of this scientist, if only to have a child on her own. The story of the scientist allowed Nadine to imagine a context for having kids that she hadn't previously thought probable without disastrous consequences. She recounted:

> I always had in the back of my mind that if I was thirty and not married, then I'll have children on my own. Then it was when I was thirty-two. Then it was when I went back to school at Princeton to get my master's degree. Then it was when I left school. And then it was thirty-six, and I had just broken up with another man.

Babies gestate in far less time than it takes most women to initiate the campaign to have a child. Most women keep postponing having children alone; often they think about it for five to eight years before acting. Even though, as I will go on to describe, the time seems short for those who become mothers "accidentally," by chancing pregnancy, some of these women have been thinking about having a child for years.

For the women in this study, single motherhood was never a snap decision. Virtually every woman postponed the decision at least once in hopes of a revelation.[3] They thought about whether to become mothers without partners. Nadine held close the biography of a scientist who became a mom without a partner. It gave her a new context for imagining motherhood. Once a new context is imagined, it opens possibilities for unfolding the sequencing of choices—including motherhood without marriage. Despite worries that single motherhood might not be something they could do, they also quietly began to think about paths toward motherhood without a partner and which path might be the best one for them to pursue.

The women I interviewed also pointed to a last relationship that blew the lid off the continued search for a partner to come before a baby. A new partner meant starting over, and why invest in starting over when there was no guarantee that this new partnership would result in a child? The risk that another man would reject them or reject having a child with them outweighed the potential benefits of the investment.

## Testing the Secret

Women's private thoughts eventually become conversations—first with their most intimate family and friends, then widening to include other important people in their lives. These people play a vital role as enablers. Women want their approval so that if and when they become mothers, they will have a welcoming community that will not disown them. They carefully craft new cultural norms that can allow their future children to be accepted members of a family-centered middle-class community. Approaching others with their story makes their situations known, and therefore not shocking or shameful.

They set about drafting their confidants to become part of the decision, giving them space and opportunity to process and accept what they were doing. This conscription of intimates does not necessarily translate into automatic acceptance of all single mothers; these women are asking permission to be the exception to the "rule" against out-of-wedlock births. They distance themselves from the stereotype of the welfare-dependent woman with children and make their claims to motherhood on the basis of demonstrated self-sufficiency, the cornerstone of the middle class. They test the waters in the hopes that having a child will not marginalize them from their work, extended kin, and neighbors. They do not want to be seen as rebels, even as they reshape family life.

Women often talk to their own mothers first, expecting them to be more sympathetic to their wish to become mothers themselves, but also because their mothers were the emotional centers of their family lives in their childhoods. Joy's mother's emotional bond to her children was an attribute that Joy wished to replicate in her own life. Her mother translated these needs to a sometimes emotionally silent father. As they did when they were little girls, women hoped that their mothers would smooth the way so that their dads could accept their decision if they chose to go forward. Mothers became pivotal supports. By including their own mothers as they wrestled with what to do, they ensured a future place in their extended family for their imagined children.

Lily continued to practice her faith, an important part of her childhood in a small town. When she moved to Boston to become a teacher, she found a church community in which she became very involved. Bubbly and outgoing, she never lost her midwestern friendliness and directness, but even she hesitated before she approached the pastor of her church with her "crazy" question: should she become a mom on her own? She fully expecting her pastor to reprimand her for defying church tradition.[4] But she was stunned by his reaction:

> I walked out of there and my eyes were just wide. I thought, "Oh no, he didn't shut down this road I am on." He said, "It's completely natural that you want to be a mother, of course you want to be a mother. And of course, it would be more perfect if you had a husband. But you would be a great mom. And this church community loves you, and I know they will support you in this."

The pastor characterized Lily's wish as logical, rational, and well thought out. He also recommended that she talk to the church elders, officials who were elected by the congregation.

> And I went to talk to them about it when I was more sure I was going to do it and I was thinking the same thing—they are not going to approve of this. . . . I was crying as I was talking about it because it was bittersweet. I really was torn. I wanted to be a mom, but I didn't want to do it this way. You know? And I finished telling them what I was thinking about, and there was this silence. And then the woman who hired me ten years earlier, she reached over and grabbed my arm and said, "Well, bless your heart! That is so brave." And then there was silence and she said, "I'm getting goose bumps thinking that we might get to support you in this."

While Lily clearly wanted their approval, she sought more than just consent. She feared not being aligned with the core people in her life. She wanted her child's birth to be a joyful community event, greeted in the same way that other members' children were received. Acceptance was essential to her. The leaders in her church agreed with her thinking, and they were united in their support.

Like other women in a liminal state, Lily sought others' opinions before she truly made up her mind. She did not go to them seeking approval for a decision she had already made. She asked them to share in her decision and to become supportive players should she choose to go ahead. But at the same time, vocalizing her thoughts made them seem a little more real.

Lily also consulted the principal of the middle school where she taught. She worried that if she gave birth outside of marriage the school board would question her fitness as a role model for students and perhaps even fire her. Her worries were acute, since she taught young teenagers. But again she found that the principal and her department head were sympathetic. The principal asked her to think about how and what she would tell her students. This gave her pause. She decided that if she went forward with her plan and if she became pregnant, she would tell the students that she had been inseminated in a doctor's office. She especially wanted to convey to the students that there was no sexual "misconduct" on her part: she had not made a mistake but had instead chosen a sexless route to motherhood.

Gina, whose story opened this chapter, imagined her future life without a child as a scary scenario in which she would need to move away from her friends and family. Often women seek help from therapists and self-help groups. At self-help groups women meet other women—"thinkers," as they are called—who are at a crossroads. Together they imagine what their futures will be like, whether with a child on their own or forgoing motherhood. They find comfort that other women feel the same way—having no one to marry but still uncertain about having a child on their own. At workshops and self-help meetings women learn about different routes to motherhood, including the best fertility clinics, adoption agencies that will work with single mothers, and things to look for in choosing a donor, as well as phone numbers and Web sites of various sperm banks.

Self-help groups pool information and pass it on to others in similar situations. Each woman's experience adds to the collective knowledge: Women discuss doctors to avoid, how to navigate insurance coverage dilemmas, what to bring for journeys to foreign countries when adopting babies, and so on. But more than swapping knowledge, each group supports its members: women call each other to find out how an insemination went; they are excited when a woman becomes pregnant or a notice arrives about a child available for adoption. Sharing the same goal, members of the group root for one another as they try various ways to become mothers. Women who become mothers and remain in the group offer evidence that single motherhood is possible. A positive by-product is friendships that continue for years, even when women stop attending group meetings. Though they may live in different towns, these friends continue to socialize over dinner. Having shared the experience of becoming moms together, they eagerly look forward to intimate evenings catching up with these friends.

The evening she went to a "thinkers" workshop, Lily also met some of the children of single mothers who were in another room for a different workshop. Getting acquainted with women who were considering the same option she was and seeing the healthy, beautiful, and well-adjusted children of women who had acted on motherhood alone gave her hope. She left the workshop feeling that alternatives existed. But she was not yet ready to change her plans.

## The Catalytic Event

Women describe the catalytic event as a defining moment when they choose to cross the threshold, realizing that even if they don't know exactly what is on the other side, moving toward motherhood is better than staying in place. Moving into the liminal phase, considering single motherhood, often brings a feeling of relief.

While a woman's age, referenced by many women as the "biological clock," contributes to some women's choice to cross the threshold, age is really more of a backdrop than a catalyst. Birthdays act as markers, reminding women that they are off their imagined life course. Often in conjunction with other factors in their life, age gives women a limited window for having a child, and surfaces as a trigger in moments of change, such as time off from work or when deciding to take a higher-powered job. There is also a social dimension to age, as women do not want to be out of sync with their friends. Women hold widely differing views on the age when they are ready to have children, but the most pressing stories are those of women who have reached age thirty-five and feel that they must decide what to do. A smaller group reaches age thirty, considers single motherhood, and sets guidelines for revising their life plan; others who arrive at thirty decide to become pregnant rapidly. Their stories reveal five types of catalytic events:

breakups, interruptions, losing a loved one, medical interventions, and cementing a relationship.[5]

## BREAKUPS

Many women in their twenties and thirties have endured breakups with those they thought would be life partners; when this relationship ends, they watch in despair as their life plan falls apart, taking with it the promise of traditional marriage and motherhood. Women report that pushing their baby agenda—their wish to have a child—in the framework of long-term relationships sometimes prompts these relationships to dissolve. By broaching the talk of children, women risk discovering that their partners do not share the same vision of parenthood. While they may know deep down that their partner does not share their desire for a child at this time and thus that this topic could break their relationship, it is still incredibly painful to hear their partner's rejection of something so fundamental to them. Some women know from the first date that the men with whom they get involved will never become dads, yet they hope their passion for this dream will become a shared passion. And they also hope their love will change their partner's mind. Other women are surprised and shocked to realize that their partner's vision of a relationship does not include having a child. They feel their partners are selfishly withholding, leaving the women doubting their judgments of the character of these men whom they loved. While the most common scenario involves men who do not want children to be a part of *this* relationship, in other cases men are willing to become dads but women doubt their long-term compatibility and their ability to parent together. Relationships collapse painfully when women decide to give precedence to the baby agenda. As we've seen, Gina thought that she could have lived a happy life with James, her first true love, but her bitterness grew because he would not agree to become a father again, and she knew she had to end the relationship; troubled boyfriend Luke's willingness to have a child with her made her realize that he wasn't the right partner for her.

Realizing that they cannot predict or depend on the relationships in their lives, women take advantage of the uncertain time following the breakup to rethink the ways in which they can become mothers. They decide that they will not risk the ability to have a birth child while waiting for a suitable co-parent, who may never be found. In a similar way, women choosing to adopt make this choice before reaching agency age cutoffs; while they forfeit biological motherhood, higher adoption age limits extend the final deadline for motherhood to upward of forty-five years.

Nadine, whom I earlier described as having found solace in the single motherhood of a scientist she admired, was not unique in learning only indirectly that the man with whom she was involved really did not want children. His drawings gave clues to his sentiments about children:

I looked at his drawings, these plans for this house that he was building. I looked at it and I said to myself, "This man does not want children." And later on we said something to each other about it that night and he really didn't want children and I said yes, I did want children. And we just parted quietly from that night. But it was funny, I could just tell from the way the drawing was done; there was no place for a child to get next to a parent. This was definitely not someone who wanted children or who had thought anything about it. . . . And after that I decided, hey, I was thirty-six, I was not getting any younger, and if I met somebody else and married him it would be a couple years before we tried having children. I worried about not being able to.

Despite her deep love and connection with him, Nadine made the painful yet necessary decision to move on and find a man with whom children would be a possibility. Thus Nadine abandoned a secure, richly drawn future plan for a life together and stepped out alone into unmapped territory. In leaving the relationship, she had to rethink how she would sequence her choices yet again, a rethinking undergone by many other women who suffer major breakups.

INTERRUPTIONS

On occasion women have the opportunity to leave their daily lives for a time. These interruptions in routines are bracketed, and provide women the freedom and opportunity to reflect upon, evaluate, and redirect their lives. For many, interruptions serve as a refresher course or an exercise in remembering and focusing on one's own life goals. Interruptions become catalysts when women realize that they do not want to return to the exact same lives they left. As a result, they make resolutions and envision their future in new and concrete ways. While vacations, one type of interruption, are often escapes from daily life, they can also provide a new perspective on one's priorities. Interruptions are points of departure.

Interruptions are the most common type of catalyst, and women experience them in different situations: vacations, job layoffs, job promotions, and retreats are a few examples. Joy, whose story opened the prologue, was offered a promotion that would have dramatically increased her time commitment and travel schedule. Forced to make a decision, Joy was pulled from the comfort of her daily work schedule as she contemplated dramatic changes in her life. The job offer interrupted her casual speculation about one day becoming a mother. Now she had to imagine accepting a job that might preclude raising a child. She realized that accepting the job would mean prioritizing work over motherhood, and she began to consider turning it down. Therefore, in her mind, letting the job go became a vote in favor of motherhood. This job offer set off a chain of events that pushed the decision to have a child to the forefront of her life.

Gina, by contrast, returned to her childhood home when her mother's illness prompted her to take time off from her life. Though her mother replaced the bedspreads and carpeting in the bedroom she had shared with her sister, Gina felt as though coming home to care for her mother meant stepping back into her childhood. When Gina first arrived, her mother slept for long stretches, leaving Gina to find ways to occupy herself. As she rearranged her childhood dolls, her memories of pretend mothering with her sister at age seven came flooding back. The two sisters, close in age and constant companions, had imagined a life where they would live in one house with their children, while their husbands, never central in their games, would visit from another home down the street. Laughing as she recalled the naiveté of this daily game scenario, she suddenly realized that her seven-year-old imagination contained the seeds of new possibilities. Instead of feeling sorry for herself that she had to shop, clean, and cook for her parents, Gina perked up. Her mother's illness forced her home, and there she discovered a way out of feeling trapped on the sidelines of her own life. Interruptions often revisit memories of the past and become clues that women rethink in the present.

Lily recalled the thinking stage, discussing the possibility of single motherhood with co-workers and friends, trying to gauge potential reactions. Since she worried a lot about how people would treat her and even more so her child, she hesitated to commit without the approval of the key players in her life. Lily described the interruption that dissolved the barriers to becoming a single mother:

> The turning point for me was my high school reunion in Minnesota. On my way home [thinking about the next reunion, five years hence] I thought, "In five years I am going to be forty-three, and what do I want to come back to this reunion like? What do I want my life to be like?" And I thought, "As a forty-three-year-old, I want to be a mom. I may not be a wife. But I am going to be a mom. I can do this." That was in August, and I spent the next several months looking for a donor and then I started the insemination process.

The reunion put her in a position where she had to present herself to people who knew her only through her childhood dreams, and the contrast between then and now made clear the gap between who she was and who she wanted to be. She struggled to understand how she could integrate her adolescent dream of marriage and children into the context of her new life and somehow reconcile the old goal to nurture with the surprising and wonderful independence and self-sufficiency that she had created for herself as an adult. In a period of intense self-evaluation, Lily finally realized that she needed her own approval to become a single mother, because even though she had everyone else's approval, it was still not enough. She had been looking for outside permission, but the reunion allowed her to look inward, crystallizing her identity as a woman who would actively seek motherhood, rather than making it contingent upon finding a husband.

## LOSING A LOVED ONE

Death unearths deep feelings about family. The death of a parent, in particular, calls attention to both the importance and the fragility of family, often compelling women to put family first in their own lives. They become proactive as part of the grieving process, mourning the loss and healing by creating their own families. Usually, these women have the support of the widowed parent, who encourages them to have a child to continue the kin line and bring new life into the family. The desire to nurture while expanding kin networks relaxes social norms surrounding single motherhood. For two women in this study, the loss of a first child also increased the wish to become a mother, and the loss of a girlfriend with whom a lesbian woman had begun to discuss co-parenting plans made her resolve to act in the present, because the future is not guaranteed.

Fran, thirty-six years old with a two-year-old, explained why she had paused to rethink what was important to her. Characteristic of women who suffered the loss of a loved one, Fran's thoughts about single motherhood crystallized as she shifted her focus from the family member she had lost to the family she longed to have:

> The big trigger for me was my dad's death. That made me think about what's important in my life. And I think there often is something that makes you say, "What do I care about?" And I thought, " I think I really want to have kids." And then in the back of my head the idea was more jelled at that point. But then I would think, "This is probably a really crazy idea, and I don't know if this is realistic."

A Jewish woman who would not marry outside her faith, Fran never clicked with any of the Jewish men she met, and saw dating a non-Jewish man as counter to her beliefs. When her father died, her desire to perpetuate her cultural heritage convinced her that it was better to create her own Jewish family and home than to search outside her faith for a possible husband. New ideas about how to expand kinship and keep her faith solidified with his death.

## MEDICAL INTERVENTION

Medical intervention can serve as a catalytic event when women learn that they have a medical problem that may lead to infertility if they do not act immediately. Usually it is endometriosis that hastens women's decision. Endometriosis is a misunderstood reproductive disease: the medical profession often informs women who have it that if they do not act rapidly, they might not be able to conceive.[6] Therefore, women feel that they cannot put off the decision and cannot wait to find a partner to have a baby.

Annette, whom I described in chapter 1 as moving up the managerial ranks, was thirty-eight years old when her doctor informed her that she had endometriosis. Startled because she had not yet thought about children, she explains her reaction:

> I woke up from surgery to be told by my doctor that I had endometriosis and if I wanted a child, I had better do it fast. I was dating no one, so I called my

former boyfriend and explained the situation. He agreed to become a known donor.

The possibility of infertility as a diagnosis catapulted Annette and other women to both think about and act on trying to become pregnant. Faced with the possibility that they may not be able to have children, these women rush to prove that they can be mothers.

A hysterectomy at age thirty caused Janica, who always told her family she wanted both birth and adoptive children, to start a family. After this sudden surgery, and still in the hospital, she sank into the beginning of a depression. Her sister rescued her: " 'What are you waiting for?' she jolted me. 'You always said when we were kids you would adopt. Now is your chance.' " Janica, whose experiences as an African American adoptive mother are explored in chapter 6, waited a year to make sure that her medical issues were resolved before beginning adoption classes.

## Cementing a Relationship

Many of the women who chance pregnancy are entangled in relationships, and some believe that they can cement their relationship by having their partner's child. They are lax about using birth control, often gambling as they forget to use protection in the passion of the moment. They also often tell the men that they are not on birth control, thus, in the women's opinion, obtaining tacit consent.

Once pregnant, these women hope that the child will cement their relationship to the biological father and his family. Even though they cite their inability to have an abortion as the reason they have the child, the women are not necessarily pro-life. Rather, they see a particular child as a connection to a particular man. They choose not to abort and not to give this child up for adoption.

During her senior year in college, Rosalie threw away her birth control pills after she broke up with her boyfriend, Javier. She describes this moment as "a fit of stupidity and rage." During their attempt to get back together again, they conceived a baby: Rosalie thought that she was using the rhythm method correctly the night she conceived, and she did not realize she was pregnant for two months. When Javier found out she was pregnant, they became engaged; neither of them believed in abortion. They planned to marry and raise the child together, going so far as to get blood tests for a marriage license before Javier, scared and overwhelmed, backed out of the engagement. They broke up for the second and last time. Rosalie, twenty-two with a nine-month-old, described how she felt:

> Part of the decision to have him was yes, on the assumption that I would get married. But even if Javier weren't in my life, I still would have had Antonio because of my religious beliefs. I'm not even just pro-life, I'm anti-abortion. I do not believe in abortions at all, whatsoever, in any case, and I've heard them all, and I still don't believe in abortion at all. So I would have had him. I can't say that

abortion did not cross my mind, because I was very scared. And I knew for one second, when Javier and I were talking about it, he said, "Are you sure you want to do this?" And I said, "No, I'm not sure." But it was that quick. It never crossed my mind again. And I just knew I couldn't do it, I knew I had to have him. So that wasn't the major part of the decision, it was just my belief.

When Rosalie first learned that she was pregnant, she believed that she would marry Javier, and felt relieved that she could have the child in the traditional context of marriage. However, when her boyfriend left again, she was scared but resolute: she held firm in her beliefs as this child tested her faith.

Women who pursue single motherhood experience a catalytic event that takes them to the threshold in their cognitive journeys. They can point to a moment where it becomes clear that motherhood has to be at the top of their agenda. It is no longer a choice but a necessity that needs their immediate attention. These moments force them to think outside the box of the expected ways to go about having a child. But even more, they feel their lives would be flatlined, that they would shrink, should they not act upon their wish to become mothers. The future can be full only with a child. Still, they do not know which route to motherhood will bring them a child.

## Conclusion: A New Vision

The liminal state is a period of shifting back and forth between remaining in search of a partner and moving forward to having a baby, bypassing marriage.[7] Women are stuck and can't easily figure out what to do. For many, the liminal state is about being caught between competing visions: their parents' married lives versus families headed by women. The latter, once a sign of poverty and immorality, has now become the way that some middle-class employed women are opting to create families. However, despite its growth as a phenomenon, motherhood without marriage is not culturally established. This, in part, is why women waver before acting.

Women stretch their consciousness in order to challenge the narrowness of prevailing worldviews: they can create self-sufficient middle-class families without plunging into poverty or marrying unsuitable partners. Suddenly a new vision comes into focus: they dare to think about bypassing marriage. However, thinking and readiness to act are separate. Often women test their own readiness by creating artificial hurdles that they must surmount before acting on their desires to become mothers (e.g., another degree, a certain sum of money in the bank, purchasing a condominium).

Looking back fondly at their own family life leads to a review of their childhoods. As gender expectations have changed, they are caught, leaving them without a clearly charted life course. While their mothers may not have articulated their role in the family, the daughters view their mothers' lives as subordinated to their fathers. These women believe that relationships can be more equal than what they witnessed as children. Further, in the workplace they experience an equality their mothers never thought possible, and want to extend this equality into their imagined home life. Prior relationships did not lead these women to "having it all," and they feel they must choose what is most important to them. As good girls who conformed when they were children, they often embraced the changing social tides by grabbing on to opportunities once reserved for their brothers. But motherhood on one's own requires a greater degree of noncon-formity. Lesbian women are already nonconformists, but they too are breaking out of the two-parent formula for family. All women waver in their decision, postponing it as they move back and forth imagining various scenarios.

Often without warning, an event occurs that crystallizes their desires, focusing a decision: a future without a child is simply unbearable. They have been talking and thinking about what to do with those closest to them for a while—wanting everyone aboard in case they decide to move forward. A catalytic event disrupts the ping-pong-like contemplation. This event makes them realize that they need to change this back-and-forth pattern that has so far characterized their adulthood. They dare to step out of line: the baby carriage is about to come before marriage. The catalyst may take different forms but always results in a woman giving herself permission to become a mother.

Their decision to become mothers on their own is in some ways a continu-ation of changing norms for women in our culture. Ironically, while their achievement in the workplace became a symbol of equality and progress, these women do not give up motherhood, the oldest expectation and centrally defining identity for women. Instead, they take a risk in order to adhere to the mandate of compulsory motherhood.

# 3

---

## MOVING ON

## When Baby Makes Two

**Lori-Ann Stuart**

After years together, my girlfriend and I had discussed at length having a child together—she was gung-ho about the idea and we had many conversations discussing how we wanted to have this baby and who would do it. I really wanted to experience pregnancy, and since I was older, in my early thirties, we thought I should have my turn first. We decided that a childhood friend of mine, probably my oldest male friend that I have known since we were ten, would be a great person to ask. We're pretty close even though he lives in Pennsylvania, so we approached him about it, just had a general conversation. And at the time, he said, "Oh, yeah, that's something I would think about."

After my relationship with my girlfriend ended, I waited awhile, unsure I would do it on my own. So when I started feeling like I was ready to think about doing it on my own, I wrote my friend Bob a letter. Even though he must have been surprised to get something from me in the mail, I wanted to give him space to think about his answer and say no if he had any doubts. In the letter, I had written, "Remember that conversation we had? Would you be willing to talk about this?" And I said, "If you feel this is not something you're interested in doing at all, that's fine, and we don't have to talk about it." I wanted to make it clear that I would still want to be friends even if the answer was no. I asked him to mull it over and really think about what this would mean. About a month later I got a call from him—he was completely open to the idea. Hearing him say that he was seriously considering this was exciting but scary—I was really torn, having heard so many donor horror stories but wanting him to be the one. Even though we are close friends, I was afraid we'd end up with a bad situation. We had a bunch of conversations and he started to have some doubts as we talked it over. He also talked to his therapist and some friends. But it actually wasn't a very long process. It took a number of months of us talking about it, a couple of months to iron out the terms. In the end, he told me I was really important to him, and he knew I wanted to have a kid, and he felt like he wanted to help. That's the simplest way to put it.

He and I have such a long-term friendship and I know him really well. He is somebody who hasn't ever really wanted to be a parent—it's not something that he really feels he has to do in his life. This made him even more appealing to me as a donor. As we talked, trying to figure things out, we decided, despite our close friendship, we needed a contract for both of us to comfortable with our decision. I can show you the contract if you want to see it, but the essence of it says that he has absolutely no obligation or responsibility, financial or otherwise, and he has no rights. He's not named on the birth certificate. I make the decisions about school, about everything. And it says that he will be known to Andrew. But it doesn't say "as the father." It says that they will see each other from time to time as it's mutually agreeable, but it's up to me basically. I can decide they are never going to see each other—I can control it. Luckily, his biggest concern was not wanting to feel like he had any sort of responsibility. And my biggest concern was not wanting him to have any. So that worked, because I wasn't looking for him to be a co-parent. I wanted this to be *my* child. If I ever ended up in a relationship, that person might become the second parent. The main thing for me was that I wanted it to be someone that my child could know and have some kind of relationship with but not have it be as a parent. And some of it, also, is the particular person—I think that Bob is really a great person. I suppose if I'd ended up with a donor that was a friend of a friend of a friend that I didn't know very well, I might have felt differently. I probably would have ended up at the sperm bank.

It was complicated to even try to become pregnant because we live in different states—but it took six times over ten months, and at age thirty-six I was pregnant. During the time I was trying to become pregnant, I began to think about how I should rearrange my life for this kid. I have a job with crazy hours and I lived alone with just my cat. I had this great single life—I could come and go as I wanted. But I wanted a life for this kid to include more people than just me and the cat. After I got pregnant, I got serious about making changes. I talked to my friends about wanting them to be a part of this kid's life in an involved way and so I pulled my circle of friends in closer.

Looking back, this was my nesting period. I also joined a baby group, a bunch of pregnant women, some single, some not partnered, some straight, some gay. In that group I could share everything that came up while pregnant and I felt like we were all in this together. It's what your generation would have called a "consciousness-raising" group, as we would share stories about the gross assumption people make seeing a pregnant woman. Everybody assumes you've got a husband stashed somewhere. Even the women in the group with husbands could laugh about the bizarre experience of having a stranger put their hands on your stomach and ask about your sex life. It didn't seem to matter that we live in such a progressive area. Between the baby group and my other friends, especially my good friend Maggie, who became my roommate, I felt my life becoming more stable. As I got big, my group of friends grew too, until my world felt big enough for this kid.

## The Departure

The idea that families can be created by women alone may not seem revolutionary, but it changed the worlds of the women I interviewed, allowing them to imagine families crafted in new ways as both legitimate and valuable. Leaving the liminal state, these women claimed the right to motherhood because it represented a promise of ultimate fulfillment that is unique to women. However, these women had to first confront the role of men in their process of becoming mothers. Society still jealously guards men's connection to children when they choose to assert it.[1] Even after women decide to exit the liminal phase, ready to make the departure to single motherhood, the route to the moment when women hold their child in their arms is pitted with societal expectations and stereotypes.

Women begin their journey by figuring out the options available to them for becoming mothers. Initially, it remains blurry as to what route to motherhood to try first, but slowly they bring their options into focus. These women store in the back of their minds the books they have read, the therapy sessions and self-help groups they have attended, and the conversations they have had with other women. They then have to figure out how to use that information in the context of their own lives.

Now on the threshold, women act on motherhood for the first time by chancing pregnancy, finding a known donor, ordering donor profiles, or putting in the paperwork to begin an adoption. Women who become pregnant through lax birth control use act twice, once when they discontinue contraceptive use and then again when they decide not to abort but to give birth to and raise this child. As they stand poised to depart on this new journey, all women are forced to reconcile the new way that men will fit into their lives for the purposes of becoming a mother.

Often women pursue more than one route to motherhood. While some, usually older women, make a beeline straight to adoption, most, including gay women, explore the possibility of biological motherhood as their first choice.[2] Taking a chance on becoming pregnant with a lover is less limited by age, cutting across women in their twenties, thirties, and forties. Women in their thirties, most of whom have all options available to them, gravitate toward donor-assisted pregnancy, caught in a quandary between locating a known donor and accepting the more attainable unknown donor. The known donor—a "bio father"—could also reveal himself in the future and satisfy the child's curiosity about his or her genetic roots, making discovery easier. Women speculate that this meeting might be important for the child's sense of identity.[3] Before considering insemination with an anonymous donor, women first ask various men—childhood friends, spouses of family and friends, and former lovers—to become donors.

Regardless of the route to achieve compulsory motherhood, women must devise a substitute for the Ozzie and Harriet family model in which many grew up. Individual contracts supplant familial obligations in the new model, reinforced by the emphasis on the individual in legal precedents.[4] These various kinds of contractual relationships, both formal and informal, regulate genetic ties and break with precedent.

Concurrent with weighing their options of how to become a mother is the shaping of a new child-friendly life. Although the phrase "baby makes two" illuminates their choice to meet these demands without partners, these women also realize that they are part of a larger extended family of kin and friends that will support them and welcome their child. This web provides a solid base for creating family life. The families these women create are embedded in a network of voluntary relationships, unrecognized by government and the law. A baby procured through one of many different means and a "chosen family" are both part of the formula for new motherhood.[5]

### What Are Men to the Making of Mothers?

As Sophie, thirty-nine years old with a one-year-old, humorously points out, sperm is easy to come by:

> While I was thinking about donors, a friend of mine said, quoting from the "Rime of the Ancient Mariner," because I was thinking, "Where am I going to go?" And she said, "You know, it's just amazing. I look around and I think, there's sperm, sperm, everywhere, and nary a drop to put in Sophie's vagina."

However, securing sperm for the purposes of single motherhood involves evading the patriarchal reach. Patriarchy is a broader system of rights and power, often reflected in the law but also part of the cultural fabric, that governs both men and women. Choosing a route to motherhood requires maneuvering around these regulations and the weighty cultural expectations surrounding reproduction. As Lori-Ann describes in her story, all routes to motherhood involve extensive negotiation and are beset with many threats to the centrality of the mother-child relationship.

Deeply embedded in these customs of reproduction that govern women's behavior is a cherished bond between intimacy and intercourse, both essential ingredients in the ideal.[6] Intercourse's unchallenged dominance as a method of conception for the majority of the twentieth century meant that it was impossible to avoid the physical involvement of men in the making of children. However, when it comes to men's involvement in their becoming mothers, today women face an array of options, some of which were once reserved for heterosexual couples only, such as the use of donor sperm and adoption. Their decisions are as much about how they will become mothers and the story they will tell their children as how far they are willing to stray from the normative path involving intimacy and sexual intercourse. For some women, in particular those who have no other option but to adopt because of their age, the decision is made for them. But even a choice to put off motherhood until it is no longer physically possible is a de facto decision that some women may have unconsciously made. Defying the traditional story of sex, reproduction, and birth—what I term the "reproduction narrative"—is a daunting task, and women vary in their willingness to undertake it.

Women who are gay have already dealt with the task of rethinking the reproductive narrative in the formation of their sexual identity. Part of their understanding of romantic relationships means accepting that they will not be able to create a baby with their partner's gametes. Likewise, there is no confusion about sexual intimacy creating a baby, as it is simply not biologically possible. Therefore, gay women do not hold on to this reproductive narrative in the same way as their heterosexual peers. These women have already reevaluated their relationship to traditional reproduction in the course of coming to terms with their sexuality. While once this reckoning might have been concluded with an either-or scenario, presenting motherhood and lesbian identity as mutually exclusive, younger generations of gay women do not feel that children are out of reach because of their sexuality. As a result of contemplating alternative families (with a partner of the same sex in mind), these women are aware of different routes to motherhood in ways that heterosexual women in this study are not.[7]

In contrast to Sophie, whose entertaining outlook on sperm opens this section, Elyce had been contemplating where to find sperm since she was in college. At that time, ten years earlier, she had teasingly extracted a commitment from a college chum that he would be a known donor for her child.

> I came out as a lesbian when I was early in college—I fell deeply in love with a woman—and so I knew I would be needing a donor if this was going to happen. Jade's father is a friend from college, so I had already started asking him when we were twenty, "Will you be the donor?"

Having already broken with the societal norms when they came out, gay women such as Elyce have already rejected a man as essential to family life. However, this does not mean that they exclude men completely—as Lori-Ann notes at the start of this chapter, men are the source of gametes. Perhaps more important, many gay women include men as friends of the family and, in one case, even a co-parent, though never as a part of a romantically linked parental unit.

Women who intentionally chance pregnancy take the most conservative path, one that maintains the intimacy narrative of two people creating a "love child." Either by refusing to use birth control or by playing Russian roulette through lax use of contraception, women are able to take a chance for the child they want, comforted that the story of the child's beginning would always include the face of the father. Though the men in these stories vary from the steady boyfriend to the casual vacation passion, about two-thirds of the women who chanced pregnancy informed the men that they were doing so. Others had various mishaps with birth control.

For these women who chanced pregnancy, another choice lay in their decision to keep their child and go it alone. Put differently, intercourse was a *technical* method for becoming pregnant that was easier than artificial insemination, a process that involves arranging semen deliveries and scheduling appointments at fertility clinics. It is the time between conception and birth, when they make the choice to become mothers to these particular children, that these women's agency is most salient, as seen in the story of Rosalie, who held firm even after her boyfriend, Javier, left her.

As they imagine being a mother, these women seek the outward appearance of the couple in love having a child, or the intimacy narrative. Hoping that the men who impregnated them will be dads, they settle for a father with a face. While these women could be viewed as having been left in the lurch, jilted by men, even this interpretation of their stories belies a larger narrative of men and male power in reproduction. This particular narrative tells of men's entitlement to parenthood: that they can stay or leave, being a dad only if they want to. Thus the story of the woman left with a child is one that serves a larger male-focused narrative, inserting men into family only if they choose it. The story line disguises women's agency in choosing motherhood, giving the illusion of men's control over families. This misdirection, while not an intentional manipulation, in effect keeps such women's bid for solo motherhood below the radar in a way that other routes to motherhood do not.

The desire to disguise their own agency is also articulated by women who use donor-assisted routes to pregnancy. Women who inseminate told me that they often prefer to let the assumptions made by strangers and acquaintances stand. A story of a man who left, not willing to shoulder fatherhood responsibilities, is preferred to that of a woman who creates a calculated child. These women's desire to "pass" is a testament to just how threatening their real story is to the cultural constructs of motherhood. To use a donor is to sever intercourse from reproduction, replacing the entire man with solely his gametes.[8] Anonymous donors become the extreme—the physical presence of a man is replaced by a paper profile, dispersing any illusion that the whole man is attached to mother. This route circumvents any claim men could make on women, and the resulting children are a strong statement of women's agency. Even the women who choose known donors usually elect artificial insemination, separating themselves and their resulting child from the men. Insemination clarifies the known donor's relationship to women and children. Women use the intentional avoidance of physical contact as a barrier to these men's future involvement. Unlike the women who chance pregnancy, women who become pregnant through donor assistance break the entanglement of an intimacy narrative and reproduction.

### Sign on the Dotted Line: Contractual Protection for Family Renegades

Even for women who deviate from the norms of reproduction, the shadow of patriarchy and fathers' rights permeates the whole decision-making process, regardless of the route to motherhood that is chosen, and so this new form of motherhood often requires contractual protection.[9] Single motherhood has abandoned the marriage contract as its legal parameters for parenthood. In its place are individually crafted contracts that break all the assumptions society makes about the connections between marriage and parenthood. In the case of adoption, these contracts also supplant birth certificates, revising the initial route of parenthood.

Some legal protection for new motherhood is established before children are even conceived. Anonymous donors are inherently contractual: men hand over their parental rights with their sperm. The donors leave behind a paper profile and a promise to never lay claim to the children that result. In the case of known donors, contracts painstakingly drawn up in attorneys' offices are meant to trump norms of genetic parenthood—there is no mistaking these donors for unwed fathers.

Women who use the donor method are not interested in socially parenting a child with the donor; they want the child to be their territory and their responsibility.[10] Because women know they want to parent on their own, men who gave any inkling that they would want involvement with this not-yet-conceived child are ruled out. Nadine, who approached male friends as possible known donors but ended up using an anonymous donor, explains it most directly:

> But I thought if I was going to do this on my own, I wanted to do it on my own.
> I couldn't do it on my own with someone who I was ambivalent about or who
> I was going to worry was going to come take my children. None of that worked.

Women looking for known donors do not completely reject a place for men in family life, but they maintain an image of limited involvement. Lori-Ann, whose story opens this chapter, picked a close friend who did not want to be a dad. Even given the trust this close friendship implied, she understood that forces more powerful than this trust could impinge on her ability to be a single mother. A contract provided Lori-Ann with the security that her personal relationship with the man could not.

The contract is meant to deny the impulse of the legal system to tie men to children. Therefore, in donor contracts, women and donors agree that the man will be a sperm donor but not a dad. His involvement is carefully mandated, always exchanging freedom from financial obligation for the relinquishment of parental rights. Children have their mothers' last names and, with very few exceptions, no father is listed on the birth certificate. Some contracts also specify that the men will be known to the child, but the specifics will be controlled by the mother. Donor contracts do not completely sever the claim of genetic fathers— in reality, these documents are merely gestures of good faith, not legally binding contracts. For instance, in one case, even though it was outlined in the donor contract, one woman had to get legal documentation of the known donor's abdication of parental rights in order to have her child adopted by her husband. This example is not only a testament to the tenacity of legal precedent regarding fatherhood but also an illustration of the legal system's treatment of donors as unwed fathers.

Women without contracts separating their children from their fathers believe they have other forms of insurance protecting their sole parental rights. The use of sperm banks is one such type of insurance. Althea, forty years old with a three-year-old, conceived her child with a friend who lives abroad as a donor:

> He knew that because I'm so damn independent that an arrangement with him would be a very good idea because he would not be in my life, literally. He was leaving the following—well, at that point, he was leaving whenever, as soon as the visa became available he was on the plane back. And he's from a faraway country, so the chance of him coming back and becoming meddlesome in my life was really pretty remote. Yes, I thought if I was going to do it by myself, I really wanted to do it by myself. So with him, it would really be by myself.

Women without a contractual agreement seek other barriers to protect the centrality of the mother-child relationship. For women who chance pregnancy, contractual protection is not established at the outset, and some women, as discussed in chapter 5, use the courts to block fathers' claims after the fact, relying on restraining orders, for example.

Adoption involves by far the most contractual arrangement of all the routes to motherhood, and for this reason it seems to promise the most undisputable claim to single motherhood. However, adoption has become more and more disputed domestically, with claims to children by birth kin making these contracts permeable. Many women choose to adopt abroad to be safe, using the ocean as a buffer, as Althea did with her known donor.[11] Others settle for open adoption domestically, hoping to avoid future struggles.

The contracts are meant to create security for women not playing by the patriarchal rules of family. Even more important, the mothers wish to establish the supremacy of the mother-child bond, since that will become the core of the family. While men might not be completely pushed aside, if there is recognition through policy or law that mothers and children are the core of today's family, men's claims to women and children would present less of a threat. While women do not want men to be tied to their families in quite the same way as in the past, it is usually not their intention to exclude them completely. As much as a particular kind of male-dominated family has declined, the legacy of fathers' claims to both women and children continues to resurface, often in new court rulings. Women wish men to play minor, steady roles, but when confronted by this enormously significant political and legal legacy, the women balk, writing them out through contracts.

### Answering the Question "Who Is Your Father?"

The choice of route to motherhood is also a decision about how women, and consequently their children, will answer to society. With the question "Who is your father?" so inescapable, women and children rehearse an answer. Those women least likely to break the rules of reproduction are the most likely to have a man to point to, or at least paternal kin to present as an answer to this question. But the question of fatherhood is complicated in the United States, as genetic paternity and being a dad are usually treated as one and the same (with the exceptions created through remarriage). In other cultures studied by anthropologists, components of what American society terms fatherhood are distributed very differently. For instance, the biological father in Botswana, as in many other African countries, is not automatically the social father and, depending on circumstances, may never become one.[12] In other cultures, the mother's brother may be delegated the responsibility for the child's upbringing, something usually within the jurisdiction of genetic fathers in the United States.[13] However, that said, the coupling of genetic parenthood and social parenthood complicates the relationship between children and paternal kin (grandparents, aunts, and uncles). For example, in the case of known donors, it is the father that is the base of the paternal kinship network, and if he is contractually excluded, so is his family. For example, Sophie, who first approached an old friend to be a known donor, was aware of the inextricable linking of the man she approached and his kin:

> And then also, Jason said at one point, "What about my mother?" And I've known his mother since I was eleven. And I said, "Well, you know . . ." And he said, "Well, Jack won't have a grandmother." So I said, "I'd kind of love it if your mom . . ." And he said, "You really have to think about that because she'll take over." It was very, very complicated.

As much as she adored Jason's family, Sophie could not fathom either their involvement or their lack thereof. Other women, such as Lori-Ann, want known donors enough to eventually expand kinship to include his family, even if this was not initially a part of their agreement.

By contrast, women who chance pregnancy, particularly those who thought they could cement their relationships by having a baby, more readily accept ties between paternal kin and the child. Regardless of the father's social involvement with the child, in these cases he is labeled as the father and provides the connection to kin. With placement of his name on the birth certificate from the start, women are weaving themselves and their children into a web of connections. Apparent from the range of reactions toward fathers and paternal kin are the multiple layers of the question of "Who is your father?" This question of a child's identity includes not simply the face of the father but also paternal lineage.

Known donor insemination provides a borderland for a child's paternal identity. Known donors are providing an identity, a tangible but absent father and sometimes his kin. Like other women with known donors, Lori-Ann wanted to know her child's father, a man to whom she ultimately could introduce her child, but she also wanted to be a sole parent without interference. She wanted intimate details of this person, such as whether he prefers preppy clothes to punk ones, is right-handed or left-handed, is a dog person or is allergic to all canines, is a couch potato or a sports enthusiast—in other words, information that a sperm bank profile alone does not reveal. Annette, who chose a former lover as a known donor at age thirty-eight, described her decision:

> I decided on a known donor for my own peace of mind. I felt like it would always bother me if I weren't able to say things to my child about who his father was. And I saw the kind of information that the friends of mine in the single mothers' group were getting about the donors from the sperm banks. And it was very minimalist. You know? It was like height, and weight, and maybe a little ethnic history, but nothing about temperament or personality. And I just wanted to be able to know that, to be able to tell my future child.

Using a known donor, however, guarantees one form of peace of mind but not another; this choice carries with it both legal and social risks for the mother and child. The choice to use a known donor, then, serves as a trade-off for future security surrounding the mother's rights. Though providing security that known donors cannot, anonymous donors (and their kin) become a collection of facts— health, demographics, and test scores become stand-ins for a more substantial identity. The paper profile is proof of a father and intergenerational kin.

Children who are adopted may trace their birth parents to answer this question of identity.[14] Those with open adoption have this more readily available as an option. However, for children who are adopted internationally, these connections are nearly impossible to make at this time. Often in these cases, it is a country that becomes a stand-in for people, an answer to the question of "Who is your father?" The history of the country is woven into the creation narrative and into the women's story of becoming a mother. Often the circumstances that were most important in leading a woman to choose a child from a particular country, whether it is a love for that country or tragic events that disrupted birth families and created orphan children, provide a gracious exit from this line of questioning, one that places blame outside the birth family's control (which is not to say the children themselves do not wish for more information). Thus, in these cases, the global displacement requires mothers and children to connect with a culture rather than a person.

The use of known donors versus anonymous donors and adopting children domestically versus internationally becomes about the mother balancing the importance of her imagined child's ability to know his or her paternal identity with the mother's need to shelter her parental rights from the reach of patriarchal family policies and law. In sum, women on the threshold figure out a passageway to motherhood that makes sense to them. Women weigh the potential for knowledge of the father against the protection of anonymity. Each choice is fraught with compromise.

## Social Nesting: Making Connections While Waiting for Motherhood

During the months they wait for their child to arrive, women take stock of a web of connections, strengthening bonds that they hope will cushion their new family.[15] They ask people to participate in their birthing classes and labor, seeing this experience as a gift they want to share with those closest to them. Women who adopt abroad make arrangements with close friends or family members to accompany them on their journey, while other friends remain on the home front, preparing for mother and child's arrival in the States.

The irony of "when baby makes two" is that, with the exception of an isolated few, the women I studied celebrated motherhood by including their close friends and families in the early milestones of parenthood. They were not mother and child against the world but part of a broader group of people chosen (and willing) to support them as they transitioned across the threshold. By talking through the sticky points with friends and family, letting them in about how they felt and what they did, they orchestrated a network to substitute for a man.[16] This is not to say that women who have partners do not make these arrangements, but the women in this study consciously went about this process in order to ensure that their needs would be met.

Lori-Ann is an interesting case in point. While pregnant, she restructured her life. Though still living by herself in a small apartment, she wanted her baby to be surrounded by loving people from the beginning. She enjoyed living alone as a single woman, but she desired to craft a different life for her child. By strategically locating people within her broad social network who wanted to be involved in the birth and upbringing of her child, she embedded her new family of two in a network of many more. These people became a part of her pregnancy experience, and knowing that she had a wealth of encouraging friends and family in the area facilitated her decision.

> Actually, part of the process of deciding to get pregnant was thinking about who were the people in my life that would be able to be supportive of me, and what

kind of support I would be able to get from whom. In some ways, I feel like he's not just my kid. He has this whole group of people who have different kinds of connections.

Lori-Ann may have valued her privacy when she was childless, but with a child on the way, she came to value the closeness of community of friends and family. This desire motivated her to change her living situation:

> I had been living by myself and I kind of knew that I didn't want to live by myself and do this because I felt like I would be too isolated. And I lived in a very small apartment. Maggie and I decided to move in together—we also work together—it was sort of a big relief because I felt like she was a person I knew and she was into me having a kid.

Maggie was not a stranger; Lori-Ann chose her because of her willingness to become involved in her pregnancy and her child's birth. Maggie and Lori-Ann split the rent, and because they worked different hours, Maggie agreed to help with child care.

Twenty-six women in this study had at least one roommate, rented space from their own parents, or rented out parts of the multifamily dwellings they owned. The majority of these women had roommates or were landlords for people who were also actively involved in their child's life. Some women reduced the rent in exchange for hours of child care per week; others made less formal arrangements and treated roommates as family members who could help out if needed. Ellen, whose mother allowed her to live in the large Victorian house that she already rented out to several boarders, took advantage of the variety of people living in the house to create a surrogate family for her child. The common living room was fair game for anyone living in the house who wanted company. These strategies fostered early ties to other adults and created routines as children age. However, mothers remained the central decisionmakers.

Friends became witnesses to each other's lives. When Claudia went to claim her adopted son abroad, she asked a very close friend, Chloe, to accompany her.

> [Chloe is] a very old friend of mine I've known for about thirty years. She lives in Northampton. She's been married for thirty years, has a son. And when I thought of going abroad, I thought, who did I really want to come with me? And I had two friends in particular who I could imagine asking, both of whom were married, had kids. . . . So I asked these two friends, and my friend, Chloe, told me she wanted to go. And since then she's been a very major part of our life.

Her friend captured on video the moment her son was first placed in her arms. The start of an adventure to create a family hooked Chloe, who also fell in love with Claudia's child. Claudia consciously chose not to ask her lover to accompany her. The relationship was too new, she did not want to compromise his status as a lover, and he did not want to be a father. Chloe and her husband were also named in Claudia's will as her son's legal guardians. As this study shows, godparents are a common way for women to tie adults to these children, with the understanding that godparents are not simply symbolic but will also provide for the child and be consistent participants in the child's life.

Extensive networks may begin even prior to birth. Lily activated hers once she found out she was pregnant. She wanted to divide up the responsibilities among several friends, all of whom had their own work, relationships, and volunteer activities. Lily astutely decided that asking several of her close friends would give her enough cover and would not overburden one particular friend with the responsibility, which was ultimately hers.

> So I asked those four to be my team during the pregnancy as well, knowing that I couldn't rely on one specific person to go to my childbirth classes. And by picking four, someone would be available at every point. And that ended up being a really good decision. And I had four childbirth classes, and so each team member came to a childbirth class. And I picked a friend of mine, who is a doula, and she was going to be my specific birth partner. But what happened is, during the birth, all the team members were able to be there, *and* the doula, so I had five women with me in the room, holding me and pushing my feet, and breathing with me, and screaming with me.

Other women describe the celebration that their friends and family brought to the hospital. Sometimes this gathering even includes the father of their child despite the fact that he is no longer involved with the mother. Take, for example, Evelyn's experience:

> His godmother was one of three people in the delivery room. I had wanted one friend and the godmother really wanted to be there. And she was so important, and my ex-boyfriend helped me deliver, he wanted to do the baby. And then a friend who was a massage therapist came because I was going to have induced labor. So she came to help me and stayed. She had been asking if she could be in the delivery room anyway, and she and I had been friends for almost twenty years. It turned out that a bunch of other friends found out that I was in labor and showed up at the hospital. So, there were by the end, when the baby was eight minutes old, twelve people in the delivery room. They brought chicken and champagne.

These women's words illustrate the diverse ways in which single mothers form support networks, weaving together family members with friends, whether these friends are strategically planned or hastily gathered at the last moment. Women alter living situations in order to reduce their financial costs and to facilitate relationship building. Shared housing that began as part of early adulthood independence becomes a lifestyle choice made to foster a more stimulating life centered on people who genuinely care for one another. Women may have moved into apartments of their own but often return to roommates or family, as this more cooperative arrangement provides mom and child with a broader base from which to craft strong adult-child ties.

Birth becomes a celebratory event centered on building family instead of limiting it, and for this reason, some women include the fathers of their children. Yet these biological fathers, as women's accounts indicate, are the least stable participants in the family groups that women build. Birth or adoption becomes the foundation upon which others celebrate the numerous ways in which children come to be part of these families. These celebratory moments mark the entry of these children into their new community openly and without shame. By sharing their struggles on the path to parenthood, women gather together a sympathetic group with whom they can spread the joy and hope of a new life and who will in turn welcome the child.

### Conclusion: Embarking on New Motherhood

The women I studied doggedly pursued secure employment while seeking out a partner, all the while holding their hopes for motherhood close. But when the search for a partner seemed as though it would block the possibility of motherhood, these women stopped following the rules. Both gay and straight women had to push aside the romance, love, and commitment that were supposed to come along with the creation of child. For heterosexual women in particular, they had to rip the seams of the package, deconstructing the old rhyme "First comes love, then comes marriage, then comes baby with the baby carriage." Consciously reordering the sequence in response to compulsory motherhood, these women made a series of decisions regarding how far they were willing to deviate from the narratives that govern family creation.

For women who choose this route, departing the liminal state involves resolving a series of quagmires. They enter territory that is unknown to them as they learn the language of sperm banks, adoption agencies, and legal contracts. They learn too that securing gametes is a difficult process, fraught with emotional upheaval. Selecting an initial route to motherhood from the options available to them, women find the moment bittersweet: the excitement of new possibilities—becoming pregnant for the first time, receiving a photo of a child that is waiting to be adopted—is juxtaposed with the lack of a partner. But the juxtaposition is put aside as women move on to focus on the possibilities for motherhood. The excitement is almost always shared as women extend their joy to friends and family—those they gather close to them become participants in their new lives.

The departure entails more than just a choice of a means to motherhood. Women stand on the threshold rethinking men. As they struggle in their individual decisions, they do so within a broader context—will they risk upsetting the patriarchal paradigm of two opposite-sex parents that seeks a mandatory tie between men and families? Some women play along, in particular those who chance pregnancy. Others take risks, often using donor-assisted routes, consciously seeking protection in new contractual arrangements.

In moving across the threshold and taking the first steps of their journey, women reorganize their lives, with roommates and friends taking on new responsibilities. Once only sounding boards, friends and family are now critical players and helpers, expanding the definition of who is a member of one's family. Women do not think that having children is the closing chapter in their lives; after children arrive, the possibility of a new and different kind of search for a partner who would love them and their children may begin. However, the process of getting a child into their arms and fitting him or her into their lives is a major journey, one in which the place of men continues to be negotiated along with race and ethnicity as well as employment and child care. To get to the point of departure is a journey in and of itself, but it is merely the beginning. They now have their answer to motherhood, but crafting their families poses a million more questions.

# Part II
# After Baby, Now What?

# INTRODUCTION

## "Where Do We Fit?"

By the time the child has trouble in life, you know, I'll be dead. I'll be long gone. By the time the kid's out stealing cars, you know, Dad will be dead a few years.
—David Letterman, late-night talk show host

David Letterman used humor to shirk fatherhood's responsibilities before his child was even born. Becoming a father for the first time at age fifty-six excuses him from his obligations as a dad to a teenager. Who could argue with death as an explanation for being emotionally unavailable? But behind Letterman's humor lies a deeper reality. His comments bespeak a larger ideal concept of being a dad, an ideal that he may fear he cannot measure up to because of his age. In the stuff of dreams and parenting books, dads are there forever—or at least through the rebellious years of adolescence. The late-night humorist is nodding in the direction of what sociologists refer to as a "master narrative."[1]

Master narratives describe something that may once have been real but which has, over time, grown beyond its original proportions to become both the stuff of legend and a powerful form of social control. Through repetition, master narratives insinuate themselves into the cultural fabric, even when the ideal is rarely seen in reality. David Letterman distances himself from the master narrative by turning his unborn child into a petty thief (another break with the usual wishes for our children) and draws explicit attention to a parental terrain unknown to Americans who have their children while in their twenties and thirties. Moreover, by becoming a cohabiting dad he has broken, on national TV, another ideal—that men marry the women who bear their children. In a few sentences,

Letterman reveals both what the American family is supposed to look like—its form and content—as well as his own personal failure to live up to those expectations.

Part II argues that single mothers are constructing new kinds of kinship to fit within the pervasive ideal of a particular kind of American family that is often assumed. While they can use the scraps of various legal precedents to become mothers, once the children arrive they cannot make a seamless fabric to protect their families from the same system that privileges two-parent heterosexual families. They may have chosen unusual routes to motherhood, but any celebration of that is trumped by their desire to have ordinary children—to fit in.

Single mothers are not out to change the world. In fact, as this next set of chapters shows, they work diligently on behalf of their children, patching together a life that resembles the so-called normal middle-class family. Like all mothers, they strive to raise an acceptable child and to organize an acceptable family life. In their eyes, an acceptable child is one who can explain himself or herself and family members to friends, day care providers, teachers, neighbors, and religious communities. Thus, while they may refashion the family through various routes to motherhood, they end up reaffirming certain kinds of kinship rather than challenging them. These women are agents in their own lives but lack power to transform the two-parent heterosexual family by themselves.[2]

As they strive to create viable families, single women confront the challenge of crafting an image and an identity of their children's fathers. Even though these women have not married the men who fathered their children, "father" occupies a lead role in the master narrative of family life. Genetic and social parenthood are supposed to overlap, and having a genetic stake in a child automatically confers on the contributing individual the role of social parent. As a corollary, individual children are not supposed to have more than one mother or father at any given time.[3]

As Part II will illustrate, these single mothers are surprised by and unsure about how to contextualize the inherent gap between the assumptions that have shaped their lives up until the point when they crossed over the threshold and the reality of single motherhood. They too presumed, prior to crossing the threshold, that biological and social fathers would be one and the same. Each of the various routes to motherhood gives rise to distinctive dilemmas over the ways in which genetic parents and social parents relate to one another.

In chapter 4, I explore how donor-assisted families construct an absent father to fit with the dictates of the master narrative that all children have physical fathers. It turns out that the women who most easily resurrect the father are those who conceive by known donors. They build into this agreement that the child will have at least a face for his or her father, even though this man is not expected to have a social relationship with the child. On the other hand, women who use anonymous donors have to construct these men from paper alone. The mother and child together fashion a suitable father, bringing an anonymous donor to life from a list of details.

When women chance pregnancy and decide to both bear and raise their children, as discussed in chapter 5, they do so knowing that their children have been created according to the deeply ingrained belief that two heterosexual parents create children out of intimacy and through intercourse. These children are aware that a physical father exists for them, despite how uninvolved he may be in the family's life. Not unlike those women who have other kinds of alternative families, other men become substitute social dads for the biological fathers, resembling the increasingly common American stepfamily. Nonetheless, these stepfamilies retain both the original father and a new man who "steps in" to participate in the child's life, even if he is a lesser parent.

Adoptive mothers do not linger over the question of genes the way that donor-assisted families do. Without a biological connection, the discovery of who their children are (personality and talents) is greeted as a welcome surprise. Some of the women, as chapter 6 discusses, have met the biological mothers (and sometimes fathers), but even then they do not focus on genetic inheritance. Adoptive mothers acknowledge an innate separation between the genetic and the social, believing that their (social) influence is critical to their child's development. However, almost all of the adoptive mothers in this study spoke of ways their children might eventually trace their birth parents, highlighting their acknowledgment of biology's ability to aid in their children's quest for self-knowledge.

In short, the chapters that make up Part II underscore the power of cultural norms to define how families should be. Often norms are revealed only when they are broken. Single-mother families not only reveal deeply held beliefs both about family membership and family content but also offer us the opportunity to rethink the confusion surrounding genetic and social kinship in America, since there is no longer a tight fit between the two.

# 4

## THE FATHER AS AN IDEA

### Abby Pratt-Evans

I sat on my living room floor with all these anonymous donor profiles around me. I had spent hours earlier that day downloading them from the Cryobank Web site. I was trying to look them over before my best friend from college came over to help me. Well, not really help me—she was more there for moral support. I was both excited and nervous, having prepared for this evening for a long time. This evening was about a new beginning, and I went through a lot to get to this point. . . .

I really started seriously considering a donor when I discussed what to do with my therapist. I had heard about a workshop through my HMO for single women considering motherhood. I didn't know anything about support groups or I was clueless to the various options for going about having a child. I remember having a hard time getting there, which is not like me. I was late. I walked in, barely looking at anyone. We went around to do introductions and as soon as I started, I just started blubbering and crying and that was why I was reluctant to go to the meeting 'cause it was real heavy-duty. I was just crying and crying and crying. The anxiety was just all on the surface. It slipped out.

The room felt like it was closing in. I took a deep breath that I learned from my yoga class. I calmed down and tried again to talk. As I talked the women around the table were nodding at me and I heard myself saying, "I thought I would be happily married by this point in my life, not wrestling with the idea that I might not meet someone in time. I really have a very strong desire to have a child. And it doesn't stop. It just keeps growing." Then I looked closely at the women who had just heard years of my life. They shared the feelings I had put to words. I could tell on their faces. I knew that admitting my preoccupation with having a baby was the first step to doing something about it. It seemed like I had entered a secret society. By then I had stopped crying and I felt my body relaxing—I felt relieved. This was a new world and I was applying for membership.

So I went to that workshop and got a lot of information. I scribbled down notes on a yellow legal pad I had taken with me from home about all sorts of things, from opinions on where to get the best sperm to which insurance plan I needed to switch to during my company's open enrollment. And I kept all that information in my head until I needed it. But that workshop turned out to be very useful.

Still, I wasn't sure that I wanted to use an anonymous donor. As I sat on the floor organizing the donor profiles, I recalled why the men I knew were not suitable as known donors. Two years earlier I had written a handful of letters to my best men friends. One was a childhood friend I'd grown up with, another I had met through a youth group and had briefly became my boyfriend, and the third was my sister's husband—this letter I wrote to both my sister and Frank. I recalled each of their responses to my conditions for complete legal rights over the future child. The complexity of those conditions made the profiles spread out in front of me seem somehow less taxing because they lacked strings. Patrick, my childhood friend, responded that his family would want to be involved even though he was "cool" with my wanting nothing from him. I adored his mother and sister and I knew they would be lovingly involved; yet I feared just how involved they would become—I didn't want them hovering around—and Patrick's child would possibly injure my relationship to them. They were local while he had moved away. George, whom I had dated, was skeptical about my motives. He called to say that he did not want to reconnect with me, even if it had been years since we were a couple, and he really thought I would hit him up for child support. Since this was about a hypothetical child, there was no way to assure him to the contrary. And then finally, my sister's husband, Frank, whom I had known for twenty years, had children of his own. He and my sister took my request seriously—as close as we are, I needed to put it all in writing. It felt easier than raising this directly. Frank thought the family relationships would just be too complicated. He said he loved me as his sister-in-law, but why mess with good family relationships? I was disappointed that there were strings attached in ways I hadn't really considered. I knew there could be possible legal entanglements, but I just didn't realize how many people this would involve. For example, I couldn't concede having Patrick's family involved, and he was the one who came the closest to being my known donor. I thought about asking a few more men, but that too seemed futile the more I thought about how a known donor might fit into my life. . . .

Back to the night with the profiles—I was really at a loss as to where to begin. I had almost fifty profiles. It was bizarre because all those profiles around me reminded me of the huge puzzles I always like to do on my floor, except this was about the kid I was about to have. The profiles were actually pretty detailed—they included information like identity release information, family medical histories, physical characteristics, education, occupation, and then there were short answer questions about hobbies, life goals, why they became donors, and their personality traits.

I didn't know how to weigh the various pieces of information. Suddenly I thought about the internship I had done at a local college's admissions office. Maybe I should come up with a formula for ranking the profiles. I thought to myself, "There must be a method." I struggled with how to equate various medical histories and translate them into phenotypic realities. I highlighted the relevant information on each profile but I couldn't find a common thread. Staring again at the profiles, I found myself rejecting profiles of men who were of different ethnic origins than my own. Short men and men with long, problematic medical histories also didn't appeal to me. But still I was left with a stack of potential donors whom I couldn't differentiate.[1] I liked the idea of an identity release donor. At least the option to meet the donor would be available. Eighteen years was a long time to wait, but it had the potential to make him less abstract.

I was so totally lost in my own thoughts, trying to figure out a system for finding the one "perfect donor," that I didn't hear the doorbell ring. Nina nearly scared the pants off me—she had let herself in with the emergency key and was standing in the doorway watching me. Nina was shocked by my floor covered in paper and immediately suggested a glass of wine. I thought of Nina as a sister—we were really close in college and now, ten years later, we still share the most intimate details. Nina was the first person I told about my plan to become a single mother. It was such a funny evening when we went through the profiles. I remember Nina picked up the profile lying nearest her, flipped to the questions, and she read out loud, "Why do you want to become a sperm donor?" And in a man's voice—she could always do great voices—she read the answer, something like "I graduated Ivy League with honors in the top 10 percent of my class. My scores on the SAT and GRE correlate to an IQ of 160. My blood relatives are intelligent, athletic, and they tend to live long, healthy lives. I consider donating my sperm to be the greatest act of charity."

I thought he sounded good, like my child would be really smart, but I remember Nina told me to get real. She told me, "Abby, your child would be a narcissistic basket case. What does an IQ score have to do with predicting your future child's intelligence?" Then she flipped over the page and pointed out that on page one, there was information about his twin, who was diagnosed with schizophrenia at age eighteen. So that profile went in the trash. Nina was great to have there; she was catching things I totally had missed.

I remember another profile that cracked us up. There's a question on the profiles asking about artistic abilities and one guy wrote, "Drawing: excellent (stick people)." I remember it made us laugh and we both loved that he had a sense of humor. And his health was perfect; he was a yes identity release, so my kid could meet him. But he was black. While I had dated black men when we were younger, I didn't know if I was prepared to have a mixed-race child alone.

Anyway, we kept going through profiles. Nina was being a goofball, grabbing profiles like she was a magician, all dramatic. There was another one, Dutch-Italian, six foot, medium build, green eyes, fair skin. He was a yes to meet the kid. I remember that one of his grandmothers was an alcoholic, but I didn't really get turned off until I read some of his answers. A couple I remember: to why he became a sperm donor, he said, "The payoff wasn't too bad." And then I was reading to Nina what he said about his math ability, a favorite line of mine, something like "I moderately enjoy math but my skills are above normal if I moderately apply myself." But his writing skill was below normal. Even though he was willing to meet the child and he was a good physical match, I wanted to toss him.

But honestly, none of the profiles really fit. No one grabbed me except the profile of the funny black man. And I couldn't help but think, why couldn't there be a funny white man who is more like me physically? I remember Nina's response to my whining—she reminded me I wasn't picking a boyfriend. She told me, "These aren't guys. This is sperm you're picking. Do you have to like the sperm? Or do we just go with physical information and medical histories 'cause you and I both know that humor isn't genetic, right?'"

With Nina's help, I finally was able to decide on an anonymous donor. I called the sperm bank to request donor number 180 and I bought enough vials of frozen sperm for ten tries. After inseminating for six months through my local HMO's clinic, I became pregnant at the age of thirty-three. Occasionally during the pregnancy I thought about the anonymous donor and what he might be like, but those thoughts were fleeting. The profile reassured me that I had at least something to tell my kid about his father.

I'm a diary keeper and I kept one during my pregnancy. When you called me about this interview, I read it over. One of the things that I noticed is that I rarely mention the donor, short of the night that Nina and I chose him. I have a friend who's pregnant right now, and I can't help but wonder what her diary entries must look like as a married woman. It must be different to be drawn closer to a partner who will share the baby. I mean, I talked to friends and family about being excited when I was pregnant, but there was no one special and equally invested in this baby to share my feelings with.

But even without a partner, there were tons of people at the birth, and the first couple of weeks I was never alone in the house, between my mom and Nina and a few other friends. But after the initial rush of new motherhood, I knew I had to establish a routine for myself and the baby. It's worked out okay. . . .

Sometimes I wonder, though. I look at my baby's face and wonder about the sperm donor. Who does my son look like and who will he take after?

## Your Father, Your Self

Abby's experience points to the utility of knowing one's biological parents in order to construct an identity. On one hand, the politics of anonymous donor-assisted families do not allow women to answer these fundamental questions of identity for their children.[2] Humanizing an anonymous sperm donor can only be approached by using the child's own characteristics to sketch the man behind the sperm. On the other hand, women who become pregnant through known donors highlight this man differently, having a tangible man separate from the child to reference.

Women such as Abby and their children grapple not only with the way they see themselves but also with the way they think others see them—something theorist Charles Horton Cooley described as the "looking-glass self." In other words, a child's self-image is composed of many things, but principal among them are how he imagines someone else seeing him, how he imagines that other person judges him (e.g., handsome or clever), and how he feels about that imagined judgment.[3] Mothers who use anonymous or known donors as fathers for their children need to help children imagine how they appear in the eyes of these fathers. In addition, the mother evaluates her route to parenthood positively, including the value of the father as having given her a gift, as we see later on. The mother decides how these traits she has identified from the father should be valued in the child (e.g., intelligence, physical appearance, talent; in the case of an anonymous donor, information she has gleaned from a paper profile). A woman who uses a known donor also helps the child to imagine the appearance of a positive father through more concrete, personal knowledge. These fathers, the women told me, often appreciate and know the child from a distance. The absence of an actual father makes the mothers' effort to create a looking-glass self (that is, how the child sees the father seeing himself or herself) more central to the child's self. Therefore, in the case of both anonymous and known donors, there is an evaluation and imagination of the self that contrasts sharply with the ideal father-present family.

While "paper fathers" and known donors may periodically enter the scene, offering glimpses of how they influence children's identities, the more enduring and impactful influence on a child's early identity is the active relationship he or she has with his or her mother. Donor gametes are only a token of the child's identity. Mothers, and then mothers and their children, are the ones who create stories about who those men are in order to help children pin down or concretize their self-images.[4] Like all valued objects, the child's sense of self is fragile; it needs to be constantly reaffirmed. This effort at affirmation—to-ing and fro-ing about who the father is and who the child is—also has an effect on the relationship between mother and child. Theorist Anselm Strauss put it nicely: "involvements become evolvements" that transform the mother-child relationship as together they imagine the father.[5]

This chapter examines fatherhood fantasies as well as various arrangements between fathers and their children. In this chapter, I argue that fathers are more ghostlike than real. I am most interested in the accounts women give to their children about paternal kinship and how those accounts arise. All families tell stories to their children of where they came from as part of the fabric that bonds children to the adults with whom they are close. These early memories are accounts of the self that children love to hear repeated, akin to favorite bedtime stories. An account of the family and each member's story is constantly in progress.

The story woven by the mother combines genetic and social identity. The importance of genetics must be considered apart from the medical perspective, particularly with regard to how much weight to give genetics in shaping lives over nurture. But from a purely social perspective, genetics is both an idea and a road map of identity. These mothers are searching for a means to "locate" their children based on the information they have. Genetics is one of the few building blocks women have to work with as they tell their children about their fathers; for instance, stories become created from anonymous donor profiles. Even though the women are sometimes confused about the meaning and importance of genes, they use them nonetheless as a road map to instill in their children an identity that assumes two parents are essential to create (though not always to raise) a child.

This chapter focuses on the thirteen women who became pregnant through known donors and the fifteen women who used anonymous donors. They are an interesting subset of this study because they represent women who deliberately sought to give birth to children in a radical way. With one exception, they had no expectations that the men who fathered their children would become anything other than gamete donors. Even those who became pregnant through known donors wrote contracts before pregnancy specifying that these men would relinquish all rights to their biological children.[6] By looking at these cases we can begin to understand the symbolic ways in which donors' absence forms a presence within families.

In short, the child must rely on the mother's imagination because the child cannot see herself or himself in the glass. Mother and child actively talk about the donor as together they imagine the donor as part of creating a sense of the child's identity. I discuss this in the next sections.

### Reconstructing Fathers: Undeniable Imprints of Anonymous Donors

Kerry did not receive unqualified support for her decision to have a child using an anonymous donor:

> There were people who came to me and said, "Don't do this. My father deserted my mother and it's always been a lifelong thing for me that I never knew him." And I thought, "Well, the mitigating factor is I'm not deserted, I'm not unhappy, I'm not bereft, it's not a tragedy." . . . And in thinking about it, I said, "But

I'm not any of those things. And if the choice is between not having a child at all and having a child who's maybe going to have to deal with some of these issues, I choose to have the child." Selfish, but I felt like I would be a good mother, and I think I am.

Although Kerry's acquaintances' opinions gave her momentary pause about having a child without a dad to raise him, she followed her desire to be a mom by using an anonymous donor. She had the foresight to know that having a child with an anonymous donor, who would most likely be forever unknown, is fraught with complexities. Her future, however, was vague and distant. Becoming pregnant, planning for the child's arrival, and giving birth are more likely to preoccupy these women than existential questions of the meaning of gametes and their relationship to an unknown man. Once children arrive, however, women try to understand what it means to raise a child with only a paper profile of a father.

The women reconstruct the father once their children are born. Birth narratives—the stories parents tell children about their histories from conception on—include the anonymous donor. As the child grows, some of his or her traits—from physical attributes to character, behavior, and interests—become attributed to the anonymous donor. The mother crafts a man out of the limited information she has from the donor profile at the sperm bank and those of her child's traits that she believes are unexplained by the maternal side of the family. That is, the father may be the source of the child's unexplained traits. In this way, the anonymous donor takes on a persona of his own—though it may be more fiction than fact. But through such creation the mother and child take comfort in giving this role of a father meaning in their lives. Once the donor is acknowledged as being unlike other children's fathers, the mother and child begin to create an imagined man who is a positive yet invisible presence. The "nice man" who helped them to become a family is a worthy human being, if an idealized one.[7]

## BIRTH NARRATIVES: CRAFTING A FATHER

In most of these women's narratives, anonymous donors have not rejected their offspring but have instead given the mothers the most awesome gift of their lives. The anonymous donor is not the "bad dad" who walked out (e.g., divorced fathers or birth fathers), but a "good man" who helped the mother and child become a family. These women recast the anonymous donor as doing something positive for them and hence for the child. The mother and child can fantasize together about the genetic father. In addition, the anonymous donor cannot disappoint the child in ways that dads often do. Creating a visual and idealized image has protective power until the child is an adolescent.

All of the children in this study who were conceived from donors knew that they had genetic fathers. Their mothers did not delete the donors from the birth story, instead finding a way to creatively include them. How do children conceived by anonymous donors make sense of a father who is not part of their lives? While mothers attempt to explain to the child his or her origin, they also explain ties to other individuals and the meaning of kinship terminology attached to those individuals. Put differently, family life occurs through naming individuals and interacting with them. In the earliest stories of how they became a family, women use the term *donor* to reinforce this concept as an ordinary way to create a family. The inclusion of a donor is an imaginary leap: the child learns that someone neither she nor her mother knows helped create her. Mothers report that their children's early questions are about kinship boundaries and formation: who's included, who's not, and who's missing. But the questions are not simply an exercise in taxonomy. They are about identity and place, that is, "Who is my dad and where is he?"

Children come to understand the social implications of blood kinship from the language of their births. Melissa, whose twins were born when she was thirty-six years old and were toddlers at the time of the interview, talked of her plans to present the children with an account of their birth:

> I've read some books and things like that [on children with donor fathers].
> I mean, they're really young and I guess I'll just tell them the basics, which is
> "Your father is in California." I think we're all going to be telling them (because
> the sperm banks are in California) everybody is going to think their father is
> in California. Because I guess that's what kids want to know at that young age.
> And then as they get older, I'll tell them more [from the profile].

Children will learn from this explanation that a human being exists who is their father. He lives in another place but not in their house or even in their town. Early on, women author narratives of a father and connect the child to him. They follow professional advice for explaining how children are created, revealing to the child pieces of his or her birth story as requested.

Women contextualize the birth stories of their children by identifying the place and events that transpired. They explain the donor not simply as sperm (a product divorced from a person) but as a man who is located in some place or who was located through someone. A father exists who values their existence.[8] For example, Nadine was under forty when she gave birth to twins. She explained to her preschool children the meaning of the word *donor* as she situated the actors and the action within a medical context. Embedded in her explanation was Nadine's gentle way of connecting the children to their donor through describing the similarities that she guessed they shared.

> Very recently, one of my sons has begun to ask me about a [father]—I have
> told them the story at other times about a doctor who helped me find a man.
> Now it's sort of dovetailed with the facts-of-life discussions. And about eggs
> and hatching. So that mommies have eggs and fathers have seeds. So I went to a

doctor who found a very nice man called a donor who gave me his seed. And that is basically how I've discussed it. And he said, "What's that word, *donor*?" And then he said, "Will we ever meet him?" And I said, "No, I don't think so. Mommy's never met him." And this was just in the last few weeks. "But he must be very smart and very handsome because look at you," you know? That's been it.

Although the mother may have received his seed, she transforms the donor into a man and crafts him in her son's image. Yet without a visual image women can only guess at the characteristics of the donor they observe in their children. They piece together the written profiles with the parts of their children they imagine come from the unknown donors. Without a real image to counter the fantasy, the women conjure a wonderful man to tell their children about to buffer the child's feelings of rejection by an unavailable genetic father. The self is fragile and requires affirmation.[9] In this case, affirmation of self occurs through the mother's socially shaped imagination about a man she has never met.

Abby, age thirty-six when her child (two years old at the time of the interview) was born, claimed that she preferred an anonymous donor to avoid potential legal hassles. But behind this legal veneer she saw the donor's anonymity as a shield against "letting her child down." By protecting the child from rejection, she also prevented the donor from embracing him. She fantasized with her child about the man they would never know, but the fantasy—like writing letters to Santa Claus—was unattainable.

> Bryan's father is the best thing that happened to us. He didn't let Bryan down; he didn't let me down, and he never will. And if it were a known donor, he can let Bryan down. I don't have any expectations of anyone, but Bryan might. But at this point, we can both be sad that we don't know who he is, but we both know that he's the best thing that ever happened to us. Or at least I know that, and hopefully Bryan will know that. We can draw pictures of what we think he looks like, and we can write letters to him in case we ever know who he is, but he hasn't let us down. Because I chose it this way. And if anything, I let Bryan down, but his father didn't.

These comments reveal a cognitive construction of the genetic father on the part of the mother as a way to protect the child and herself from the "less-than-perfect" way she went about having a child and becoming a mother. Abby, like the majority of women who became pregnant with anonymous donors, could not find a donor in the sperm bank registry that she liked who agreed to have contact with the child at age eighteen if the child wished it. She settled for a donor she thought was a better match even though he would not accept future contact. Few anonymous donors give their consent to later contact with the child. Further, the broader cultural values of privacy and anonymity of donors structure the psychological price the children may pay. The child is denied full knowledge of his or her genealogical heritage and the face of the father.[10]

## HALF ADOPTED: THE FANTASY FATHER

From the partial information women have about their donors we can see how they construct a notion of a whole man—the fantasy father. Instead of denying or remaining silent about him, women make him present in everyday life and conversation. Often these mothers think of their children as "half adopted," a term used by one woman. "Half adopted" is a way to explain the traits that the mother cannot identify in her own extended family. Differences—both physical characteristics and personality—are tentatively assigned to the genetic father. As Nadine commented: "I can see more what comes from me. It's hard for me to know what comes from him [the anonymous donor]. That's the mystery part."

But regardless of whether they believe in environment or nurturance as the primary factors shaping their children, most women would still like to know more about the anonymous donors. Melissa explained why she would like to exchange photographs with the donor:

> Their personality, I see their personality as things coming from me, and I think the other things must come from him. Some of their looks come from me, definitely; some of their looks must come from this other person. And I think that those things are important. So I think this person is important, I don't think this person is just nobody. . . . So I would not mind exchanging pictures or things like that. . . . To give them a sense of genetic identity, of who this person is, and who they look like.

Before conception, Melissa believed that environment was more important than genes. But her children's unexplained mannerisms have challenged her former beliefs. That is, the social implications of blood kinship arise as a mother notices parts of the child not recognized in herself.

Melissa's realization is a reminder that the self is not a thing but a process that is developed, sustained, and transformed through social interaction.[11] Her child's unrecognizable gestures, personality, talents, and physical traits transform Melissa's awareness: she must rethink how to engage characteristics of the child that come from the father's genes. In effect, a profound revelation has occurred. The mother not only perceives the child as containing elements not from her, but also acknowledges that she must socially interact with and embrace those elements in order to affirm the child's sense of unity of self.

Susan, who was thirty-nine when her daughter was born, described how the child's attributes caused her to rethink how to integrate the donor into daily life as an actual person:

> See, initially I didn't talk about him much and I sort of put it off and I didn't really want to treat him as a person but just a sperm donor. But as time went on, I began to think of him—I changed my attitude about the whole thing and began to see it more as she's half adopted. And that she has, there is this person and he

is her biological father and she does have a father . . . and so we talked about him more as a real person. If there are certain traits I don't have in my family, or myself, I might say, "Well maybe you get that from your father." But, like, he was musical and played the piano, and she's musical. And he was athletic, and she's *very* coordinated. So I just kind of introduced it and then we've talked about him as more of a real person and his different ethnic background . . . and then also, he's someone I can talk positively about. He is a physician. I can say he's smart.

Susan indicated that conceptualizing her child as "half adopted" is a process of normalization for her and her child that occurred as her thinking shifted from denial to acceptance of the donor. The concept of being "half adopted" may legitimate a procedure that carries great stigma—being created using donor sperm.[12] But "half adopted" may not be sociologically accurate. Susan equated her child's anonymous donor with a birth father. But her child was not adopted. In the case of adoption, the birth father has legal standing until he gives up his legal rights. The anonymous donor never has any legal standing. Fatherhood is given meaning at conception through the social act of intercourse that does not occur when artificial insemination has taken place. The body of a father is missing from the creation of the anonymous donor child. A mother grounds the donor in what she sees in her child, using her child as a reflection of the man she has never met.

The sperm is a detached product that helped to create a baby, what clinical psychologist Diane Ehrensaft refers to in her 2000 article "Alternatives to the Stork" as the part-object father; it does not make the producer of the product, the donor, a dad. Put differently, these mothers may feel the absence of a parenting partner and create a fantasy father for the child, but they are not imagining that man as a parenting partner. Instead, they refuse to leave "the sperm from the vial" in limbo, preferring to construct a man from the gamete. What is the psychological status of the father when the father is only a sperm? It is difficult to imagine that the child is an offspring of a mother and a sperm. Because this situation is psychologically problematic, Susan borrowed adoption terminology to give meaning to her child's genetic (not birth) father.

The use of adoption terminology allows mother and child to discuss the meaning and implication of genetic heritage and how "pieces" of the child are unexplained and might come from someone else. Children learn to internalize the biological inheritances assigned to them, even if they are fictive. Further, adoption scholars have argued that the search for birth parents by adopted children is a search to establish their genetic heritage and solidify their physical self; that is, the physical traits that they share with other family members are affirmed on meeting genetic kin.[13]

Searching for birth mothers and the relief and realizations that result from such reunions is an important theme in the open adoption literature. Maternal knowledge seems to provide the missing genetic heritage necessary for self-unity. Adopted children find themselves reflected in their biological mothers, and this seems to satisfy the self. In contrast, the children of anonymous donors live with their genetic mothers, whose physical presence echoes in their sense of self. This is not to suggest that birth fathers are not essential. I am only noting that there is an absence of information about birth fathers and how they might contribute to the self of a child created through anonymous donor insemination in ways that might be different from how finding the birth mother operates for adopted children. Certainly these mothers of anonymous donor children sketch fathers based upon profiles that list height, build, eye color, hair color, skin tone, and in some cases other pieces of information about bodily features.

Perhaps more important, the mother and child together consciously help the child see themselves as the offspring of *two* parents, thus recognizing the father as blood kin, if only in their imagination. In this regard, "half adopted" also represents the idea that the sperm is not simply a deconstructed part of a man but is connected to a human being. Therefore, the pieces that the mother regards as unknown become clues to the human being that the mother and child are trying to put together. This process is similar to solving a puzzle without an accompanying picture to guide what the completed puzzle looks like. Putting these clues together provides a way for the child to visualize and identify with the self as an object and the father as an object. By giving an object—in this case, the father—a name, mothers help children figure out how to relate to it and what to expect from it.[14] Of course, a certain mystery remains. In addition, since donors have no place in the nomenclature of the family, their reality is entirely contingent on this talk between mother and child.

Mothers carefully store, as though they are cherished mementos, second-hand information and passing comments given to them by various medical personnel who actually met the anonymous donor. The mementos are eventually passed from mother to child. These clues indicative of a man not only become central pieces but are inflated and conflated as *the* man. Susan continued: "The receptionist in the doctor's office said he was incredibly handsome, drop-dead handsome. So he's handsome, I can describe what he looked like physically, some of his hobbies, things like that."

Even though Susan's child's father was not an anonymous "yes" donor (a man who has agreed to contact with the child when the child is eighteen years old), she and her daughter talked about half siblings and what they would say if they could meet him: "The likelihood [is] that he's a lot younger than I am. And so by the time he went off and got married and had kids, they will probably be a lot younger than she is. But I've talked to her about the possibility that she might someday meet him and that he might have—there might be a whole extended family, half siblings."[15]

These imaginary conversations reinforce the child's bond to a biological family that extends beyond the mother-child dyad. Susan recounted the fantasy conversation she had with her nine-year-old daughter about what each would say if they could meet the anonymous donor.

One time she was saying she thought she would like to meet him sometime, and I said, "Why?" And she said, "I'd like to see what he looks like and if he's nice and if he likes me and things like that." And I said, "Yeah, me too." So we got into this great conversation and I said, "I'd like to meet him too." And she said, "Oh, why? What would you say?" And I said, "I would hug him and kiss him and tell him how much I loved him and how wonderful he was to give me a wonderful daughter and how grateful I was and how I just love this man to pieces even. If I ever met him, I would just thank him and thank him." So she was beaming by the end of the conversation because it made her feel good about him and herself.

Paradoxically, children learn that although men helped to create them, the men remain unavailable to them—even a photograph is lacking. The notion of a father whose presence is felt continuously and may be incorporated into conversations is still more ghostlike than real. They are asked to accept on faith that they have genetic fathers who gave their mothers the most important gift of their lives, but these men do not wish to meet them.

Mother and child cannot help noticing that the genes of an anonymous man have left unanswered questions in their lives. These stories of unknown donors point to the continued importance of blood ties. Mothers believe that their children want the acknowledgment that all children desire: they are loved not only by the people who raise them but also by the men who provided the gametes. Having a social dad might mitigate this importance. Yet grown children whose parents used donor sperm and kept it a secret, as the medical profession once advised, often had haunted childhoods. They felt that they did not belong to the families in which they were raised.[16]

When a child starts to ask questions the mother cannot answer accurately, the mother sometimes returns to the sperm bank to ask that the donor be contacted, despite knowing when she became pregnant that she would never have access to the identity of the genetic father. Since the majority of women in this study had children who were young (under age six) at the time of the interviews, they had not yet actively lobbied the banks for more information. Older children, mothers report, want more information about their genetic fathers than donor profiles give. The women and their children find the present donor system problematic for this reason. However, bureaucratic control over which pieces of information women can receive in personal and genetic profiles means that they will get, at best, only clues to a genetic father. The profile is static. Updates on medical histories do not exist. Personal information is limited to hobbies, interests, physical traits, and any additional comments the anonymous donor might want to add. Sperm banks are private and self-regulating, and the information a woman receives varies.[17] Susan attempted to relieve the pain of being unable to answer her child's questions by creating a human being for both herself and her daughter. Abby, Susan, Nadine, and Melissa may never know if attributing to the genetic fathers the traits and abilities that they could not find on the maternal side was simply a jointly constructed fiction that they and their children created.

## Providing Alternative Ways to Genetic Knowledge and Kin

Politically, these mothers believe that children have the right to meet their genetic fathers, but they have reached this conclusion only upon realizing that sperm is not just a product but also an aspect of a person and a part of their children's identities. Sperm donors, however, do not have to disclose their identity because our culture values the privacy and anonymity of the adult donor.[18] As few donors agree to meet their offspring after they reach the age of eighteen, mothers must accept anonymity in exchange for a gamete.[19] Therefore, mother and child relinquish knowledge and settle for a sketchy medical profile, despite a continued cultural belief in a tight connection among blood, kin, and family.[20] Donors sever their legal, social, and moral obligation to the children their gametes create. Ultimately, however, the women seek to reconstruct genetic lineage and its relationship to identity and family for their children. Undeniably, the vast majority of women in this study would have liked to be able to contact the donors of their children.

Even those women who believe that nurture triumphs over nature underscore the importance of the donor to a child's identity. No one mentioned future medical issues as a reason for a more open donor system. But, lacking such a system, women try to devise ways to locate the donors. Some women hope that leaving paper trails in the donor's file or maintaining contact with clinic personnel will someday lead to the missing person. They treat the information they have like an insurance policy they will use if their child wishes to know more or actually meet his or her genetic father. Teresa described how she laid the foundation for future detective work:

> So I talked to this woman, Cindy, in the sperm bank, and she gave me the information about the donors. And I wanted a medical student for two reasons. One, I wanted someone who, when they asked the medical questions, would understand what they were talking about. If I was going to get clean genes, I wanted clean genes.[21] And second, I figured if ever my baby wanted to search, it would be easier narrowing down the profession to that. . . . So anyway, I got all this information about this guy. And then I knew someone who worked at the university. And I said, can you give me a list of graduate students—because I knew when he would graduate from medical school. And I got the list—and maybe I'm wrong, maybe I didn't write it down correctly, but I do believe I have the list of his graduating class and I very nicely wrote out the characteristics of what I had and I took the list that I had and I put it in a safe deposit box.

Another woman, Corina, believed that local clinics should be more open to providing information not listed on forms. Because the clinic from which she had obtained the sperm she used for her first tries at insemination had run out of that donor's sperm, she shifted temporarily to another clinic with an on-site sperm bank. She thought that the odds were against her getting pregnant because she had been unsuccessful on numerous previous tries. But she decided to risk having less information about the donor at this new clinic rather than pass up a chance at conception. She became pregnant that month and hoped that continued personal connections to staff members would facilitate her ability to get sealed information about the donor if she should need it. For example, each year she gave the staff a letter to put into the donor's file about the child's progress in case he contacted the clinic wanting to know about or meet his genetic offspring: "One of my things is to leave a passive trail of information in case the donor should wish to be in touch. And I understand that they have files. . . . Also, I suppose I try to just build a connection with the individuals at the clinic. It's probably been a couple years since I've been in touch with them."[22] In this way, she is like some adoptive parents who hope that certain clues they have will uncover a birth parent in the future.[23]

OTHER OFFSPRING

Women usually purchase enough vials of sperm for six months' worth of attempts. Earlier, other women may have purchased this same donor's sperm, and additional vials may be purchased by a third or a fourth woman, or even more. When Abby chose donor 180, the line that read "other children" did not factor into her decision. She was preoccupied with trying to figure out her likes and dislikes on the donor profiles in order to narrow her options to a few suitable donors. Information about other offspring was extraneous. She only thought, "Gee, donor 180 has a good track record and I hope I'm as lucky." It did not occur to her that this meant her future child would have genetic half siblings somewhere.

This thread of information on the donor profile means that there is a possibility of having genetic kin without the presence of the genetic father. Even though Abby, as was the case with the majority of other women, would have liked her child to someday be able to contact donor number 180, she discovered another way to find paternal kin: nothing prevents donor-assisted families from locating other mothers and children who share the same donor's ID number.

Some women in this study (as well as a large number who are presently listed on national Internet registries) wanted to meet other children who shared the same donor father. They viewed meeting genetic half siblings and the other mothers as providing paternal kin ties and additional social identity.[24] Although the majority of women in this study reported that they did not deliberately pursue strategies whereby they would share donors with other women, oftentimes they wanted to meet the children sired by the same anonymous donor, and their mothers.[25] The management at Corina's sperm bank agreed to an unusual request because it had no bureaucratic regulations to the contrary:

After you pass your first trimester, you can ask for a more in-depth profile of the father. And they sent it and the one thing in it that really caught my eye, that

I hadn't expected to find out, is they tell you how many other children he has successfully sired. Which means that my son has at least six—he was the seventh—half brothers or sisters out there. And I was like—whoa, if I were my son, that's who I would want to meet. I would want to know my half brothers and sisters, and there are these six other kids running around who may look like Andy. So I called the bank and asked about getting in contact with those families.

*Did you feel like you had any relationship with those other mothers?*

I felt I would like to, even if it was only at some point to let our children meet each other if that's what they wanted. Privacy is absolutely utmost, but . . . No one had ever asked them that before and they were quite taken aback at the request and finally came back to me and said, "If you want to give us a letter, we will keep it in your file, and if any of them"—they said, "We won't send it to them, but if any of them also sent in such a request, we would send this letter."

Corina left a letter addressed to the other mothers in her donor's file. She hoped that they would search on their children's behalf, looking for genetic ties to other blood relations. These genetic ties would create a family of horizontal lineage wherein half siblings provide the links that children's genetically unrelated mothers foster.[26] Since Corina left that letter, donor registries have sprung up on the Internet, giving her another way of finding women who share the same donor number.

The gametes from an individual donor may produce several children with different women who are unknown to one another (and to the anonymous donor), which challenges the traditional boundaries of genetic kin and how families are usually created. These half siblings whose mothers choose to meet or who are old enough to do so on their own are forging families in ways unforeseen. This one-generational paternal side of the family, presently without other generations (e.g., uncles, aunts), could one day have multiple generations. But these donor-assisted families will be disconnected from the original donor source. Meanwhile, the anonymous donor may have his own family, with paternal relatives who exist separately yet share the genes of children he sired.

## Known Donor Fathers: Ghosts, Uncles, or Escalating Dads?

I know when we were doing the contract, you sit there and you talk about these things, but everything is so abstract and that's kind of what this feels like. It's so abstract; you're talking about this being that's not even there. And until it actually happens, you just can't really think about what it's really like.

*But you did say that he did in fact agree that he would have a relationship with her, which sounds like that was important to you.*

Well, originally, I didn't know. Mostly, I wanted her to know who her father was and have something—I wanted some kind of history, I wanted her to know who he was. I didn't want some anonymous person. And I don't know what I had in mind in terms of a relationship. Even he said, like when we were talking about this contract thing, "I'd like to see her this many times," like who knows? Neither of us really knew. We were just kind of grabbing at what seemed like it might be good.

Known donors are not simply sperm donors, as the preceding quote from Deborah makes clear. A physical man to display to her child is critical to the woman's decision to become pregnant with a known donor. Men typically selected as donors are either old friends or former lovers for whom the mother has a special fondness. All the known donors agreed to contractual arrangements that stated that they had neither rights nor obligations to the children.

The child is told that the donor is a special man who helped Mom "make" him or her; the donor is not the child's dad, only a family friend or the equivalent of an uncle who visits on occasion. That is, he remains an interested party but not obligated emotionally, socially, or financially. He is not a provider, a pal, or a male role model, as a dad is supposed to be.[27] The relationship between a father and his child does not automatically translate into dad and son or daughter. The child knows the donor as a good friend, calling him by his first name. Known donors may spend time with the child and mother as someone special to both of them—even someone who has special feelings for the child. But the child has no fundamental ability to turn this man into a social father; adults define and set the boundaries of relationships even though children may try to exert some influence.

All the children in this study who had known donor fathers, with the exception of one family, had met their genetic fathers. The children and fathers had a range of relationships: some men had minimal contact with the children, and some were considered dads. In the former case, what is the relationship of the donor to the child? Is he simply a genetic abstraction? Although at the time of conception all the men agreed to be bystanders, a few men became dad after the birth.[28] That is, the child had explicit emotional ties to the donor as a daddy, but he was not a co-parent. What makes a known donor a dad? And under what conditions will a contractual agreement escalate into a different arrangement?

THE DECONSTRUCTED FATHER: GHOSTLY BUT PRESENT

The known donor becomes a more complicated figure once the child is born. The mother, through her talk, can help her child navigate the challenge of the "looking-glass self." However, when a physical person enters and leaves their lives, certain contradictions arise and have to be dealt with by the mothers. These include terms or names used for the donor father ("uncle," "friend," etc.), the context of the past, present, and future relationship between the mother and donor father, and the potential network of kinship. In short, all of the matters that emerge over time to create a family are mediated through the mother's activities and wishes to include or exclude the known donor, and the donor's wishes as well. Thus the idealized version of the father and the everyday reality of the actual man come into tension in various ways.

The known donor's image resembles a negative of a photograph. The negative offers a glimpse of a person who is there but missing. The child knows his or her genetic identity, but the man remains in the shadow socially. Ironically, the mother knows him as a whole person (the positive print) because of a past relationship. The child still must imagine what it would be like to have a dad, even if the mother's history and memory form the basis of talk with the child about her imagined father.

In the first account below, by Lori-Ann, the known donor had a continuous relationship with the mother and child. In the second account, Jennifer's known donor appeared sporadically as a shadow.

Lori-Ann, featured in the opening to chapter 3, became pregnant by means of insemination with the sperm of a good friend, Bob, whose family she had known since her childhood. She thought of the known donor as an "uncle" who occupied a parallel relationship to the child as her brother, the child's real uncle. In cases such as this, the father is more of a constant figure in the child's life with whom some relationship can be shared. However, he too remains in the special category of part-object father. To return to the photographic negative metaphor, the known donor appears visible on the unprinted negative, forming an image for the child, but not as a developed self of the dad.

Lori-Ann's son, Andrew, at age four had a relationship with his father, but not as a dad who was raising him. Lori-Ann, forty-one, explained how she gradually introduced her child to the concept of father. She knew that the questions from her child would become more difficult and would challenge her to explain why his genetic father remained only a friend and not a dad.

> So they have a very particular relationship. I mean, they have a strong relationship, and Andrew thinks of him as "Pennsylvania Bob" because he lives in Pennsylvania. My brother's name is Bob too. So my brother is Uncle Bob, so this is Pennsylvania Bob. And ever since he was a baby I've said, "Pennsylvania Bob is important because I wanted to have a baby and he helped me have you." And when he was little, that was as much as I said. So he knows that Bob has something to do with him being around.
>
> And more recently, I had a conversation with him where I was a little more concrete about it . . . "So Bob gave me sperm and I put it with the egg and that made you." Because we were talking about how some of him looks like me and some of him looks like Bob. But I've never used the word *father* and he hasn't so far made that connection, although at some point I'm sure he will. He'll figure out that what a father is is that person. But I haven't used the word because I feel like it's not the relationship that he has with him. That his relationship is much more like an uncle or something. And I don't want him to have some confusing ideas about what Bob's relationship to him should be. And I imagine at some point he'll have questions like "Well, if Bob's my father, then how come he doesn't live here?" Or "Why don't I see him more?" I'm sure that those things will come up. But I feel like it's like he's always known. It's like "This is the story: I wanted to have a kid, and Bob helped me. Bob is important." So he knows that Bob is special in a different way than other people, that Bob has a particular kind of role in his life. And I'm very fortunate because this is exactly what I wanted. I wanted somebody who would be known and who would be important to him but who I wouldn't feel threatened [by] because he would suddenly want custody.

If Lori-Ann's son wanted a deeper, more intimate relationship with his genetic father than her friend was willing to have or could give him, her son might feel cheated and angry. The future concerned her, as she felt caught between having to protect her child from being disappointed by his father and having to protect the donor, who had no obligations and a contract that freed him from fatherhood. This dilemma underscores the rationale some women give for their choice of an anonymous donor as a preferred route to motherhood. Lori-Ann's choice of Bob as the donor for her child generated the potential for a tangled web of hurt feelings:

> There's something about the father thing—and you know, Bob and I actually haven't talked about this much recently, but part of it is protecting Bob because he really doesn't want to be a father. So I don't want him to feel like Andrew sees him as something that is not what he wants to be. So I think that is all to be worked out, still. Because as he gets older, there are going to be more questions about it.

Lori-Ann wanted Bob to be the donor because she thought that his ambivalence about becoming a dad would keep him at a distance. She also believed that he would be less likely to claim paternity than another man eager for a child. Lori-Ann and Bob have yet to figure out answers to future questions. Donors have no clear place in kinship systems. But Bob agreed to known donorship, and he had a contract with Lori-Ann that specified he had no parental obligations or rights. As Deborah pointed out at the beginning of the section, however, who could predict how the child's presence might alter the contract? For the time being, the contract between Lori-Ann and Bob remained the guide: Bob had no obligations to become a dad, and Lori-Ann was the sole parent. She hoped that if she should find a partner, that woman would become the co-parent. In this regard, Lori-Ann had no baggage of other parents to feel conflicted about or to compete for the child's affection.

Bob came to town a few times a year to visit his mother and siblings. He always made sure to schedule a few extra days to stay with Lori-Ann and her child, just enough time for the child to know "Pennsylvania Bob." Lori-Ann saw the distance as important for maintaining boundaries that would not allow the donor to become more involved even if he wanted a different relationship: "It does help that he doesn't live around here, I think. I mean, I don't know, it might be fine if he did, who knows? But it gives the relationship certain kinds of limitations, you know."

This child also had some contact with the donor father's relatives, who knew this child as Bob's biological son. The relatives would have liked to be treated as "real" kin, but Lori-Ann remained ambivalent about these ties because she did not know how to name them and could not give them the same weight as ties to her kin. In such situations, the mother's kin ties determine kinship relations; the donor's family raises too many unanswerable questions. How can he be a friend to his genetic child while his kin become grandparents, aunts, and cousins? Without the father these relatives exist in the abstract.

Jennifer, by contrast, believed that it was important to have special feelings about the man who fathered her child. She rejected the idea of an anonymous donor because she could not imagine herself having a child with a man she had never met. Jennifer and the donor, Sam, had been ambivalent lovers who finally decided to end their relationship but try to have a child anyway. Jennifer could convey intimate knowledge of the father to her child because they had been lovers. Jennifer explained how her feelings about her former lover made him more than a deconstructed father, which was how she saw using an anonymous donor:

> It was real important for me and my issues of control to know. I know that I can tell Zoë about her father. I also love that I have feelings about him as a person. I feel like there's a history I can share with her about him. When he was over here the last time, I asked him to create a genealogy of his family for her, and although there really isn't control there's the illusion of greater control and I feel like I got good genes for her and that was very important to me. Because I feel like I wanted her to be healthy, I wanted her to be smart, I wanted some of those things that I felt I couldn't get from a written document [from a sperm bank]. And the other very significant thing for me is that I have his support.

When Zoë was ten months old, Sam wanted Jennifer and Zoë to celebrate holidays with his new wife and his children from a previous marriage. Jennifer was ambivalent about such kin gatherings. She did not want to be drawn into circumstances that resembled the ties of divorce-linked families.[29] She set limits on socializing as a way to define kin, deliberately not sustaining the social interaction necessary to establish kin ties. Sam was a deconstructed father to the child: the child had a genetic father but not a social dad. They met in a public place a few times a year so that Sam could see the child, but he was more of a stranger than anything else. While Sam would have liked more contact, Jennifer created a tightly controlled boundary around her daughter, establishing herself as a single mother and her child's father as someone who would not be a part of her and her daughter's future. She then was able to present her daughter to the men she dated as "daddy-less," as she put it. These actions set the stage for finding a man who would not have to compete with another man for her child's affections. The result was a known donor who lived in the shadows.

Did she hold tight to her strategy? A second interview, two and a half years after the first, revealed that not only was Jennifer engaged, but her future husband planned to adopt the child. As she described it, Charles, her fiancé, understood that since she had deliberately left the father's name blank on the birth certificate blank, he could freely adopt the child. Jennifer and Sam's pre-birth contract had specified that he would not contest an adoption. However, Jennifer suspected that the reality of another man becoming the dad would hurt Sam's feelings because an adoption would push him further away from the child. She told me in both interviews that she had "feelings for Sam as a person," which was an "important history [she could share] with Zoë about him."

However, Jennifer did not wish to erase the known donor from her child's life. Beneath the physical resemblance lay a deeper psychological tie between mother and donor. She hoped he would retain "some spot" of feeling for the child, though reciprocity from the child was not likely at the time. I asked Jennifer about how she felt about the known donor when she was on the verge of getting married to another man:

> I would like him not to be absent from her life. But I really don't want him to be, which he wouldn't be, too in there. I really want Charles to be her father and her daddy. But I would like Sam to have some spot for her. I really do still feel connected to him, and she looks like him and me. . . . And there are things about her that remind me of him and I want her to know that they come from him. So I have some investment in him, but I don't know the answers. It feels like a mess to me.

During the first interview Jennifer remarked, sounding a bit hurt, that Sam had not bought the child a birth gift. But the last time they had met he'd actually bought the child, then three years old, a few things. She noted this detail in both interviews even though I never inquired about gifts. Jennifer had never asked Sam why he suddenly bought gifts, but she explained to me, "I have no idea what possessed him to do it. He said they looked cute." I suspected that she had never said anything to him about this because gift giving made him more like kin. Neither she nor the donor felt comfortable with this designation, even though she was hurt by the lack of presents, and so she did not pursue a deeper meaning behind a first-time gift at age three for their child. This exchange of gifts symbolized a *social* relationship between the participants, the meaning of which was laden with entanglements and intimacy. Yet they shared only minimal time, always in a public place.

Kin is constituted through chosen ties to biological and nonbiological individuals.[30] A social distance between fathers and dads is not uncommon in other cultures; dads who are not biological kin frequently have a more important role than biological fathers.[31] But in Jennifer's case, the social ties defined kin, clarifying the meaning of a donor. Sam, the donor, did not really have a place in the kinship system except as a shadow figure who appeared occasionally. Jennifer tried to find the language to locate the donor within a socially based kinship system, comparing him to other individuals who are important but not legally family (e.g., the fiancé's ex-wife). The donor is a past lover of the mother's. But for Zoë, the child they jointly created, the relationship between father and child was only genetic. Jennifer made a choice to foster the social kin relationships through her husband-to-be and his kin because they would be the basis of emotional and social interactions. Her child's genetic family remained in the shadows.

## The Donor as Vague: Dad at a Distance

Known donors who live far away may be termed a dad by the mom and child even though they are not easily accessible to the child. While Jennifer's daughter, Zoë, saw Sam, the known donor, he was never called a dad. By contrast, one woman in this study, Althea, used the term *dad*, not *donor*, when I asked about how her child's known donor fit into their lives. Since an ocean limited the potential for contact between her child and this man, she did not worry about gatekeeping in the same way that Jennifer did. Further, both she and the known donor agreed that maybe when the child grew up and became a young man he would travel to visit and perhaps stay with his "dad" and paternal kin. The donor wanted this child to be his son—even at a distance. Althea agreed to a possible future relationship for her son with his paternal kin when she decided to try to become pregnant by her friend.

Althea knew the relationship between her child and his genetic father would never amount to anything more than sporadic contact until perhaps the child reached adulthood: "Before Josh's father came to visit, he had pictures of him, but he hadn't heard his voice. But we talked about Ethiopia, he knows his daddy's a doctor there." This child has a photograph of his genetic father, which demonstrates the father's existence. But images are objects to fantasize about; they can generate a wish to know the person behind the photograph. The photo of a genetic father who lives far away signifies an identity, but it is unlike other photographs that allow a child to recall a lived moment (e.g., a picture of the child with Donald Duck recalls the trip to Disneyland).

When Althea's child was three, his father visited for the first time for a week. She described the moment they met:

> So he did get off the plane, he came over and gave me a big hug and I guess Josh just stood there. And then he picked up Josh and just this look on my son's face—this big smile came out and they hugged each other, and spun around in circles. And it's been love at first sight.

Though the child's half siblings did not know about him, his father told Josh about them, showing him pictures. Josh and his dad grew close as they played together that week. He visited Josh's day care center and met his playmates and day care providers. His dad provided a momentary but monumental presence:

> I hope that the visit will ease two things: I hope it will ease his mind that *for sure* he has a dad. You know, if he had any questions about "Well, is my mother lying to me?" or any of that kind of stuff, hopefully that will be dispelled. And second, I'm hoping that he will not feel like the odd one out when the other kids are talking about their parents or any of that stuff. Again, fortunately (or unfortunately) he's in a day care center with a lot of creative families anyway. So it's not as though every child there has a father who lives in the house, or even a father. But

still, I just figured that it might be a little bit easier for him to say, "My dad lives in Ethiopia, I haven't seen him for many years," and that's it.

Having family in another country did alter the donor's ability to visit his son. He acknowledged the child differently than the men presented earlier. He was called dad when Althea and Josh talked, but he was not involved in any consistent way in this child's life at that time. However, the genetic father considered the child his son—more for his own self-image than for the child's. That is, he knew he had a male offspring. A fading memory of a visit from a father in a photo made Josh like other children in his day care center who may have had fathers but not involved dads.

ESCALATING RELATIONSHIPS: THE DONOR AS DAD

Despite contractual agreements, the relationship between the known donor and the child may escalate. These known donors become "bio dads." That is to say, fatherhood grows out of their genetic contribution to the child; being a dad, the social part of fatherhood, is an afterthought. They set out to become not dads but fathers in the shadows. The mother acts as gatekeeper, regulating the known donor's ability to physically spend time with the child. Sometimes the man may want to be more involved but the mother does not want more involvement. Other times, agreements made between the known donor and mom-to-be before conception change once the child is born. Two of the women interviewed had been involved with the donor in the past, as what they characterized as "ambivalent lovers"; for a third woman, the donor had wanted to be the woman's lover (he had a common-law wife) but she was gay, and the intercourse that produced the child was solely instrumental. The fourth woman became pregnant with a good friend who offered his sperm as a favor.[32] In these four cases, the genetic father was dad to the child. But while he might be emotionally and socially involved in the child's life, he did not pay any child support. The child typically spent time with him alone. The donor's extended family was socially involved in the child's life as well. In effect, the role of dad was not assumed from pregnancy on but evolved over time. The women allowed this even though they might be ambivalent about shifting the original terms of the donor's role.

The need to deal with ambiguity gives rise to innovation and new values, and in rare instances dramatic transformations can occur.[33] The bio dad is conceptually interesting because he intersects with and acknowledges both the social and biological aspects of kinship that attempt to reconcile an initial gamete donation and a social relationship. The nomenclature of kinship expands. Additionally, it leaves room for the possibility that in the future the mother might marry and the child could have a second dad living permanently with him.

Sometimes the known donor's relationship to the child changes over time, escalating in ways initially unanticipated by the mom or the donor. As powerless as children may be, occasionally they do influence this change. Eavesdropping and observation help children to frame an understanding of their social world and the norms that govern the relationships in their worlds.[34] Children absorb both factual information and the affective load attached to that information—who is kin, who is not, and whether their mothers are happy with the respective relationships. Children interpret their mothers' affect in the context of what they already know about the structure of their social world. Those children with mothers who are vigilant boundary keepers may sense their mothers' firmness, making it more difficult for them to negotiate time with this "special" man than it is for children whose mothers are ambivalent (and who may want more time or emotional investment from the known donor). Young children sense their mothers' ambivalence and ask their mothers about future plans with this "uncle": this is a way young children may facilitate further and extended contact. Even mothers who have set limits on contact know that as their children grow older they might initiate closer relationships with these men. But these men would have to be willing to participate in their children's lives differently, abandoning the vows of limited involvement agreed to in pre- and post-conception contracts.

Although the man Heather selected as a known donor was a good friend and liked having a child in the world created by his genes, he did not want to be a parent himself. The donor's friendship with the mother—they were, as she characterized it, "pals"—precipitated his slowly growing relationship with the child. It was the friendly part of the dad relationship that had evolved. When Heather's daughter, Sydney, was younger and needed more physical care, the three of them would go on vacations together, looking like a "traditional" family to strangers, but at ten Sydney was old enough to take care of herself on the first solo weekend the known donor and child spent together.

> He knows her. He visits. We go on vacations every year. Some kind of family vacation thing, where we look like a nuclear family. He is a close friend of mine. When she was very little, he would sort of not know what to do with her. He was just all thumbs. But he and I were friends. We'd go on vacation, the three of us. And slowly he got to know her. And actually this year, for the first time, he's gonna take her for a weekend skiing without me. And now he's just starting to take her by himself, now that she's older and old enough not to be too fragile and they're kind of buddies now.

Sydney loved to replay these weekends for her mom, and at the end of the retelling Sydney would ask, "When are we going to see Uncle Mark again? I had so much fun with him and I love him so much." Further, even though her child and her good friend had seen each other infrequently over the years, Heather was startled by her observation that the child had grown up to be more like him than her. This cemented the importance of letting the known donor become more actively involved in Sydney's life. Remarking on this observation, Heather was attuned to the importance of noticing the man, not just the availability of his sperm:

Now that I've had Sydney, now that I've had my daughter, she is just like a carbon copy of her father. There's an amazing amount of things that are genetic. She danced exactly like him. But they'd never danced together. She's never even seen him dance. And when she started dancing, I went, "Oh my God, you dance . . . ," all the body movements were the same. There were just so many things. They furrow their brow the same. They look a lot alike. The same school issues. Just an amazing number of things are genetic. And I feel like I'm sort of a case study for what's genetic and what isn't. Because really for the first few years, he had very little impact on her at all. He'd visit two or three times a year. And they weren't close.

This realization changed her views about the known donor remaining at a distance, and instead she encouraged him to become a bio dad. In effect, she saw her close friend in her daughter constantly. She could pick out his reflection and imprint. Heather knew the whole man when he became the donor, but her daughter was only just beginning to know the man whose genes she shared. The donor for this child was not a complete dad. She knew only pieces of him—the pieces her mother told her about. The mother, in contrast, shared a history with the known donor, particularly because they were old friends. This knowledge about the donor was asymmetrical. Further, the known donor masked his identity—Sydney knew him as "Uncle Mark," a family friend who helped her mom have her. Both Heather's and Mark's views changed as Heather encouraged Mark to become a dad and as Sydney became older. Her genetic father, once an external figure in the child's life, was about to become more involved. Sydney and her dad were developing an independent relationship in which Sydney could replace her mother's memories of the man with her own experiences of him.

While Sydney and her dad may continue to grow closer, into more than pals, Annette's friend John became her child's dad early on. Annette had severe endometriosis, and after treatment her doctor told her that if she wanted to have a child, she should try to become pregnant soon. She told the doctor that she was not involved with anyone, and the doctor responded that her practice had many single women. At age thirty-eight, Annette became pregnant with a former lover, a relationship that had ended years before. Annette told how the donor's feelings toward fatherhood changed:

> That was a surprise because going into it, this donor was not particularly keen on the idea of fatherhood in the sense that he made the statement, "Having a child is just not part of my life plan, it's not something that I'm yearning to do, wanting to do, have always wanted to do and 'Oh, great, now's the chance.'" It just wasn't part of his horizon. But his motivation was because he really cared for me and he could see that this was something that I very much wanted and he wanted to help me out. So he wasn't anticipating that he would glom on to this kid and that it would be all fulfilling and wonderful. But he didn't anticipate that he would fall in love, kind of, that he would be so emotionally bonded. And that's what ended up happening. He got very involved when Ben was born and just through the months and years of parenting, he's not faded into the background.

It's like all exciting when the kid's first born, you know? You might sort of expect he'd be around there then. But maybe when it got kind of tough, that he might have disappeared or gotten less interested. But that didn't happen. He just kept getting more and more interested. And at this point, there's not any wavering about it. My son has a dad.

Annette had been skeptical that the donor's initial enthusiasm and euphoria about the baby would last, but it did. The donor did not fade into the background as she had expected and as they had specified before conception. In fact, the first thing she did every morning when she got to work was to leave a message for John about how the child was doing. She described a weekly routine that resembles those worked out by cooperative divorced parents:

> We don't have set times. We didn't negotiate it or go to court and sign a document. But it's evolved to a pretty patternized kind of thing which involves one night a week that Ben stays at his house without me, and one night a week after school like on a Wednesday or something. The overnight I just said happens on a Friday, usually, sometimes Saturday. And then usually Wednesday nights (but sometimes Tuesday and sometimes Thursday) his dad will come over to our house around seven-thirty or so and spend an hour and a half, or however long it takes, to do the visiting and bath and bed routine and put Ben to bed. So that's a time, for those couple of hours if I want to go out, I can also go out because I know that I've got that coverage. So that's what we've evolved to.
>
> We also spend time usually on Sundays all together, the three of us; sometimes on Saturdays too. It depends. Every weekend somebody always has something, whether it's Ben having a birthday party, or me having something, or John has something that he's got to do. So we're very flexible about that. But we certainly do try to have some time in the weekend where we're all three together, because that has become very important for John. He really—that's what keeps him in this, is the family time. He really likes that a lot, much more than he anticipated.

Whereas the donor particularly liked the time spent as a family, Annette was much more uncertain about its meaning, seeking therapy to sort out her feelings toward John and his unexpected reemergence in her life.

> I have kind of mixed feelings. In one sense I do like it that it's a lot easier to take care of a kid when there are two adults around, I won't deny that. The part of it that I don't like is I feel a little bit false in that it's like playacting, or pretending to be a family when we're not a family. And I feel a little bit like living a falsehood there. What does the world see when they see these people going along with their kid? But I guess I'm not going to worry too much about what the world sees because if that had bothered me a lot I would have never gone this way in the first place.

The child had always gone back and forth between the two apartments. He was used to the differences in how his mom and dad lived. I asked her how her son felt, and she explained:

Well, I haven't asked him how he feels about it. I mean, he seems to go along pretty well with the notion of "Okay, we're going over to Daddy's house now, and you're going to stay at Daddy's house tonight." I mean, it's a whole different scene over there; it's a whole different house. Very differently ordered and paced. He's got a different place to sleep there. He doesn't sleep in his own bed at our house; he sleeps at this other bed at Daddy's house. And there are other toys there. And his father has all these entertainments. He has a big, big, big-screen TV, so they are always renting videos. And that's just not something that I do. I have this decrepit old TV that's like twenty years old. I barely get color most of the time, you know? So he has different things that he does there. His father really likes to play baseball with him. And I'll play baseball with him a little bit because I know that he loves it, but I just can't get into it for hours and hours the way a guy can. And his father loves it. So that's a real joy that they share. Hey, I'm all for it.

In addition to checking in by phone in the morning and evening, this dad was concerned on other levels not mentioned by other women whose children were fathered by known donors. For the most part, known donors were brief visitors who played with their children in the mother's presence. But John was actively concerned.

And he is very—oh, how can I say this?—he tends to be a little bit hypochondriac. He's very keyed into medical things and kind of takes a gloomier view of things than I might be inclined to otherwise. But it's kind of a stabilizing influence. Because if I'm going to let something go by, he's never going to let it go by. So together we make sure that Ben's welfare is always being taken care of. So if he notices something about Ben, he'll always mention it to me. And he likes to get daily reports, basically.

Annette viewed her relationship with John as platonic, but he would have liked a romantic involvement with her. He was the father of her child but not her partner. John is the best example in this study of a known donor who became a co-parent. But as a result of what Annette called a "non-relationship relationship," the boundaries were murky. Not setting boundaries and allowing the known donor to become the child's dad left the mother wondering how men she might meet in the future would view this situation.

## Conclusion

Even as mothers affirm some important ties—most prominently, kinship by blood—they undermine others by separating reproduction from marriage, intercourse, and love. The intimate accounts of these women afford glimpses into how these mothers and their children experience the contested terrain over family life, namely, the power of a two-parent ideology. In part motivated by a cultural ideology that emphasizes the importance of fatherhood and marriage, these women attribute unexplained characteristics of their children to imagined fathers. But ironically, as new reproductive technologies create the possibilities of multiple types of fathers (and mothers), these women work hard to protect the boundaries between social and genetic kinship, in the belief that only one man can be a child's dad. These women protect these boundaries in the hope that another person will come along, marry them, and adopt their children—the ultimate fantasy.[35] Adoption will then give the child a legal second parent. In the uncertain future, middle-class heterosexual women may more readily accept multiple fathers for their children, thus acknowledging genetic ties and social ties as distinct dimensions of family life. However, as children grow up they may make their own set of demands and call for anonymous donors to reveal themselves, not unlike adoptees. Children may also negotiate different relationships with known donors than the ones they currently have.

Although it may be possible to know everything there is to know about our children and ourselves genetically, medical testing cannot produce a man to touch, to hug, or to share the child's deepest hopes and fears. The self emerges in relationship to significant others: the search to know them is deep, and as a culture we deny these children a fundamental right by allowing anonymous donors who never have to reveal themselves to these families. Perhaps the use of anonymous donors needs to be rethought in light of the data I have presented on "imagined fathers."

As medical technology makes possible the ability to uncouple genetic and social parenthood, new forms of families will continue to emerge that challenge kinship boundaries. One of the most fundamental issues is that of self and other within the family context. In this study I find that biological, social, and sexual sources are distinct but have to be unified in some way that I have called, after Cooley, "the looking-glass self," as mother and child imagine a father. The women's stories show in rich detail the many nuances that anonymous and known donors must cope with in order to sustain the idea of the father for the child and for the mother. There are important distinctions between anonymous donors and known donors. In the former, the crafting of a father is an act of imagination that belies concrete description (characteristics such as smells, sounds, feelings, voice, etc.). A woman must bring to life pieces of information that she feels comfortable loving about this man and, by extension, in their child. The child becomes a looking glass, refracting an image of the man they will probably never meet (which is why contact with other offspring of the same donor becomes an important linkage).

Through deepening love for her child, the mother gradually crafts a man the child believes is a "good" father, and because the mother created this image and mother and child jointly imagine him through this image, the child's self is positively reflected. In the case of known donors, an asymmetry exists between the mother's knowledge and experiences of the known donor and the child's firsthand knowledge of this same person. The mother has intimate knowledge of times shared with the donor that does not usually become the basis for the development of father-child relationships. Children's expectations of known donors are often limited. But innovations that include these men, even in vague and unspecified ways, may have some transformative value and power within individual kinship systems. Although the child is at a distance from the father for the most part, the child sees himself or herself in the man even if he is not a father in the conventional sense.

Donors may become relevant to family life in ways the women themselves do not foresee. Both anonymous donors and known donors are deconstructed, but in different ways. Anonymous donors are fantasy men who provide their sperm without taking on any legal, moral, or social obligation to the child it creates. The deconstructed father is reconstructed by the mother-child dyad as they search to give meaning to the donor in their family. Genealogical lineage remains severed from social kinship on the paternal side, even though the mother and child wish they could meet the man who lives as a vague presence in their lives.

Known donors are also deconstructed because their social role as dad is detached from their genetic relationship to their child. In these cases, the metaphor of the photographic negative is critical: the child knows his or her genetic identity, but the man remains in shadow socially. The asymmetrical knowledge of the mother's relationship to the man versus the child's is striking. Her choice of a known donor derives from a former (and often present) relationship with him, yet she remains a gatekeeper determining how and if a relationship between father and child develops. While multiple kinds of relationships exist between known donor fathers and their children, in this culture kinship boundaries are tied to particular types of acknowledged paternity that these women and donors prefer to leave legally vague. However, as I have demonstrated, some of these women have expanded the boundaries of kinship, and their children do have relationships with their genetic fathers. Policies that guarantee sperm donor's anonymity may change, and other mothers with biological half siblings may come forward. We have yet to label this possibility or discuss it as part of the broadening of kinship through these new family forms. This transformation of kinship terminology that rests on the relative power of gametes to unravel master narratives is "kin claiming."[36] Attempts by women to label sperm donors "bio dads" is an example of kin claiming. However, kinship that continues to be rooted in traditional marriage will preclude the possibility of expanding the ways in which donor father/child relationships develop within the United States.

# 5

---

## ROMANCE, INTIMACY, AND PREGNANCY

### Father Involvement Outside of Marriage

**Ellen Hammond**

I spent my twenties bouncing around Europe. I met someone, got married in Amsterdam, and just in time for my twenty-third birthday, I got pregnant. I wasn't ready to be a mom at that point, to tell you the truth . . . so I, we, aborted the pregnancy. Two years later we divorced, and eventually I returned home to the States. . . .

I was twenty-eight when Gavin and I started dating. We'd known each other as kids but never got serious until then. It was a good time for me: I'd landed a good job as a financial analyst making pretty good money. Gavin was starting his own business as a plumber. He had a child—with a woman he married but who left him for another woman. He never divorced her but she lived in another state. And, frankly, it didn't matter that much to me because after my experience, I wasn't too keen on marriage as an institution—to put it mildly.

Well, I got pregnant. Let me put it this way: I never was a regular pill taker, so I guess you could say I got pregnant accidentally. It seemed like the right time to have a baby. I was getting awfully close to thirty, after all. Still, I practically fell apart when I told Gavin because I wasn't sure what to do. I couldn't go through another abortion and yet I didn't know what to expect from him. He hadn't really established himself in plumbing and sometimes I wondered if he ever would. Let's just say he didn't score really high on motivation and responsibility.

So I was pretty straightforward with him. I said, "Gavin, this means that we have to make a commitment. It changes things." And he said that he wanted to have the baby. Mind you, he didn't say that he wanted a long-term commitment. I wasn't listening for that at the time. I heard "long-term commitment," but what he said was "Let's have the baby." A big, big difference.

Neither of our families was thrilled about the pregnancy. I'd known Gavin's mother for years and she was pretty blunt with me. She said, "You're a beautiful girl, you're articulate, you come from a wonderful family, and Gavin really cares for you and may even love you, but he doesn't have the means to support a child." My mother wasn't thrilled either, but she did offer me our old house in Boston to live in. She was renting it because she'd moved to Florida. Gavin was pretty handy so we figured he could turn the top floor into a separate apartment just for us and we could rent out the rest. That was important because Gavin's business was off to a slow start. Well, to be honest, it wasn't going much of anywhere, but that's another story. . . .

Unfortunately, Gavin and I broke up before the baby was even born. I'd had it with his lack of motivation and responsibility. He slept all the time I was at work. It was ridiculous.

When I took our baby home from the hospital at twenty-nine, I felt all alone, even with a house full of renters. I'd always pictured myself having a partner when I had a baby. I did keep that part of the fantasy alive, in a way. I made sure Gavin's name is on our daughter Skyler's birth certificate even though I gave her my last name. I want Sky to have a record of her father, no matter what.

Well, not long after Sky was born, Gavin stopped by to see her. I was angry at him, yes, but I felt I owed it to my daughter. And you should have seen how much in love with her he was from the very first minute he laid eyes on her. He stayed a week, sleeping on the living room couch and helping out any way he could. Then he went away. Then, maybe it was five months later, he kind of reentered our lives. I was feeling guilty that Sky didn't have the kind of dad I imagined for her. Gavin was pushing all the time for us to work on our relationship for Sky's sake. I don't know, I guess I just gave in and tried to work it out with him.

He didn't pay me anything in the way of child support, but he did offer to take Sky to his house sometimes on the weekends. Believe me, I needed the relief. I was still working and I felt exhausted all the time. I could afford to have her in full-time child care, thankfully, but it seemed like I never had a minute to myself.

At first things were working pretty well. His business was slow and he had the time. He liked taking Sky to his mother's house. She loved Sky, too. I liked the fact that Sky has two grandmas, not just one. This went on pretty well for about a year and a half.

Then, like I feared, he turned unreliable when I needed to rely on him. His work was sporadic but he wouldn't commit to picking up Sky at day care on Wednesday nights, when I desperately needed to be at a late staff meeting. He started showing up late on Saturdays. He would have a softball game or an old friend would be in town for the weekend. What made it tragic was that Sky would say, "I want to see Daddy. I want to go to Daddy's house." I didn't tell her that Daddy couldn't get his act together to come pick her up.

After months of him sometimes being there and sometimes not being there, we had a whopper of a fight and he walked out. He was sick of playing daddy and went back to his houseboat and his bachelor life.

## Chancing Pregnancy

Clearly, marriage does not a mother or father make. Women in this chapter who chance pregnancy by using inconsistent contraception believe, however, that if it does not take a marriage to become a mom, the same logic should apply to the fathers of their children. The cultural climate has changed, and children, not marriage, determine fatherhood. Put differently, biological parenthood derives from sexual intimacy, not marriage, and it is this biological union that determines rights and obligations to children.

Chancing pregnancy is not a tidy solution to women's wish for motherhood. It may give these children the potential for dads, but it doesn't mean that these men will make the necessary commitment to their children or former girlfriends. While a third of the women in the study who risked pregnancy were betting that a baby would cement a relationship with this man, the rest were unclear at the time what they really wanted from their lovers.[1]

Once pregnant, these women made a conscious choice to become mothers. Maternal love and feeling took over; they were ready, they said, to take responsibility and nurture *this* particular baby, as distinct from previous pregnancies. Ellen, for example, had been pregnant in her mid-twenties but felt at the time that she was not ready for motherhood, and so she decided to abort. These women knew they were chancing pregnancy, but they took the risk anyway. In other words, though some may have been walking with their eyes closed on the route to motherhood, no one was sleepwalking.

With the inevitable complications that result from this way of having a child, why, then, do women chance pregnancy to become mothers? Why do they entangle themselves with these men and their kin? While they may not have considered donor assistance and adoption as viable options, this in itself is a symptom of their entrapment in a certain mind-set.[2] For these seventeen women who chanced pregnancy, calling it accidental is a misnomer.[3] What these women did in order to become mothers cannot be confused with the passive stereotype society attaches to "accidental" motherhood.

Women who become independent agents in the reproduction narrative are defying the traditional story of giving in to men's wishes for sex in order to find intimacy. Those who chance pregnancy more easily tell everyone (including office co-workers and strangers) of their route to motherhood—their chosen story line, the old tale of "accidental" pregnancy, is close enough to the traditional heterosexual creation of a baby to hide their decision to forgo birth control for a chance at motherhood. However, by calling these pregnancies "accidental," society strips unwed pregnant women of their agency in their decision to have a child outside of marriage. The control that is undeniable when a woman orders gametes from a sperm bank is disguised by chancing pregnancy.

Women who chance pregnancy also act with intent by technically orchestrating their own pregnancy. A closer look at the contraceptive use of the study women at the point at which they became pregnant reveals the following: only one woman who routinely used birth control reported that contraceptive failure led to her becoming pregnant (the condom "fell off"). On the other hand, eight women deliberately did not use birth control, taking chances in the hopes of becoming pregnant. They told their partners that they were not using birth control, and because the men did not object, the women believed that the men consented. These eight women wanted a baby fathered by this particular man, and so they took advantage of the romance of the moment to get the child that they wanted. Unlike known donors, these women did not discuss or agree upon the place of this man in the future child's life (or their own), preferring to stay in the here and now. They believed they were creating "love children." Finally, eight other women, including Ellen, claimed to have been using birth control, but admitted that it was erratic.[4] They took chances by using inconsistent contraception.

The women in the study who chanced pregnancy represent a broader range of age, race, and class compared to the women who used donor-assisted routes or those who adopted. They ranged from their early twenties to their early forties, with the average point of conception falling around thirty. While I met practically all of these women in middle-class settings, this group included the most diverse array of occupations and income, from women who worked multiple jobs at hourly wages to higher-paid professional women such as Ellen.[5]

Choosing to have a baby that was conceived through intercourse does not always make both sexual partners responsible for parenting the child. There is something about the act of intercourse—the intimacy and momentary passion—that allows women to believe these men will become reliable fathers. Even some women who at conception think they do not want these men involved change their minds later, for reasons I will discuss. However, there is no predictable formula for which women end up with a dad for their child. The expectations these women hold for the fathers of their children are not uniform. Some women are constantly grappling with the question of how to keep "good" dads involved, while others fight to keep the "bad" dads out of their lives. Without a marriage certificate, which, in the past, ideally obligated men (good or bad) to their family of procreation, the relationship and obligation of these men to these children is unclear and open to interpretation. The women described in this chapter demonstrate the tensions that exist as they attempt to transform biological fathers into socially involved dads, with consistent contact and participation in their children's lives. In contrast to donor-assisted families (and adoptive families), women who chance pregnancy often have a contentious relationship with the fathers of their children, sometimes taking the form of financial disputes. This chapter explores the variations, the different kinds of fathers and dads these men become.

## How Important Is a Dad, Really?

Colleen, an artist, had her baby girl just shy of her fortieth birthday. The man who fathered her child was Colleen's long-term lover. She never really thought about the implications of his involvement (or lack of involvement) with that child when she became pregnant, but she knew she didn't want to be his wife. When he asked her to marry him, she said no. It is only after Colleen made the decision to reject him as a romantic partner that she grappled with how she wanted him involved in her child's life.

> I feel as if I should have made a better choice about who would be a father to her. It's nice for kids to have a father. It seems to be important. Daddy this, daddy that.

Colleen did not realize that she wanted a dad for her child, not a husband for herself, until after she had embarked upon this route to motherhood. However, Colleen's long-term boyfriend, like many men in this chapter, did not want a paternal relationship with the child without a romantic relationship with the mother.

Some women who chance pregnancy think that they can craft families without fathers, and a few in this group successfully did. For others, their own deeply ingrained belief in the importance of the father surfaces, forcing them to redefine the place of their child's father. Maeve, a thirty-year-old with an eight-year-old she had during the final weeks of her last year of college, described her thoughts on her son's father: "I think Hunter has a right to know his dad. And I try to keep him safe from any harm that might come with the relationship while at the same time keeping a big enough crack open for a better relationship to grow." While Maeve went so far as to move across the country so that her child's immature father would not hurt her son, even she emphasized the importance of this man to her son. She sent him regular letters about his son's growth, and, having returned to Boston, she still hoped Hunter's father would be a "good" dad and visit more consistently. Maeve was maintaining the symbolic importance of her child's father, hoping that a social relationship, a "dad," might be a possibility in the future.

When men begin to pull away from their biological children, women are forced to decide how they want these men involved. While some simply cut them out of the mother-child family they have created, others try to keep these men on the periphery and connected to their children. Often they go back and forth between what they want when pregnant and what they want after the birth of their child.

Cara, thirty-two years old with a three-year-old, is an example of a woman who actively sought to become pregnant. She wanted a passionate moment, not a husband, she thought. She had already been married and divorced and was on the rebound from a marriage that fell apart over her aborted first pregnancy. Cara's decision to become pregnant this time from a one-night stand represents a common scenario in a broader culture where women find that what they want and what they can reasonably expect diverge. A one-night stand, a place where most women never thought they would find the solution to creating a family, may at first seem irrational, but often it is an act that takes on a logical progression of its own.

Cara began to flirt with a handsome man while on vacation with her sister at an adult-oriented resort. That afternoon was more than just base sex. They aroused each another through talk of their respective striking features, painting a picture of a beautiful girl they were in the act of producing.

> I came out of the room and my sister's just like, "Where the heck have you been?" And I said, "Linda, it's a girl! I'm pregnant." She goes, "You're out of your mind." I said, "I'm telling you, I know it happened. I can feel it."

That afternoon when the two parted ways, Cara was exhilarated by believing the afternoon's passionate lovemaking had rendered her pregnant, and that was enough to sate her. At the time, she never expected to see him again, though she took his phone number. It wasn't until later that day when she bumped into him at dinner with his wife that Cara learned about his "open-marriage arrangement."

The father is not a known donor, but he consented to Cara's lack of birth control and to the possibility that he might impregnate her. As her pregnancy progressed, Cara contacted this man under the guise of wanting information for medical purposes. Cara's decision to get in touch with the father months after they parted contradicted her initial decision to become pregnant through a one-night stand with a stranger. This phone call opened the door to his continued contact with her.

Cara did an about-face. Her desire to provide her child with a father reversed her initial belief that the "Club Med man" was a momentary apparition with no potential for becoming a reality in her life. However, things changed dramatically with the birth of her daughter, and even knowing he had a wife did not deter Cara. She wanted to believe his wife accepted the situation because it made Cara's own new desire to have this man become a dad for her child less painful and fraught with the complication of another woman:

> He came out to visit when April was eight months old and that's the last time he's seen her. And he'll probably come out this year. I send pictures. I call his mother. She needs a family. If you're gonna make a decision such as this, you need to have an open mind because you cannot be selfish. She didn't ask to be born. I would love to be selfish. Protecting her. But it's not protecting her, it's

protecting me, and that's where I gotta draw the line. I can't hurt her. I gotta be
fair to her. It is her father. I don't really care about the money. He pays me
no child support. He sends some money but not often. I have to set a border
for him: "This is what you need to do if you want to have a relationship. You need
to give of yourself."

While Cara expected nothing of this man for herself, she did not want to accept
the no-strings-attached paternity that a one-night affair would afford her child.
Caving to the idea that dads are necessary for healthy kids ("I can't hurt her"), she
attempted to pull this man (and his family) into her child's life. Colleen, Ellen,
Maeve, and Cara all wanted something from these men as dads, but did not always
succeed in getting it for their children. They learned to cope in different ways
with what they got.

### Paternity on Trial

The court is a tool available to women who chance pregnancy, but how they use
that tool varies. Most women prioritize the emotional relationship between father
and child over financial support—if they can afford it—and use (or more often
avoid) the courts to that end.[6] Women generally try to avoid court-ordered child
support, preferring voluntary contributions if any. Even though they may have
chanced pregnancy, they assess their ability to support a child on their own. The
majority are financially stable and able to make ends meet for their children. In
general, women avoid taking the fathers to court for purposes of child support.
They do this to preserve and not inflame the possible father-child relationship.

Mary, who makes her living as an educator, tiptoed around issues of financial
support and possibility of future involvement by the father of her child when she
was pregnant. She knew she had the emotional and financial ability to raise a child
on her own, though she did prefer that the father of her child be involved. She
intentionally became pregnant at thirty-six with this particular man, though she
felt the best way to establish a lifelong tie with the father for the child was not to
make any demands and to just let a relationship unfold:

It's a little easier on everybody if there are two people raising one child and they
are doing it together immediately. And it would have been nice. Which is why
I didn't block him out, close doors, or sue or cause trouble. I wanted to see what
would happen and only wanted good vibrations coming.

In Ellen's case, she settled for the Pampers Gavin brought when he came to pick
up his daughter for a day each week. She knew if she forced him to pay support she
would run the risk of estranging the child from her father.

Men's financial contributions are not unwanted, but single mothers perceive
the court to be a contentious arena, and the wealthier women fear that their children's fathers' affections could be undermined by the act of seeking child support.

Men's affections for their children thus become emotionally priceless, a luxury that distinguishes the worth of the father from his historical provider function within the family.[7] In these cases, men's financial responsibility for their children is seen as an act of kindness, not an expectation of fatherhood.

Children whose mothers employed the courts to force the children's fathers to contribute are more likely to already have strained relationships with their fathers.[8] Ironically, court-ordered child support generally amounts to very little money, and few men comply with these orders anyway. Women are often surprised at the paltry amounts. The sums never cover the costs of day care, after-school programs, or summer camps, let alone food and clothing. Thus mothers of these children are left to bear the brunt of full financial responsibility for their children. Excerpts from two different interviews illustrate the tension that emerges from court-ordered awards that men say they cannot pay, even if the amounts appear negligible. Jasmine, age twenty-seven with a three-year-old, felt the court's decision was unfair:

> So we went in front of the judge and I almost did everything but cry. But I knew that I couldn't yell because I knew that I'd get arrested in there. I said, "Your honor, I worked eighty hours a week last week alone. I owe $2,000 in child care. I'm two months late. I don't have any heat in my house because it's too expensive to keep on all the time." He told the judge he worked twenty-five hours a week and he made only $8 an hour. The judge ordered him to pay $220 a month. Ross said to me after court, "I can only give you $20 a week." And I said, "This is for *your* child."

Crystal, age twenty-eight with a four-year-old, couldn't count on support:

> Her father gives me child support every now and then. I don't count on it. When it comes we just put it in a savings account, but most of the time it doesn't work out that way.

The fathers are not expected by the courts to find better-paying jobs to support their children. Support payments are based upon how much a man earns, not his potential. For example, the father of Jasmine's child was in college and the court order only instructed him to pay a portion of his part-time salary, a drop in the bucket of the child's expenses. Of course Jasmine would receive more money once the father had a full-time job after completing college. But in the meantime Jasmine shouldered the financial burden, working an extra job while she struggled to finish her degree. Men without good-paying jobs are men without money and are not good providers, whether in or outside of marriage. The courts cannot turn them into being the kind of providers the women would like for their children.

Courts can assign only a financial contribution to fathers, not an emotional one. However, courts can establish paternity. Colleen, who admitted that she chanced pregnancy with the wrong man, discovered that he was not willing to be the dad she wanted for her child. When he refused even to meet the child, let alone have a relationship with her, Colleen took him to court, hoping to give her daughter some symbolic proof that she had a father. The court forced this wealthy man to pay child support. Even though the situation was far from ideal, Colleen made sure to spend the monthly check with her daughter as if what they bought were gifts from her father.

The intimacy that produces a child is rarely enough to morally obligate these men to their children. Women think the cultural value of traditional fathers as "providers" will compel men to help support their children, but they are wrong to assume that the support will be substantial. While not all women count on these men to be a dad, those who do so are often disappointed. What they find is that being a dad is not an enforceable obligation. Fathers cannot be made into dads who visit. Financial obligation is the only aspect of traditional fatherhood within the courts' jurisdiction; the courts can grant visitation but cannot enforce it or emotionally bond men to children. While paternity testing can identify beyond the shadow of doubt a father, it cannot produce a dad.

### The Cat's Cradle: Paternal Kin

Mothers who chance pregnancy often expect that they and their children will become part of their children's father's extended kin networks, setting them apart from the other women in this study. Similarly, the father's kin frequently claim these children (and, in doing so, their mothers) as part of the traditional kinship system, which remains problematic for the families of known donors. Naming a father, with his confirmation, entitles children to his kin. Contact with the father's extended kin brings the social standing of an additional set of roots to these children. In this way, kinship then is based upon blood ties, and the biological and social become aligned.

The father's extended kin frequently become involved independent of the biological father's social involvement in the child's life. They can do this because the mothers claim a particular man as the child's father. Jasmine remarked upon her child's paternal grandmother's active participation:

> Her dad's mother is the grandmother that makes cookies and she was the one who didn't want to have any part of this in the beginning. And she's constantly under me, all the time, and she is the type of person who calls every day: "I want to see her, can I come and get her? I want to spend time with her." And she spends more time with her grandmother than her father. Her dad, who was in college when she was born, will have her every other weekend but he will go off and play softball and leave her in the house with the grandmother.

Fathers often facilitate the bonding between the child and his kin, either intentionally or for convenience. These fathers receive help from their own mothers and other female kin who care for their children, and some of these women remain close to the fathers' families despite their withered relationship with the fathers of their children.

Brandy, twenty-six years old, inserted her child into her former boyfriend's family in another way. Alex, the boyfriend with whom Brandy broke up when she was three months pregnant, was invited to see his child immediately after she gave birth even though they hadn't spoken during the rest of her pregnancy.[9] From then on he came by daily to see his daughter, Ali, his namesake. Brandy, in order to keep her job, sent her three-year-old daughter to spend half the week at her mother's. Alex was welcome there and used to visit Ali at both Brandy's home and Brandy's mother's house. Though Alex's contributions were limited to his time and various gifts to the child, Brandy was impressed by his commitment to their daughter. Unfortunately, when Ali was eighteen months old, Alex ended up in prison. Brandy and Ali, however, retained their status as an accepted part of his family. Ali's place within her father's family is indisputable; she has a biological father, and from that stems her "rightful" access to his paternal kin networks.

> His family? Yes, we both see them. We see them every weekend, the whole family. She is part of that family. They come take her, they buy her things, they've always come to her birthday parties. We go to all their family events, even though he's not around; that doesn't stop me from going to see them.

Brandy honored Alex's brother by making him her daughter's godfather, which pleased Alex and further cemented Ali's standing as a member of his family. She had no idea that her decision to include Alex's family would bring such lasting and influential consequences to her daughter's life. Even though Alex's brother was a part of Ali's biological family, he was much more than simply a biological link to her father. Ali's godfather manifested as a surrogate father by taking his responsibility as a godfather seriously, but he also occupied a biological place within kin terminology as uncle.

> I feel like Alex's brother is the closest thing to a father that she has right now. Luckily, it's his brother, it's not like some stranger that he doesn't know. So I felt like that's who the gift [the Father's Day card that Ali made at the day care center] should be given to. He's the guy who is taking care of her—he's the godfather, he's the uncle.

Brandy was making an important kin claim by deciding to give Ali's Father's Day card to someone other than her biological father. In this case, the godfather occupied a socially known and understood relationship, but it was possible that another man could enter their lives and also serve as a step-daddy to Ali. Brandy knew Alex was relieved that his brother was filling in for him, as that left him room to resume his role as a dad after completing his prison sentence.

Mothers become gatekeepers, patrolling the boundaries of their children's extended kin networks, which include their child's father's new girlfriend or wife.

These are nuanced relationships. While mothers may befriend these women initially, in order to continue to smooth the path for father-child relationships, such friendships sometimes turn sour. Brandy, whose ex-boyfriend married another woman (with a child from a previous relationship), explained the complexity of these situations:

> I used to let his wife take her. Later, I felt his wife was just using my daughter to get closer to him because they were having problems. So I just cut his wife off altogether. So I have no contact with his wife and her daughter. I just deal with his family, not with his wife or anything, not anymore.

By contrast, Ellen, whose vignette opens this chapter, found that while the father of her child was inconsistent, his girlfriend could be counted upon more readily. Ellen viewed his girlfriend more as a reliable babysitter:

> Kelly's his girlfriend who he's living with. She is really a very nice girl. On Friday evening I'm running late, so I said I'd drop Skyler off after supper. So Kelly calls me up at seven and says "Gavin's sleeping." "Oh, what happened to his stopping by to put in an estimate on a job?" "It got cancelled." "Why doesn't he come get her?" "Oh, well, I'll come get her if that would help." "Great, cool."

Both Brandy and Ellen were agitated at having to negotiate relationships with other women in their child's father's life in order to maintain father-child relationships. Ironically, Ellen, who initially was upset when Gavin found a new girlfriend, discovered a way to incorporate her in their lives to her advantage. However, Brandy, who amicably parted with Alex, found his new wife's behavior to be inappropriate and thus had to patrol the boundary between Alex's new family and her own. These new girlfriends became members of the extended kin networks with which the mothers interacted in order to keep their children involved in their fathers' lives and to retain their own positions within his family. In such cases, the child is a reminder of kin obligation, of ties that remain intact when the father (or the mother) moves on to new romantic relationships.

Naomi, thirty-three years old with a one-year-old, did not realize until after she became pregnant that she was being two-timed. Moreover, both women ended up pregnant—in her words, the "doggiest thing" a man could do to a woman. After the birth of her child, Naomi sought out the woman whose child was her son's half brother, a relationship she did not see as insignificant.

> Last Saturday we went to New Jersey and saw her and her son. [The boys] don't look a thing alike, and we are raising them very differently. But we feel strongly that they should have some kind of connection, because they are half brothers. She would like for me to get pulled into their lives a lot more, but I have to set certain limits because I'm not part of her life and I'm hoping that eventually I will meet someone else and have a life and a family.

Both mothers separately rejected this biological father as a suitable dad, aware that he could not be counted on financially or emotionally or as a role model. Naomi still chose to keep as kin her son's half brother, but everything else was less than ideal. The women, who live in different states, stayed in touch for the sake of their children, expecting to visit at least once a year. In this case, the kinship system has been modified, though it is still based on the power of genetics. A type of "co-mother" relationship resulted from this deceitful situation. Unlike anonymous donors, these women did not have to construct a fictionalized father; yet, despite already knowing that these half brothers would be raised independently and under very different circumstances, these women vowed to maintain ties for their children's sake. In Naomi's case, maintaining kin ties through a half sibling provided a less painful way for the child to know his father by re-creating him through the genetic similarities of two children.

In all but two cases, the women in this chapter were embraced by the father's kin, even though a few of the paternal grandmothers had initially suggested abortion or adoption when they learned that their son's girlfriend was pregnant.[10] However, most became supportive relatives who often spent more time and gave more lavish gifts to these children than the fathers did. Ironically, many of the fathers who left or ignored their offspring had kin systems that absorbed the child and often the child's mother. The importance of the extended family continued for these women in spite of the "irresponsible" fathers of their children. Therefore, in another way, a paternal extended family continued despite the absence of marriage because of the women's decision to label and acknowledge these men as fathers (not dads).

In such cases, science provides added proof: DNA tests leave little room for lies or doubt regarding paternity. The concept of genetic family, now bolstered by science, holds more weight than ever before among paternal kin networks.

### What Makes a Dad?

Some women in this study, many of whom appear to be very similar to women who used known donors, were always very clear about what they wanted from these men: nothing. They used distance (sometimes an ocean) as a buffer. These men had all but disappeared. Those who did want a dad for their child or simply did not know what they wanted when they became pregnant lived in a world of "good dads" and "bad dads."[11] Women described in this chapter were struggling with what fatherhood means in the absence of marriage. However, just because the man's name is not on a marriage certificate does not mean that it does not appear on records relating to the child. Unlike women who used known donors, the closest counterparts to the women who chanced pregnancy, these women did not set up legal barriers between father and child from birth. Birth certificates with the father's name were a rare exception among known donors and simply did not exist among women using anonymous donors or adoption. However, ten of the seventeen women who chanced pregnancy listed the father on the birth certificate. Moreover, a third gave the child the father's last name or included it using a hyphen.[12] Naming was a lasting symbol of women's willingness to consider including the men in their children's lives as dads, and it also served as an acknowledgment of a past relationship between father and mother, an emotional tie that might move into the present between father and child.[13] While naming the biological father either on the birth certificate or in the child's legal name set these women apart from others in this study, it did not determine who would be a "good dad."

Social involvement was a recurring theme in every woman's account of what makes a "good dad," even among those women who expected nothing from the men who fathered their children. Economic support was also valued; however, most women, even those with serious economic constraints, were willing to settle for consistent social involvement of the father, as opposed to court-sanctioned support. Women constructed their children's fathers as "good dads" if those men willingly engaged themselves in the children's lives on a consistent basis. Of the seven involved dads described in this chapter, all but one, who lived out of state, saw their child at least twice a week, and usually for an entire weekend. Women talked of love between the child and his or her dad, indicating an emotional relationship. Other women assessed whether the father was "giving enough of himself" to the child. That is, the man's circumstances colored her assessment, as in the case of the imprisoned father of Brandy's child. Women expressed over and over that "good dads" love their children and demonstrate that love through not only visiting them but also sharing time with them independent of the mothers. Women were reluctant to label fathers as "bad dads," but many men in this group did not fulfill women's expectations of consistent contact. Eight women noted that their children's dads were ambivalent and minimally involved. At best, these men saw their children a few times a year, with an occasional surprise phone call. While two women who viewed their child's father as threatening to their families had obtained restraining orders, the greatest fault of most "bad dads" was being "inconsiderate" of their children's feelings, canceling their time together, or not being around enough. For most "bad dads," changing their label required upping their level of involvement. Social interaction was the key ingredient to being a "good dad," trumping financial support in the opinion of these women every time.

In this study, women facilitated the interactions of "good dads" with their children or tried to encourage ambivalent dads who lived locally to be more consistently available to their children. Visits were seen as keeping alive an emotional bond that might lead to more frequent dad-initiated involvement. As Maeve aptly summarized, "I will always work very hard and strive towards Hunter having a very close relationship with his dad." Maeve and other women in this chapter can be described as kin keepers, prioritizing the maintenance of the father-child relationship—their commitment to keep fathers connected is what distinguishes them from gatekeepers, who either shut men out or control their access. The most extreme gatekeepers are women who used known donors; they occupy one end of the spectrum, while the kin keepers in this study occupy the other. Women who chance pregnancy range from kin keepers to gatekeepers.

Mary's story is typical of the women who became kin keepers, though she was more successful than most. From the time she knew she was pregnant, Mary hoped that the father would participate in the child's life, even though Mary was prepared to be a solo parent. She recalled thinking about the child as "hers," lining up the financial resources and the child care to raise her daughter as a single mom. Mary knew Blake did not want to be a "daily" dad, as he had already done it with his two grown children from a previous marriage. Nonetheless, Mary was not ready to give up on Blake as a potential dad. Although all decisions regarding the child were Mary's, she believed in the importance of a father:[14]

> A man gives another point of view. He gave her another set of skills that I couldn't give her. And he gave her security. I have memories of my father and he was important to my intellectual and my emotional development. So I assume that children need close people to help them and a father is a likely candidate. And she has this other life down there.

Once the child was born, Mary took her every weekend to visit Blake. She carefully facilitated the beginnings of the father-daughter relationship. Most women in this chapter, like Mary, thought that the two-parent model for a child was important, though it was not essential for the other parent to reside in the same household. Initially, Blake might have been a reluctant dad, but Mary rekindled their romantic involvement six months after Lizzy was born, paving the way for the development of the father-child relationship. Mary described their weekly routine:

> We saw him every weekend. She got to know him. That was her life. Her life was here with me during the week and it was different than the life that kids she knew had, but it was her life and it was always like that. From the time she was little, she was going there on weekends.

Mary and Blake amicably ended their relationship a few months later, the age gap between them becoming a bigger strain. However, by this time the father-child relationship had been cemented. As a result, Mary's child had a consistent "daddy."

> Lizzy continued the relationship because it didn't really change all that much . . . well, it did change 'cause I wasn't there, but she continued to go there and it was just a slight adjustment. And it actually was a little freeing for her because she had her relationship now unencumbered by me. Everything else stayed very comfortable and compatible and she continued her relationship with him and her half sisters and nieces.

Even though Mary claimed that she made all the decisions regarding her child, it is clear that at least on weekends Lizzy's dad was the parent in charge, often giving Lizzy more freedom than her mother did. Starting at the age of five, Mary's child spent weekends alone with her dad. Despite the consistent relationship between Lizzy and her father, Mary stuck with her initial plan of treading lightly, continuing to make no demands of Blake.

Maeve, mentioned earlier in this chapter, is a classic gatekeeper.[15] She became pregnant in her senior year of college but, unlike many of her friends, could not go through with an abortion. The father of the child, whom she described as a "New Age loser," had largely disappeared by the time of the birth. With the father making only irregular visits, Maeve and her son moved out of the area, feeling no obligation to stay on account of the father. Maeve kept in touch with his sister, and her return with her four-year-old son to New England some time later sparked a resurgence in the involvement of the father, who lived a few hours away, though Maeve continued to be skeptical of the father's behavior (and ability to keep a permanent job). Three years later, Maeve explained her view of the father-son relationship and why she continued to tolerate Hunter's dad:

> I understand that children have a basic biological need to understand where they came from. And I'm glad I did, because now Hunter has the most wonderful relationships with his uncle and aunt and grandmother on that side of the family, and so do I. I love them like family. And when the kids at school say to Hunter, "Do you have a dad?" he says, "Yes." He has a dad that he has a relationship with.

Maeve's quote highlights several different issues common for other women described in this section. Despite minimal involvement with his father, Hunter could point to a dad who sporadically attended soccer games. This acknowledgment served as the foundation for positive ties to paternal kin. Further, Hunter felt just like other kids, because on the surface he too had a dad.

However, Hunter's dad was unreliable. When Hunter began acting out at school, the school counselor deemed that his father's inconsistency was the root of the problem. Using the school's diagnosis as evidence, Maeve very directly told Hunter's father that he needed to be a better dad. The dad, to his credit, altered his behavior and started spending every Saturday with his child. Maeve described her son's dad as dedicated, but she still had doubts about his parenting ability:

> I would never let Hunter go alone with his father for a weekend. I think that Hunter has this sense of his father being a regular presence in his life without having the detrimental effect that his father is totally inept as a parent. He really is. But he is loving. He's never mean, never abusive. He just ignores him, and it's weird.

As Hunter's dad became a more consistent part of his life, he also became more demanding, which scared Maeve:

There have been times Hunter's father threatened to sue me for unsupervised visitations. And I was petrified because the courts are just ridiculous. Their standards are this high as far as what they think is acceptable [Maeve pointed to the floor].

Maeve agreed to let Hunter's dad visit more often in order to avoid legal involvement, but she still would not let Hunter's father see him without her supervision. Ironically, if he sought unsupervised visitation in the courts, he would most likely end up being ordered to pay child support, which he had never paid. Maeve's predicament is what many women fear about having a child without legal protection from the father's claims. While Maeve never regretted her decision to raise Hunter, Hunter's father certainly complicated and disrupted her life. Interestingly, when Maeve decided at twenty-nine that she wanted a second child, she chose to adopt in order to keep another father totally out of their lives. Maeve was attempting to transform Hunter's dad into one that she believed would suit her—and Hunter—better. She was stuck with Hunter's dad, and she had already made the choice to include him in their lives; thus her only recourse was to patrol the borders of the father-child relationship.

Darlene's situation is representative of that faced by women who chance pregnancy thinking they have no expectations for the father. However, the future is often unpredictable, as women sometimes wish for dads for their kids long after the fathers have gone. Darlene refused the father's offer of marriage when she became pregnant with his child at twenty-four; she told me, "My only reaction— I can still see it to this day—was I couldn't imagine making four sandwiches every day for the rest of my life." Because of this rejection, Kendra's father wanted nothing to do with her. Instead, he paid regular child support—the honorable thing to do, as was his offer of marriage when the pregnancy occurred. Darlene may have refused marriage, but she did not refuse the child support checks he sent, as it was the only acknowledgment Kendra's father gave of her existence. For the first eleven years of Kendra's life, Darlene's father, who lived down the street, was actively involved with Kendra. Kendra loved animals, and her grandfather allowed her to use the allowance she saved from doing chores around his house to pay part of the cost of a horse (he covered the remainder of the cost). He taught her to care for animals, and she loved being with him. When he died suddenly of a heart attack, the void his death left made Kendra long for her own father. Darlene wrote to him asking him to consider taking Kendra out to ice cream. He never responded to this request, which was sent by certified mail. However, when the next month's child support arrived, Darlene was surprised by her daughter's reaction:

I showed her the support check. And I said, "Look, I can't make him love you, but every month he supports you. So he's a responsible person, Kendra, he just cannot feel what we want him to feel for you." Her father had gotten new checks, and there was a coyote on them or something, and Kendra loved it. It was from

Daddy. Well, she looked at it: $70 a month! Well, that was like $7 million. She looked up at me and she said, "Mommy, do you know how many guinea pigs you could buy with this?" And I looked at her and I drew myself up and I said, "And we're going right now to spend it."

Darlene figured that if her daughter's father was unwilling to be emotionally supportive, she might as well make sure that he was financially obligated. That way, she felt, her child would at least know that her father existed. As she put it, "She'll see that she has a father. He pays for stuff. And it's better than nothing." Darlene does not discourage her daughter from creating a portrait of her absent father. Instead, she splurged that month and took her daughter to buy another guinea pig. No woman can make a man give his emotional support; she can, however, make demands financially (though not all men will pay).

For the most part, women are interested in more involvement from their children's fathers. Mothers cannot control a dad's inconsistency, and they feel helpless. Maeve may have been able to get Hunter's dad to change some of his behavior, but most women fear that if they voice too many complaints, their children's fathers will shelve their children permanently. Most of these women settle for minimal financial support from their children's fathers and varying degrees of father involvement. These women believe dads to be important and that fathers have the right to see their children, which ties in with their adherence to the larger narrative of what makes dads and family. However, overall, the women's accounts show that these men do not necessarily feel obligated. In Ellen's words, "you can't get blood from a stone"—mothers seeking emotional involvement or, less often, financial support for their child often find that men come up short. While women will use monetary support to establish a father, money is rarely a substitute for emotional ties and routine social involvement. What makes a dad is contentious for these women, who are struggling to make sense of their lives juxtaposed to the master narrative of the married nuclear family.

## Conclusion

One might ask why women settle for this. Romance, intimacy, and pregnancy follow an older sequence that once resulted in quick marriages before women showed signs of pregnancy. The women described in this chapter followed this traditional sequencing to a substantial extent, deviating from it only in their failure to marry the fathers of their children. Whereas in the past women who became pregnant outside of marriage suffered harsh penalties, today the social sanctions of "scarlet letters" and labels of illegitimacy are in the past. Middle-class fatherhood in the absence of marriage is unknown territory. DNA testing may force men to acknowledge paternity, but it does not compel them to undertake social fatherhood. Women may wish to keep genetic and social fatherhood coupled, but they come to realize that they cannot make biological fathers into social dads if the men are not interested and willing. Women who leave the door open for fathers to become socially involved with their children are willing to live with the burden of constant patrol. However, women do not have the answer of how to make men show up at their child's school play or cheer them on at a soccer game; there seems to be no formula for social fatherhood.

On the other hand, proven paternity has replaced marriage as the basis for inclusion in the paternal kin network. Mothers can now call upon the help of science as they attempt to make the child a member of the paternal social circle. As a by-product of applied science, mothers also gain access to these circles, which may provide them with help caring for their children and afford them some of the rights and privileges of an in-law even if the father marries another woman.

The disparity between biological and social fathers is increasingly common in the United States. This is in part because economically self-sufficient women often choose not to make financial demands of the fathers: the amount of child support courts order tends to be so little that women do not see it as worth risking the alienation of a father who might become a social dad at some point.[16] These women are not initially unraveling the biological and social aspects of fatherhood, which they see as intrinsically coupled. Instead, they believe that dads bring something special to their children. To pin down in words what these men bring to these children is difficult. At the very least they hope for emotional closeness, though few really have it. It is for this reason that the women in this chapter settle for varying degrees of father involvement.

Women know these men can walk out of their children's lives at any moment, and some men do. Women's talk of men's stability in their child's lives is reduced to consistent contact (e.g., showing up when they say they will, so as not to let their child down). Put differently, dads become a luxury whose main purpose is little more than being a playmate to their children. They have been absolved of their historical responsibilities as breadwinners and authority figures. Grappling with the meaning of fatherhood in a time of incredible flux, women struggle with "good dads" and "bad dads," vacillating between their roles as kin keeper and gatekeeper. Chancing pregnancy may give a simple answer to one of the questions prompted by single motherhood, namely, who the father is, but it brings up many questions about the place of fathers overall.

# 6

---

## ADOPTION AND FITTING IN

**Rebecca Thompson**

I remember one day where I was running along the river and thinking, "My God, this could be ten years ago. It's like everything is the same in my life except that I'm older." I wanted a change. I wanted to move on. I wanted to do something.

I had tried to get pregnant with the help of the fertility clinic for four years, on and off, starting when I was thirty-six years old. A couple years into it, I started moving through the adoption steps, like attending workshops for prospective adoptive parents. By the time I'd run out of sperm, I had started my home study. As hard as that was to finally give up becoming pregnant, I decided to stop trying. At least in terms of turning my energy to a new set of activities. At that time, the adopting part just came out of wanting to have a baby and then continuing on that path. But I think in the waiting period, which is very hard, some of the stuff that I hadn't thought about became central.

When I made the mental transition from giving birth to adopting, it was with the image of a white baby. I wanted a baby like me. I did the home study, not with the agency that I eventually used, but with an independent social worker. She told me that the chances of my adopting a white baby from the U.S. were slim—next to zero. She recommended that I think about adopting from overseas.

She also stirred up all this stuff. She recognized in talking with me that I am an intensively private person, and yet since the child I was going to adopt would never appear to be my own biological child, I was going to be visibly an adoptive person for the rest of my life. She was blunt: "How are you going to deal with curious stares from people at the playground? Will it bother you?" Her probing started this internal dialogue about what kind of children I could parent comfortably as a white woman. Russian? Cambodian? Chinese? Domestic baby of color? I kept going back and forth in my head knowing that what I cared most about was simply having a child of my own.

The plus side of adoption which I thought about at the time is that for any-body, and maybe for me more than a lot of people, being reminded that she is a different person, she is not me redone, might be a good thing. I'm excited to see who she is and how she's different. But when I first thought about adoption, it was imagining somebody who looked different from me. After the home study, having people raise the idea of not having a child who *did* look like me, then I got confused. I sort of moved back into that thing of wanting somebody like me. It was trying to figure out who's going to be like me.

The social worker's questions haunted me and I wasn't sure about what was important to me. I knew I would have to make a set of tough compromises. I guess I was really uncomfortable with adopting a child who had been through the Department of Social Services. Even though my daughter had been in a less than ideal situation while living in an orphanage for several months, that seemed better to me than a child who might have been abused or abandoned. Besides DSS, the other possibility was where you would make a little book and try and sell yourself to somebody who was willing to give up their child, but that seemed dismal. I wouldn't pick me. I'd pick a two-parent family. There are so many couples, why would you pick a single parent? I might find somebody at some point who would be interested in that, but it would take too long. So that just seemed out of the question. So I wasn't going to be getting an infant with a known parent.

And after thinking about racial difference, I realized that mothering a child of a different race would have another set of issues. I had worked in a Head Start program with largely Hispanic children and I am bilingual. But as the years went on, I didn't feel like that was a culture that I was so attached to. And I also thought, once you adopt from whatever culture, you need to bring that culture into the life of the family. And it just felt like more than I could take on. I wasn't sure if I was in a place in my life where I could be both a single mother and also be a part of a culture other than my own. Making a family that is interracial is different from working with children of another race. In my heart I wondered if this was a good decision for me and I felt uncomfortable thinking that as a pro-gressive, liberal person. I fought against my own feelings. I weighed and mulled over and weighed some more what I cared most about as I decided how to proceed with my adoption plans. I just had to decide how to compromise between want-ing a child that matched my race and just wanting a baby. I had to ask myself, would I be comfortable having people look at my family differently because we didn't look the same? Maybe I would get used to it and ignore other people's curiosity.

## The Changing World of Adoption

Rebecca, like many of the twenty-one other adoptive mothers in this study, wants to adopt a child who will not only fulfill her desire to be a mother but also fit into her preexisting private and public life. At first glance, adoption might seem like an ideal social institution that meets the needs of both childless parents and parentless children. Certainly the number of U.S. children needing stable, loving homes far surpasses the capacity of the domestic foster care system. Although there are more than enough needy children within the United States for each potential American couple or single parent, adoption is not always a win-win transaction. Race and age complicate the process and blur the lines between the needs and desires of all parties involved. Most potential parents desire certain kinds of children, who will blend into their established lives—meaning that most Americans want children of their own race (or at least be able to pass in public) and want to raise their children from infancy.

Legal adoption, a revolutionary innovation of the mid-nineteenth century, severed blood ties between birth parents and their children in order for adoptive parents to create a legal tie "by convention and by choice." The law created an "artificial" way for strangers to become kin.[1] Adoption law and social policies were implemented to imitate biological families: two parents of opposite sexes would share the same race as the child. Adoptive families would thus blend in, appearing as "natural" blood families whose children could have been born to them. These "as if" families would be matched by experts as closely as possible for race, religion, ethnicity, and sometimes social class background.[2] This normative model of the "as if" family has mutated into new family variations as the market for adoption has changed.[3] Single women are a new segment of the group of potential adoptive parents; children from all parts of the globe are finding homes in the United States; U.S. birth parents, while still relinquishing their legal rights, are increasingly requesting open adoptions to facilitate some contact with their birth child. However, single mothers find that the original legal and social policies of the "as if" family shape the segment of the adoptive market that is open to them in the United States. Since other countries have their own adoption policies, often single mothers seek children elsewhere.

In order to build a cohesive family, potential parents explore the pros and cons of domestic versus international adoptions. They search both private and public agencies to determine which one will offer them the greatest possibility of adopting a child of the right race and age to fit comfortably into their lives. The adoption process is often long and painful, requiring prospective adoptive parents to fill out stacks of paperwork, confront difficult decisions, and make compromises. Many prospective adoptive parents agonize over the decision of whether to adopt interracially or wait for children of their same race, yet, surprisingly, studies show that families who adopt interracially and those who adopt same-race children seem to be about equally as happy. In the end, no matter what they decide, the result is usually successful for both parents and children, but the process is always grueling.[4]

For a single woman desiring to adopt a child, the journey is often more difficult than for heterosexual couples. The bar is set higher and the hoops seem endless. Single women rank low in the adoption system hierarchy. Like their coupled counterparts, single women also worry about how an adopted child will affect and fit into their extended families and greater communities. Since these women have fewer healthy infants offered to them, they must make difficult compromises and choose one criterion to supersede others in their adoption search.

### Hegemony of the Nuclear, Heterosexual Family

How does a woman such as Rebecca, typically in her late thirties to early forties, end up the mother of a different-race child? Biological motherhood prevails as the dominant way in which women become mothers; adoption remains a second best alternative. Sociologist Katarina Weger, in her article "Adoption and Kinships," observes that in the U.S., adoptive mothers are often stigmatized as "inherently less capable of providing 'good mothering'" due to "the assumption that mature, healthy womanhood is intricately linked to biological motherhood" (p. 46). Further, those with husbands are part of a two-parent family, which many believe will provide a greater network of support than would a single parent.

The ranking of parental desirability within the adoptive system speaks to broader assumptions about women and men. Women without husbands appear to be incomplete—even though all women are accepted as having the emotional qualifications essential for mothering. Unspoken is a tacit cultural agreement that only women who successfully build and maintain a marriage prior to adoption are capable of mothering, even if they are not the biological parent. A woman proves she is worthy of approval for an adoption through the initial love and nurture of a husband—still the foundational building block of the contemporary U.S. family. Single women are suspect, presumed incapable of providing stable family lives. Conventional wisdom holds that family stability rests on the heterosexual two-parent partnership because it offers a child both men and women as role models, as well as a way of interacting with both sexes. Therefore, the adoption system is more sympathetic to married couples not only because they are less "risky" parents but also because, ideologically, adoption will allow them to fulfill their marriages by creating families. In this way, the adoption system supports and legitimates marriage and its obligations to procreate.

The reach and power of the adoption hierarchy, which places married couples at the top, is substantiated by these women's own comments. As Rebecca explained, "I wouldn't pick me. I would pick a family. I think my daughter would be much better served with two models, with two parents, with two different people to learn from. . . . But I'm still hoping to find a man and a dad." Marli told of a rumor that exists among U.S. parents who adopt Chinese children that "adopted girls who are the prettiest are placed with single mothers to counter the lack of a father in their lives." The assumption is that a pretty face, and the advantages that come with it, will help compensate for the missing dad and corresponding lack of opportunities for the child.

In addition, cultural myths—based upon publicly known, media-based stereotypes of divorced families and poor teen mothers—perpetuate the assumption that single mothers will produce juvenile delinquents and adults who might not be fit citizens. In short, single women are perceived as at risk for producing social misfits; only single men fare worse in the adoption hierarchy. Gay couples also are contentious as potential adoptive parents, and some states continue to ban gays from adopting.[5]

The white adoptive mothers in this study said they would have chosen white U.S.-born infants if that choice had been available to them. But only one woman in this study, who worked in the system, was able to adopt such a child. To hold on to their dreams of becoming mothers, the women thus had to expand their searches, answering the question "What kind of child am I willing to adopt?" The women in this study began to explore the possibility of adopting an "at-risk" child, a catchall term that includes children with physical disabilities, older children, and siblings in the foster care system. They also began exploring adopting children of a different race and/or children from another country. Women who adopted internationally were matched to children and brought them back to the United States much more quickly than women who adopted domestically.[6]

By contrast, black and Hispanic women could more easily adopt children of the same race because there were more children of color available in the United States. But they were told that couples would be given priority for babies and that they should think about adopting toddlers or older children or go abroad in search of an infant.

Single women's stigmatized status in U.S. culture as a whole and subsequently in the adoption system, which reflects deeply cemented beliefs about the superiority of marriage and family, forces women into a narrower position of choice in creating families. Private agencies are more likely to work with single mothers and cater to their special needs, but the cost of adoption through a private agency averages $20,000.[7] In many cases, the women's privileged backgrounds offer them the financial means to adopt children that otherwise would be out of reach for single women. Adoptive mothers are typically well established in careers that offer stable incomes and good benefits. Additionally, the majority of women who adopt are more likely to have grown up in a middle- or upper-middle-class two-parent family than women who select other routes to motherhood, and the women's parents are thus often able to contribute funds for adoption fees and child care costs.

The hegemony of the nuclear family—an invisible power that draws its legitimacy from historically entrenched gender relations—frames adoptive mothers' needs for stable financial situations and guides their personal decisions. Women also often consciously or subconsciously hold off on their dreams to become mothers in hopes that a suitable partner will enter their lives and instantly improve their desirability as adoptive mothers. Many of these women's "waiting periods" last into their mid to late thirties or forties, which means decreased fertility and often leaves adoption as the only route to motherhood.

As this study shows, adoptive mothers are also more likely to form transracial families than women who have biological children. In their journey toward motherhood, the importance of biological kinship fades.[8] Questions of family identity and the acceptance of an adoptive child are further complicated by the international and/or transracial circumstances of the adoption. These women must negotiate a very different path en route to motherhood.

### Difficult Compromises: The Dilemmas of Age Versus Race

Women's routes to motherhood and adoption are often dominated by a struggle in which they must weigh the age of an unknown adoptive child against his or her race.[9] Mothers who give priority to the criterion of age in their searches hold the belief that intensive mothering is about sharing in the child's infancy. U.S. culture puts great emphasis on this early bonding experience. Feeling this cultural pressure, many of the women fear that adopting older children, and subsequently missing their children's infancy, will mean an increased risk of damaged children and diminished mother-child experiences. Women who hold this belief correlate the age of the child with the extent to which they feel they will bond with their adopted children and integrate their children into their private emotional lives.

The criterion of race, on the other hand, is more connected with the mother's desire to integrate her child into her public life. Having a child of a different race may complicate her extended family's acceptance of her new family. Different skin colors of mother and child could elicit unwanted and uncomfortable questions and assumptions.

In the beginning stages of the adoption process, social workers often ask potential mothers which characteristics in a child are most important to them—including age, race, gender, health, open adoption, and citizenship. Rebecca's social worker was not unique: in the initial home study meeting, social workers confirm that receiving a white infant domestically is a privilege typically reserved for married couples. Women articulated in the interviews the process of making a mental hierarchy of different races they were comfortable adopting. Rebecca, who finally adopted a nine-month-old when she was forty-one years old, overcame her discomfort with adopting a child of a race different from her own, with her desire for a healthy infant taking precedence:

> I started worrying about—was China right? Was somebody who was going to look different from me a child I could love? So, I started thinking about Russia, and then I asked would it be Russia, China? Russia? China? I finally just picked China. It was torment and it was pros and cons. . . . I finally picked China because there was [an] age limit there and I wanted to be sure I would get an

infant before getting too old. . . . The key thing for me was I really wanted a smart child if I could pick one thing. I wanted a healthy child. So, it is trying to think [in] which country am I going to get the best.

At the time she was searching for an infant, agencies in China had available abandoned or orphaned infants. Russia did not guarantee that she would be placed with a baby, although they had plenty of white children to adopt.[10] Further, she relied upon racial stereotypes in the United States that Chinese kids are smart, and this was important to her. Rebecca felt that by choosing China she had better odds of getting a smart baby even if the race of this baby was not her first choice. Further, Rebecca revealed how she categorized skin color and prioritized it: "Thinking about the race thing—it did seem like adopting a black baby would be harder for me. It felt too different. I also looked at Cambodia. So skin color felt more different than different features." Feeling "too different" is a comment I heard a lot in these interviews. Rebecca deconstructed race into two categories —skin color and facial features. She felt that skin color that was darker than her own was more problematic than the shape of a child's eyes.

As women wrestle with issues of race, they ask themselves: "What kind of child can I comfortably and properly mother?" Unlike the question of the age of the child, race is less about the mother's fears and hopes for early-age bonding with her child and more about how an obviously adopted child of another race will fit into her family and community. In the years and weeks leading up to the decision to adopt, the issue of how a child of color will fit into a white woman's circle of family and friends plagues many women. Many of the white mothers are disappointed and hurt if their extended family's reaction to the decision to adopt a child of color is initially unsupportive. Many women, in realizing that they need financial and emotional support from their families and communities, worry about adopting children that will not be welcome or comfortably "fit." In this study, however, all these fears and rifts within the biological family melted away once the adopted child was brought home and the woman's parents became grandparents.

For women who firmly believe that intensive mothering during infancy will significantly shape the quality of their future relationships with their children, adopting infants is critical. Many know that placing utmost importance on the age of the desired child will mean greater possibility of receiving a child of color. Their single status compounds their ambivalence as they try to predict what they can reasonably handle, as Rebecca noted: "I knew it would be easier to adopt a biracial child because for whatever reason, they were not recruiting enough families of color. But I just thought if I remained single, and now adopt a transracial infant—was I stacking the deck? I wondered about whether I was up to the challenges. Was I spreading myself too thin?"

Claudia, featured in the prologue, kept postponing single motherhood each time she thought a new relationship might progress toward marriage. Her journey to becoming a mother also took many twists as she thought about the child she could comfortably parent. She began with imagining a child abstractly, but as the details of her story below illustrate, her imagined child was not just any child regardless of race and age. As she began to think deeply about her own biases, she realized that motherhood was specific and a "universal child" was not the solution. She eventually adopted a two-year-old Russian boy when she was forty-five years old. I met her when she was fifty-two years old and settled into a routine of squeezing her work into a four-day schedule, mostly during the time her son was in elementary school. As with many of the mothers, her process of deciding what age and race child she could comfortably mother was a long, arduous one. Lacking support from her mother and friends in her desire to adopt, Claudia agonized over her decision to adopt a child for over nine years before actually beginning the adoption process. During these nine years, she briefly considered asking a previous boyfriend to be a known donor. Quickly she rejected this idea, as she feared a known donor might in the future reverse his decision and decide he wanted to share her child. As she succinctly put it:

> So in a sense I had already crossed the line where I saw myself doing this solo . . . Of course, I could've done it with an anonymous donor, but I thought if I had done it with somebody it would be more complicated. I [didn't] want to share this child with anyone else. Or if the person said, "I don't want to be involved," but later came back and wanted to be involved, how much do I want him involved if it's not a committed relationship?

Claudia gave up the dream of having a child with a partner and knew that she would be doing this solo, but couldn't picture herself alone with a newborn. Unlike most of the women in this study, she realized that she didn't want to be single and pregnant and then alone with a newborn. She said that "the idea of being with a baby felt more isolating, felt more overwhelming."

As a clinical psychologist herself, she knew that single mothers have little chance to adopt white children domestically. Furthermore, she feared that adopting a child out of foster care might mean being the mother to a child who had been abused or abandoned. She also believed that the risk of birth parents coming back and claiming her child was higher in the domestic system. Adopting internationally "seemed cleaner." Claudia wanted to be sure that the child she adopted not only would be hers permanently but also would comfortably blend into her preexisting single life. She worried that she could not handle a child who was "too different" or "the responsibility of bringing the child's original culture into the life of the family." She said, "It all just felt like more than I could take on." Claudia decided that having a child of the same race and similar culture was more important than sharing in her child's infancy.

Claudia originally had looked into adopting a child from South America, but for reasons that were difficult for her to discuss, she realized that she could not take a child of color. It gnawed at her that maybe she could not love a child of another race, and this caused her to adjust her imagined child. She said that following this painful first attempt, she spent a year of "soul-searching" in therapy during which she reassessed her criteria for her ideal child. She gravitated to her own family's genealogy to clarify her decision—a weak link to relatives she barely knew, but one that gave her peace of mind: "Russia was very appealing because my roots were Russian. My grandparents were all from Russia and I just felt a real connection. . . . It feels really good for me to say to William that my grandparents—his great-grandmother—were born in Russia, and it just feels really nice. . . . He has a strong identity about having been born in Russia." Claudia decided to adopt from Russia not only because adoption from a faraway place reduced the risk of birth parents surfacing, but also because she wanted a white child. For Claudia, race took precedence over age in her journey to create a family and adopt a child that would fit into her white extended family and social network. Other women like Claudia who desire a white child find that international adoption through a private agency provides them with the closest racial fit— even light-skinned Hispanic and Asian children seem less different than African American children.[11]

Women want to be the best mothers that they can be, and so each woman wrestles with the question of what kind of child would be the best fit for her life. Rebecca prioritized age over race, while Claudia chose race over age. However, setting these priorities is a compromise in itself. Arriving at approximately five months of age, Rebecca's baby was not a newborn. Claudia would have preferred a white American child but settled on identifying with her Russian heritage.

Women's political consciousness of international and domestic policies is also a burden they carry forward in their adoption decisions. Race, social class, and citizenship become identities that clash, sometimes for the first time in these women's lives. The history and politics of black-white race relations continue to lead to racial segregation and questions about adoption across race lines. International adoption has a different twist. Prospective adopters' social class standing in conjunction with their U.S. citizenship makes them desirable candidates, and adoption creates a migration of babies from poorer countries to wealthier ones.[12] Because the exact circumstances that severed birth parents from their babies and toddlers are sometimes either unknown or undisclosed, the politics of each country that releases children for adoption elsewhere become central to the narrative of how children are left in need of homes. Stopping the flow of children who are adopted from second- and third-world countries is part of an ethics of globalization to which women have no easy answers. Each woman must craft her own story to explain how her child landed up halfway around the world.

Marli, forty-six, also decided to adopt internationally, her decision shaped by her sensitivity to identity politics.[13] When her chances at biological motherhood were diagnosed as not good because of fibroids, she immediately shifted to figuring out what the adoption route would entail. She was bisexual, and a significant concern for her was what she would say about her sexual orientation to the social worker who came to do a home study. She ultimately decided not to mention her bisexuality when she was asked about her past relationships, and she presented herself as straight.[14] But for her, the pivotal issue in the adoption process was her political consciousness. One of the lenses through which she saw adoption was that of globalization and its relationship to adoption. Are international adoptions, which largely involve children from poor countries going to parents in wealthy ones, saving children from poverty or a life in an orphanage, or are they feeding into a system of abuses, disruption of local families, and social distortion in which children are little more than commodities?[15] Marli framed her choice to adopt a child from China as a way to reduce, though not eliminate, her concerns on this front, and assuage her guilt:

> Once I decided to adopt, then it was unbelievably tortuous. I checked out every-thing, everybody. I went to the different agencies, but for me, the hard issues were around what kind of child, and the politics of it. The politics of it were prob-lematic. . . . I mean, I identify myself as a leftist, so it mattered very much to me what were the conditions under which a child became eligible for adoption and how was I going to create a family which would be affirming of the child's culture of origin. Those were the two issues. And the obvious choice at that point was to do a Central American/Latin American adoption and those were much more my plans and I had a lot of trouble with that because it felt like that these were children who were available because of U.S. imperialism.[16]

Another issue for Marli was the debates around the issue of interracial adoptions. Unlike one of her friends, Marli decided she did not want to get tangled up in the domestic politics of white families adopting black children. She continued:

> And then I debated at one time about doing a domestic transracial adoption, like some my friends did adopting an African American child or a biracial child. And that felt really problematic. I mean, given this very politicized position of the black social workers—a whole articulated position against white families adopt-ing black children—a cultural genocide . . . I felt very awkward getting involved.

She eliminated various possibilities through one criterion after another until she found a country, China, that offered children for adoption in a way that did not contradict her politics.[17] However, she was concerned by her lack of knowledge about Chinese culture and her ability to integrate that culture into her daughter's life. Ultimately, she decided that her own ignorance of Chinese culture was some-thing she could remedy, whereas acquiring a child under politically problematic conditions would permanently weigh on her conscious:

> In some sense, it's funny. On that score, I actually felt much more comfortable, like at least I knew how to begin. And I knew a lot, not oodles, but as an American, I knew a fair amount about black culture, history, literature. For me the big stumbling thing for me about doing the Asian choice was I felt like I knew nothing. And how would I ever . . . I would never learn Chinese.

While she still wondered how she would tell her daughter that being born female in China had made her unwanted and was the reason she was abandoned, she felt relief knowing that this issue was not one that her country had responsibility for. She still had concerns about how to give her daughter a cultural identity and how she would create a transracial family, however.[18] At the time of the interview she was already involved with one of the many area centers that taught Chinese culture and language. In addition, she stayed in touch, meeting frequently, with the other adoptive families (four of the six families assigned to the group were also single parents) with whom she traveled to China to adopt infants. The children were fictive kin insofar as they all came from the same orphanage. Knowing neither the birth town nor anything else about these children, the parents of the children of the same orphanage created a group tie. Marli knew little of her daughter's history except that the child was abandoned at ten months.

Another mother, Patricia, was from a large Irish Catholic family, and among her earliest memories was the wish to have a big family; her ideal situation would be to have both adopted and biological children. She was a nurse who worked for a public agency, and she saw many foster children who needed permanent homes. It was important to her to adopt a newborn as young as possible because newborns are less likely to come with emotional baggage. A domestic adoption made her feel more comfortable because the agency would have more information about the infant than international agencies would.

The child she eventually agreed to adopt was her fourth match from a private adoption agency. Even though she specified that she wanted a healthy infant of any race, the first two calls she received were placement attempts by the agency for terminally ill babies. She refused these infants. The third match she lost because the birth mother decided to keep her baby. Exactly one year after applying, she received a call saying that the agency had a newborn African American girl still in the hospital whose mother had taken drugs through the pregnancy. Since from her nursing work she had experience with crack babies, she decided that this was a child she felt comfortable accepting. Her daughter, age four at the time of the interview, had never shown signs of drug-related problems.

I asked her directly if race was an issue, and she explained her own priorities alongside the politics and arguments made against black-white adoption by segments of the African American community:

> I lived out of the country for a while. I've done a lot of Central American work. And just from my own exploration, I just felt like there was too much of a black market situation there. I just felt that I couldn't do that even though the child would be Hispanic and probably lighter. As much as the agencies I spoke to were saying there are reputable lawyers and stuff, from all that I could tell there, I wasn't confident of that. There was just something about it that I felt there was less control that I had, or that the agency had. But also that I am gonna live here in this country and there are children here and I think I just felt more responsible doing it here. I haven't quite figured out how to word that, but it was more like a gut feeling. I just felt like I needed to do it here.

Well, the race issue is of course an issue we deal with every day. But I felt that I had the personal resources to deal with whatever issues were gonna come. I basically said I want a healthy infant girl. And it didn't matter what race she was. And the way our society works, children of color probably are more available at this point. Now, there's a lot of people who feel that's really wrong. Cultural genocide, you know the black social workers are *very* much against it. A lot of that has come up again recently. And that was hard for me. It was a struggle. But I felt that I really wanted to be a parent and I wasn't saying, "I want a black baby." I just said, "I want a healthy infant girl." As it turns out, Maya actually was exposed to cocaine, and perhaps that helped me get her. I haven't said this to a lot of people, but I've worked with cocaine-exposed children. They weren't threatening to me. I feel like I can deal with it and actually she's totally fine. Some people might think she's pretty enthusiastic, and who knows what that's from, but anyway, that didn't intimidate me. There were some things that perhaps intimidated other people that really didn't intimidate me.

Patricia did not set out to adopt an African American baby, even though she knew that she was more likely to be offered a child of color if she pursued adopting a newborn domestically. She confided in her sister that she did not have the $10,000 domestic agency fee. Immediately her sister called their parents and asked them to offer Patricia as an adoption gift the money they had already set aside for her wedding. Reluctantly they did, assuming that she would adopt a white child. After she hung up with the agency, she excitedly called her parents to tell them the good news: "I have a baby who is African American. I am so excited I can't wait to hold her." Patricia's parents' reaction was less than enthusiastic. Caught by surprise about the baby's race, her dad asked her to rethink her commitment to this child. They were worried about how an African American child would fit in their large extended family of only white grandchildren and whether Patricia would to be able to overcome the troubles of the interracial families they saw in their community. Although Patricia's excitement was temporarily dampened, she stuck to her position that she would adopt this particular child. Patricia's sister, who was six months pregnant, was thrilled when she heard the news. Her sister's embrace was important because Patricia knew that it meant that at the very least her child would have some extended family and a cousin her own age. And in the end, once her parents saw the baby and how happy she was, they become loving and active grandparents.

Janica, a fifty-year-old African American with two teenage daughters, fourteen and sixteen, explained how the adoption process discriminates differently against black women. She adopted her second daughter just three years before Patricia adopted her infant daughter:

I'd seen these two as little kids, and then I saw them again [in the adoption book] when I went back to adopt a second child. The little boy was biracial, and the little girl was white. And I asked then would they let me adopt the two of them. And she said no, because she's white. "If you had had a white husband, they would let you adopt them." I said, "That's ridiculous." So these two kids, they were

siblings and they wanted to be together. So they would have taken a single person
if it was a biracial single person, or a white single person. See? So that's the bias.

These siblings were not available to Janica, even though they were available to
be adopted. Patricia, by contrast, could have adopted a biracial baby and even
a healthy black baby. The racial discrimination within the adoption system
between white and black women who are offered different children is in many
ways similar to the practice of redlining in certain neighborhoods. Janica was
better educated, had a salary twice as large, and had a better support system
than Patricia. But Janica was subject to a different scrutiny.

The social worker who was assigned to Janica's case also asked about skin
coloring as part of the matching process to find the right child for her. A holdover
from earlier points in time about creating a "natural" appearing combination of
family members' skin colors was deemed critical to configuring a black family.
Janica explained how this preference about color worked in her broader community and how it was used by adoption agencies:

> In terms of race, I wouldn't say "race" but "color." Growing up, I'm dark. And
> my brother is dark, and my two sisters are lighter. We have a lot of Indian blood
> in our family. . . . It was funny when I got my first daughter. There was a social
> worker who brought up the fact that she was light. And I said it didn't matter
> because that would match fine in our family because that's the way our family
> was. So most people don't realize that they are adopted because my younger
> daughter looks very much like me, and my first daughter looks very much like my
> mother and my sister. So for our family, that didn't become an issue.
>
> It only becomes an issue to other people. I don't know if you realize this, but
> there is a race issue around color that black people have to put up with. For me,
> I'm very much aware, for my children, in a way that my mother wasn't aware of
> when we were growing up, because people did make a difference between my sis-
> ter and myself. She got to go to a school that was just beginning to be racially
> integrated, and I didn't get to go because—I know you've heard of the "paper bag
> test."[19] I didn't pass the paper bag test. So sometimes I see it happening with how
> my daughters are treated. I stop it.

Janica prepared for a toddler, since she was told the possibilities of her being
given an infant were not good. However, when Sharon, her older daughter, was
two months old she was offered to a few couples who passed. Janica went to see
her because she was told that if she did not see every child that was possible the
agency would not consider her a serious potential parent. Sharon looked sad and
was very small. But the moment Janica held her in her arms she perked up, and
Janica fell in love. She kept asking questions about the birth mother and the process, since she did not want her heart broken if a couple came along. She received
a call telling her Sharon was hers a few days later—she felt she was lucky that there
were no couples at that particular time who wanted the child.

Two years later she was thinking about adopting again, and she returned to
the agency to look at the picture books with the children that were presently

available. She really thought about a toddler this time, partly because it would be easier for her mom, who was caring for her children, while she worked. She had put her search for a second child on hold when she received a call from another adoption agency. Sharon's birth mother had given birth to another child whom she was relinquishing, and requested that priority be given to the family who had adopted her other birth child. Janica was stunned. She conferred with the significant people in her life to see if they were on board, including her siblings, and especially her mom, who would have the greatest responsibility, caring for a toddler in addition to a new baby. Notably, she did not confer with the man who had moved in with her but was not a co-parent.[20] Her mom said, "This is Sharon's sister. You have to take her." Janica called back the next day and said yes. She also told her agency that if the birth mother had more children, she did not want to be contacted. She felt two children was enough and her family was complete. The agency rushed to do an expedited home study, waiving the fees because the children were siblings. The fact that this baby was her child's sibling became the overarching reason for this match; the factors that determined her adoption of Sharon—color and age—were not part of this second adoption. Even though love and legal stewardship were the basis of her family, blood ties between her daughters cemented her decision.

Patricia had options for children that Janica did not have. Race matters differently for black and white women, and its use in matching children with potential mothers is itself racially biased. Also, Patricia paid almost ten times the fees that Janica paid because Patricia went through a private agency, while Janica went through a public system. White women are more likely to use private agencies because they feel they will have support in their attempts to become single mothers, while public agencies will be less sympathetic.

Single mothers agonize over the choices they make as they try to find a way to comfortably adopt a child who is different from themselves and whose reflection they cannot see within themselves. They learn to accept the public gaze that marks them as adoptive mothers who do not easily blend in with the majority of families around them. Yet women also consciously attempt to create new ties to affirm their child's racial and/or cultural identity, even if these new worlds are foreign and without precedent in the mothers' childless lives.

## Birth Families and Adoptive Mothers

Several women in this study undertook a bold and risky venture to include contact with the birth mother as part of an expanding kinship system that is not reflected on birth certificates or through other legal documents. When the adoptive family incorporates birth parents who have given up their legal rights to their biological offspring, the social family expands in ways somewhat similar to families that use known donors (discussed in chapter 4). While known donors rarely function as dads, they do often have some social relationship to their offspring, even if they have no legal rights. In both cases, these single mothers believe that knowledge of the genetic parent can be beneficial to the child. Women believe that nature supplements nurture in the social development of children. Therefore, the inclusion of genetic parents by adoptive mothers reflects a new social reality in which it is possible to have multiple parents. But birth parents are not the same as donors. In today's construction of motherhood, the birth mother is considered as another mother, even though she has relinquished parental rights, in part because of the transformative role ascribed to pregnancy and birthing (the fact that birth fathers are of less consequence than birth mothers reinforces the significance of these factors). By contrast, when a woman becomes pregnant by a known donor, he is not socially considered the child's father; donating gametes is not equivalent to the transformative process of pregnancy and birth.[21]

Historically adoption has been a way to protect a child from the illegitimate circumstances of his or her birth through legal means that hide the truth, such as sealed adoption records and an altered birth certificate. While the majority of adoptive mothers in this study wanted adoptive children whose parents would remain unknown, two women adopted infants whose birth families maintained contact, and two other women adopted siblings out of the foster care system whose biological mothers raised them, even if briefly.[22] The inclusion of the birth mother as a recognized part of their family was not initially the way in which these women thought they would create a family. Each woman came to her decision slowly and with much trepidation, worried about how her and her child's relationship with the birth mother would unfold. They were not really concerned that the birth mothers would share in their daily lives, since contact would be limited; however, they were concerned that the relationship between the children and their birth mothers, who were not solely fantasies to the adoptive child but instead real people, might bring new complications. With a mixture of ambivalence and hope that their child might feel more complete than their adopted friends who grew up not knowing their birth mothers, these women decided they had the emotional strength essential for open adoptions. They felt that they would forever share a child at a deep psychological level with the woman who birthed that child (and possibly the birth father and both sets of biological extended kin) and that an open adoption was a demonstration (and statement) of this shared bond.

Birth parents, particularly birth mothers, live in a borderland of shadows for both the adoptive mother and her adopted child. This situation is not exclusive to adoptive single mothers; it is also true when a heterosexual couple has an open adoption. Two women claim the child differently—and to a large extent the child holds a place in both of their lives even if contact with each woman is radically different. These mothers do not share parenting. The adoptive and birth mothers of the adopted child are not partners who physically share a life, even if they may coexist emotionally in the child's life. And they are not likely to be peers, as couples are; often the birth mother is significantly younger than the adoptive mother. The birth mother and the adoptive mother have made very different commitments to the child both legally and socially.

Many women who eventually decide to open their lives up to include birth parents do so because they see this as the only viable way to become mothers within the constraints of the adoption hierarchy; with a shortage of available infants, birth mothers aided by private attorneys who act as conduits can pick the family who will receive their child. And a number of single women seeking to become mothers start their search for adoptive children with the belief that it is essential to them to locate children whom they will know a lot about and whose biological families are not hidden. The four women I interviewed who adopted openly reported that to adopt internationally would have precluded the possibility of tracing biological kin for their future child. Since this knowledge was important to them and they knew that the chances for domestic adoption were slim, they turned to other ways to adopt children—through either private agencies or the foster care system. All four women adopted children who were either biracial or of another race. They had mixed experiences with their children's birth mothers.

Gina, whose narrative about men and liminality opens chapter 2, met her adopted daughter, Isabelle, on the day of her birth. The birth mother, with the help of her own mother, who is a few years younger than Gina, selected Gina as the adoptive mom. On the day they left the hospital, the birth mother, Bethany, a white tenth-grader, placed the baby in Gina's car. Gina had waited for this moment for a long time and was excited beyond her wildest imagination; when Bethany closed the car door, tears of joy rolled down Gina's cheeks. She had been through a lot to get to this point: leaving her last serious boyfriend at thirty-six years of age, she tried becoming pregnant with an anonymous donor for about a year; when that failed, she was matched three times with birth mothers, and for different reasons each match did not work out. Her baby was beautiful, with curly dark hair that matched Gina's own. Hesitant in the beginning to adopt a baby who was biracial, Gina was delighted that she had decided to consider children of other races after the other potential adoptions fell through.

Gina had been invited to meet Bethany's family, so when they left the hospital parking lot Gina followed Bethany's mom's car to the local high school, where they picked up the birth father, who was in the eleventh grade and African American, and together they all returned to Bethany's family's house. Gina was introduced to family and friends, and the few hours she spent with this extended birth family gave her a window into their lives. She concluded that they trusted her with this baby, and in return she would keep the lines of contact open so that when her daughter was old enough they would be available.

I got to see where these kids met and went to school and then went to Bethany's house for this remarkable five or six hours where no one got up to go to the bathroom. And there was a parade of people. Bethany's father was there, too, and

John [the birth father], who I thought was remarkably brave to sit here with this extended family. And then Bethany wanted me to meet her best friends, who also stopped by.

Once this meeting ended, Gina boarded a plane and flew home with her baby. Since Isabelle's birth, the only form of communication has been an exchange of letters and photos directly—not through an attorney, which is more usual. A few years after the adoption, when Bethany was a young adult and Isabelle was seven, Gina began thinking about the possibility of a reunion of sorts. At the time of the interview, Gina had recently had her first phone conversation since the adoption with Bethany and her mother. I asked her, "What does Isabelle want?"

She's interested in meeting them. And she has very poignant questions around her birthday. She will say, "I'm really missing my birth mom." She now is beginning to understand genetics and she knows that her height—she's tall—is not going to come from me. And she has a lot of questions: "Can I ever meet them?" Yes, those words have definitely come out of her mouth. She was asking me even at five, "Who named me? Who held me first?" She'd like to go back and see the hospital where she was born. She's a thinker and she's curious. . . . After Bethany graduated from college she moved to New York. And Isabelle told my friend, "My birth mother moved to New York to be nearer to me." So fantasies are there.

Gina's underlying philosophy about what her child would need was the result of the losses adoptive children face who do not know their genetic roots because of an ideology of closed adoption.[23] Gina saw closed adoption as a loss for all the parties involved. She felt she would rather share her child, even if it might be painful for her, than raise a child who continued to have questions about herself. She thought that an open adoption would be a cushion for Isabelle because she could offer her a relationship to her birth family:

I want a happy and whole and healthy child. And I believe not having to give up entirely one family to gain the loving family which she has will in the end give her the least hole or emptiness. And I'm trying to do it in a way that supports her, that's not out of my imagination. I really, if all things were equal, wanted to have a tremendous amount of first-hand information. I think adoption is hard. I think it's another layer for children to process.

The more I learn as a parent, the more I know that this is the best way to go. You can't wait. In some ways I want it to be her choice. You can't introduce her to strangers at age eighteen. I care about these people. I have tremendous affection; I am very, very lucky in that I trust them. I'm not saying that if we would have a more open adoption that there wouldn't be an issue once in a while. But I feel very confident.

I think Isabelle can only gain, whatever questions she will have about her identity, I think she can only gain in having a relationship, regardless of how intense or how often, from knowing them and having direct access to them. Not only for questions, but just the opportunity for them to know her. Who knows? But I believe it's true. So that's why I'm doing it.

And what I hope is that in the end, the closeness with your child—because I'm not a martyr—comes from offering them support. Again, whatever my losses are, she's not responsible for them. And I think her loss is a big one. I don't want her to feel like adult adoptees in their fifties and sixties who feel that their lives are ruined lives, I don't want her to feel that.

Gina, however, wanted to make sure that if she allowed a relationship to develop between Bethany and Isabelle, it would not be fleeting.[24] She described what she was seeking from the birth mother on behalf of her daughter:

The only thing I have to make sure about and talk to Bethany more about, who is still a young person, is that I do see this is a sort of lifelong commitment. So if we move forward I'd like her to be available and not just a one-time thing. I'd really like her to think about this as a commitment—that she feels she's willing to do that before we go to the next step.

Gina sized up both Isabelle's and Bethany's readiness for this first meeting. Similar to other mothers in this study, Gina was the gatekeeper of information, telling Isabelle about her birth family and the letters they wrote. However, Gina wanted to control this reunion. At the time of the adoption, Bethany had been a tenth grader and unable to make a commitment to becoming Isabelle's mother, but Gina had been ready to be a mother. With this reunion, though, Gina did not want Bethany to give Isabelle up again and open Isabelle up to feeling twice abandoned. Gina realized that contact with the birth family was an emotional risk for both herself and Isabelle, yet it was a risk she was willing to take.

For Caroline, who adopted a sibling group out of foster care, the risk of maintaining contact with the biological parents was much higher. At the time of the adoption Caroline was thirty-seven years old and the children were nine and ten years old. The children had been placed in foster care because the parents were alcoholic and abusive. This knowledge prompted Caroline to request a closed adoption. The four children from this sibling group had been in foster care for most of their childhood, yet when Caroline decided to adopt, only the younger two remained in the state's custody; the older two were young adults and living on their own.[25] Caroline was determined not to let her adopted son and daughter be hurt further by their biological parents. The children were angry and wanted no further contact with their biological mother, as they had been in foster care for years. They wanted a fresh start, which Caroline had hoped to give them. Somehow, however, despite the closed adoption, the biological mother managed to learn the children's whereabouts—which Caroline had assumed could never happen. At the children's request, she intercepted the biological mother's attempted contact.

When the children were fifteen and sixteen she received a call from a social worker in the foster care system, who informed her that the biological mother was extremely ill. Caroline was torn between wishing to protect her children and wanting her children to have closure. She took them to the hospital for what she thought would be a final goodbye.

> The biological mother was in an alcohol-related seizure and went into a coma and she was unconscious for two weeks. Somebody called me and said, "Just so you know, the kids' birth mother is in the hospital." So I said to the kids, 'cause they were like fifteen and sixteen at the time, "I think it's really important to go see her and say what you need to say." I told them that even though she was unconscious, she could hear them or they could write it or whatever. And they were saying, "No way. We're not going. We do not want to." And I said, "Well, I know that." And I can't believe that I was kind of pushing that. But I really felt it was important that they have some closure and get to say what they needed to say to her. And of course she survived! Which then turned upside down the apple cart for those poor kids, especially my daughter. Because now she felt so guilty. Oh, my goodness! So it's been quite the adventure.

When the biological mother left the hospital, the children were again inundated with phone calls. Both Caroline and the children, having already created a new life separate from the biological mother, agreed that her attempts to contact them were unwelcome. Caroline told her so directly. And then she said:

> "You really cannot call here anymore. The kids have your number. It's sitting on the refrigerator. And if they want to call you, you need to let them call you. You can't keep calling here." But of course she didn't because she started drinking again and then she called up while she was drunk.

Interestingly enough, even though Caroline agreed legally to a closed adoption, because the children had two additional older siblings, she also willingly agreed to allow contact among the four siblings, the former foster parents, and the children's biological grandparents. Yet even this arrangement proved to be an emotional roller coaster ride. While Caroline and the adopted siblings established a close relationship with the eldest nonadopted daughter and her husband, their ties to the other nonadopted older sibling became more problematic.

> So we stay in touch with their older brother and sister all the time. And the older brother wasn't so much a good idea once he started doing a lot of criminal things. But the reason I finally cut it off with the eldest brother was because the birth mother was trying to use my son. The birth mother called him at school wanting to know if Joe would give his Social Security number to the older brother, who was in trouble with the police. She lied and told the school that she was in a coma. At that point I said to her, "Okay, no more Mr. Nice Guy. That you would be willing to put at risk this child is not acceptable to me. Please don't call here again." So . . . I mean she drank. So it's like telling the wall.

When Caroline decided at age forty-six, the year I met her, to adopt a second sibling group out of the Department of Social Services—three Hispanic children ages four, seven, and eight—she made sure that it was indeed a closed adoption, unwilling to have the same kind of emotional pull repeat itself. Despite the legal status of the adoption as closed, Caroline was not opposed to allowing her children to contact their birth mother in the future and would be willing to ask the agency to help them in their search.

Gina and Caroline represent two different routes to expanded kin situations. Gina's first meeting with her daughter's birth family gave her confidence that these were decent people whom she trusted and respected for their decision that Bethany was just too young to raise a child—the reason Isabelle became Gina's daughter. By contrast, Caroline's adopted children did not come from a loving home environment and instead had spent years in foster care. They were at risk because of the instability in their young lives. Caroline felt that their biological mother and older nonadopted biological brother could only bring more heartache, not offer anything positive.

When adoptive mothers seek to expand kinship ties in order to fill in identity gaps for their children, they also act as gatekeepers of their children's outside relationships and seek to limit contact to only biological kin who will be beneficial to their children. In an ideal world, adoptive mothers would welcome genetic kin in their lives in order to bolster their children's sense of self. However, women who adopt out of the foster care system—and particularly those who adopt older children—often know from the beginning of these placements that the biological parents may be harmful to their children's formative identity. Caroline was torn between resisting a biological mother who tried to push her way in and hoping that that mother might reform her ways. Time proved that her children's biological mother would only continue to be a persistent source of pain. Yet it was much more difficult for Caroline to simply close off all contact because she and her adoptive children did have a good relationship with some of their other biological kin. She said that she did not fully recognize how problematic adopting adolescent children out of foster care could be.

## The Dominant Culture and Questions

Children try to make sense of their situation as they confront definitions of families and life experiences their adoptive mothers can't control, although mothers are prepared to ease the difference. The experiences their children face are not always ones that their adoptive mothers know firsthand. White mothers have not experienced the same racial discrimination that their child of color faces, nor have most of these mothers experienced the absence of a father. Therefore, the mother's social construction of the family's everyday experiences is insufficient to address and anticipate the child's questions. While all mothers face this in varying ways (from differences in history, generation, social class, etc.), the creation of transracial families makes family members more obviously not blood kin. Later, the challenge is to answer the child's questions about things the mother has never experienced.

These women's experiences point to both the continued hegemony of the nuclear family and the racial assumptions about its members. The most telling rendition of the power of the hegemonic family comes from Gina's experiences as she tried to protect her daughter. She realized that her work exposure to African American colleagues, supervisors, and clients might give her insight, but it was no substitute for the actual experience of race that her daughter might have. She found race to be more complex than she had imagined. She lived with a double lens: trying to imagine her child's everyday racial experience while sharing the cultural privilege of her own whiteness.

Gina heard a certain amount of inquisitiveness in the voices of acquaintances when they remarked that her daughter was beautiful. She interpreted their comment about her daughter's beauty as a question about the child's father and her own tie to a man: "People will say, 'Your daughter is beautiful.' It isn't, 'Oh, is she biracial?'" Some mothers when they are alone with their adopted children— particularly those of biracial children—report that they sometimes find it easier to pass as their child's biological mother, particularly if the person asking is a stranger. The mother conveys the impression of a biological family in order to minimize any negative repercussions that might lie behind a stranger's comments. Interestingly, Gina believed that her own appearance contributed to a mother-daughter match:

> I've been told over and over again that most people who are meeting me think I might be part African American. I guess I am not aware of this. The over-whelming assumption seeing Isabelle and me—of course they think we look alike—is that I am married to someone of color, or I was in a relationship and she is my biological child.

Without the other parent present to complete the family picture, the assumption is often that this is a biracial biological family. The presence of a man is presumed, as is that the child is the product of the small percentage of biracial marriages in the United States. In public the mother can hide behind the hegemony of the nuclear family and blood ties as the basis for kin.

Similarly, Janica, African American with two African American daughters, rarely told anyone that her daughters were adopted. She preferred to blend in, as if her children were biologically hers. But without the presence of a dad at various school functions, she too was unable to mimic the nuclear family template. She recalled that when her children were in middle school other parents would ask, "Where's your husband?" Or they would say to her daughters, "Where's your dad?" Even though she adopted her daughters in her thirties, she felt as if she was usually being judged on the basis of a stereotype, in the same way as a teenager who "accidentally" became pregnant—no man in the picture. She did not dispel this stereotype of herself because she felt it was her teenage daughters' right to tell or not tell friends they were adopted. She was willing to live with other people's bias about single black women rather than expose her daughters as adopted.

Therefore, one day she developed the strategy of telling acquaintances, "We don't know where he is." This response silenced them, and as she told me, "It is the truth. I don't know where their birth fathers are." Even close friends were surprised to learn that her children—who are biologically related to each other—were adopted. The power of the biological nuclear family, with two opposite-sex parents of the same race, shaped her belief that her children's privacy about their birth origins was not a topic she wanted to discuss openly. These were her daughters, and that was all people outside of her immediate family circle needed to know.

Yet when their children's own self-awareness grows and they begin to ask questions about how they fit in with the family, the mothers deflect the difference by separating out blood ties from social ones and by absorbing the void through fantasy talk. When Isabelle was seven years old, she and her mom were driving home from an extended-family vacation that included grandparents, aunts and uncles, and first cousins. Suddenly, Isabelle who had had a wonderful time, asked her mom: "Is there no one in my family with brown skin? And I was the only one of my cousins that didn't have a dad." When I asked Gina how she responded, she told me:

> Well, I would say right now that the single part is a little more prominent. Sometimes we go with a fantasy. "What would you like about that [having a dad]?" We've done a lot with that and that's given her some outlet. Sometimes we'll go with a reality check about whether that's likely to happen, under what circumstances it would happen. I can't do anything about that. The way we talk about it is that she does have a father, her birth father. She has pictures. She doesn't have a forever dad. And that's because I'm not married. It's clearly trying to completely keep the focus. So, it's like, "Get yourself married. I want a dad."

But it was one thing to fantasize when Gina and Isabelle were alone together and quite another to have a playmate raise this absence, however innocently:

> The only time it ever came up was with another child—the second year of pre-school, where I walked in and overheard a child who said, "Does Isabelle have a dad?" And there is my daughter. And what came out of my mouth was, "Isabelle has a birth dad. She doesn't have an everyday dad. I'm not married." Then another question, "What do you mean, a birth dad?" I didn't answer her further. The first question she asked was enough. I tried to validate that [Isabelle has a dad]; it was the best I could do. I wasn't going to say no, and I wasn't going to say yes to something that wasn't true. Basically, for what she was asking me, the answer was no. But I thought it was important to say that first part.

Even though a four-year-old playmate does not understand, the teacher standing nearby certainly does. Gina's words spilled out as she answered for her daughter. She did not want her daughter blamed or, worse yet, teased for something that was Gina's "fault"—not having an "everyday dad" certainly wasn't Isabelle's doing. Yet Gina realized how guilty she felt for not even recently attempting to find a man who would become an "everyday dad," that is; a man who would be a consistent presence in their lives.

During preschool Isabelle tried to figure out how she could have two parents like the other children in her group. She made the following equation:

> When she was learning in the second year of pre-school about Gay and Lesbian Pride Day and they read *Heather Has Two Mommies*, first she said, "Well, that's like us. I have two moms." True, but we're talking birth mom and adopted mom, not two everyday moms. But then she said, "If I can't get a dad, I'd rather have two moms." I said, "I wish it were that easy to just change overnight!" And that's when I thought, "You know, some of this is about having another person."

When Gina told her friends this story, they assured her that Isabelle missed having another person around, and that was why she placed her birth mother as the other parent in her life. It was not a confusion about the separation of kinds of mothers in her life; but the wish to be like other children in two-parent families—even a gay family would do. Gina, like most of the mothers I interviewed, admitted to me that to some extent it was true that it would be nice for both of them to have another person around to give Isabelle attention even though they had a rich life of friends and family.

### Building a Transracial Family

Adopting a child of color catapults women into an experience of scrutinizing and then organizing their lives through a new lens: race. They have never previously seen their whiteness as a socially organizing frame that segregates their public life from those they include in their intimate circle of friends.[26] Their status as white women determines their friendships, their cultural activities, and the public spaces they frequent. However, often they have co-workers, supervisors, or clients of another race. They learn the language of diversity in the workplace, which rarely translates into intimate friendships. The women talk about how their time is now consumed with calculating ways to place their child in public places frequented by people of their child's race and cultural background.[27]

While finding such public places or cultural activities in the greater Boston area is not difficult, these spaces do not easily provide gateways into intimate circles of people of color because of the mothers' whiteness. Gina reflected upon how her views of places to swim changed when she considered her daughter's race:

> We go to the public town pool, which if you had asked me ten years ago would I go to a public pool, I was probably a big snob: "Is the water clean?" But actually the public pool is a really nice pool. It is clearly 70, 80 percent black. . . . One day we go there and then one day we go to this private pool in the suburbs that my sister joined that has few people of color.

However, the separate pools of water symbolize, in this case, both racial and social class divides. Gina did not have to talk to anyone at the public pool. She was an invisible overseer of her daughter's play—a space she occupied that allowed her daughter to be camouflaged with the other kids. She was caught between the white world and the world that her daughter fit into. There was no in-between or mixed world in which both she and her daughter could comfortably exist and be affirmed as a family unit. As she shifted between swimming areas, so did her own comfort level.

Marli also articulated a similar struggle to find both public and intimate communities that would affirm both her whiteness and her daughter's Asian identity. Marli talked about being able to easily find and integrate herself and her child into networks and groups made up of white parents and Chinese kids, but not the Asian community. As the numbers of transracial families in Boston rise, these families band together as a hybrid community.

> But how to then create a multicultural, multiracial, white/Asian family, now that seemed like a really daunting challenge. There is this tremendous network of people who have such a family configuration in Boston. So you can be part of that network, which is not the same thing as being part of the Asian community.

While adopted Asian children of white families have a huge network of similar families, the white mothers do not have the personal experience of growing up Asian to rely upon. Similar to religious converts, they learn the culture and language hoping that authentic members of the local Asian community will accept their child foremost and themselves secondarily. These adopted families sometimes hire authentic members of the Asian community to school their children (and themselves) in the cultural knowledge they lack.[28] They have to consciously work at creating Asian identities for their children immersed in a white world.

> We order the books about China from the adoption places up the kazoo. And then we recently hired someone who comes in to teach the kids Chinese songs. It's just Chinese songs so far, and I would say it's a flop, but it will get better. And we try to go to holiday things like something the Children's Museum puts on, or we go down to Chinatown. I assume that we're gonna have to do a whole lot more things and I don't know all of what they are yet.

Rich and complex cultures are reduced to more easily accessible events or experiences for themselves and their children. This is not all that dissimilar from the experiences of first- or second-generation children of most ethnic families. Cultural knowledge declines and becomes more symbolic; foods, holiday celebration, and some language skills become symbolic reminders of a family's history.[29]

Marli was savvy. She offered a complex statement about intersecting identities and where, theoretically, a family that is transracial could find a place. Yet the social world is structured in such a way that the intersections she sought are often absent.

How would you create a multicultural life, affirming of being black and white together? If you were Christian and you go to a Christian black church, and that maybe would work for you. But where would you live? Who would your friends be? Where would you be welcome? Where would your child be welcome?

Her statement points to the structural constraints that women need to overcome if they are to foster not only a multicultural world that celebrates diversity but an intersecting world that embraces overlapping identities.

Mothers who create transracial families search for day care situations that include other children who are of diverse races. Unlike for white parents with white children, racial safety—the tensions that a child feels being a token minority—weighs heavily in their day care decision making.[30] They do not want theirs to be the only child of her race or the child who is used to fill a minority quota.

In an ideal world, Patricia explained, she would have friends and a community life that included African Americans. She lacked this diversity and therefore sought a day care center that would provide ongoing diversity for her daughter. Patricia selected a setting where the majority of children were African American. Her selection of a predominately black day care setting complicated her relationship to her daughter, who at age four saw skin color difference between herself and her mother. Her mother repeated what her daughter had recently wished:

I have used the word *adoption* right from the start. There's somebody on the *Barney* show that's adopted: "Oh, she's adopted just like you." I don't think she fully understands it yet. But interestingly about the race, she's actually in a day care where there are all children of color. And the majority of teachers are people of color. So she's pretty much in a day care world that's pretty brown. And she came home about two months ago and said to me, "I want you to be brown like me." On the one hand, I was glad. On the other hand, it's like right there. So we talk about it. And it comes up—it's not come up now for a few weeks, but we talked about it and I said, "Mommy's never gonna be brown like you. We're different colors." And she calls me gray, which is fine. And adoption has come up too around that, because she came out of a brown woman's tummy is how she put it. Also for her, that issue came up very early on, which I was totally surprised it wasn't the daddy issue: "Where's my daddy?" The way she seems to have got it is that we don't have a daddy that lives with us right now. That's how we say it. I feel like at this point I've been able to answer her questions, what she's asked. It's obviously gonna get more complex as she gets older and I'm trying to be prepared for that.

Patricia believed her daughter fixated on her racial difference with her mother. Patricia's strategy to place her child in a school where her daughter was part of the racial majority made Patricia the minority in her daughter's social life. Patricia's daughter had access to a racial world of which Patricia was not a part, and the child wished she could change her mother's race so that they could share this world her daughter loved going to each day. Further complicating this scenario was a home life that included few people of color. Patricia was concerned with how her life and her daughter's was so segmented—further divided by a working-class day care setting and a more middle-class home life. She worried about the composition of these worlds and how to better align race and social class in their everyday lives.

### Forced Versus Organic—Personal Versus Public

All women who become first-time mothers begin to see their lives in terms of life before baby and life with baby. For these mothers who adopt children of a different race and culture, this divide between their previous and present lives is further fraught with the process of building a transracial family. They are concerned not only with making the adjustments of motherhood but also with carving out a multicultural space that neither negates their own identity nor excludes their child's heritage. There appears to be a number of different layers in these intersecting social worlds. There are multiple, sometimes overlapping resources to tap: (1) resources from the hybrid adoption network, (2) resources from the mother's single life, and (3) resources from local communities of color.

Marli distinguished between connections that developed naturally and fit fluidly with her present life and those that felt more forced. She found these organic connections through lifelong friendships and the adoption community: "My best friend is Chinese American and she is about to go to China. She is lesbian, about to come back with a child. So that is an organic connection in our life." The people in her adoption group who went over to China and adopted from the same orphanage considered their children "cousins," and this group remained close. However, Marli acknowledged, these connections did not fully represent Chinese American culture, and she sought out connections that were more authentic even if they were also more forced:

> Because basically it's a white culture. And even though the kids are physically Asian, and the reality is, identity stuff is incredibly complicated. Zoë is not just Asian and she will be Asian/Jewish and whatever that means. But I definitely think some link into actual Asian communities to me seems significant, and to be aware there are Asian adults, so it's not just kids. I think that's differently affirming than just knowing white families who have Asian kids. And then of course that all collides into all the rest of the realities of being a single mom. Which are, how do I do them all together?

In the above excerpt Marli circled around her own principal identities, including being single, lesbian, and Jewish. All were interlocking and constituted who she was. In her life prior to adopting, she had constructed a tapestry of relationships that affirmed these other identities. Now with an Asian child she had to weave together her preexisting identity with her child's cultural background:

> I feel like it's a very conscious task. I feel like I'm only at the beginning. Although I clearly have categories that I'm trying to fill in. Personal relationships, culture

. . . Definitely I've got to get somewhere on the language school, at least so I can read the transliteration correctly. It's not adequate enough to be just good friends and hanging out with other people from China.

Marli wanted to create a life in which the interlocking identities that formed her family would all be acknowledged in varying ways. They did not all need to be acknowledged simultaneously; for Marli, the task of reweaving a new life was more about building an authentic multicultural family. Marli saw herself in contrast to other white families who would rather gloss over their child's race:

I definitely do consider myself adamantly in contrast to the color-blind school, which I think is unfortunately extremely mistaken. Do I think you could be obsessive about this? Yes, I do think you could be obsessive. Do I come anywhere near that? No. I mean I think there's a real tendency, if you're white, and particularly the way Asian culture is quoted in this society, you could start to think your kid's white because you're mostly in a white world.

Single white mothers who adopt children of color have to be intentional and creative in linking their families to authentic communities of their child's race. For instance, Gina sought out an African American pediatrician so that her child would have a professional role model. Similarly, she attended cultural events to expose her daughter to famous people of color in the arts. They vacationed in a part of Martha's Vineyard that is a summer destination for upper-middle-class African Americans. Social class concerns were equally important in her decisions. Yet while she had the economic ability to place her child with middle-class African Americans, she remained an outsider:

I am just trying to put a little more emphasis on raising a resilient child. I want her to stay strong in how she feels about herself. I'm trying to expand who is really in our lives. It's harder to go beyond even play dates and to go beyond mixed birthday parties and really be intimately connected with families from different racial groups. I've made some inroads but not as much as I'd like to. But we've slowly identified Oak Bluffs as our vacation spot. Each year we are meeting more and more people. Race is part of each decision I make. So far so good. I'm more in awe [and] not that articulate about this—but I'm more in awe of the tremendous responsibility of parenting a child of color. And the additional responsibility for parenting a child who is African American in this society than I ever was before.

Gina decided to force the authenticity of intimacy in order to place her child in affirming and visibly diverse social circles. The friendships such children form with people of the same race and/or culture may lead to relationships the mothers may or may not share in the future. Whether the children's friendships become the catalyst for multicultural communities that are less intentional and more organic remains to be seen.

Ultimately, we do not live in a multicultural world. These women's stories and concerns about how to fit in make this point abundantly clear. Single mothers are at the forefront of creating transracial families in the United States. Ironically, the hegemony of the adoption hierarchy, which gives priority to heterosexual couples, makes it unlikely that these white single women will be matched with a same-race child. Single mothers weigh race and age as they try to figure out how to craft a family that blends in with other families around them. They need to feel comfortable with the child's race, cultural background, and age at adoption in order to bond with the child. In the process of trying to figure out their own comfort levels, they discover how their own race has privileged and shaped their worlds. Often their white privilege is unrealized and unconscious until they try to figure out spaces where their child will meet other children of his or her racial background. Overlapping and diverse communities are rare.

Mothers sometimes become the "minority" in order for their child to be a member of the "majority," but even then women feel that it is difficult to find middle-class environments with the right racial and ethnic mix—or a multicultural world—where both mother and child would feel comfortable. These adoptive mothers become conscious of a world in which segregation and ethnic enclaves are often variably open to outsiders. Slowly they are making inroads and hoping that intimacy and deeper relationships with authentic members of their child's background will become possible.

## Conclusion

Like Rebecca, whose story began the chapter, most of these women's journeys toward motherhood begin with a reflection period in which they look at their preexisting private and public lives and begin to ask what kind of child will fit in their worlds. As the women look at their social circles they realize that a child of color would glaringly stand out. Among those who decide to adopt children of color, even the most self-conscious, such as Rebecca, eventually become immune to the sometimes hostile gaze of the predominately white world they live within. They survey the geography that surrounds them in order to head off attacks on their child's positive identity. But even Gina, who made a conscientious decision about a day care placement, found the curiosity of a young playmate almost unbearable, and she became defensive. Gina learned as her child grew that she needed to better make her child's racial identity matter while also sharing her own identity with her child. That is, she saw herself in her child—the mark of bonding and motherhood—even if they did not share the same race. Yet in public she had to heighten her awareness of race and create a game plan for dealing with the questions and curiosities of strangers.

The white women in this study who adopted children of color discovered emotional resources that they'd never known they had, and they were able to successfully carve out a space for their children within their private and public lives.

They discovered ways to create structures and a map for mothering a child of another race or culture. However, some women decided that bringing issues of a different race and culture into their families would be unnecessarily complicated. They therefore compromised on the age of the child they adopted in order to secure a white child and deflect the uncomfortable public gaze—and prevent themselves from being marked as visibly adoptive mothers.

In addition to struggling to piece together different racial and cultural identities to form a cohesive family unit, these single women are also confronted with other kinds of difference and disadvantage. The domestic foster care system is full of "at-risk" children who are seen as "unfit" by many of the players in the adoption system. Due to their high-priority status in the system, heterosexual couples typically are not offered these types of children. If couples do see these children, they often do not feel compelled to adopt them since they have a good chance at a healthy white infant.

On the other hand, after a few months of exploring their options within the adoption system, single mothers are fully aware of their low-priority status, even women of color. Like at-risk children needing homes, single women are also given the label of "unfit," in this case in connection with their motherhood. Both parties longing to be a part of a family are thrown together into the same potential adoption pool. Some women, on realizing that these types of "at-risk" children are what is available to them, opt to adopt a child internationally. In a sense, the slim pickings of white children in the domestic system drive these women out of the country in their search for a child. However, quite a few women see these at-risk children as not so undesirable. Their desire for a child outweighs any misgivings about labels of "unfit" and "at-risk." These women, in a sense, embrace their own "unfit" status and become mothers to children who also have been overlooked because they are considered less-than-ideal adoption candidates. In fulfilling their desires to be mothers, these women almost unknowingly are altruistically adopting the neediest children and doing the greatest service for the U.S. adoption system. Ironically, the women who are deemed by our culture as being unfit for motherhood are taking on the difficult task of carving out a space for their adoptive children and their newly formed mismatched families to finally fit.

# CONCLUSION

## Ordinary Lives, Extraordinary Circumstances

I wanted a normal child to enter my abnormal life.
> —Jennifer, known-donor route to motherhood

Garrison Keillor's *Lake Wobegon Days*, based upon his radio show, *A Prairie Home Companion*, posits a community in which "all the women are strong, all the men are good-looking and all the children are above average." In this parody of the perfect American community, families all have extraordinary children who live ordinary lives. The women in this study have created families in extraordinary ways, and since these single mothers know there is no community where all the children are above average, they, like Jennifer, wish for children and families that will simply blend with their own average communities. These women may live their lives and create their families in nontraditional ways, but they do not want their children to suffer the consequences of those choices. They also want their children to live ordinary lives—that is to say, a middle-class, orderly life where their children fit. They do not want their children stigmatized by lifestyle decisions that they themselves have made about becoming mothers. However, the more agency that women take on in creating families on their own, the more fearful they become that their children will be marginalized by the dominant culture.

The concept of liminality is salient in the process of women's decisions to go their own way, in terms of their respective routes to motherhood. As women leave the liminal state, they cross the threshold of what is socially accepted; yet, after crossing the threshold, they want their children to be seen as ordinary, separated from the extraordinary circumstances that brought them into their lives.

However, single mothers and their children cannot avoid confronting their birth narratives and struggle with how to include them as they present their family to the world. Faced with pervasive ideas of women and children's place in the family, they must resolve the conflict between the master narratives and their own lives. While Part I of this book celebrates women's slow discovery of alternative routes to motherhood that exclude marriage, Part II argues that once children arrive, "fitting in" trumps the celebration of crafting these same alternative families. These three chapters are also about three crucial contradictions that single mothers perpetrate on behalf of their children: denying agency, the weight of genetics, and resurrecting the father. These contradictions are less reflective of women's regrets and inconsistencies about the way they have created their families than they are demonstrative of the power and omnipresence of the master narratives governing family and its members.

Part II highlights how women craft families to make their own look more like the "ordinary" American family. To do so, women backpedal from the three bold confrontations of traditional family that they make en route to motherhood, instead bowing to various narratives embedded in patriarchy. They rewrite their stories to conceal their agency, not wanting to break with the broader prescriptions of gender that a man's inclusion validates the family as a complete unit. They separate out genetic and social families by deconstructing men, but then build back up the preeminence of genetics. Finally, mothers go to great lengths to protect themselves and their children from claims of the father (or birth parents), only then to resurrect these figures in order to conform. While the women pull at the threads of the heterosexual nuclear family, unraveling it en route to motherhood, as they raise this child they attempt to reconstruct it. Women are patching their lives onto the acceptable pattern of middle-class family—no less ordinary than what Garrison Keillor posits.

The template of the two-parent heterosexual nuclear family is inescapable. Everyday life reflects, particularly through institutional spaces, what family is supposed to look like. Schools, unavoidable for children, and religious settings, which many women choose not to avoid, often subtly or overtly reinforce the normative two-parent heterosexual family. The process of constructing identity and origin is a yearly assignment in many classrooms around the country. Certainly this is the case in eastern Massachusetts, where the women in this study reside. Each year the majority of these women's children come home with an assignment that forces them in the early grades to identify family members through photos and in later grades to create family trees that include written reports on relatives' lives and achievements. These activities reinforce the uniqueness of each child and celebrate classroom diversity, as well as teach the child about the rooting of self in history and heritage. This task proves difficult for many of these families because as much as uniqueness is to be celebrated, to stray too far is isolating and often leads to uncomfortable conversations and questions about family composition.[1]

Children whose families are crafted in nontraditional ways need to be explained, even if at the most basic levels. While the mothers in this study want their children to proudly answer questions about their family heritage, there is an imbalance in what they know and how they know it regarding their paternal side of this heritage. It is not simply about genetics and the family tree, but also about the memories and social relationships that children accrue over time (ideally with members of the "biological tree") that give meaning to the self and allow children to compose an identity through kin interactions. In a culture that masks the possibility of having more than one mother and father at a time (with perhaps the exception of stepparents, who are second-class parents, with their standing again derived through marriage), this becomes problematic even in the most liberal communities. Being unable to display a picture of a father to complete these assignments marks these children as different.

Those women who had either open adoptions or known donors for their children are more readily able to provide their children with a picture or family tree, conforming at one level. But on another level, these children confront the nontraditional reality of multiple parents or parents who are biologically but not socially involved in their lives. Similarly, the bits of information in donor profiles while providing less information, do offer some sense of identity, which, as I have already argued, allows the mothers to imagine with their children a fantasy father. They pass along any information that might help their kids fit in—that is, their children could say, "I was born here," and point to a place on a map in China, or "My father is a musician." As much as family diversity is accepted, children spend much of their time in day care and school settings in which they are constantly being asked to explain themselves and their families. Therefore, the other children who, in their curiosity, ask about a child's dad and where he is notice children whose fathers do not come to day care or school events. While educators have training to be sensitive to a wide range of family diversity issues, the lack of a father remains a delicate matter. These families find that other institutions in which they participate expect them to mirror the path dictated by the master narrative of a two-parent, heterosexual, married family, which opposes their own reality.

After setting aside the rule book to become mothers, in raising their children women choose to conform rather than rebel against the dominant nuclear family. The reality is that these women's children will have to live in and move between (at least) two worlds—one steeped in the hegemony of the two-parent heterosexual family and another that intrinsically defies it. Mothers do not want their children to have to defend their daddyless family or become a visible poster child for a social experiment. To that end, women attempt to build a bridge between these two worlds, one that their children can use to fit in. The bridge can be a father crafted out of a paper profile, a reluctant dad's sporadic visits, or the half sibling of an adoptive child. This push for conformity, made up of the three contradictions discussed earlier, is motivated by women's aspiration not to implicate their child.

Once these hard-won children arrive, women confront institutions rooted in normative family structures. While these institutions might grapple with diversity and discuss alternative families, in fact the assumptions of the nuclear family are deeply embedded. For example, one child came home reporting to her mother that his teacher, tired of lining up the class by first or last names, decided to be creative and ask the children to line up for recess by father's first name. The last thing single mothers want for their children is for them to be the odd kid out, and this situation brings to life that fear. It is for this reason that single mothers arm their children with information about imagined fathers in anticipation of an inevitable confrontation with this assumption. In the opinion of these single mothers, children just need enough information so that they can fall into line. The child in the class who did not have a dad but a known donor instead found his place in line because he knew his genetic father's name was Marcus. Even though the child's close friends in class know that he has a donor, the child is not outed to all as fatherless. For the moment, the child blended into the line, passing for no less ordinary than the other children on the way out to recess.

While American society has reached a new marital low point and has begun the reconstruction of family life, it has not seen the demise of the master narrative that still privileges the two-parent heterosexual genetic family. At the epicenter of the master narrative is the father, the patriarchal puppeteer of the family. Single mothers begin to cut the strings en route to motherhood, only to find themselves dancing, on behalf of their children, to the master narrative once again.

# Part III

# Composing a Family

# INTRODUCTION

## Recycling and Reconstituting Families

The sun in all his light and glory was to rise upon a new world; in this world woman was to be free to direct her own destiny. . . . My hopes also move towards that goal, but I hold that the emancipation of woman, as interpreted and practically applied today, has failed to reach that great end. Now, woman is confronted with the necessity of emancipating herself from emancipation, if she really desires to be free. This may sound paradoxical, but is, nevertheless, only too true.
—Emma Goldman, "The Tragedy of Woman's Emancipation," 1906

Having liberated themselves from the paralysis of childlessness, the women in this study are faced with integrating their new lives and selves with children into the world. This world is not as hostile to alternative families as it once was, yet it remains unyielding to the twenty-first-century needs of all families.[1] The new world for women described by Emma Goldman at the beginning of the twentieth century holds the same promise and contradiction as that facing single mothers today. Goldman expresses frustration with the reality of freedom, asking, "What has she achieved through her emancipation?" This question remains a century later.

Women who have managed to free themselves from the social norms of married motherhood have done so as reluctant revolutionaries. They did not set out to break new ground, but wanting a child before time ran out took precedence over following tradition. With a child in their arms, these women must again forge their own path as they organize their family's daily life. They relieve themselves of the burden of chasing marriage, only to be shouldered with the new trials of single motherhood. The world in which they have freed themselves is still flawed—integrating their new family with their social life, their work life, and the world around them leaves them with little wiggle room. These women have what Goldman calls "external emancipation"—they have the job, the home, and the child. But larger forces premised on a particular type of job structure, home life, and mothering trap them in their emancipation. Essentially, these new opportunities for women do not form a cohesive package. In the United States, making it all work is left up to these women individually.[2]

Today, women can be single mothers as an alternative to the nuclear family, with one catch: making this choice means making a promise to stay below the radar. That is to say, as long as they and not the government finance their motherhood; as long as they make their children fit society, not force society to fit their children; and as long as they reshape their individual jobs, not the workplace as a whole, they can be single mothers. Further, they must yield to one final societal concern: they must now also work hard to include men they had initially excluded from their family's formation. As single mothers, they are outside the bulkhead that continues to shelter the nuclear family, leaving them exposed to the storm of social problems that currently batters all families. As women are treading water, trying to keep their work and family life from capsizing, I recall Goldman's question: is this really freedom? These women are directing their own destinies but navigating through the same quagmire.

Part III begins by examining the nuances of how these women are defined as single. When I initially began this study, I took single to mean unmarried and not cohabiting at the times of the first interview and the birth or adoption of the child. At the outset, I was more interested in routes to motherhood for middle-class women that did not entail marriage or living together, paying little attention to comings and goings of lovers or the exceptions of children with a second parent. In terms of the lay definition of single—not married—both lovers and parenting partners are relevant.

With the increase of motherhood outside of marriage (leaving aside cohabiting couples having children), today's families have at their core not the adult couple but the mother-child relationship. Like the "housetop" tradition of quilting in which each quilt is built around a solid medallion of cloth, these women patch together a life for their family around the mother-child dyad.[3] The centrality of this dyad as the stable foundation of middle-class family life is a recent phenomenon. For the majority of women in this study, this twosome is the most common family structure and leaves the potential to reclaim the nuclear family. Where does romance fit in the mother-child family? While it may exist, it is not the center of family life, often only a tangent to the mother-child twosome.

Nothing is more salient for these women on a daily basis than the drama between work and family. Chapter 8 illustrates how women streamline their employment to finance their mother time, sometimes turning to other resources when their paychecks do not suffice. But all women rely on good child care to make employment possible. Counting on their alliances with child care providers, women form a long-term relationship with these individuals, enlisting them in their one-woman struggle against the American work-family dilemma.

What has happened to men in these families? If women are no longer in search of a man to make a baby, what role do men play in these children's lives? Chapter 9 raises these questions, which so many people ask of single mothers. It explores the contradictory reasoning behind including men, seeking to reveal what is so special about what men offer to children. Regardless, women are including men. However, they further struggle with the conflicting messages of a gendered system, socializing children to fit in while aspiring to raise feminist kids.

Where do romance, work, and men fit in? Single mothers grapple with their freedom from marriage, attempting to answer the serious questions that arise with their new families. Ambivalent as to what children need, how they should be socialized as girls and boys, and how the "private" life of families interfaces with the public world, these women face dilemmas that highlight important issues that remain in question for families overall. These women bring to light what is not settled by either researchers or policy makers: what is best for children, families, motherhood, and men. Without consensus, these women must decide on their own what is best for their daily lives.

# 7

## WHAT DOES SINGLE MEAN?

The term "single mother" is in many ways a misnomer. The lives of these women challenge the idea of singleness as a monolithic concept. While all these women are legally single because they are not married, *single* implies they are alone, and these women are anything but. In one context, being single—the opposite of being married—implies that these women are available for romantic partnering. In another context, being a single mother, defined by politicians discussing poverty and out of wedlock births, is taken to mean parenting alone, in absence of the child's father. Thus singleness can be taken to mean two different things: either that a woman is without a romantic partner or that she is without a partner with which to parent. These two connotations of singleness interact to create four different categories. As the number of children born outside of marriage increases overall, the loving couple that parents together is becoming less and less common. Divorce implodes the romantic relationship, leaving two parents to work out a way to share their child (with help from the legal system). As deviant as divorce might have been at an earlier point in time, parenting together without once having loved each other is still not commonplace these days. This began a revolution that separated parenting from romantic partnership.

As much as the women in this study were reluctant revolutionaries, they too separated love from child rearing in numerous new ways and at earlier points (such as conception or adoption). Some women loved elsewhere, choosing romantic partners who had no connection with their child. Other women parented with another person with whom they had no romantic relationship. Some women had both parenting and romantic partnerships, separating their lover from their parenting partner; others had neither, choosing to define themselves via motherhood.

When women decided to put motherhood on the front burner, they were launched into a decision-making process that included how they would love once mothers and sometimes with whom, if anyone, they would parent. Most of them hoped that they would find one person whom they could love and with whom they could co-parent after the child arrived, in effect reversing the nursery rhyme —putting love and marriage after the baby carriage. They could then abandon the rubric of single motherhood for a more traditional two-parent model, rejoining love and parenthood with a partner who hoped for the same.

As I interviewed the study participants in depth, I discovered that the label *single* is incredibly nuanced and multifaceted. Women revealed longtime lovers who did not live with them and other figures in their life who also were parents to their children. Regardless of which category they fell into at the time of the first interview, these women's situations shifted easily. As life unfolded, families changed—women might find lovers, genetic fathers might become dads, and lovers might turn into parenting partners.

Table 1 demonstrates that when the nuclear family is pulled apart—romance separated from parenting—women craft families in new ways.[1] Choosing motherhood does not necessarily mean choosing celibacy. And in choosing to have children without marital vows, they do not necessarily forgo a parenting partner. Put differently, Table 1 illustrates the variations that can occur when the romantic couple is no longer the center of a two-parent family. Ironically, many women would have preferred to build their families on the romantic couple model, and they continued to hope that with baby would come love, which in turn would lead in the direction of a nuclear family. Women had a vision in which their partners shared equally, loved them with respect, and tenderly cared for their children as if they were their own. However, for now, they have unraveled the model of which they aspire to be part.

### The Consummate Mother

The consummate mother is the archetype of the middle-class single-parent family. This woman, without a romantic relationship or a partner in parenting, is alone. She is both provider and nurturer, but there is no question of which role takes precedence—when she is not in the office, she is selflessly caring for her child. In this caricature, the mother's life revolves around being a mother, existing in a child-centered home where all free time is devoted to caretaking. Weekend activities and evening hours are monopolized by play dates, soccer games, and other enrichment activities. This woman's job, outside of her formal employment, becomes introducing her child to the larger world as she carefully oversees his or her development. Without a partner to sub in as another parent, her life is a constant merry-go-round of childhood activities. Homes are visible

Table 1 The Single Motherhood Rubric

| Partners in Parenting | Romance: Low | Romance: High |
| --- | --- | --- |
| Low | I<br>**The consummate mother**<br>*No other parent, no romance*<br>• Mother-child dyad is core<br>• No other parent<br>• Mother is technically responsible 24/7<br>• Mother has no romantic partner<br>• Mother relies more heavily on extensive social networks | II<br>**Splitting lives**<br>*No other parent, romantic partner*<br>• Mother-child dyad is core<br>• No other parent<br>• Mother is technically responsible 24/7<br>• Mother loves elsewhere<br>• Romantic partner has no interest in parenting |
| High | III<br>**Transacting family**<br>*Another parent, no romance*<br>• Two (or more) parents collaboratively parenting (to varying extents)<br>• Other parent is either genetic father, extended kin, or joined by contractual arrangements<br>• Splitting parenting<br>• Mother has no romantic partner | IV<br>**Transacting family with love elsewhere**<br>*Another parent, romantic partner*<br>• Two (or more) parents collaboratively parenting (to varying extents)<br>• Other parent is either genetic father, extended kin or joined by contractual arrangements<br>• Splitting parenting<br>• Mother loves elsewhere |

reminders of the monopoly of the child, with toys littering the living room, easels in the kitchen, and bottles in the bedroom. Adult space is nowhere to be found, overrun by children's blocks and books. In short, the child is the sun in the mother's universe, with all life revolving around him or her.

The family exists only as mother and child, and that dyad is particularly intense. While motherhood is fulfilling and sole caretaking gives women control of family life, after the first weeks of motherhood, filled with the parade of well-wishers and helpers, have ended, the reality of being on call every minute of every day sets in. The reality of consummate motherhood crystallized for Jennifer during the baby's first illness:

> And I actually thought, when my daughter fell ill, what it would be like if there was somebody here, a man in my life? We probably would have fought about whether or not to go to the hospital. There was nobody to process anything with, which was very hard. . . . I called a friend at two-thirty in the morning, who said I should bring my baby to the hospital. So I did. The doctor checked her out and

we were quickly released. Standing at 6 a.m. waiting for a cab to take me back home was really upsetting. I had this overwhelming sense of aloneness. And me, who thinks I have the most amazing support system—which I really do—felt so incredibly alone. And then I came home, and I said, "You know, I could have had a husband who was on a business trip," and very quickly reality set in about how you're alone no matter what. It was amazing. Really, I felt so pathetic. The sun was coming up—I'll never forget it—here I am, standing with my daughter in my arms, taking a cab home! And probably there were a million people I could have called, and I just didn't want to do it.

Jennifer acknowledged that a partner is not always insurance against these situations, but she also felt alone in a way that could not be ameliorated by supportive friends and family. Veronica described it in more abstract terms:

If you're a single parent, it's just different, and I think people who are single parents, who have another parent involved, also live a different life than those of us who are parenting 24/7, seven days a week, week after week, month after month after month, and not having the breaks that other folks get whose kids goes off with another parent, even if it's one or two nights a week. It's still one or two nights a week that you sort of have yourself back in a way that if you don't have family or friends who are taking your kid for you regularly, it's just different, a different life.

Veronica captures the undiluted responsibility of single mothers in this category. Jennifer may have called a close friend in the middle of the night over her daughter's rising fever, but she did not ask her friend to accompany her to the hospital. That night Jennifer realized that it was not the absence of people to help that made her feel so alone, but her own unwillingness to cross the boundary of middle-class self-sufficiency to ask them. In response to the 24/7 life of the consummate mother, some women come to rely more heavily on social networks that challenge the do-it-yourself parenting model, to be discussed later in this chapter. Even after tapping social networks in creative ways, these women are still the only parent, and as a result, they find it difficult to make time to become romantically involved.

The consummate mother model, for all its intensity, is attractive in that it leaves a lot of room for both a romantic partner for the mother and a second parent for the child. It is this structure that can be most easily transitioned into the two-parent family model, and that is its allure. Even though the baby carriage came first, women still hope to find love and marriage. By guarding the mother-child dyad, most poignantly by keeping the genetic father at a distance, women free up their family for the introduction of a partner who is both lover and parent. Among the four variations of single mothers, these women show the most commitment to the two-parent family model, hoping to end up with the ideal package in spite of the less than ideal sequencing. Joy, a classic consummate mother, rationalized, "Anyone that I would meet would have to love kids anyway, so what difference would it make that I already had a child?" and clearly *at this point* imagined herself eventually finding a partner. This first child also leaves room for a second with a partner, easily mixed into a different family structure. In short, this consummate mother could easily transform herself into the consummate wife, regardless of sexuality. All she lacks is a partner who loves children.

## Splitting Lives

Some women are parenting alone but not sleeping alone. Women form romantic relationships, but this does not mean that these men and women become parents to their children. The mother moves between two distinct loves—maternal love and romantic love. She is splitting her life. The key point in this arrangement is that the person who shares the romantic love with the woman has no interest in the responsibility of parenting. These relationships, far from the casual dating a divorced woman might engage in, have continued for many years and involve a serious commitment, but that commitment does not include parenting.

Claudia, who was featured in the prologue, began a new relationship at the time she filed the adoption papers. She is a classic example of women in this category, as she described her "two lives"—one as a mother to her child and the other as part of a couple with her boyfriend, Carl. Carl had never taken on a parental role to her child and kept busy being a parent to teenage kids of his own. Claudia's son did have contact with Carl, and while they had a special relationship, Carl excused himself from becoming this child's dad.

> Carl does not want to be a dad again. He's been a parent for twenty years, and a very primary parent. His work life really picked up and he's gotten a promotion and his life has just filled out in so many ways. So I think we're in different places. And you know he took up golf. He wants to launch his own life. So I'm sure there are trade-offs for both of us. And I guess I mean we really care about each other and I don't feel like I could start a new relationship now. I really don't think . . . I'm not that available. I mean my commitment is to William [her son]. And so that's one thing. So even though there are things I wish were different, there are a lot of good things.

Carl was not likely to do things with Claudia's child alone, nor was he involved in decision making about this child. They rarely discussed the child as parents might do, she reported. Two other women in this study at the time of the interviews had a similar arrangement, in which they had long-term lovers who did not live with them and were not dads or co-moms to their children. As Claudia pointed out, such women maintained "two lives" in order to have a companion for themselves and, independently, to mother a child.

At the time of the first interview, Sienna's family life resembled Claudia's, with the exception that her lover lived with her.[2] She was not cohabiting when she adopted her daughter, but the man she loved moved in with her shortly after she arrived home with her child. While she invited him to become a legal parent to her child, he refused and remained only her lover but not her child's father. She described the situation:

> So he entered the family, but he hasn't become a co-parent. And he's very close to my daughter and they have a very good relationship. But it's a very evolved au pair kind of situation, rather than a parental one.

Sienna used the vocabulary of paid child care to distinguish between someone who is a reliable, committed parent and someone who occasionally helps out or does so as a job. Even though they lived in the same apartment, they had not combined their lives.

> He had a world that was separate and more compelling to him than anything a domestic life could offer. But for me, a domestic life was an incredible adventure. The minute I became a mom, the clarity of my ability was there. I was absorbed with being a parent and working.

While Claudia and Sienna were both adoptive mothers without contact with the birth family, Evelyn took a different route to motherhood. Her son, the result of chancing pregnancy, was in contact with an out-of-state father only by phone. This man was not a parent, though the child called him dad. In some ways, that clarified the role of the boyfriend, who was not a permanent household member. When asked if her boyfriend, Paul, was a father figure to her son, Evelyn responded,

> I'm not sure yet. Nicholas [her son] calls him his best friend. I'm not going to push it. I let Nicholas decide where he wants Paul to be. It's not for me. It's kind of for Paul and Nicholas to decide and for me to kind of watch and make sure it's healthy. I'm not pushing it either way.

Like the consummate mothers, women who split their lives still maintain the mother-child relationship as core. Evelyn reiterated the centrality of her relationship with her child: "I've chosen to allow closeness in my life, but I'm not going to take care of any man. I'd rather have a partner and a friend, but I'm very self-sufficient. I take care of two people: my son and me. That's it. And if I have other children, okay." These women all pour their energy into raising their children; however, they also must maintain their romantic relationship. Still, they monitor the relationship between their romantic partner and their child, noting sometimes with regret that this person is not a co-parent. Since family comes first and these men (or lesbian lovers) are not family, they are distant physically and emotionally. Knowing that their partners do not necessarily want to be fathers or co-parent, women limit the time they spend as a threesome in order to shield their children. Split lives are sometimes juggled in the hopes that one day they will become unified. Most of the women in this category hope that their situation is transient. Whether romance for these women evolves into parental partnership as well remains unclear. However, for the moment women are making the compromise of compartmentalizing their lives.

### Transacting Families

Transacting family is about using formal and informal arrangements to create parents for a child. A smaller and very important group of women in this study have thought outside the box of the nuclear family that centers around two parents—straight or gay—bonded by love and companionship. Whether true love in earlier historical times was anything more than a manufactured belief, a scripted tale that justified a union, is unknown. However, if it is fiction or reality, love remains the most popular theory of what holds a family together. Even for homosexual couples, whose families challenge the traditional model on the grounds of sexuality, the common refrain is that love makes a family. But the women in this category question romantic love as the glue that holds a family together, often noting that these families fall apart. Trish, a woman who had contracted co-parents, voiced her skepticism:

> I made a really clear decision that I would not have a child with a romantic partner. I sort of lost faith in that kind of relationship as being one I could count on over the long haul. . . . I felt like there was a lot of denial going on among couples about the implicit trust in that arrangement, and having a child with your romantic partner. Everybody thought that was the way you did it, and that was what made sense. It *never* felt right to me. It always felt like "How are they so sure?" I feel like that's where I go, I always am skeptical about whatever the conventions are. I don't inherently trust them.

Avoiding romantic partnerships in the formation of their family, these women are contracting parenting partnerships with the idea that these will be more stable. These contracts function to allow autonomous individuals to make their own bargains outside the normative organization of the culture. These are *transactional families*, where the adults agree that they want to share a child together.

Trish, a gay woman, did not conflate the creation of a child with the possibility of love with a partner. She pointed out to me the difference in transactional commitment to parent with a partner. Unlike other women in this study who were gatekeepers or wanted to control their child's time with fathers, Trish willingly entered into an arrangement of sharing her child with other adults. Trish explained what she sought: "I wanted another parent whose relationship is about the kid and not about our romantic situation. My strategy was to find a parenting partner, not a romantic partner to have a child with." Trish co-parented her daughter with a gay male couple, after having initially approached one of the men, who subsequently found a romantic partner. The triad of adults decided to continue talking about the possibility of a child.

For her daughter's two dads, Alex and Ron, the other models of gay parenting that their friends had chosen did not interest them. They did not want to find a surrogate to have a baby for them and include the surrogate as an "aunt," nor did they want to be known donors on the margins. As she put it, "They wanted the real McCoy—dads. They didn't want to be supplemental caretakers." It took almost two more years of talking and planning. Alex would be the genetic father, but he and Ron would become co-dads. With the help of an attorney, they drew up a lengthy agreement that laid out in detail parenting arrangements, spelling out the rights, obligations, and routine of the involved parties. The yet-to-be-born child would split her time between the mom's home and the dads' home.[3] In some ways, Trish attributed the clear boundaries of her arrangement to her sexuality:

> I actually thought this arrangement was much better for me as a gay person than it probably would be for most straight women, where there would be so much more ambiguousness, or there could be. Whereas with us, there's no ambiguousness because both he and I had been gay for a million years, before we ever did this. So it was always clear that it was kind of a business relationship, in a way. It was really about the business of having and raising a child.

Having removed romance from the equation, Trish had a good working relationship with her daughter's two dads. The three adults met to make decisions about their daughter at an important weekly meeting, including scheduling events and filling each other in on the week in order to make parental decisions.

Angie was about to order sperm from one of the banks and even had an appointment to begin the process of inseminating when she decided to answer a personal ad that caught her attention in a local paper.

> The man said in the ad "wants a would-be mother." "So I thought, "OK, I'm a would-be mother." And then it went on about him and what he would offer. And he had decided that the only way he was going to have a child was to find a woman who already had a child [i.e., he was looking for a divorced woman]. We went to dinner [and Angie explained to him what she was planning]. And Jack said, "Oh! Do you want a volunteer?" And I said, "That's the most ridiculous thing I ever heard. We've known each other an hour and this is a thirty-to-forty-year project."

The man Angie met had not thought of anything besides the usual ways to parenthood (marriage or remarriage). Angie told him of another way, and she was surprised when he jumped to volunteer. But she was drawn to Jack; she couldn't really put words to what it was except to tell me that she liked him enough to consider his offer. A close friend with whom she talked at length advised her that another parent would provide "company and sharing," a reason to pursue this offer. Unlike Trish, Angie said that she would have preferred a lover, but she settled for a transactional relationship.

Jack made clear from the beginning what he thought he wanted as a parent, and even though she had a different vision they went ahead with a limited partnership, which created a new sequencing to parenting. Angie winced at Jack's swift, blunt, and sealed position, which he never shifted from:

> At the beginning, Jack's whole vision was "I'm helping this woman out." Not "We have a child together." Even though I answered his ad. But he was never simply a known donor. Now he considers himself my co-parent. He said, "I'm going to do this, but I want you to know, I will never marry you, I will never live with you, I will never be romantically involved with you, there will be absolutely no emotional romantic stuff between us."

They signed an initial contract written with the help of an attorney, and later updated it.

In both Angie's and Trish's cases, the child rotated between two separate households. Angie, Jack, and their shared daughter spent Saturday afternoons doing some kind of outing together, and one night a week they might eat together. They were parenting as a unit but not living as a unit. While they had separate relationships with the child, they were also a family joined by this child. When asked if she considered her arrangement a family, Trish reiterated that at the base of this family was a transactional agreement. There were moments when they did "family things" as three parents and child. However, they did not spend the kind of time together that Angie described. Alex and Ron were not Trish's family, but they were her child's.

> There's ways in which we function as a family, but I'm not even sure that we're even good friends with each other, particularly. It hasn't changed. It was never that way. We were never best friends. We were never close friends. I feel like our relationship with each other has really been about this kid. So I think we're family in that we do her birthday together. We celebrate some aspects of each of our birthdays together with her. I've done Christmas with them from time to time, Thanksgiving from time to time.

Trish did not feel connected to Alex and Ron outside the bonds they shared with the child, Sarah. However, they occasionally spent time together during family holidays, a symbol that their strong bond with their daughter fostered a weak tie to one another.

Trish still felt very single, especially given her weak social networks and distant kin. Angie also felt single, and despite the many activities that filled her nights when her child was at Jack's, she lamented the absence of deep intimacy that can come from a romantic partner but can also be supplemented by friends. While both these women were not single parents, they were still single in that they did not have romantic relationships. Having intentionally separated out romance from family, they strategically created a family for their child that included two or more parents, though they still lacked a partner for themselves.

Both Trish and Angie had actual contracts cementing their transactional relationships with their parenting partners. For Janica, her co-parent had no legal obligation and there was no document outlining their arrangement. However, Janica's parenting partner was not a stranger to her—it was her mother.[4] Unlike the other two women, Janica parented simultaneously with her mother in the same space. When Janica, featured in chapter 6, decided to adopt her first child, she was thirty-four years old. She described the adoption process and her mother's involvement:

> My mother was living with me . . . and she went with me to a lot of these things about adopting because she was living with me and she was going to be very involved. We talked about the commitment, prior to that, and she agreed to be a partner with me in this.

Since Janica adopted via a public agency, she was offered a choice among several children who needed homes, and her mother accompanied her to each appointment. Even though the child was given to Janica by the social worker, the decision to accept that child into her home was made by both Janica and her mother. Unlike Angie and Trish, Janica and her mother lived in the same household, parenting together under one roof. And though it was Janica, as the legal adopter, who later got a call from the adoption agency offering her the half sister of her daughter, an infant, for adoption, it was Janica and her mother who made the decision. While Janica did want another child, she had never thought she would have a baby in the house again, thinking that it would be too much for her mother to handle. She was so sure about the decision that she had given away her daughter's crib and all baby paraphernalia. However, when the call came from the agency, her mother played a critical part in making the decision.

> My mother said, "We're talking about Sharon's sister, so why don't you just do it?" I said, "Ma, it's a baby." And she said, "I'll have her walking around here in six months!" I said, "We don't have anything. We've given everything away." She said, "Then we'll just get it back." So I went back into the other room and called the woman back and I said yes. I heard a stunned "Oh," and she paused and said, "Well, are you sure?" And I said yes. So I just asked if she was healthy, and she said yes. So I said okay.

While formally Janica was the mother and the decision to adopt was hers legally, clearly parenting was a partnership between her and her mother. Janica retained her status as mom by being the parent who set the limits, established moral guidelines, and disciplined her daughters.[5] She left each day for work as a high-level state employee secure that her mother was parenting her kids, meeting them at the bus after school, and scheduling their activities. Unlike in the matriarchal family that is part of the culture of poverty, Janica was solidly middle-class, educated in elite institutions, but sharing parenting with kin.[6]

A risk in Janica's informal arrangement to share her children with her mother is that family relationships can blur and clash over control issues. When her children were young, Janica was very comfortable sharing her parental authority with her mother. Her mother took on the responsibility of primary caregiver for the kids while Janica went to work. As the children entered their teenage years, the tension between Janica and her mom over who had the final say grew more pronounced. At the time of the interview, with her children fourteen and sixteen years old, Janica was insistent on establishing herself as the authority figure in the family: "So I think we get into normal teenage/parent squabbles and sometimes it's accentuated because my mom's voice gets in the middle of it. The bottom line is, I'm the mother."

By sharing parental responsibility, single mothers in this category give themselves a gift that their counterparts do not have—they are not constantly on call. Whether this gives them more flexibility in their jobs or time for themselves, they are able to maintain their identity outside of motherhood in a way that consummate mothers are not. Trish wanted to add a child to her life without becoming a consummate mother:

> I really wanted another parent because I wanted to have built-in time when I wasn't going to be responsible for a child. I also felt like there are other parts of my life, separate from motherhood, that I really love and care about, and I didn't want to give it all up. I didn't want to turn my entire life into being a mother. I really like my life with grown-ups, and my dating life, my sexual life, and my romantic life—all these kinds of things that don't include children. And I wasn't willing to give all of that up.

For the women who are single because they are unattached romantically but are not parenting alone, they are able to retain their lives outside of motherhood in a way other single mothers cannot.[7] However, like the consummate mother, these women do leave room for the possibility of a partner to love and live with them as part of their family. While the bonds between parents and the child are the center of transactional families, the arrangement between parenting partners is not heartless. Even Trish and Angie, who contracted with men they were not close to, acknowledged that the connection to the other parent or parents through the child obligates these adults to one another. The transactional obligation between the adults arises from feeling connected because of a mutual concern that they share as parents in raising this child. Commitment to the family as it is formed around the child does not mean romantic commitment between adults. Instead, responsibility to one another comes out a shared obligation to the same child. This could extend to the child's kin network through the other parent, as illustrated by Trish's choice of example:

> I definitely feel it has elements of family, or whatever. It definitely has elements of that. Alex's brother-in-law was killed in a car accident recently. I'm not around

his family enough to have really gotten clear about who everybody is. But I busted my butt so that Sarah and I could be there at that funeral, even though that meant driving across the state very early in the morning to be at church and taking a day off from work. But it felt really important to me to be there, and I felt like his family appreciated my being there. So I definitely feel like in some ways we're a family. But it's a real hybrid, and I think that it works okay for me, and it works okay for them because we're not black-and-white kind of people—it either is this or it isn't, or if it is this, it has to look this way.

When Trish said, "It felt really important to me," she was giving a nod to the obligation she felt to the other parent of her child. While their formal contract had no mention of her involvement with his family, she felt a connection with these people because of their relationship to her daughter. Trish had a relational bond, not an emotional bond, with her co-parent's family and more strongly with her child's other parent, leading her to act not out of love but out of mutual concern.

In these new families, the idea that a family should be based upon a transactional agreement in itself signifies a change in the way that families have been formed in the past. The multigenerational model that Janica was adapting is structurally old, but refreshed by the shared parental responsibility and its movement into the middle class. Trish and Angie are among a small group of women in this study who methodically arranged a business-type relationship in which the child was shared, a new use of legal contracts to make families.[8] These new kinds of families tie people together through children, obligating them to one another through the joint project of a child. They refute romantic love as the essential ingredient between co-parents, using formal or informal arrangements to provide their child with more than one parent. The stability of these families is noteworthy: despite occasional friction between parenting partners, the long-standing commitment to children has been honored.[9] The label "single" applies to their romantic status only, as they are not parenting alone.

### Transacting Families with Love Elsewhere

If the women previously described in the transactional families found romantic partners, they would easily move into this category. Women who both form parenting partnerships and find love elsewhere challenge what is meant by single, melding together the transacting families arrangements with split lives. They decidedly separate romance from parenting but have a partner in both.

Like Janica's case, Barbara's mother was a parenting partner. Her mother lived a floor below Barbara's apartment, and her son easily traveled up and down the inside stairway.

Having my mom around means he has another steady, everyday family member to go to. He goes up and down between apartments and we eat together about four days a week, we have meals together. There's an inside stairway so he goes up and down. And he plays with her. The first year, she's a wonderful playmate. So they would build things, and she reads to him, and works on letters and writing. It's really great. And I think she plays in a different way than I do.

This arrangement had not been in place at her son's birth. Barbara's mother volunteered to be her parenting partner when the child was a year old and the stress of work and consummate motherhood became too much for Barbara. "It's allowed me to do more things with my job, you know, like when I was climbing the ranks. So that's changed things, and that's been great."

Barbara also had romance, a woman she met after her mother moved in downstairs and gave her some time for a social life of her own. At the time of the interview they had been together for a few years, but her girlfriend was still far from a parental figure to her six-year-old.

I think he kind of sees her as his friend. It's interesting. She doesn't parent—she helps out, but she doesn't bathe him . . . she doesn't really discipline him except inasmuch as something comes up while they play. She doesn't put him to bed or get him up. She's not really an authority figure or a parent. And I feel like that's probably appropriate for right now, until we decide, or even if we decide, we're more serious.

Barbara wanted a second parent who was not her mother but rather her lover. She had a current lover who did not parent her child. The lover was willing to take on parental responsibility, but there was a catch: the lover was seriously considering having a biological child. The lover wanted Barbara to co-parent this hypothetical child, joining their families. Barbara faced a quandary—while she would have loved a second parent for her child, she was not sure she wanted to become a mother again, and the decision was still up in the air at the time of the interview. Even though her mother's presence gave her child another parental figure with which Barbara could share responsibility, still she wanted a romantic dyad to be the basis of parental partnership. Her mother was aging, and Barbara felt that ultimately she would be left alone with her child.

Mary, who chanced pregnancy, as described in chapter 5, expended considerable energy to foster a relationship between her daughter and the child's father. As a result of her careful cultivation, she had a second parent for her daughter. They lived about an hour apart, but Mary delivered her daughter every weekend to spend time with him. Mary and her daughter's dad had no formal contract outlining parental responsibilities (including distributing the financial burden), which was a deliberate move on her part in order to foster an emotional relationship between father and daughter.

Mary also had a man in her life, a boyfriend who came over regularly during the week and at whose house she spent the weekends. She said of her daughter's relationship with this man:

> She likes him a lot. He's not her father. He never disciplines her and we work
> hard that he never has to discipline her. She isn't a discipline problem. She gets
> a little mouthy sometimes. But basically they have a very nice relationship and
> they tease each other.

It was very clear that this man was not the child's dad. However, Mary had
decided not to combine households, a deliberate move to curb romance in order
to successfully mother:

> The image in my mind is that my job right now and for the next, say, six or seven
> years is my daughter and anything else is a distraction. So if there's a conflict
> between what he wants to do and what I want to do, or what my daughter wants
> to do, I don't have a conflict. I am very clear that I'm not married to him. He's not
> my primary responsibility. It's pretty stable and it's not very demanding. And
> it works.

For Mary, her daughter was the priority, and romance was a separate affair. This
decision did not make her a full-time mother juggling a relationship the way
women who are splitting lives must, because she had a second parent for her
daughter as well. Even though she had a partner in romance and another in parenting, she was still considered a single mother because these men were not one
person, and she did not live with either one.

These women have both romantic and parenting partnerships, creating an
interesting interpretation of what it means to be a single mother. While these
women are not single by either of the two definitions of the word, they are also
not part of a romantically tied couple that doubles as a parenting team; thus
neither of their partnerships exempts them from single status. In essence, they
have dodged the nuclear family. However, their children have the benefit of two
stable parental figures, and mothers do not have to be on call 24/7, freeing them
up for romance on the side.

### Rotating the Rubric: In and Out of Romance
### and the Elusive Parenting Partner

I have illustrated the rubric of singleness using snapshots of moments in these
families' histories, but it is important to acknowledge that their lives were fixed
only for a frame. I used the point in their narratives that best located their particular circumstance in the four categories, but these are not representative of
the whole picture. Many of these women moved around the rubric as they told
their story, movement that will be discussed here.

Maeve was a consummate mother at the time of the first interview, though
she revealed in that conversation that she had had two romantic partners after the
birth of her son, who was eight at the time I met them. She had spent the last eight
years dividing her time between the consummate mother category and that of

splitting lives. She moved in and out of romances. As was true for most women in this study, romantic partners, not parenting partners, were the most inconsistent aspect of her single status. Maeve recognized that her family also experienced her romantic involvements, as much as she tried to maintain the split between her lives:

> I think when you have children, you have responsibility. You created a family, you need to keep it stable. I think introducing new partners on and off, living with people, that doesn't seem responsible to me. And even though I never lived with my [ex-]boyfriend, Riley, and as far as Hunter was concerned he was my best friend, not my boyfriend. There was never any indication that there was a romance . . . Hunter just knew my ex-boyfriend was around a lot. He was really really close to us. And that was painful enough. I would never let that happen again. Because I can't. Can you ask some guy that you are dating to be a lifelong father figure to your child? No, and can you demand that your child not form that bond with someone who's there all the time, who's fun and friendly and loving to them? No. So you shouldn't set that situation up, I don't think. I think it's irresponsible. I think I was irresponsible in doing it.

Maeve, as a mother, entered romantic situations with a certain degree of caution, mindful that her child could become hurt if the romance fizzled. She noted that not every romantic partner wishes to also become a parenting partner, a lesson many of these women learned on the route to motherhood. The "best friend" explanation is one that mothers often use for children under ten to explain a kind of intimacy between the mother and her lover, and children sometimes borrow this label to explain their own bond with that person. Like many of these women, Maeve felt that her responsibility as a parent took precedence over her inconsistent romances. Her life was split, but the half that remained constant was her role as a single parent. She performed a delicate balancing act between trying to love elsewhere and guarding her son, even as the three went to the playground and had dinner together.[10]

Janica, who co-parented with her mother, had one major relationship in the time between the adoption of her first child and shortly after the arrival of her second. They had dated for six months, and because he was spending over half the week in her home, he moved in with them, much to the chagrin of her mother. Even though he lived in her house, he was neither a parent to her child nor a voice in family decisions. Before getting the call from the agency offering her daughter's half sister, Janica had returned on her own to look at the picture books of toddlers to adopt through the state agency, without her boyfriend. As previously mentioned, when the call out of the blue came offering a baby, it was together with her mother, not her boyfriend, that Janica made her decision. Even though he wasn't opposed to the second child, she was insistent that since they weren't married, it was not his decision to make. Nor did she intend him to be a father to her first child when he moved in:

He moved in, even though my mother, who is a little old-fashioned, was not happy. Even so, my mother had a good relationship with him and Sharon really liked him. I have to say, maybe that wasn't the right thing to do. He was a little younger than me, but he was still very immature and a little selfish. So he wanted *me, me, me* and not *us, us, us*, although he was very good . . . I think he would have been a good father, but he needed to grow up a little bit. I didn't have time for that. I had two kids, you know? I didn't need three!

Concurrent with her adopting her second child, Janica gave her boyfriend an ultimatum: marriage, including fatherhood, or moving out. He chose the latter. Adding and then subtracting a romantic partner moved her briefly from a transactional family to a transactional family with love elsewhere and back again. Once again, it was the romantic partnership, not the parental partnership, that waxed and waned.

It is the rare case that an unforeseen parenting partner, without romantic intrigue, appears in these women's lives. For the vast majority of women, the parenting arrangement that they had set in place at the point at which they became mothers remained constant. The women who struggled to make dads out of the men with whom they chanced pregnancy sometimes succeeded. Ellen, whose story opens chapter 5, and Mary, mentioned earlier in this chapter, both made dads out of men who initially had resisted paternity. By the time their children were two or three years old, it was clear whether or not the men were going to be involved and what that involvement would entail.

Known donors are constricted by contract and thus usually remain in the shadowlands, yet they too occasionally carve out a niche in the family, becoming what I have termed earlier "bio-dads." Most women, however, are vigilant gatekeepers, not allowing the few donors who have an interest to develop more than a superficial relationship with their children. Often checking in once or twice a year is sufficient for mother, child, and known donor. Annette, who allowed John to escalate his involvement from known donor to dad in chapter 4, is an exception. They talked each morning about the child, who moved between their separate households. Annette and John provide a good example of an unanticipated parenting partner. Annette thought she would be a consummate mother, but instead she allowed herself to enter into a transactional family as the donor emerged from the shadows. As with other transactional families, such as those of Trish and Angie, the child moved between two households. However, Annette's story is rare and was made possible only by her compliance with his wish to be an involved dad; it soon took another turn, which will be discussed in the epilogue. There is not much movement along the continuum of parenting partners—if anything, they are more likely to be lost than gained.

Exiting the rubric is an attractive possibility for many women. At the end of the first interview, many thought of themselves as only reordering the traditional sequence. They had yet to abandon the idea of the nuclear family. Now that they had fulfilled their dream of motherhood, many hoped that absent the pressure of aging without a child, they would find a partner in both romance and parenting to complete their vision of their families. Already mentioned in chapter 4 was Jennifer, a woman on the cusp of exiting the rubric when I interviewed her a second time. A consummate mother at the point at which she was first interviewed, at the second interview she was weeks away from her wedding and attaining the elusive nuclear family, even in a blended form. This marriage would make her a stepmother while securing a father for her daughter; she hoped he would adopt her child, conceived through a known donor. Despite the hope for adoption, Jennifer had not excluded the known donor, an interesting twist on her otherwise tidy ending. It is easier for some than for others to follow Jennifer out of the rubric of single motherhood. Without a parenting partner, the hope of finding that person in a romantic context is palpable. Even for women who have a parenting partner in the form of kin, they too can inject the romantic partner into a parental role, a possibility that Barbara revealed that she was considering. However, for women who have transacted family through a contractual arrangement, a substitution in any form is not possible.

# 8

## DOWNSHIFTING CAREERS WHILE FINANCING MOTHERHOOD

### Relying on the Gift-Giver, the Roommate, and the Careworker

**Joy McFadden**

I work at a hospital and I also work in research. Except when I am attending at the hospital, my hours are very predictable. But I've had to shift things around to get it this way—I mean, I turned down a big promotion and some other interesting opportunities just to have a child. I'm thinking of moving out of the clinical side, because the hours aren't regular. It would be hard to spend less time at the clinic, but honestly, weird hours aren't compatible with babysitters. As it is, I already have a bunch of different people who help at high-stress times of the day, and the kids are in day care. Having an erratic schedule just makes it that much more complicated.

**Claudia D'Angelo**

I'm between jobs [as a clinical psychologist] right now. The schedule I had was four days a week, Friday off, two nine-hour days and two eight-hour days. I mean, if I had my druthers, I would work part time, twenty hours, getting involved in school stuff. But that isn't what I can afford, even with my mother giving me $10,000 a year, enough to cover William's day care. So I have to figure out if there is some work I could do, maybe some consulting, I don't know. I'm sorting work out, shuffling through several offers. How can I make more money? Is there something I can do that would get me more money? Maybe have a base job that would get me health insurance. Right now I have COBRA. Maybe I'll go back to private practice.

### Lori-Ann Stuart

I always have to be there from three to six-thirty, and on Wednesdays from twelve to six-thirty. Those are the hours of the program [she is a school administrator]. However, I also have administrative hours which are kind of up to me to figure out when they are going to be. So some of the schedule is because it works for me and some of it is because I *have* to be at work until six-thirty every day. And by the time I put away the materials from the after-school program it could be seven before I leave. Since Andrew is at a different school, this means that I have to figure out a plan for Andrew every day but one.

### Abby Evans

Work was a default position. My career [as a teacher] became important because it was the major thing in my life and major area of success. It never felt to me like, "Oh, I would rather have this career than a family." It also never felt to me like I just wanted to be home with my children and have no career. But being a mom definitely means I can't make the same decisions about my job. I had positioned myself in line for a principalship before I got pregnant, but once I had decided to do this, I knew the evening hours just weren't going to work. I know I passed up a big jump in salary, but I don't even want the headache of being an administrator of any kind, given that I have a preschooler.

### Ellen Hammond

Ideally I'd probably work [as a financial analyst] four days, but I just can't slow down my job. I asked, I talked to my boss about it, but it was not an option. Honestly, I really don't think he cares that I have a kid at home, and [he] just will call a meeting on a Wednesday night. Anyway, I've had to be a little creative with finances after day care expenses and with Gavin contributing absolutely nothing. One solution is my mom owns this big house and gave it to me to share it with four other individuals who pay me rent. It bumps up my income, but it doesn't really help my long hours or late meetings.

### Jasmine Duarte

Usually I would just do the one job, one that had something to do with my associate's degree in business, but since I got laid off, I got paranoid. I got as many jobs as I could [as a secretary, cocktail waitress, and housekeeper] because I went a whole month and a half without working, without doing anything. I exhausted all my savings and I had no health benefits and no resources. So it was like, "What am I going to do?" So I got one job, which was a part-time job, and then another part-time job came along, and then I started temping. These jobs just gradually built up. And it was like, "Oh, okay, I *can* do this." My kid is in school in the day-time and then in the evenings when I work as a waitress she'll go either upstairs to my neighbor's house and she'll spend one evening with my mother and I'll pick her up on my way home from the club. I might sleep over my mother's house too. Usually I work Mondays and Thursdays nights. It's really hard. I have to be there at ten o'clock and I'm done working at two if I'm cocktail waitressing. If I'm working the door, I'm done at one-thirty, one forty-five. If I work until two, I'm not out of there until about two-thirty because we have to help the bar guys and we have to pick up the glasses and stuff like that. On the alternate weekends when she's with her father, I'm cleaning cottages on the Cape. Not that her dad helps at all with the financial situation. Since I took him to court, I have to twist his arm to get the whopping $50 a week in child support that was ordered.

\* \* \*

Work that once filled time now steals it away from family. The majority of single mothers do not have a parenting partner, and none has the luxury of a partner's paycheck. There are bills to pay, and when savings run low, credit card debt can only help them to avoid more hours per week for so long. For every hour these women are home with children, they are trading money for time. However, they refuse to put a price tag on parenting—this labor of love is not about cost efficiency. Inevitably, they must confront their workplaces, changing the contours of their employment to fit their families. Whether they are career women or those living on an hourly wage, women creatively patch together the means to be a mother. However, single mothers struggling to establish their individual balance between work and family cannot afford to be isolated. The topics covered in this chapter discuss the struggle of primarily middle-class single mothers as they attempt to strike a balance between work and family.[1] How do they finance their own mother time? How do they use their individual resources to make ends meet? How do they use the market for child care?

Dual-career couples often misdirect the tension between work and family at individual spouses when the real culprit is the historically gendered division of labor and a workplace modeled to reflect that division.[2] Single mothers, with no partner to shift the focus, see clearly that their opponent is the workplace. Workplace cultures they once embraced now become an obstacle to their family lives. Most women reduce their employment expectations, using creative strat-egies as they cut back. Professional and managerial women are most able to place family first, resting upon the gains they made when their paycheck only needed to support themselves and they could labor long into the night. Less skilled single mothers often improvise more, as their work life is frequently unpredictable in a way that professional moms do not experience as readily.

However, all women strive to draw a boundary between hours of paid work and family time. This tension, a major fault line for all employed women, is espec-ially salient for women who are on call as parents twenty-four hours a day, seven days a week, with little relief. Even with help in various forms, women face a difficult task as sole provider *and* sole nurturer. While motherhood among middle-class women continues to presume that these women have an option to stay home, in fact few women, regardless of marital status, have the choice to do so.

These women operate within the capitalist market economy, generating income and paying for services. However, their paycheck is not their only resource. From the very earliest interviews, I sought out the hidden exchanges that purchase a middle-class life for these families. Almost half of the women in the study (thirty-two of the sixty-five) have income that is supplemented by gifts, rental income, or both. Women have to recognize the potential of their existing resources and redefine their use.[3] In short, middle-class life is not simply supported by income from a paycheck alone—these women have paying jobs, space to rent, and gift givers in their lives. Regardless of the dollar amount attached to these additions to a paycheck, these gifts and exchanges are often mixed with friendships. Friendships may grow out of what starts as economic relationships, just as a monetary gift may be tangible evidence of intimacy.

Relationships also develop around areas of expenses, such as child care. Many women intentionally foster emotional bonds between the child care provider, their children, and themselves against the backdrop of an exchange of money for services.

Women bring new people into their lives and build relationships off economic exchanges. There is a huge gray area for these women between economic and family life, and in that space the boundaries of these families are expanded into a more permeable and fluid system.

### Redirecting the Flow for Family: Changes in Employment after Children

After years of being the last person to leave the office, often carrying armloads of work to finish at home, when women become single mothers they would like to be the first to walk out of the building on time and empty-handed. After years of enjoying employment, many women downsize their jobs in order to expand their role as mothers. They are placing children at center stage, not unlike some dual-earner couples in which one or both spouses make the same decision. The strategies individuals adopt depend upon their position in the labor market, as well as their marital status.[4] This does not mean that the arrival of children leads women to slack off at work. The vast majority of Americans simply do not work eighty hours a week, but prior to motherhood, some of the women I interviewed did work these kinds of hours.[5] They expanded a nine-to-five job to fill evenings instead of returning home to an empty house. When they become mothers, some women are able to work fewer hours because they increase the intensity of their work time, skipping a lunch break or stepping up their pace to produce the same amount in a shorter period. The voices of the women who open this chapter show the variety of possible work-family juggling acts. Their sound bites lay out a range of choices that they have made about employment and children. They have reinvented themselves to not only bring home a paycheck but also serve up dinner.

Even among dual-earner couples, work hours are a result of strategic decisions, which may be different for husbands and wives. These arrangements are neither static nor linear, and they may vary over the life cycle. Just as there is no prevailing work-hour strategy among dual-earner couples, there are various ways that single mothers manage family and work.[6] The major difference between single mothers and dual-earner couples is that single mothers cannot decide to opt out and make motherhood their sole pursuit.[7]

For some women, like Joy, motherhood means using their skills to open up new professional spaces. For others, like Abby, making room for kids means passing up advancement opportunities, choosing to spend at home the time that otherwise would be eaten up by schmoozing with colleagues and volunteering for committee work. Still others, like Claudia, are trying to escape the institutional model of rigid hours, often moving into private practice or entrepreneurial ventures, only to then confront worries about health insurance.[8] Working conditions, such as nonstandard hours, are sometimes in direct conflict with parenting—for example, Lori-Ann struggled to smooth over the gap between the end of her child's school in early afternoon and the time when she gets home in the evening. Other women, like Ellen, are subsidizing their income in creative ways. Finally, the subset of women who work multiple jobs on an hourly wage, like Jasmine, precariously juggle motherhood with unsteady employment.

This study included both salaried professional women and women working for an hourly wage.[9] While career women, understanding the intimate contours of their chosen career fields, are able to streamline their employment, women who are piecing together a paycheck by working multiple jobs prior to motherhood have fewer options for employment transitions. Bargaining power, in the form of education and skill sets, is key in their negotiations with employers.[10] While their success in molding their employment to fit their family varies, all women are slowing their pace at work. Weighed down by the responsibilities at home, many women would rather work fewer hours, though few wish to exit the workplace altogether. Meeting the needs of both their employers and their children becomes a delicate balancing act, falling primarily on their shoulders alone.

Annette, a manager who decided to change firms just after her son was born, explained how this move enabled her to shape her own work life. However, she admitted that she could do this because of her advanced technical skills:

> I'm going to have one-third of the number of people reporting to me than I used to and I'm going to walk out of work at 5:15 p.m. . . . And that was a very conscious choice. I didn't want a job that was going to consume me right now because I know that my priority needs to be taking care of Ben. . . . So it's constantly this balance of how much time at work and with my child. How deep does the foot go in? Is it the toe, up to the ankle, up to the knee? How

deep am I in the work world with still my arms and my head free to be with Ben? And it's a balance that I anticipate continually needing to adjust as the years play out.

A variety of strategies is employed by these women as they pull their limbs out of the corporate quicksand. They still work full time, but they assess what is really required of them in their jobs. Some strip jobs of nonessential "face time," reducing their hours and streamlining their careers. Others use technology to be present but not in the office, making conference calls while in the carpool line. Others become contract workers, accepting the insecurity of project-based employment for the sake of flexibility of hours. Still others shift organizational settings and take jobs more compatible with their children's school hours. Patricia used to care more about the kind of specialized carework she loved than about the nonstandard hours she worked. But when her daughter arrived, she concluded that not all hours of the day were equal, and sought a change in her career:

> As much as I loved being a neonatal intensive care nurse, I worked twelve-hour shifts and decided once I adopted my daughter, and after an entitled paid maternity leave through the hospital, I would find work as a school nurse. I wanted the same time off as my daughter so I could be there for her in the afternoons and she could have the childhood of hanging out that I had growing up. I also couldn't work nights and leave my daughter as a single mom.

Finally, other women, like Fran, take their more established careers in new directions. Unable to negotiate with her corporation, Fran was stuck until she discovered a more creative, entrepreneurial route to support her family.

> Before I had my kid, I was a corporate consultant. I love the travel and being an expert; I'd pop into a city to see a client for a day. But the hours were terrible and I was always living out of a suitcase. Making the decision to become self-employed gave me more control over my hours. I probably work the same number of hours, but now I decide when.

For some women, redirecting their careers is about more than hours. Rebecca, a lawyer by trade, mentioned the logistical details that become more important on a mother's already packed schedule.

> It is the little things that make the difference. At my new job, I have greater flexibility. By this I mean I work regular hours, but I can do so from home if need be. The government agency I work for has installed a computer at home so I can manage my staff without being there face to face. But the best perk is a downtown parking place in the building I work in, not the building next door or down the block. A parking place allows me to get my kid faster. When my parking place was in the building next door, it added a half hour onto each day. Days that already don't have enough hours.

Women realize that it is tough to maintain the same commitment to their jobs as they had when they were child-free and often served as the reliable backup person who worked later to finish the project so that their colleagues with children could go home earlier. Their own hard-won children have put a new spin on work. Not only is the office no longer a substitute for their home life, but they also realize that few bosses either care or have the power to change the workplace norms they have lived with for years. Some are able to negotiate special deals with their employers (such as minimal travel or working one day a week from home), but most seek "mother-compatible hours." They figure out ways to match their children's schedules by morphing their careers or changing their employment tracks, usually while continuing to utilize their degrees and expertise. These women leverage their experience in the workforce in order to create a work/family balance; often they opt out of meeting organizational goals and agendas that do not fit their conception of motherhood.

Low-wage women negotiate, too, but there is less to be asked for and won. Many of these women are simply stuck in pockets of the economy that just do not pay. For example, Brandy, twenty-six years old, had been working at the same day care center for ten years, starting in high school. She negotiated with the center owner that her child would have a free slot at the day care two days a week.

> Yeah, my supervisor just figures I was there for ten years, why should she make me pay for my daughter to be there? Luckily, she's just that kind of woman who really cares. She just felt it wasn't going to make or break her if my daughter is there, which is good. I just can't see myself behind an office desk typing and answering phones. That, to me, is boring. I like to be out there. I'm a very very active person and I love the energy level of kids. My goal has always been to own my own day care.

While Brandy would have preferred having her child there the full four days a week she works (her mother watched her daughter the other two days), she considered herself successful in her negotiation because relative to her pay, a two-day-a-week slot was a major bonus. Brandy used longevity and experience at her job to get a perk that, like the parking places and the company-provided home computers of her salaried counterparts, eases the tension between work and family.

Other women who do hourly work, such as Jasmine, face a more daunting challenge. While they may have made ends meet working a series of jobs prior to the arrival of a child, now they too would like time with their children. There are only so many hours they can shave off their work time and still make enough money. These women are the most likely to work nonstandard hours, and they also usually have mothers with whom they leave their children a few nights a week.[11]

After having committing themselves to employment for many years, women, especially single mothers, are between a rock and a hard place—they are choosing between commitment to their workplace and their children. They quickly discover (or already knew) that their commitment to the workplace, the very thing that kept their careers on an upward trajectory or made them successful employees, will preclude them from making a real commitment to their child. In short, no one in this study was willing to use a twelve-hour-a-day substitute, whether it was a nanny or her own mother, in order to continue working at her former pace. In order to spend time with these long-debated and hard-won children, women allow their employment to plateau. Being a good mother means being a good provider as well as nurturing children at home, but juggling providing and nurturing as one person is a daunting task.[12] These women understand work and family as competing but not separate worlds. Negotiating between these two worlds takes incredible energy. Women come to realize that fulfilling the ideal—being both the model employee and the model mother—is simply not feasible. As much as women once enjoyed their work, children now overshadow their jobs. Formerly an end in itself, employment is transformed into a means to an end.

### The Gift-Giver: Gifts as a Substitute for Wages

> If there's one thing I could change about single parenting, it's the financial burden. An extra $10,000 a year net, if I had someone who would sleep on the couch and bring in $10,000, it would be *great*!

While conventional lore dictates that middle-class status is established by self-sufficiency through one's own efforts, Rebecca's comment above and the stories of other single women undermine the assumption that a paycheck alone is the basis for middle-class standing.[13] Gift giving, the monetary equivalent of Rebecca's wish, is an important part of the economics of family life that is not obvious at first glance. These women challenge the tenet of middle-class self-sufficiency.

Grandparents provide financial support, which serves to pull kin closer, obligating their daughters and grandchildren to visit and call frequently.[14] Grandparents' gifts pay the day care expenses (or even private school tuitions) that allow their grandchild to be well taken care of while their daughters are employed. Few women expect these gifts to stretch to supplement a college education. These income transfers from parents to children are not insignificant, even though they are without a lifetime guarantee. This money often becomes like the "second income" their own mothers once brought home when their fathers were the primary breadwinners—slightly unstable and not quite as lucrative, but important nonetheless. A quarter of the women in this study had received nonwage income in the form of a gift or trust within two years of their interview.[15] Often this gift giving begins at the point at which a child enters the woman's life. Women with working-class origins are not likely to receive this financial help from their parents, with the exception of financial help to defray adoption costs.

On a different scale, a smaller group of women receives "pennies from heaven," inconsistent monetary assistance from friends or family that provides a financial cushion, such as the loaning of money with no expectation of being repaid.[16] This kind of income supplement is the alternative for women who do not have kin who are financially well-off enough to provide a regular monetary supplement. The idea of this financial help as a "gift" is somewhat of a misnomer —women devoted considerable time and emotional energy to the cultiva- tion of relationships in which generosity can be comfortably received. Often these "pennies from heaven" begin with the entry of the child into the family. Sometimes these gifts are given in unusual forms, such as the six months of rent-free living that Brandy's landlord gave her as a baby gift. The psychological safety net created by these gift givers cannot be underestimated, as often these women feel inches from the economic edge. It is interesting that many of these women view their financial situation as precarious, because in actuality these women often fare better than many two-income families. Still, because they have only one income, they worry about losing their jobs and slipping out of the middle class.

Despite the fact that Patricia could afford to pay her own taxes, Connor, a good friend and former lover, covered the cost, freeing up her money for other things:

> He would be the person I would be able to go to with no strings attached. I don't have to pay him back. . . . Like I had to go to him to pay for my last year's taxes. I'd go to him if I was running short for the month and he'd just give me a couple of hundred dollars to get me through the month.

Another woman, Valerie, also received money from a former boyfriend:

> An ex-boyfriend of mine, Sandy, gives me money. He's so great. He wants me to have a housekeeper and I didn't want a housekeeper 'cause I don't want to pay. I make money, but I owe back taxes and with a business, so much has to go back in the business. Which, it's not like that one time, he always does that. So I don't ask him for money, he just comes in and whips out his checkbook all the time. He's a mensch.

Some women, such as Patricia and Brandy, work in the less lucrative end of the service sector. While they may not have much cash on hand, they have stable jobs and solid incomes. Still, wealthier friends are easy to tap and happy to help. While Valerie, quoted above, does not work in the service sector, she is one such example. She has a business with a cash flow problem but is hardly living on the edge. More important, perhaps, she allows good friends to help her out, feeling comfortable with their generosity.

Despite the mothers' skillfulness, they cannot guarantee that a gift will be given or that a given individual will always come through. Out of the many gift givers, former boyfriends are the most unpredictable, but for the time being the additional support is welcomed.

## The Roommate: Supplementing Income with Space

Single mothers quickly discover that their own homes can reduce the economic expense of a child. Roommates or tenants generate income in addition to the mother's paycheck. The result of this arrangement challenges class conceptions that there should be one family per home. Ironically, by abandoning the middle-class sensibility of living independently as a nuclear family, single mothers are able to maintain their middle-class lifestyle.[17] Space becomes an economic resource, a bartering tool, or a place where strangers become friends. Large one-family homes have been reclaimed by single mothers to accommodate their family needs. Mothers in this study often purchase housing once intended for nuclear families and then reconfigure the space to generate both income and company. In short, households comprise elements both of the market (renters) and of families (the mother and her child). This found source of money is an alternative way to shore up the family finances.

For most women, their decision to buy property was not motivated by a long-term plan but rather was a short-term economic move. Renting out space in eastern Massachusetts is a common and lucrative venture, as there are always students looking for a room and the real estate market is incredibly inflated. The income from a rental unit can be the equivalent of day care fees for a year. Women seek to plug the drain on their income by purchasing multifamily homes. Janica explained:

> It was kind of silly to pay that much rent when my sister and I thought we could go together and purchase a home. So we purchased a three-family, with three bedrooms on each floor, with the thought that it would be a starter home for each of us and we could rent out the third unit. We had originally planned to move out to the suburbs from there, each going our own way, but we're still here.

For many of the women in this study, the market shifted in their favor and their houses appreciated substantially, leaving them with economic leverage that they had not anticipated. However, when these women became mothers and realized that something had to give as they tried to juggle work and children, space became a flexible resource that they could draw upon. By becoming a landlord, either using an inheritance to purchase a house or acquiring it through their own devices, women readjust their time and money, particularly once these properties are paid off. Some women are able to cut back their work hours, the income generated by the property making up the difference. Others transform the property into a job in itself (a bed-and-breakfast), while some who own a duplex sell off one unit, allowing them to live rent-free. Still others use the space to bring other adults into their children's lives, usually a roommate.

Colleen, an artist, decided to transform her Victorian home into a bed-and-breakfast after her father, who lived with her and her daughter, died. To replace the contribution of his Social Security check to the household budget, she rented out seven rooms that were decorated with the family's heirlooms. She discovered herself again as the owner of a bed-and-breakfast:

> There are a lot of aspects that just work well for me. I like decorating and that's sort of related to art. So it was fun to be able to afford to do a lot of stuff and keep everything in good shape. I like to cook a lot and I found out I seemed to be more sociable than I had thought I was gonna be. So I enjoyed my guests a lot. And it also takes a lot of time away from work, which is hard. I'm so independent. I like working for myself. So, mainly when I considered how to make a living, rather than applying for jobs, it was "What can I do? How can I market whatever?"

The bed-and-breakfast slowed down the pace of her artwork production, which frustrated Colleen, but it allowed her to maintain her lifestyle. The smells from the kitchen were a wake-up call to her ever-changing guests, and while they ate their eggs and hot muffins, she sipped coffee and enjoyed the adult company. The space that Colleen could trade gave her something more important than just the income as she was raising her adolescent daughter.

> I like having people around to talk to. One of my big complaints with my life early on was that I was lonely a lot. Having a daughter and having people live in a house provides me with people to do stuff with. "You want to go to the movies tonight?" "Sure, let's go to the movies." "You want to take a walk?" Whatever.

While superficially her decision to make her home a business appeared to be purely economic, for Colleen having people in her home was about more than just the money. It provided her with an instantaneous, though ever-changing, community.

When women rent out a room, the line between the market and family becomes especially blurred, as roommates share kitchens, living rooms, and bathrooms. Patricia initially expected her roommate to simply be a check. Instead, she found that the woman who lived with them became close to both her and her daughter, despite the economic transaction of rent.

> The other person who is really becoming very supportive is Marielle, our roommate. She and Gemma have . . . Marielle is pretty important to Gemma. Gemma can be really tough, and I feel like she's toughest on me and Marielle, 'cause we're the ones in her life. So she feels like she can get angry at Marielle or whatever. Marielle is quite reserved, but she has exposed Gemma to a lot of different music. She's from Spain and she is a flamenco dancer. She does have a full-time job, but they dance together a lot and though she doesn't actually babysit a lot, she keeps this house. She actually does a lot of the housework, which is great. It just worked out that way. She's folded my laundry and things like that. She uses my car sometimes and it kind of works out.

While Patricia and Gemma did not routinely share meals or food supplies with Marielle, and did not name her as family, Marielle had taken on more importance than just being a renter. Not all roommates work out as well as Marielle, but in this case the tenant gradually became more intimate with Patricia and her daughter. Gemma was a toddler, unable to distinguish between family and tenant, when this living arrangement began. Indeed, Marielle did not fit perfectly into either category. When Marielle was home, Patricia often invited her to join them for dinner, and Marielle loved playing with Gemma. Though the two women were a study in contrasts, gradually they discovered they had a lot in common. Patricia introduced Marielle to her activism, and in turn Marielle shared her cultural experience. While there had been no initial expectation that she would take on this place in their family, Marielle was important as another adult in both the mother's life and the child's.

Ellen, whose story opens chapter 5, spoke candidly about the flexibility of having another adult in the house. While Ellen maintained her own separate space in the apartment she created in the top floor of the house, her renters would keep an eye on her daughter occasionally.

> It frees me up so I can go out in the evening after Skylar's gone to bed. If they're staying in, I say, "Okay, you're on duty for fire rescue or whatever." And then I can leave. So it gives me a lot more flexibility than I would have if I were literally living just me and Skylar alone in an apartment or whatever, which I think would be much harder.

Even though the renters were paying Ellen for a room, there was still a measure of support and flexibility afforded by having other adults in the house, though the relationship between her daughter and the tenants was very casual. The rental income was an addition to Ellen's sizable salary as a financial analyst, but Ellen clearly valued her tenants beyond just their rent checks.

Some women include their renters more formally in their lives. Kerry's arrangement with her roommate, reduced rent for child care, began with an unusual baby gift from a friend who specialized in recruiting and interviewing potential job candidates. Kerry's friend offered to screen roommates to find the perfect candidate.

> I had this seven-room apartment and I needed help. It was way too much for me. And although I have a lot of wonderful friends who help me a lot, it was just on the day-to-day, run-of-the-mill things, that were hard. Basically, you can't go to the grocery store. For my baby shower, a friend of mine said, "If you want, as your present, I will put an ad in the *Tab* and I will interview people and present you with a couple of finalists." So after the first year and a half, I thought, "Okay, now it's time." So she did and she found Eleanor.

Kerry struck a deal with Eleanor, exchanging fifteen hours a week of child care for board. This gave Kerry some evenings off to be with friends and the ability to meet some work demands.

> We are very happy with the arrangement. Eleanor is in school, she's going to nursing school. She's not doing as much day care as she was the first year because she's doing more intensive school things. But you know, I was able to go away on business and leave her here with my child. So there are ways that it works out.

By sharing her private space, Kerry was able to met the demands of her job and relieve pressure at home. Skirting the market for child care, Kerry made a trade, using her space rather than her paycheck to add another pair of hands to her family. Her example is unique in that the arrangement was structured with specific expectations in a way that was not typical of the other women who traded in space, such as Patricia and Ellen.

While the majority of women may be parenting alone, that does not necessarily mean they are living alone. Whether they derive income to pay day care and household expenses or they barter child care for a room, the economic use of space brings other adults into the lives of these single mothers and their children. Figuring out how to shape and sell what used to be space once inhabited by and designed for the middle-class nuclear family is a creative way for women to shore up their paycheck, giving them flexibility as they integrate work and family. Tenants dance with their landlord's kids, hold on to the baby monitor as the mother runs to the store, and provide adult company when the mom feels lonely. While the use of the market and space to bring outsiders into families has its roots in the market economy, these relationships have a tendency to grow into more. The home, once a private haven for its kin members, now includes boarders. These individuals not only change the family finances but also alter the dynamics of daily living. They blend the public space of the market with the private space of the family.

### The Careworker: Paid Child Care Provider as Partner

The expense of child care also blurs the boundaries between the market and the family. Employment for single mothers is dependent upon arranging adequate child care. Without the option of staying home or a partner to care for the child, women, with the exception of those whose children are cared for by their kin, use the market to free them for employment.[18] The majority of women depend upon one main type of child care while piecing together additional coverage as needed. The most popular form is family day care, not only because it resembles a family setting but also because it is cheaper than center-based care. A few women have nannies, but for most, private child care in their own home is economically out of reach. Single mothers are unique in that they explore different ways of incorporating child care providers into their lives, in search of individuals to provide another pair of hands, windows into their child's life, and child-rearing experience and wisdom. In this section, I have conceptually divided these relationships to illustrate the different forms of child care providers as partners, though most women in this study blend these archetypes.

Child care providers are providing more than simply a service. Single mothers do not see child care providers as competing for the role of primary nurturer.[19] Instead, the majority of women view their relationship with child care providers, whether they are full-time nannies, part-time help, center-based child care providers, or the woman running the neighborhood home day care, as an important partnership. Lacking a spouse, single mothers embrace the involvement of another person. As Jennifer said, "What I really realized around this child care thing is the profound disorganization. And really how dependent I am on it. I don't have a partner except the child care person who essentially is a partner in this deal. I really can't do it without her. So that's a really critical piece." Often they say there can never be too many adults in their children's lives. Single mothers do not feel that child care providers threaten or undermine their role in their children's lives. Instead, they view child care providers as engaged in another form of partnership, with roles such as the buffer, the mentor, the picture provider, and the fictive grandmother.

THE BUFFER: BUYING ANOTHER PAIR OF HANDS

The buffer is seen as a stand-in for the lack of a partner. In order to reduce the stress in the most hectic parts of the day, women hire help on a limited basis, particularly to handle day-to-day tasks. They prefer that the time that they spend with their children not be occupied with the frustration of not enough hands. In this strategy, the market is used not only to secure child care but also to buy out of routine household tasks. As Abby said in response to what she wished she could do if she won the lottery, "I would hire people to do the things that take me away from him, to do shopping, and cleaning, the kind of routine maintenance." Whether this person is doing the laundry or picking up the child from day care, the buffer is there, in lieu of a partner, to relieve the pressure points of the day. The absence of a partner made the high-stress times all the more visible to Joy, who hired several stand-ins, a luxury afforded to her by her substantial income. She believed that help by way of the market was much more reliable than help by way of marriage:

> Many of my friends who face a pretty similar end-of-the-day situation, because there is a spouse, don't give themselves the luxury of saying "Well, I'm only one pair of hands, what can I do to make the situation pleasant for everybody?"[20] I didn't want to be in the position of yelling at my kids because we were all frustrated from our respective days. Dinner needed to be on the table and I didn't have time to play with them. I didn't try to do it on my own between work and bedtime. I knew that period before dinner was the witching hour for everybody, so I always had help. I was always the story reader; I was always the play person. I didn't want to be frazzled at the end of the day. And I knew if there was another pair of grown-up hands around, that I would be more relaxed. Which is true. And it would be true for many of my working colleague women, but there is this notion that the husband is going to help. And a lot of them don't.

Joy recognized her limitations as the sole parent in the family, knowing that having another pair of hands around would allow her to be more relaxed in the evenings. She counted herself lucky in that she did not have false expectations for a husband to help her shoulder the "second shift." Instead she just hired helpers. Also, when work had her on call, Joy needed someone on call at home:

> I needed the flexibility. If I had a late meeting or late rounds or emergencies, then there was someone else who could pick up the baby, get him started on dinner, bath, whatever, depending on when I got home.

At times her hours were irregular and she was unable to pick up her child when day care ended at 6 p.m., so she hired someone to help at the end of the day as well. Joy was good at delegating tasks at home so she could meet the responsibilities of her career. More interesting, perhaps, is that she knew which parts of mother-hood were important to her and found other people to relieve her from doing everything else. She hired people to be there at the stress points in order to have the kind of time she wanted to enjoy and parent her children.

For Beth, her stress point was the morning routine. Having to arrive at work early to meet with clients meant that getting out of the house was her greatest struggle. To solve her problem, she found a college student to help for a few hours each day: "I actually hired somebody to come in in the morning, get the baby dressed, put together his stuff, and take to him to day care. She also does the laundry and then leaves the house after I do." Those who can afford to do so high-light the most important parts of motherhood that they want to retain, buying help for the remainder—they hire someone to make dirty dishes in the sink, unmade beds, and hampers of dirty clothes disappear. The stress of trying to do the custodial tasks of the household and children is cut out from women's days once those tasks become recognized as something that can be accomplished through bought labor. Women want motherhood to be filled not with main-tenance activities but with quality time. In short, women streamline home life as they do their careers, handling the most essential parts of each.

## The Mentor: Transferring Experience from Child Care Provider to New Mom

Another partnership that can form between mothers and their child care provider is one of mentorship. This is especially common with women who use family day care. Not only is this type of child care centered in a home setting, but usually the provider's spouse and school-age children are present for some part of the day. Mothers see the family day care provider as counseling them when they have questions about their child's development. New mothers have no guidebook as they take on the responsibility of raising a child, no one with whom to learn what to do when a child is sick. Some rely on their experience babysitting younger siblings or on advice from their own moms. However, on a day-to-day basis, it is the wisdom of the experienced paid family care provider, who usually has already raised several of her own children, that becomes the resource.[21] The care provider becomes both an educator and an employee, offering a positive spin on the trials and tribulations of first-time parenting, such as colic or tantrums. Having passed through the gauntlet of motherhood themselves, often several times, they know how to instill confidence in the new mother without making her feel incompetent. Claudia explained:

> I felt like there was a mother in the house. And I loved it. Not that I needed to do all her suggestions—follow her rules about bottle washing—but I really felt like somebody knew something and it was great. It was this incredible sense that there was an adult here.

Nadine, who had twin toddlers, relinquished control, trusting the experience of the family day care provider.

> Some people talk about feeling threatened by day care providers who become kind of substitute parents. I don't feel that way. I've been very good about letting her have more and more say over what the twins do and what they eat. She does better than I do, so I just let it be that way.

Nadine clearly viewed the family day care provider as a partner who had different strengths rather than a "shadow mom" to whom she dictated what to do in her absence.[22] Further, an added bonus of her child care situation that Nadine discussed later was the presence of the provider's husband, whom she saw as offering a positive male relationship with her children. Family day care providers blur the line between labor for pay and labor for love, which may have consequences for the providers. However, for the women who employ them and for their children, child care providers become critical teachers for the mothers and nurturers for the children. Mothers without kin in the area seek out family day care settings in pursuit of this type of relationship, linking their children to the provider's family. Often the tricks the day care providers can share with the mother are culled from years of experience and not to be found in a book.

## THE PICTURE PROVIDER: A CONDUIT TO THE CHILD'S DAY

Day care providers often either speak directly to parents about their child's day or (in larger center-based care) send along a written summary of the child's day. Mothers sought day care that would offer a more complete picture of the child's day. This is the kind of detailed information about the child that one partner who was home all day might tell the other upon arrival from work, providing a vicarious picture of the child's day that allows the other parent to be present in a sense even when she or he is not physically there. For single mothers, day care providers paint a picture of a child's life from nine to five and interpret it in developmental terms, some even going so far as to send out nightly e-mails. Leigh placed her child in such a day care setting.

> I don't mean the usual day care report, you know, "Maya did a poop at two o'clock, she ate four green beans, she wouldn't drink her milk." This is a complete story, a narrative of what the children have done all day in terms of their play. If they have built castles, what did Maya do in building the castle and what did she have to say? What was an idea that she had at one point? And then if the play turned to hospital, was she the nurse or did she want to be the doctor? And how did she and Nathaniel get along? It is this *very* strong narrative that weaves through. So that's a storytelling that takes place, that I'm a part of as a listener. So I would say that those are the ways that I do it.

Leigh might not be with her daughter during the hours she was in day care, but that did not exclude her from her child's life. She engaged via these narratives in order to make herself a witness to her child's day, even when she was not a participant. The e-mails also allowed her to monitor her child's development and ask questions of both her daughter and the child care provider. Leigh kept a file folder of such records as a sort of diary that she planned to one day give her daughter.

## THE FICTIVE GRANDMOTHER: CREATING CHOSEN KIN

Often women seek out a partnership with the child care provider that mimics family. Those who did found a certain comfort in relationships that more closely resembled a family tie for their children, such as that with a grandmother. While I am using the term *grandmother* to reflect the gap of age and experience between the care provider and the mother, women describe them as second parents in some ways. Nadine easily relinquished her control over her children's feeding, partially because she viewed her neighborhood family day care provider as a kind of kin.

> And they started going to Marissa's. And Marissa is lovely. They think of her and her husband as their second parents—no, they probably think of them as their first parents. Every day I told her I didn't want to bring them out, and she said "I'll help you," so she comes over and we bring them both to her house. And then she helps me bring them home.

Nadine described Marissa and her husband as parents, an important statement about the ways a child care provider can become more than simply an employee. Nadine willingly shared her own status as parent because it inserted both her and her children into a larger family network. Further, the day care provider's children bonded with Nadine's twins:

> And Marissa's kids, they love the babies. It's almost like a family relationship now with Marissa. And she and her husband love the kids. Her husband came to this

country about four years ago. They spend a lot of time with the kids. And she loves them. She absolutely loves them to death.

In a way, Marissa embraced Nadine's children as an extension of her own children's childhood. With her own children in elementary school, she still had two babies to care for during school hours. At first glance, her caring for children was a market transaction, but this paid relationship easily blurred the line between work and family. Clearly, all parties were emotionally invested. Oftentimes such partnerships have longevity, as women in the study who had school-age children often reported that providers continued to care for these children, supplementing after-school programs.

For Nadine, who had no kin in the immediate area, the child care provider's love of her children came as a happy surprise. That sort of warmth is not usually found in the market economy. For other mothers with older children, caregiving relationships dilute the intensity of the mother-child pair. Interestingly enough, as children become more independent, they often continue to seek out their early providers on their own, unable to classify these adults who remain so important in their lives as simply hired employees. In short, while child care relationships start in the market, the emotional bonds can continue throughout the child's teenage years, as former child care providers become confidants and dispense advice to their former charges.

Single mothers' employment is dependent upon access to quality child care. This dependence prompts the majority of women to see child care providers as more than simply an invisible presence. In fact, mothers emotionally tie child care providers to their family, building a place in their child's life as another caring adult.[23]

## Conclusion

Single mothers *have* to work outside the home. Beyond that, they *want* to work. However, how much they work is highly contested. The number of hours they spend in the workplace varies based upon their resumé and their manipulation of other resources. They use space and gifts to subsidize their motherhood. Further, motherhood gives them an opportunity to redefine themselves in their jobs. Some mothers who are older and have already proven themselves in one career use the arrival of a child as an excuse for a transition to a less demanding or more streamlined career. Even some in their thirties are looking at ways to use their skill sets and degrees in new ways. Regardless of age, women's employment plateaus with the arrival of a child. Whether this was a conscious decision women made, a consequence of facing a glass ceiling or exhausted career opportunities, or simply the result of the workplace's inflexibility toward motherhood is unclear. What is clear is that women wanted to shake up their lives by having a baby and were willing to place motherhood at the center of their focus, rather than on the periphery.

The image of the welfare single mother haunts single-parent middle-class families. Even those women with desirable skill sets and high levels of education fear losing their jobs and not being able to provide for the family. A fall such as this would tar them with the same brush as their poorer and often government-assisted counterparts, the very stereotypes they try to combat in choosing motherhood. The paycheck (and other resources) is what facilitated their motherhood from the beginning—to lose financial stability would be to lose what secures their family and their lives, their foothold into the middle class.

Financing motherhood goes hand in hand with finding a trustworthy person to nurture children in their stead while they work. It is for this reason that child care providers are incorporated as friends, not foes. Far from imagining usurpers, single mothers embrace these individuals out of need, looking for ways to build emotional bonds to strengthen what starts out as an economic relationship. Women massage these relationships, avoiding friction instead of inviting it, as their coupled peers sometimes do.[24] In order to shelter these interactions, women treat child care providers as esteemed professionals, shifting this construction only to view these individuals as chosen kin. Relying on the kindness of paid child care providers together with believing in the resiliency of their children is the only option for single mothers who must support their family financially.

The forces that shape the workplace often make it incompatible with parenthood. Women's workplaces in this study are not inherently family-friendly (a point that often becomes clear early on, when women seek maternity leave). Unable to form a comfortable partnership with the workplace, women form other alliances, primarily with the gift-giver, the roommate, and the careworker. It is these alliances (and those discussed in the next chapter) that help women both provide for and nurture their hard-won children.

# 9

## A WORLD WITHOUT MEN, AMEN?

Fatherlessness is a heated topic in America today. Some observers worry that fatherless families could lead to a generation of children with behavioral problems, to juvenile violence in schools, to adolescent childbearing, and to future economic malaise.[1] The executive branch of the U.S. government has proposed marriage incentives in the belief that female-headed households might be retrofitted with provider dads.[2] Conservatives contend that single mothers have purposely shut men out of their lives and those of their children as part of a feminist, anti-male statement.[3] Their unstated worries are nonetheless clear: What will become of men left without the comfort of families? And if men are no longer needed, will families disappear altogether?

In this chapter, I suggest that the crisis is exaggerated. Single mothers are deeply concerned about having men in their children's lives. Many would prefer to have dads as integral parts of the family. However, the interviews also reveal an intense and deepening confusion about what exactly fathers bring to families.[4] Indeed, as women seek to create children without gender stereotypes, they find themselves grappling to explain to their children what is special about men.[5]

### Raising Children

Single mothers are constantly asked about the men in their children's lives. The implication is simple: men are essential to raising children. The reality revealed by my interviews is that—far from trying to create a world without men—single mothers and their children deliberately strive to include them. For this reason,

I will pay special attention to men's involvement with single mothers and their children in this chapter. Having built small female-centered families, these mothers struggle, on one hand, to assimilate their families to a male-centered world, while on the other hand, they continue their reluctant revolution. While men as individuals can just be another friend to the family, on the whole they come loaded with masculinity and what it brings to children. Thus, before discussing the way in which women connect their families to men, it is important to first understand how women confront gender stereotypes while raising their children.

As much as women seek to incorporate men into their children's lives, they also are vigilant about how they portray gender to their children. Women are looking to give their children the opportunity to develop both "masculine" and "feminine" qualities. They are especially concerned about providing positive messages for boys when they are young. They want their sons to identify as male (with men), but they want to broaden the definition through their own example as women. Without a manual, women are tinkering with existing formulas in order to create a world in which boys can be nurturers while also being able to throw around a football, all the while reinforcing masculinity through their recruitment of male role models for their children. Noted Abby: "I want him to know all sides of it and of life, male and female, and to make choices based on what he wants, not on what traditional roles tell him he should do." Ellen echoed this: "I mean, we're all affected by stereotypes, and that will always be true. But I would just hope that in some ways I could either eradicate or at least lessen the impact for her." "He sees me going to work every day, having a career. If something breaks, he says, 'Mom can fix it.' And that's true, I can do most things," said Annette.

These women are raising children at a time in which women are capable of providing their child with a full range of ways of being in the world, as the above quotes indicate. They are concerned about their daughters also, but when the children are younger it is the mothers of boys who most often remark without prompting about how men in their lives give their sons masculine behavior to model. In short, these mothers are still concerned that men be around as they raise their children. They respond to this pressure through deliberate inclusion of men in their social networks.[6] It is not that they believe that men provide a critical difference in perspective that women cannot supply; it is more that their very presence signifies the continued importance of men in our culture. Single mothers are seen by the larger society as threatening the social fabric by making men outsiders to family life.[7] In response, women seek out the presence of men for their children, with the emphasis on that mere presence rather than particular behavior models or skills.[8]

## Raising Feminist Children: Male Privilege in the Way?

We live in a society that has a residual gender hierarchy of which single mothers are acutely aware and to which they feel they must respond.[9] Therefore, as much as these mothers talk about raising feminist sons and daughters, poised to break through gender stereotypes, they bow to the pressure of the notion that masculinity continues to be privileged, prompting women to consciously cultivate men in their children's lives. These women are a product of their social environment, having witnessed male privilege their entire lives, sometimes clashing with it in graduate school, the workplace, and their own family. To reject the normative perspective of male privilege would be to become more than the reluctant revolutionaries they are. At this historical moment, women know that male privilege is not inherent, but they are not willing to be the ones to strip that privilege away. Instead, these women opt to connect their children to that privilege, unwilling to risk making them a casualty in their gendered fight against the hierarchy.

While individual men might also believe in gender equality and relaxed gender roles, these mothers are aware that the broader culture continues to privilege men, valuing them and what they do over women and what they do.[10] These contradictions reflect the broader conundrum that exists in our culture today— women cannot unravel the paradox of power while men (as a group) are unsure of how to share privilege. As is apparent in the words of the women quoted above, they want their children freed from gender stereotypes, but at the same time they do not want to fully reject the idea that differences between men and women may exist. Therefore, these women still buy in to the worship of masculinity, unwilling to shun men in the event that exposure to masculinity is the key to a well-adjusted child. This is contradictory, and women do not know how to reconcile this tension, especially as they raise sons who at times seem to be born with the innate vocabulary to describe every piece of machinery at a construction site. Perhaps more important, it may be easier to gain power and privilege than to give it up. Sons have more to lose in this regard, a struggle of which women are acutely aware. Further, they want their daughters to know male privilege when they encounter it and to be prepared to combat it. This dynamic of privilege is especially charged in the middle class, a group strongly invested in the class hierarchy with a tenacious foothold in the middle.

As much as male privilege may frame how they raise children, women, even those who take for granted feminism's influence on their own lives, frequently mention how feminism influenced their views of child rearing, including the values that they want to give their children, starting with everyday small aspects of life such as balancing the "male" and "female" toys that they give children and making sure that when they visit the local firehouse both women and men are on duty.[11] They have strong views that children, regardless of gender, should not feel pressured by gender role stereotypes. Mothers of both girls and boys express fear that the ubiquitous and subtle sexism that saturates our culture will creep into their children's minds and affect their way of viewing the world. At times, women catch themselves perpetuating sexism; for example, two mothers talking one day realized that "the boy got the truck and the girl got the doll," and they tried to fix it by reversing the gifts in order to create more gender-neutral play. However, as one frustrated mother noted, "What do you do when your son's third word is *backhoe*, a word I never knew when I was young?" While not discounting that genetic tendencies may exist, these supporters of the nurture side in the nature-nurture debate believe that environmental differences can overcome nature, though at times they wish they understood better how genetics and social influences work together.[12]

As much as the women try to eliminate sexism, it proves more pervasive than they had originally thought. They are surprised by how often sexism crops up at day care and how young children pick up on it. Mothers thus become somewhat resigned to sexism as an inevitable part of child development and subsequent thinking. Claudia, whose son had just entered kindergarten, reported:

> There was this really big thing going on in that classroom around "boys are this and boys are that and we hate the girls." And it is the first time I saw this division. I want him to be able to be with both boys and girls and be comfortable. I would like him to be in both worlds comfortably. Maybe there shouldn't be two worlds.

These mothers' views about raising boys and girls are similar to those of many partnered mothers. Mothers of girls seek to teach their daughters that they can do whatever they want, and to instill self-confidence and respect. In the words of Ellen, "I want her to enjoy herself, respect herself and have faith in herself. I don't necessary want to affirm her as a woman. I want to affirm her as a person."

Mothers repeatedly speak of wanting their daughters to have positive images of female power and to see that women are capable. They are very conscious of their positions as role models for their daughters, as are the mothers of boys. Having careers and raising a family, they present a model of women as free to make whatever choices they deem necessary for their own well-being, while successfully coping with the pressures those choices entail. In addition to talking about employment, women tell stories that focus on learning new skills in order to show their children that they do not need to rely on men when performing daily tasks and so as not to perpetuate division-of-labor stereotypes at home. Gina, who reported that she grew up thinking that science, math, and anything spatial were her weak points, went to great lengths not to pass on this fear to her daughter.

> I have literally stayed up until two and three and four in the morning to put together certain things—toys that require assembly and most recently a new bike—so that I did not rely upon my brother-in-law, and she really thinks I can do all that stuff. And she is great at it. She's always improvising how to fix something, grab the tape, or whatever.

Setting an example that challenges gender stereotypes is often a priority for these women. Without taking on the feminist label, they are determined to present themselves as capable beyond gender expectations.

Raising boys presents more challenges and contradictions. Often women wish that there was a guidebook on how to raise a feminist son. They want them to be aware that manhood comes with privilege, which mothers hope they will use responsibly. At the same time, they want their sons to express themselves as individual people, acknowledging gender as only one of many important components of their identity. This concept is hard to grasp and to translate into practice. Hillary captured this sentiment:

> I want to be careful how I raise my sons. On some level with a feminist attitude, but I also want to respect him as a man. That's what I've tried to do with my older son and want to keep doing with my newborn son. It's funny, though, I think a lot about the fact that I am essentially raising white men and that's when I get a little anxious and a little angry at feminism. I mean, I am raising children who are considered the primo repressor worldwide. I want to raise them so they are conscious of the fact that by virtue of who they are they have a certain amount of privilege.

Hillary articulated a theoretical position of gender domination that most women in this study did not express so consciously. Often, mothers of boys told me that having a son meant rethinking how easily in the past they had labeled all men as similar. But this reasoning falls apart as they come to see their son as a unique individual with his own potential. They can no longer simply nod in agreement that all men are this or that. The shock of birthing her first male baby led to the transformation of Hillary's extreme views, as her baby represented a challenge to her previous thinking about men: "Here was this little man that I really loved a lot; I kind of had to change my senses around after being a man-hater for many years. Or be more sensitive to some of the things I didn't like about men's behavior, such as their constant need to tell me how self-important they are." This child was not anonymous, nor could he be a generic stand-in for all men. She loved her son and wondered how she could raise him, and after him his younger brother, to equally respect the abilities and accomplishments of both sexes as well as protect them both from the view she once had.

Raising feminist sons challenges these women to go against another cultural message they have also internalized: the notion that being less masculine translates into being gay. This is not unique to the straight women in this study, but women's concerns reflect the tension between the gender fluidity available to girls and the resistance to feminizing sons. Melissa, the mother of twin four-year-old boys, realized the contradictions and differences between them in their play:

> It gets into what kind of men I want to raise. I just bought a couple of books about this because they are now in this very aggressive phase, which seems developmental. They want things like Power Rangers and it's driving me crazy. They're talking about killing. It's everything the literature says, because they make guns out of Legos because we have no guns. Yet one of my sons wanted a Barbie and wanted Barbie stuff for him on his birthday. And the whole thing about do you

feel comfortable doing it that way even though you can buy your daughter trucks? And I have bought him Barbie stuff.

Committed to raising feminist sons, she nonetheless struggled to figure out a middle ground. She recognized that guns are a stereotypical form of male aggression and did not want to instill this in her sons. But at the same time she worried about buying her sons traditionally "girl" toys even as she recognized that this would not be an issue if she had a daughter who preferred trucks. She knew she was being hypocritical and fought against it, but the primary cultural message remained strong.

In short, the male identity, if more narrowly defined, makes it difficult to raise feminist sons. Often, girls' ways of being in the world are more expansive. The women discussed in this section lay out the dilemmas of trying to raise a feminist child, concerns that are not unique to single mothers but rather resonate with all mothers who wish their sons had more opportunities for self-expression. Boys may be harder to raise without a social consensus on what qualities matter or without revising notions of how men can be equal participants in family life (even if these mother-child families do not have the daily reality of a present dad). Mothers struggle with raising sons, unclear how to free them from stereotypes in the ways their daughters have been freed.[13]

Women experience tension between the freedom that they hope to provide for their children and the role models that they feel they must provide—the tension between ideology and practice. Women provide their children with gender-neutral toys and the option for boys to be sensitive and girls to be aggressive, but they also have the sense that their children must fit into the world. Their vision for their child's future is not that of a social exile; thus they are mindful that they cannot ignore the attitudes and stereotypes of larger society. This translates into women's belief that they must include men in their children's lives in order for their children to gain familiarity with and thus to be able to participate in a world that still privileges men. For sons, mothers want boys to understand the power of that privilege as well as the ferocity and weight of masculine ideology. For girls, mothers must prepare them to fight the stifling cult of femininity as well.

### A World with Men

Women in the middle class are not looking for men to become surrogate dads; they are cultivating relationships for their children with men as a way for them to know men up close.[14] That is, women want to make sure that their children have the same opportunities for having a successful middle-class life as children with dads. If the presence of a dad in the house is proven in the future to give children an advantage, then women have to figure out how to provide some equivalent so that their children do not fall behind. Whether men are a source of cultural capital is not conceded, but without dads these women are covering all their bases.

Women feel they must expose their child to men as part of middle-class tutelage, in some ways much as they think they should expose their child to a musical instrument or a sport. If there is something to be gained from men, then women want their children to have that knowledge as well. Since these children are often without dads, mothers seek to provide their children with continuous exposure to men in order that the children feel comfortable around them and have knowledge of men to draw upon as they grow up. It is this worry of insufficient exposure that spurs a conscious search by the mothers for significant male involvement and relationships in their children's lives.

Women do not feel like they need to teach their children about men. Lessons about growing up gendered are readily available. Masculinity is woven into the dominant culture, and no child can escape knowledge of the supposed differences between men and women. Rather, women believe that children should experience a variety of types of people and personalities, men included. There is also an irony here, however. Women ask these men to teach their sons how to knot a tie; the company of a man with their child at a baseball game is more valued than that of a female friend. The male entitlement to spaces such as the baseball diamond is a privileged perspective that women want their children to experience, as American as the game itself. Women look to men to instruct their children on the subtle cues of certain kinds of male behavior, despite the fact that women could be equally qualified teachers. Women want their children to experience men firsthand in order to expose the kids to what has been traditionally viewed as masculine behavior and to illustrate their own opposition to gender stereotypes. For instance, Charlotte told me that her dad pushed her brother to enter engineering even though she was the one who excelled in math. Hoping that her dad would notice her talent if she received good grades, she worked hard—harder than her brother—so that she would merit his mentoring. It annoyed her that her dad began to advise her only once she had proved herself to him. She felt that her brother had received her dad's attention solely because he was a boy. Yet, in Charlotte's view, it was her dad and her brothers who gave her own daughter critical encouragement. Charlotte also encouraged her daughter to achieve, but she clearly felt that it was somehow different coming from men who themselves had achieved in the workplace. Charlotte's belief that male encouragement was critical reinforced for her daughter the message that much as women are in the workplace, it remains a man's world. Recruiting men to instruct their children exposes a clear contradiction: women seek men out to expose their children to male privilege, but doing so reinforces the idea of this privilege and undermines their attempts to raise kids who are not wedded to traditional gender ideology.

Dads, uncles, grandfathers, and older male cousins are important resources that women draw upon to integrate men into their family life. Women act as kin keepers, regulators of contact and intimacy, in regard to their own families and, for those who chanced pregnancy, the father of their child. The male kin of the mother often play an active part in the children's lives. Charlotte wove her male kin into her adopted daughter's life, noting:

> The male members of my family adore her, even though we usually see them only a few times a year because they aren't local. Her grandfather is always on my daughter's side, even in her most mischievous moments. She's a very physical kid and my brothers like to rough house with her. My nephews are in their mid-twenties and they visit frequently and love to take her out. They are her favorite people. I'd say there's little contact time, but on her part there is a lot of imaginative time with these family members.

Charlotte included the men in her own extended family, involving them as often as they could visit. She wished they lived closer so that their visits would be less sporadic and they could be a more routine presence in everyday life. These mothers are exercising considerable agency in deciding on what male kin members (both maternal and paternal, if available) are excluded or included. Genetics does not equal unlimited access to children. For instance, children's fathers whom women feel they cannot trust with their children are not welcomed as providing "good modeling" for their children, and their visits with children are limited.

Women note that there are many opportunities to involve non-kin men in their children's lives. Most women can easily rattle off a list of men their children see on a regular basis. Often this list include coaches, teachers, principals, religious educators, day care workers, after-school personnel, camp counselors, babysitters, and other extracurricular instructors from music teachers to martial arts trainers to theater directors. As more men enter what have been traditionally female fields of employment (though they are still underrepresented), women actively pursue them.[15] Women often request male teachers for their children if available in a given grade, hoping to provide their children with a caring male role model and positive interactions.[16] Some children spend more of their day in the classroom of a male schoolteacher than with their moms at home. Women believe that these men are sensitive to their family structure and go out of their way to develop special relationships with their children.

Rebecca viewed her daughter's soccer team as an important structure that brought men into her daughter's life, though she also deliberately volunteered as a coach herself:

> Most of them have their dads out there, but she doesn't have a dad, so it's important she have a parent out there. This year I co-coach with two men who are clearly father figures for her. Clearly. She related to them in that way. And at the end of the year when she's saying, "I'm gonna miss my teacher, Mrs. Richards, and I'm gonna miss them at after-school care. But you know who I'm *really* gonna miss? Brian and Eric."

Big Brother organizations provide another institutional structure for boys and men to interact.[17] The vast majority of male children in this study were involved at some point in this program, with the exception of those children who had contact with their fathers (children of women who chanced pregnancy). This is a voluntary institutionally mediated relationship, in which men agree to commit to being a Big Brother to a boy for at least one year; the woman owes the man nothing. (While some women with daughters are involved in the Big Sister program, this is far less common and, in these cases, women talk about their daughters having an older sister rather than a female role model.) Male children have had very positive relationships with these placements, as the organization deliberately matches children and men who have similar interests. The Big Brother program is premised on providing adult male friendships in children's lives, and often the men remain involved with the children for many years, accompanying children to father-son school activities and otherwise acting as quasi-parents. Explained Hillary, whose son was a participant in the Big Brother program, "A classmate of his asked him when he was no older than seven, 'Do you have a dad?' He told his classmate, 'Everybody has a father, but I don't have a father that lives with me. I have a Big Brother and he does things with me like a dad would.' "[18]

Men also are recruited within less formal settings as well. Women do not live in a sex-segregated world, and all have men in their lives as friends—either friends that the women met on their own or the husbands of their girlfriends. Friendships between men and women are rarely studied, even though the women in this study report strong ties to male friends going back to elementary school.[19] Male friends are called upon in various ways and are consulted as part of the discussions that go on with close friends during the early liminal phase.[20] Lori-Ann met Ned and his wife at a local self-help group years before she became pregnant. While Lori-Ann's network is predominantly female, she attaches special importance to the role Ned plays in her son's life. Ned began his relationship with Andrew when he and his wife, who had grown children from a prior marriage, used to watch him for a few hours after day care one day a week. But as Andrew got older and Ned's wife's hours of work changed, Ned began picking Andrew up one day a week by himself. Lori-Ann described their relationship:

> Ned, in his early fifties, he's never had kids at all, and he totally loves Andrew. He has a truck and he picks up Andrew in the truck and that's their thing—they go off on a truck ride. It's been really, really good for them because they have this whole relationship that they wouldn't have otherwise. . . . They're pretty close. Because he'll say—like, we've talked about safety issues and he's not to go any place with strangers. And he'll say, "Well, I'll be safe with Ned because he's part of my family." It's definitely part of his image of family.

Lori-Ann's son extended the term *family* to include individuals who cared for him, and Ned was considered part of the family. Ned was particularly special for Andrew because they did "guy things." Interestingly, Lori-Ann is typical of mothers who seek out examples of men or contexts that represent traditionally masculine behavior in order to explain to me how their children acquire intimate understanding of what constitutes male activities. Women are turning over the instruction of masculinity to either specific men or institutions so that their sons acquire some semblance of information about societally reinforced masculinity. This is a strategy that they use to ensure that their sons will have a foothold in the dominant culture that privileges men, even if they do not support that culture and are not perpetuating that privilege in their home. The irony of using these men to do "guy things" with kids is that it essentializes men in ways that directly contradict women's wish not to define gender so rigidly.

Joy's story is a direct example of this contradiction. Asked about male role models in her second interview, she mentioned that she sent her son to a boys' camp, drawn by its large male peer group, the male counselors, and the male director. What happened on the ride home from camp the first summer exposed the contradiction between what Joy accepted in her home and what she exposed her son to. In the car, she noticed that her son had added lots of salty language to his vocabulary while he was at camp. She said to him, "I hear that you have learned many new things at camp, which is terrific. But when we cross the bridge into Massachusetts, I would like this language to stop. It is not language that I want in our home." She knowingly exposed her son to "boy talk" but reined in this language, as it was not consistent with her family values. "Boys' worlds" such as summer camps (and their girls' counterparts) provide contained same-sex environments, fertile ground for gendered bonding activities that often involve trying on extremely gendered behavior. Joy's son displayed the language on the ride home as a sign of newly acquired masculine knowledge. Yet while salty language might be fine at summer camp, it was not so in the middle-class suburb where they lived. In sum, even though Joy was pleased with the sports skills he developed at camp, she did not wholeheartedly accept all aspects of what he learned there.

Children also are active participants starting at very young ages in broadening opportunities for intimacy by inviting both adults and children to interact with their families. "She draws people to her," said Erika about her daughter. Erika continued, "It has become a challenge to manage it all. They want both of us so we both get invited but they definitely want her." Since these families include men and the mother-child family is easy to incorporate into the lives of other families, children have other avenues for knowing men up close (for instance, as a by-product of friendships, children become close to the dads of their friends). From early on, mothers become accustomed to their children acting as the conduits to other families, part of the way in which all families become tied through children's peers. In a second interview, Nadine discussed the shift in her group of friends when her children entered elementary school: "My primary network of support includes both new and old friends, friends I knew before kids and new friends I have made through my kids. Recently, I have been switching alliances to the newer friends because the kids are involved and these are their closest friends." The child is initially absorbed into the mother's existing network of friends; however, this changes as children form their own friendships with peers and spend time with their friends' families.

Children's peer groups, especially once they are in school, expand into larger webs of friendships that draw in their parents. Hillary used the relationships her children built with other families through elementary school not only as communal support but also as a type of male support for her child:

> As my kids get older, their best friends have become very important in our lives. Not only do we get together for barbecues and things like that. One of the fathers likes to include all the little boys in our circle when he gets tickets to a baseball game.

Children make connections and build friendships that are not restricted to just other children. Individual adults also become enmeshed in the lives of these children and their mothers in new ways. In some cases, these relationships start out as paid arrangements. For example, Susan hired a dog walker whom she rarely saw during the early years of his employment. When her daughter started tagging along with the young man on the afternoon walks, she began to talk at dinner about the fun she had had that afternoon with the dog walker. When the original afternoon babysitter graduated from college, Susan asked the dog walker to pick up her daughter on Wednesdays, the half day of school in her town. The relationship escalated, and the dog walker started occasionally going with the family to movies on the weekend and to cheer at the child's sports games.

While many women can expose children to adult men from their friends and family, many also express regret that their children are not witness to a positive romantic relationship between their mother and another adult. Of course, a large percentage of women in this study do have romantic relationships that their children might have eavesdropped on, but the child's ties to this person have limitations. In short, some women feel culpable for not having found a perfect mate, but as they explain to their children who ask about the absence of this partner, it is better to have no one person in that role than to have one person do it poorly.

Rebecca's daughter, Sarah, actively asked about a missing dad during preschool, but she remained silent on the subject for several years afterward. During a second conversation with me, her mother told me how her daughter startled her with a more complicated question one day:

> A year ago, when Sarah was twelve, out of the blue at dinner we were talking and laughing about a recent trip to the beach when she abruptly changed the conversation and got this serious look on her face. She said to me, "Do you think my personality would be different if I had a dad?" I said to her, "That depends upon how much time a dad is around. And there are good dads and bad dads." Then we talked about different kinds of dads and I told her again, "It is hard to find a good enough one."

Rebecca was caught off guard by her daughter's question. She carefully chose to focus Sarah's attention on all the other men in her life, from the soccer coach to her close uncles, grandfather, two adult male friends whom they saw for a "family dinner" once a week, and her male teacher. Still, Rebecca did not know how a "good dad" might have made her personality different.

At one point Sarah, like many other young elementary-school-age children, started to come home from school with recommendations of men her mother might think about dating. Sarah hoped this would lead to marriage for her mom and, more important, a dad for her. At one point Sarah saw potential dates for her mom everywhere—the school bus driver, the mail carrier, and a real estate agent who was helping Rebecca find a house. About the last of these, Sarah asked her mom, "What's wrong with him?" Rebecca pointed out his wedding ring, which they both knew made him ineligible as a potential date. This phase ended about the third grade, at which time Sarah stopped suggesting possible men for her mom to date. Rebecca felt sad that she had not found a suitable man to marry— maybe even more so for Sarah's wish to have a dad than for her to have a husband.

Melissa also understood how her twin sons wished for a dad when they too came home one day and suggested that she might like their male day care teacher. She took a different tack, since they were younger. She tried to give them a sense of how the family dynamics might change. Over dinner she told them that she liked their day care teacher but that he was too young for her to date. She was not sure that her twins understood that a ten-year age gap was too large for her. But they did understand this part of the conversation:

> "If there were a dad, he would be a dad for you, but he'd be a husband for me, and that would mean some changes. We wouldn't have all the time we do together, for instance." "Oh, okay, well, I don't want a dad anymore," one of the twins responded. But he will evolve out of not wanting to share me, I'm sure, and actually want somebody.

While Melissa would have liked her children to witness her in a loving relationship, she realized that her children were thinking about a dad for themselves, not realizing he also would have a separate relationship to their mom.

Mothers are expected to be the emotional center of family life, and not having a romantic love is a particular regret that reflects the entrenched belief that women are responsible for modeling all emotional behavior. While the literature on divorce warns that children suffer from watching parents who don't get along, more research is necessary to understand the importance of romantic modeling in children's lives.[21]

## Conclusion

Men and masculinity become a piece of cultural capital offered up to children as an additional resource, not an essential component. Ironically, the fact that women seek out men as a form of cultural capital reinforces the very gender ideology that they hope to displace in raising their children. This dilemma may be an artifact of wishing to raise children in the middle—both in the middle class and in the middle of the cultural spectrum—not on the margins. To do so, women feel pressure to accept certain aspects of gender stereotypes in exchange for rejecting others. Women are caught between appeasing the dominant culture and raising feminist kids. Even as they try to raise their children to counter a gender-biased world, they are not interested in creating a world without men as a solution. The fear of marginalizing their children leaves these women stuck between the gender hierarchy of daily life, which they really can not control, while simultaneously encouraging their children to resist it.

Men are important recruits to the mother-child families. Unlike poor single mothers, who struggle to find men to involve with their children, these middle-class women expertly provide male companionship, using the same resources with which they provide other enrichment activities. Like music lessons, soccer camps, and language classes, men are offered up to children as an essential luxury that mothers can afford: essential in that men are seen as necessary to raise successful children, and a luxury in that it is women's resources that ensure men's involvement. They are the soccer coaches, the father of a classmate, and the dog walker, all certified to teach children whatever nebulous and intangible things men bring to children's lives by their very presence. With nothing definitive about what men as a group have to offer, women struggle with the meaning of gender as they raise their children. However, they do understand that men as a group have privilege and therefore they must introduce their children to it.

In order to be good mothers, women perceive the necessity for integrating their families into larger networks of people who bring a host of ideas. Each individual brings an identity, a composite of that person's history, and his or her place in the larger social world and its ideology. Connecting to these individuals, sometimes to other families, women graft themselves and their children to larger groups, forming alliances. In more concrete terms, they want other people present to share and celebrate their children and their families. Incorporating elements of the old and new, mothers embed their families into a web of people that will ultimately contribute to a child's life as well his or her identity and success in the world.

# CONCLUSION

## What Does It Mean to Be a Good Mother?

How better to circumvent the power of the new women than with the idea of mothering not as care but as creation. Every moment for children is a teachable moment—and every moment missed is the measure of a lousy mom.

—Anna Quindlen

No woman in this study wants to be called a "lousy mom," especially as her route to motherhood so easily exposes her to critique. However, unlike their coupled peers who sometimes convince themselves that intensive mothering is within their reach, these women know that being a full-time mother is simply not an option. Unable to leave the workforce, these women settle for resting the measure of motherhood not on being there every moment but on being visible at key moments and logging what many call "family time."

With only twenty-four hours in a day, women must not only be mothers but also finance their mother time. Streamlining employment is the compromise for these women, and their success in this attempt depends on their skill sets. Adding hours onto mother time and subtracting them from paycheck hours is the foundation of placing motherhood at center stage. Another approach to reducing employment hours is ferreting out other sources of income, such as gifts and rental income. Other women spend down savings accounts, while some run up credit card bills. Women are giving up their personal time, social life, and outside hobbies so that they can be home on time for day care pickups or in time for dinner, things that are essential to them. In fact, the successful orchestration of these events, such as school pickup and dinnertime, becomes symbols of good mothering.[1]

While some mothers may use the time after their child goes to sleep to catch up on work brought home from the office, reading the bedtime story and the rituals of baths and brushing teeth are a priority. Weekends are sacred, but during the week, mothers are employees. Motherhood might have been a choice, but employment is not. Women can streamline their employment, but they cannot stop working. Women in dual-earner couples can often forfeit or at least minimize their identity as an employee, knowing that they have the safety of another paycheck.[2] This is not the case with single mothers. Single mothers integrate their identities of employee and mother as they must be both. In this way, these women are at the fault line of the work/family dilemma.

Crucial to these women's survival on this fault line is help with child care. No matter if these individuals are paid or unpaid, mothers must have someone to take care of their children so that they can work. Faced with the inability to give their identity as mothers undisputed supremacy, these women come to understand child care in a different way than those women who might have the option to stay home. In order to rationalize missing their children's "teachable moments" (essentially any moment, as Quindlen observes), they conceptualize the child care provider as an equally capable teacher. This understanding of child care providers is far from normative—in fact, the normative assumption of motherhood dictates that only mothers can provide children with what they need. Single mothers do not have the luxury (or the curse) of holding themselves to that standard. For these women, the child care provider is not invisible, but rather is part of the team.

Further, child care settings are spun as beneficial, helping to socialize the child. The child stands to benefit not only from being around the child care provider but also from becoming involved with other children. As children grow and transition to school, these single mothers rejoin with the norm, as teachers and schools have always been accepted members of the team. Staff of after-school programs, however, hold a place similar to that of the day care provider of earlier years (and in some cases, the children are returning to their original provider for the after-school hours). For these women who know that child care providers are an inescapable reality of motherhood, they prefer to see these individuals as capable partners rather than mediocre substitutes. In their descriptions of these relationships, it is clear that another tenet of good mothering is the careful selection of the people who will be there for the "teachable moments" that they will miss. For the new motherhood practiced by women who cannot be there for every moment, creating a team symbolizes their success as a mother. In short, women parcel out "teachable moments" to other carefully chosen adults, ideally a constant presence as the child grows.

Women are making other adults important in their family as part of their motherhood. While they may discuss child-rearing decisions with other important people in their lives, the stamp of good mothering is making the final decisions alone.[3] While this is never described as easy, many women relish their role as the sole decision maker. Ultimately, the responsibility is the mother's alone and making these tough decisions is the mark of a good mother, in the eyes both of these women and of the people around them. As Anita Garey poignantly describes in her 1999 book *Weaving Work and Motherhood*, good mothering is wrapped up not only in self-evaluation but also in others' expectations: "Ensuring one's maternal visibility is a response to the ever-present, scrutinizing gaze—a gaze with an eye on the performance of mothers *as mothers*" (p. 31). Being single means that these women are subject to extra scrutiny, so mothers are especially attentive not only to their own expectations but also to those of the people who are watching. With such a critical audience skeptical of how these children will turn out, the weight of the decision-making process is increased. These women are aware that in the eyes of the public, the mistake of one single mother is the failure of all single mothers.[4]

Besides surrounding their child with people who care, the final test of good mothering for these women is providing the social capital for middle-class citizenship. This is especially important because it distinguishes these children from those of poor, young single mothers. These enrichment activities, the piano lessons and soccer camps, are indicative of women's concept of achievement, very much entrenched in the values of the middle class. Providing this kind of social capital is central to their effort to make their children just like children whose families have two parents and two paychecks. Yet what distinguishes these children from those born to the nuclear family is that men become included in the social capital these mothers provide. As much as men are part of the gendered world that these children live in, women still seek to give their children the luxury of having men around, though still unclear as to what that luxury will mean for their children's future. Providing adequate social capital, men in particular, is the final testament to their good motherhood.

Women's lives are filled by work, children, child care providers, roommates, kin, romantic partners, and, in rare cases, parenting partners. While most have not given up on finding one person to be both a lover and a co-parent, in the interim they are preoccupied with fulfilling the charge of being a good mother. Each reinvents what good mothering in the middle class means within the constraints of their own limited mother time; however, from their stories, consistent refrains emerge. Placing family at center stage means streamlining their lives and making hard choices. Making their dream of motherhood work in a cultural climate that is still grappling with the place of mothers is the major challenge for these women. They are at the vanguard of the struggle to blend work, family, and partners. These new families are simultaneously revealing the tears in the social fabric and mending them for their particular families. These women hungered for motherhood. Once it has been achieved, they must make sense of their family that was created in extraordinary ways, inserting it into ordinary life. These women are committed to steering their children toward conventional success, successfully navigating institutions not built to fit their families. What keeps these women from real freedom, restraining them as merely reluctant revolutionaries, is their hopes for their children. They will forgo real revolution and real freedom for themselves in order to ensure that their children will be successful adults and not another single-mother statistic.

# Conclusion

---

## PROJECTING SINGLE MOTHERS
## INTO THE FUTURE

Middle-class single mothers are here to stay. However, the future is less about women who chanced pregnancy or chose adoption and more about donor-assisted families. These women are challenging norms of both family *and* reproduction. While it is news that single motherhood has moved into the middle class, and important legally that these women are allowed to adopt, it is women who had donor-assisted children who are casting light on the future. Science and technology are moving families in an unanticipated direction, changing the way we have babies and parent children.

Women who choose single motherhood are most often at odds with their biological clocks, bumping up against the constraints of their fertility. Science has the ability to change this—in fact, change is already under way. The options for extending fertility are quickly increasing. Older women are using the eggs of younger women to become pregnant. Older women's DNA is being inserted into younger women's eggs. Younger women are freezing their eggs or even ovarian tissue to be used to gestate at a later date. Beyond that, it may eventually even be possible to restock a woman's egg supply using bone marrow stem cells, adding to what is generally thought of as a limited stock at the time of birth.

Science not only extends fertility but also reinvents the way babies are made. Parthenogenesis, the development of an embryo without sperm, has already been successful in mice, and reproductive cloning is already possible, though heatedly debated. The reproductive technology with which the world is already familiar has been used by these women, and even something as nondescript as artificial insemination challenges the way in which families are conceptualized. The simple fact that women can now reproduce without men physically present (as a whole human being) holds a world of possibility, already realized in this book. But the implications of not needing any part of men, not even a gamete, are even more far-reaching, and the scientific realization of this possibility is around the corner.

This science holds special potential for women. The ability to put off children indefinitely could enable women to wait even longer to find a perfect partner, no longer slaves to their biological clock. But more likely, women will turn to science in order to give birth to their own children rather than pursuing other routes to motherhood that involve large adoption fees and having to prove to social workers that they are qualified to be mothers. Even for the reproductive technology that is now old hat, increased accessibility is changing its meaning in our world and changing families. Ordering sperm over the Internet brings this technology into anyone's home, making families without dads within reach. New generations of women are savvy to options available for timing their child to fit their life, some of which might not include a partner. In the future, reproductive technology, particularly artificial insemination, will no longer be a last resort, but an option for women of all ages. Future generations of younger women may prefer to take intercourse out of the reproduction narrative by ordering sperm off the Internet rather than chancing pregnancy with a lover in order to become mothers.

## Does This Marginalize Men?

High-tech science, such as parthenogenesis, may be slow to reach the masses, but families created without dads are here now. As this book has discussed, the place of men is already being questioned by these women, and the best conclusion many can muster is that men are a luxury item. For children without dads, mothers supply men as mentors, friends, and kin. This involvement does not secure a place for men as dads in families. In fact, men are not needed in the family—even the act of sex and the job of financially supporting the family, both of which traditionally bound the man to the mother and child, no longer require men. The possibility of creating children without the act of sex detaches the genetic claim men make to children. This revolutionizes the meaning of men in families.

Consequently, men need to rethink their place in the family because it is no longer implicit. Without automatic membership, men must find a different basis for connection to families. This will mean that men will have to exert new energy to claim a place. If we strip away the assumption that men are entitled to a special place in the lives of children on the basis of gender, what will men have to offer? I suspect that in order to have men rethink their place in the family, they also need to rethink their place in the workplace. The workplace remains hostile to both men's and women's involvement in family. Perhaps this will be what finally reshapes the workplace significantly—men as well as women pushing the workplace to accommodate the family. Under these conditions, men will reemerge as a different kind of player in the family (though clearly such a statement assumes that men want to be part of family life, and that is by no means necessarily true). Becoming more involved in the daily lives of children may make them more a parent and less an antiquated symbol. But what will win men a place in family, making them once again important to women and children, is the question. What men offer today is obsolete, and I am hopeful that they will revise their offerings. What will they bring, and will every family want it? Further, will they have to be a dad to offer it?

### What Is Holding Women Back from Female-Centered Families?

While social parents have solidly established their places as primary in children's lives, I am not ready to completely disregard the weight of genetics. It is difficult to separate the cultural lore surrounding genetics from its importance in identity formation; it is often overemphasized in a society that builds families around blood ties. Genetic ties have meaning beyond the nuclear family, extending intergenerationally, an accepted basis for who is in and who is out of the family. However, as the open adoption movement gains momentum and women reiterate frequently the special place of the donors in their child's life, it is clear that while genetics may not make a parent, genetic parents offer children pieces of their identity.

New reproductive technologies have opened up the possibility for intentionally crafting genetic ties; however, the women sketched in this book shy away from playing with genetics in nontraditional ways. These women initially prefer to conceptualize the donor as theirs alone, even when faced with the number of children sired by their donor on the paper profile. Implicit in a decision to use an anonymous donor is the decision to forgo direct access to the donor. But he is not irrelevant. When questions of paternal identity are unanswered, women turn to a new search for other donor siblings as a stand-in for more information about the child's paternal identity. Donor siblings are an extension of the anonymous donor, which is why women try to provide their children with them. The increase in donor sibling matches and the growing number of individuals registering on Web sites for that purpose indicate a new way in which kinship is born.[1] Yet while women scour the country and the Internet in search of genetic siblings and half siblings of their children, they adamantly refuse to share the same donor with their friends.

While donor registries could provide one answer to the absence of paternal genetic identity, the use of reproductive technologies could provide another. Imagine if a group of women—say, a circle of friends from college—got together and decided to share the same anonymous donor. Each could order sperm using the same donor number without even having to leave her own home. These mothers would not be pledging to become co-mothers to each other's children, straying nowhere near the vision of a female-centered social order presented in Charlotte Perkins Gilman's *Herland*, nor would they be forming one seamless family without a patriarchal head. Rather, they would be creating many families connected by genetic ties. This would provide their children with genetic kin raised by like-minded mothers who want a social relationship. The depth of these relationships would vary based on the expectations of all involved, but at least this alternative would provide a genetic safety net without requiring the women to undertake the search for donor siblings. Energy could be better spent developing relationships rather than tracking down individuals.

Obviously genetics are important as a window to identity, or else women would not be putting so much energy into maintaining genetic ties and searching for genetic kin. Instead, they would simply establish a chosen family bound by social ties. But this is not the case, and women say that creating genetic families in new ways, such as sharing anonymous donors gametes with friends, is not an option they would consider. This is a step women are simply unwilling to take.

What stops women from taking advantage of this possibility? Presently, female-centered families are threatening to patriarchal control of the family, and the women in this study are only reluctant revolutionaries. Women still prefer to parent with one other parent, and the wish among heterosexual women for a dad for their children remains strong. In order to create a new social order of families, the implicit control of men would have to be fully disassembled (though I doubt this will happen in the near future). Once that disassembly is complete, the opportunities presented by science could be capitalized upon and a new ideology of family would be possible. Already this study has shown that the mother-child dyad has become the core of family life.[2] Other relationships that embed the family in larger webs will be spun from this pair. A mother-centered culture could be the future if what these women have reluctantly began becomes a full-on revolution.

## Motherhood Against the Odds

Mother hunger—the concept with which this book began—is also here to stay. Women, regardless of movement into the workforce and changes in gender equality, still feel the pull of children. Whether this is the continuing pressure of compulsory motherhood or the long-standing wish for a child to love, the women in this book demonstrate the triumph of motherhood against the odds. *How* women pursue the dream of motherhood is changing and will continue to change, particularly with the help of science and technology. The potent combination of the age-old desire for motherhood and the new possibilities of science is well on its way to creating major changes in the formation and functioning of families. This is a projection of a possible future, one that reevaluates the place of women and men in families. Ultimately, building families from a mother-child core is the future.

# Epilogue

## COMPLETING FAMILIES, COMPLETING LIVES

During the winter of 2005 I called all the women I had interviewed at least four years previously.[1] As many had only been in the beginning stages of family building at the time of the first interview, I asked them how their lives had changed in the intervening years. When we had first talked, most of the women had toddlers and young children, and none of the women had live-in romantic partners. Eagerly they told me about the life changes that had occurred. Somehow over the years I'd begun to feel as if their lives were fixed in time, as if their first interviews were a reflection of their lives in the future. I was surprised to find out just how much their lives had changed.

There were three questions that motivated me to pick up the phone. Prompted by my own curiosity about what had happened in the lives of these families, I wanted to answer the very questions with which people peppered me when asking what my research was about. Had these women succeeded in resequencing the nursery rhythm about love, marriage, and the baby carriage? What had become of the fathers, especially the known donors, as well as other men in their lives? Finally, had single motherhood led directly to financial disaster, or were women still successfully juggling work and family years later?

When I began this study, if I had been asked to predict these women's futures based on their wishes as expressed in the interview, I would have guessed that single motherhood was a transition on the way to the coupled two-parent family, reversing the sequencing. I might have predicted that those who found partners would have more children. However, I certainly did not imagine that women would have more children on their own. Even if they sometimes wished for one, they had told me that they could not afford the second alone. As I reopened these women's stories by picking up the phone, I discovered my predictions would have been inaccurate. Many surprises awaited me on the other end of the line.

One of the biggest surprises was how the women had "completed" their families. Despite some women's objection to the term *complete* and their preference for *finished* to mean that they were content with their family size and did not wish for additional members, most women happily used the term, though it was interpreted in different ways. By the time of the update, the older women were in their late forties and fifties and most likely finished having children; however, the smaller group who had graduated from college in the late 1980s and 1990s may continue to add more children in the future. Contrary to my predictions, women did not wait for a partner to move on with their lives; instead they had second children on their own. As much as the master narrative of the nuclear family as the ideal continues to be pervasive in our culture, these women's lives are telling a new story, one in which single motherhood can create a planned family of more than one child. The addition of another child brought closure to the families of a smaller group of the older women. This act, the second child, trumped conformity, reluctantly taking the revolutionary act of single motherhood one step further.

As for romance, less than half of the women described themselves as currently romantically involved. However, 23 percent (ten) of the women I spoke with had increased the size of their family through marriage or civil union.[2] One woman married the father of her child, while an additional four spouses had adopted their partner's child. On the surface, these women had achieved the coupled two-parent family. But as I discovered, even among this smaller group, the addition of a second parent often did not translate into the exclusion of other adults tied to the child through blood or social parenting.

Other women found "completion" without marriage or another child. As much as women may have wished for partners in the first interview, for many, that wish for a partner in romance and parenting never became reality. They therefore revised their take on family, bringing closure without a partnership or marriage. They had redefined family completion as feeling embedded in a chosen family and their own maternal kin. As much as a partner might have added a new dimension to their life with a child, they did not feel that they were lacking anything in the absence of a partner/parent. They now staged their families as a whole, no longer waiting for the entrance of a missing member from the wings. By the time of the update, they had revised this projected scenario of marriage, and the mother-child pair in the process was recast as a family finished or one unto itself.

All these women reiterated the great joy their children had brought them. Their children had transformed their lives as parenthood took center stage. This is not to say that 24/7 parenting was not stressful at times, particularly when they had young children. However, women adjusted their personal lives and employment, and often were surprised to discover that having children energized them.

Even though each of the mothers completed her family in a different manner, they all found ways to move across the threshold into uncharted terrain and settle comfortably into accomplished lives.

## Diluting the Mother-Child Family

Joy McFadden, whose story opens the book, had reorganized her life to better accommodate the growing number of baseball, basketball, and soccer games that occupied a substantial portion of her children's time. One of the few women to have two children when first interviewed, she preferred to be in the cheering section at those games than to be at the workplace. At the time of the update, not only had she figured out a more flexible way to make a living to accommodate her kids' schedules, she had also made time to campaign for a seat on city council. She had sold her first home to buy a new, larger house in the same community. Over the years, she had managed to not only raise her two children but also embed herself within the community; she now felt that her life was full, even though she had not ruled out someday finding a companion when she wasn't so busy with other parts of her life.

Even though she was still without a partner, Joy considered her family complete, as she had told me when I first interviewed her after the birth of her second child.[3] The other women that I interviewed fulfilled the need for completion in the intervening years between the first interviews and my update calls. Many women by that time had followed Joy's lead, adding a second child to their family.[4] To them, the way that their families felt finished would be through the addition of another child. Some adopted, while others gave birth to another child. These mothers often voiced that the mother-child dyad that they had been living in needed another participant to feel balanced. Sienna's story was unremarkable insofar as she was one of several mothers who had adopted a six-month-old from China.[5] When her first daughter was seven years old, she returned there to adopt a second child, a toddler. Even though money was tight then and she was still paying off the expense of a second child, what she termed her "MasterCard baby," she said, "You need to take a chance to get a chance." She wanted the chance to expand her family, to complete it. To her, two people were only the start of a family. Her daughter was becoming more and more independent, but Sienna said, "I'm not done yet stomping in puddles and struggling with how many more times down the slide until we have to go home." She wanted her older child to have a sibling to mentor, struggle with, and love. For herself, a second child gave her the chance to "continue the challenges and adventures of childhood" and to not separate so quickly from her first daughter's early years. Further, Sienna hoped to build a team, leaving the relationship of a twosome behind. As a family of three, she told me, they all had to renegotiate their lives and reconfigure them, "from the dog on up."[6]

In the first interview, the vast majority of women expected that after the child, they would reenter the dating scene, looking for a third member to add to their pair—a companion for themselves who would also become another parent for their child. Rosalie, now married and the mother of two more children with her husband, was still adamant that when she became a single mom, she formed a functioning family, though she almost contradicted herself when she explained the transition:

> It was equally as complete when I was a single mother. You are a family once you have a child with or without a man in your life. I never thought I would meet anybody who would want to take on a young woman and a child. I had resigned myself to being a single mother. But I met my husband and we fell in love. I thought, "This is the person I want to share my life with." He closes the circle. Now I have someone to share the burden of parenting with, as my oldest son's father isn't involved on a regular basis, seeing as how my son only spends a couple of summer months with him.

Both single motherhood and married life have their pros and cons. A partner brings new negotiations about daily life and adds another dimension that can be challenging. Other women who had not added a partner or another child also said their lives were complete, and they wanted it noted that it did not take a partner to feel that family life was fulfilled.

However, among those women who found partners, some did say that a partner made a big difference in their family life in various ways. Kerry, who became pregnant with an anonymous donor, represents a new sequencing to family formation. Kerry fell in love with a wonderful woman and welcomed her into her family as both a second parent and partner, expanding the mother-child dyad. She and her partner went to Vermont in order to obtain a civil union (a substitute for marriage, then not yet allowed in Massachusetts) around the same time that her partner adopted her child in Massachusetts. Kerry explained an important way in which her partner completed a missing element in her child's life: "Elizabeth is the perfect addition. It is great to have a partner, but it really fills out that side of our son, as they both share a similar mind-set." Their child's interests were more similar to his new mom's, and this helped Elizabeth forge a bond with him that was central to their family. In Kerry's case, completion was about the quality and dynamic of change that occurred with the addition of a new family member.

While it is often within a woman's control to add a second child, and thus easier than finding a partner to share her life with, both kinds of additions create a similar shift in family dynamics, especially as it pertains to the mother-child relationship. The intensity of the mother-child dyad was a recurring theme that women expressed to me in the updates.[7] Many women told me that their family needed to be expanded to dilute the intensity of that mother-child relationship. These women told me the family did not always feel "finished" until there were more than two people. To dilute the dyad, women added either another child or a partner.[8]

These women really wanted more family and were able to figure out a way to have it. They directly experienced what Simmel theorized—that the dyad is qualitatively different from all other types of groups.[9] As a pair, mother and child confront each other as an interlocking unit. The addition of another child or a second parent creates a different group dynamic. Usually it is the relationship between adults that changes when couples become parents.[10] The triad formed with one child redefines their partnership in structural ways.

When a second child is added to the original mother-child family, new alliances are also possible. The children have a relationship with each other, the mom has a relationship with each separately, and together they are a close-knit group. Two children might gang up on the mother, or the mother might become a balancing force between the two children, or the mother and one child might go off and do something alone while the other child visits a friend. The processes that are possible in a triad involve authority and hierarchy; even when the adult is outnumbered, adult status trumps children's wishes. Further, the mother must mediate if two children are arguing, such as over which movie to see. Such mediation establishes the mother as authority in a way that is not always asserted when there is only one child; a second child creates an equal pair within the triad, one that the mother must then manage. With the addition of either a second child or a partner, there is the same numeric outcome, opening up new opportunities for coalition formation. Three creates a group life in which individuals have to make concessions for the collective good of the family.[11] However, the ratio of children to adults creates different authority dynamics, even if the number of family participants is the same.

Beyond the changing numbers of family life, I was struck by the other motivations behind the decision to have a second child. The first time around, as women actively entertained the reality of having children, they focused on moving from non-motherhood to motherhood. The family formation that they struggled to consider and redefine focused on one child. They were moving from zero to one, breaking social norms through this particular pairing of mother and child. Considering a second child, single mothers often worried that they did not have the time or the money.[12] However, adding family comes not out of a calculated formula but from a feeling of deep longing for more children. Their "emotional thermometer" motivated these women to expand their families, as they thought that a second child would make them feel they were done having children (and not putting it off for a partner a second time). A second child, a sibling, brings security to the family in another sense. A sister or brother brings continuity beyond the mother's lifespan for this *particular* family, as the children are bound together through the parent they share. Despite the complex conscious and unconscious thought processes that lead women to have a second child, they did not agonize over their decision in the same ways. Even though it did stretch their resources, the majority who added more children did not grapple with having another child the way they did when they decided to go from zero to one child. The second child, though a monumental change for their family, was not the major adjustment that putting aside a partner in pursuit of a child was the first time around.

Remembering that at the time of the first interview women had expected to put aside the search for a partner, I asked women over the phone about romance and lovers in the intervening years. What I discovered was that romance was more about compromise than completion for the subset of women who even had it in their lives. While at the time of the first interview women believed romance would lead them back to the two-parent family, the majority of those who were dating or had a significant other were living the split lives I had described earlier to varying degrees. Take, for example, Claudia, who in the first interview had a classic split life. While she has since bound her romantic life and her motherhood closer together, Claudia presents the best-case scenario for women who are now living under the same roof with the men they love.

Claudia, who was profiled along with Joy in the prologue, was raising her young child when first interviewed while continuing a relationship with a man who did not assume a role as a father in the child's life. She told me that she had continued to function as a single mother until six months ago, when Carl, her longtime lover, moved in with her and her son, William, now ten. Despite many interruptions over the years, their relationship had blossomed, and they decided that they had reached a point in their relationship at which they had to live together in order for it to continue to grow. He was becoming more of a father figure to William, but he maintained that he was not William's dad. Claudia felt her life shift when Carl moved in. Not only was there someone to help out with the daily chores, but also psychologically she no longer felt that she was alone in raising her child. William delighted in gaining another adult in his daily life. Quickly, the two dyadic relationships that had once occupied Claudia's life separately now merged into a triadic bond that was *almost* complete. Claudia still wished for marriage, which would make Carl her son's dad and her husband. However, as much as she wanted to institutionalize this relationship, she knew that state recognition would not make them a family; rather, day-to-day living is what would cement the bonds. Claudia moved one step closer to having both a partner in parenting and romance, her ideal, but for many women, loving elsewhere, as Claudia did in the earlier chapter, is as good as it gets.[13] These women are still roaming the single rubric, presented in chapter 7.

The rest of the women reported that they either had not dated anyone or judged these romances as too fleeting to elaborate on—they remained consummate mothers. While some voiced that they would like companionship but did not have time, others simply told me it was not a priority. Women discover that between raising their child and fulfilling the demands of their jobs, they have no time for meeting potential partners. Further, as their children age, they realize that adding a romantic and parenting partner would stretch their family life in a direction that might prove more problematic than positive. Feeling that the partner they had hoped to find after motherhood was unattainable, they revise their views, casting family as the mother-child dyad. Having held a place in their imagined family for a partner, they close that space by asserting their family is finished, rejecting completion as a structural necessity or a functional imperative. These reluctant revolutionaries have come a long way toward embracing the revolution they started—finally seeing their families as complete without a second parent or more children. Consummate motherhood equals a complete family to these women, who, like Joy, express that they are content.

## Woven Families: Celebrating Entanglement

The idea of holding a spot for a potential second parent to love both mother and child interested me from the very first interview. I remained curious about the future of women and their donors and whether or not "accidental" fathers would want more of their children than women were willing to give. While I was confident about the longevity of open and closed adoption agreements, particularly those that were international, the reality of these women's lives is more interesting than my imagination. The phone calls were revealing, sometimes even surprising, showing how far these reluctant revolutionaries had gone. Even the most vigilant gatekeepers of biological or genetic kin had expanded their vision of family. Just as their lives continued to develop, their understanding of donors, birth parents, and blood kin had been rethought.

I was particularly curious about families with known donors, perhaps the most attention-grabbing of the four routes to motherhood. Despite all the concern women had felt over the possibility of known donors wanting to share custody or even wanting rights to their genetic children, these donors had stayed in their place. Not one had revoked his contractual agreement, though three had revised their agreement, escalating into dads, already discussed in chapter 4. Similarly, I wondered about the "accidental" fathers. While the law views known donors and "accidental" fathers as one and the same, "accidental" fathers were without a contract and had even more potential to claim the children. Contrary to what I had thought would happen, it was the "accidental" fathers who had more frequently faded away, while the known donors typically held fast to their commitment to the mother and child, providing a face that did not fade even as it remained at a safe distance. Either the patterns established in early childhood stabilized or, if anything changed, the fathers' involvement declined.

Even when mothers found partners who adopted their children as their own, the donor was not expected to disappear. Jennifer's husband, Charles, adopted Zoë, the known donor relinquishing paternity (a legal aspect not covered by the donor agreement) so that Charles could adopt. However, Sam, the known donor, did not remove Zoë from his family health insurance policy, a symbolic act for everyone. Sam retained that special "spot" for Zoë, as Jennifer hoped he would. The two families, which came to include Charles's daughter from his first marriage and Sam's wife and two children, saw each another a few times a year. Jennifer considered this entire group kin, with varying obligations to Zoë.

Lori-Ann, whose story opens chapter 3, found her life partner right under her nose. She ended up marrying the "Wednesday woman," one of the group of friends who volunteered to take care of Andrew during the gap hours between the end of day care and Lori-Ann's return from work. The "Wednesday woman" also adopted Andrew. However, Lori-Ann and Andrew still maintained contact with Pennsylvania Bob, the donor. Pennsylvania Bob, despite Lori-Ann's belief at the time that she asked him to be a donor that he never wanted to be a dad, subsequently married and had other children to whom he was an active parent. Lori-Ann emphasized that Bob was still important in Andrew's life: "He never articulated missing a dad because he had Pennsylvania Bob and he knew he had a special closeness." But the second parent to Andrew was indisputably the woman she had been with over the previous few years, who had been a daily presence in his life since early childhood. Unlike Jennifer, Lori-Ann and her donor kept their families separate, but Pennsylvania Bob still visited Andrew without his family when he was in town.

By contrast, Annette's relationship with her child's known donor had not worked out so neatly. John, the known donor, had had a relationship with their child that escalated to informally sharing custody. In the years between interview and update, John went from the best example of an escalating dad who became a co-parent to a distant dad in sporadic contact with his son. Annette, who had been initially ambivalent about resuming a romantic relationship with John and becoming a family under the same roof, allowed him to move in with her after they went to counseling and things seemed to be working. But when he lost his job and became deeply depressed, they parted. Their child, now thirteen, continues to see his dad regularly. When we spoke, she was currently involved with another man, but her son was not so welcoming.[14] Annette tried to make the genetic family work—but as much as she loved her child's father for giving her her son, she needed to move on, and found another romance that was more satisfying.

Some women maintain less contact and more distance from the beginning than Jennifer, Lori-Ann, and Annette. Althea, whose child's known donor lived an ocean away, arranged a visit when her son was in preschool, described in chapter 4. The summer before the update, she had arranged a second encounter, traveling with her now middle-school-aged son to visit the donor and his family in Ethiopia, meeting his other children and extended family. During the interim years, he and Althea's son e-mailed from time to time. Hillary's two sons by a known donor were content with an occasional glance at a picture, expressing no interest in meeting him.[15] The donor likewise had not approached Hillary for contact with the children. Althea and Hillary illustrate the variation between relationships with known donors and reinforce how with the passage of time women who become pregnant with known donors no longer feel at risk because of their route to motherhood.

Women who chanced pregnancy, discussed in chapter 5, likewise settled into a routine regarding their child's father and his extended kin. Ellen and Gavin, featured in chapter 6, were still disagreeing over Skyler and who was responsible for what, including setting boundaries for their daughter. When I called, Gavin, who had married the woman he was dating, had recently taken Skyler on a family vacation, but he usually saw her when it was convenient for him. Ellen continued to make plans for Skyler to spend time with her dad through her child's stepmom. In many ways, nothing had changed—they were still bickering. Brandy, also featured in chapter 5, eventually took Alex to court for child support after he got out of jail. The routine paternity test shocked them both, revealing that Alex was not the father. Regardless of genetic parenthood, their daughter, Ali, remained a part of Alex's extended kin, and Alex continued to let her refer to him as "Dad." The paternity test absolved him from back child support and future mandatory child support, but he still occasionally bought gifts for Ali. Though Brandy had no child support, she prioritized having a social dad for her daughter over tracking down a genetic father. In essence, nothing had changed for Brandy either, despite the shocking news of the paternity test.

Beyond fathers, siblings and half siblings were an interesting twist to these women's updated stories. Naomi, mentioned in chapter 5, knew from the time that her son was an infant that there was a half sibling, the result of her two-timing then-boyfriend. Naomi, who never married or had more children, remained in contact with the mother of her son's half brother, as they had originally agreed upon when they met for the first time when their children were under a year old. The two families continued to meet from time to time, though Naomi unlisted her phone number to keep her son's father away.

For women who used anonymous donors, half siblings take on a new importance as well. While most women have abandoned the hope of contact with their anonymous donor, many have posted on donor registry Web sites in search of genetic half siblings. One of the pieces of information they were given from the sperm bank was the number of other children sired by this donor, a figure taken from self-reporting on the part of other mothers. They hope that eventually another mother who shares the same donor will happen upon their posting, bringing their children who are genetic half siblings into contact. Something I never anticipated was the way in which half siblings become important links to genetic identity for children of anonymous donors. Abby, who called on her college friend Nina to help select an anonymous donor, was among the first women to register her child's donor number on a new donor registry Web site. Abby, whose child was in elementary school at the time of the update, couldn't answer her son's questions about his father. As I wrote in her vignette, she was never clear on what role genetics played. "Who did he take after?" she wondered out loud to me. Trying to find some answers, one night she opened the locked box in which she kept important papers and keepsakes and reread the donor profile, hoping maybe there was a clue to something she had missed. She had ordered additional information about donor number 180, her son's father, when she was pregnant but had only quickly glanced at the papers before locking them up. Now, startled, she realized that she had not noticed that five other women had reported having conceived with using this donor's sperm. Abby was excited, and that evening she posted on two donor sibling registries. She wrote, "Hi! I am the mom of a child whose donor is 180. Seeking other women who have children from the same donor." Within a week, she received a message posted back. "Hi! Our children are siblings. Let's talk." She had found "instantaneous family," she told me. As much as she would have liked to meet the donor of her child, she had found a new way to connect to the donor, even if the anonymous donor was unaware of these new kin ties. Donor siblings (genetic half siblings) are now creating extended families without knowing the father. Abby said that the children had identical smiles—crooked to the right with one gorgeous dimple each. She now knew that this came from her son's paternal side. Her child and his half sister began to e-mail, and even though they were several hundred miles apart they met a few times a year. Her son had a picture of his sister to take to school to share with his teachers and classmates. Also, Abby felt that she and Margie were co-mothers, connected through their donor and their children—they considered themselves closer than in-laws, who are tied to family through blood members. This new kinship arrangement of co-mothers and half siblings weaves together strangers based on genetic information, every day revealing more about the connection between social and blood ties. Who would have thought that the Internet could produce an "instantaneous" family?

Interestingly enough, adoption also holds the possibility of bringing genetic siblings into children's lives. While it was not surprising to me that Janica, who adopted domestically, was offered her daughter's half sister unexpectedly by the adoption agency, the emergence of siblings out of international adoptions is shocking. Charlotte, a minor figure in the adoption chapter, told me an important story about her closed international adoption. It turned out the U.S. agency she adopted through had a contact agency in Eastern Europe, and consequently all the children from one orphanage were sent to the same geographic area. What she had no way of knowing was that the birth parents of her adopted daughter had placed several of their children up for adoption, one child at a time, through the same orphanage. Charlotte discovered that her internationally adopted child had full siblings living nearby. As uncomfortable as she was at first with the idea, she eventually arranged outings to introduce her child to her genetic siblings. She told me, "Her siblings are an investment in her future. They are an important part of her identity—not only do they look alike, but they share various traits of siblings, and when they are together they play as if they have always been together. It is amazing to witness." The other adoptive family and Charlotte created a broader kin set, forging new bonds that brought together both genetic and social kin on soil far from the birth country—and distant from the personal expectations for adoption that both these families had once held. While Charlotte had presumed that international adoption would be a tidy way to create a family, she eventually embraced her role as the weaver of a broader kin system outside the traditional boundaries of family. For mothers with children who do not have kin miraculously in the area, many travel to their child's country of origin in search of not only cultural heritage but the thread of kin connection. Any scrap of informa-tion, such as from a visit to the orphanage or a meeting with a foster mother, can provide another bit of identity for these children, which their mothers now eagerly seek. Unlike Charlotte, these women have found only scraps.

Women who had open adoptions could provide their children with more than just scraps. Birth parents were available but kept at a distance unless women set relationships in motion. I asked Gina how she resolved Isabelle's meeting with her birth mother, Bethany (described in chapter 6). Gina and Isabelle flew to visit Bethany and her kin when Isabelle was nine years old. There was a second meet-ing when Isabelle visited her birth mom by herself for a weekend, and in between there were many e-mails while Bethany completed college. Bethany and her mother came to Isabelle's bat mitzvah. As part of the ceremony at their congre-gation the Torah is literally passed from one generation to the next before the child reads from it. On the podium stood Gina and her mother as well as Bethany and her mother, and the Torah passed through both birth family and adoptive family to the child they all shared in common. Isabelle often wondered out loud to Gina about what life would be like if her birth parents had stayed together and kept her, a picture of an alternative family that is a usual fantasy for adopted chil-dren. Despite these fantasies, Gina still thought that Isabelle was better off with concrete knowledge and contact with her birth relatives. Recently, Isabelle had asked if they could try to find her birth father, because as a biracial child, she is presently engaged with issues of racial identity, and her African American father, who had all but disappeared, is an important link. As much as Gina tried to find space where she and Isabelle could be together as a multicultural family, Isabelle had a different perspective on race and the significance of it in her life than her mother. At the time of the interview she liked to spend time at the homes of her black friends as she worked out this part of her identity. Gina continued to incor-porate Isabelle's birth kin in their lives in private and public ways. Her teenage daughter confronted the complexities of her identity with a mother who offered her many pieces and opportunities to engage them rather than deny them over the course of her life. Her child was resourceful and turned to others to work out aspects of herself, a process that her mother wholeheartedly endorsed.

Unlike Gina, not all mothers have the answers to their children's questions, nor can they weave together the various adults who helped create their child with their family. Women are not magicians who can produce genetic or birth parents out of a hat when their children start asking. However, the children of these women must eventually reckon on their own with the master narrative of the two-parent heterosexual nuclear family that is considered normative. Children become weavers of their own stories, using the birth narrative their mother gave to create their own explanations of how they came to be. When they were young, the mothers spun the stories of fathers they had never met, or they became the gatekeepers to those who lurked around the edges of family life. However, at a certain point, children must articulate on their own answers to the barrage of questions as to where they came from. During early school years, children developed pat answers. One woman told me when her adopted child was in preschool she would say to her friends, "I have a mom in America and my birth father lives in China." Children who are adopted usually indicate that they have birth parents elsewhere, and this seems to cover the issue of fathers—at least that everyone has one, even if he is not a dad. Other children from donor-assisted families reiterate their mother's version of their birth stories. In the case of anonymous donors, they tell their friends that they have a genetic father (whom sometimes they call their donor) and maybe they will meet him someday; in the case of known donors, they say they have met their genetic father, but he lives elsewhere.

The father question is really about a tangible dad, though young children are answering it by conflating biological fathers with social dads.[16] Children's answers became more sophisticated in the elementary and middle school years, sometimes diverging from the story their mother gave them. When asked about his "other parent," one male child conceived with an anonymous donor would boldly comment, "There is no father and my mom did not have a boyfriend when I was born either." This child is making a definite claim: that no man is his father and the subject is closed. Other children give vaguer statements to their friends.[17] In fact, often the language of donors is made commonplace in preschool and kindergarten classrooms, where children are expected to describe their family, as is the possibility of adoptive and birth parents. The complexity of these family structures may have eluded children initially, but the presentation of these structures by children as possible and even normal has expanded acceptance. As harsh as kids' peer groups may be, as they age they begin to find common ground and shared interests with their classmates. Their athletic abilities, their beautiful singing voices, their humor, or their leadership becomes the stuff that results in friendships and admiration of one's peers. Further, the curiosity over birth stories becomes stale and the questions eventually stop. Since these families did not move around, consistent relationships and stable communities with many different forms of family save the children from having to continually explain themselves. Diversity of families has made the single-parent home just another structure in the spectrum rather than an oddity. In short, women's fears that their child would be ostracized because of their family structure (including the way their family was formed) never materialized, partially because of their commitment to weaving their families into local communities as well as their birth narrative into their families.

## Not on Welfare: Exploding and Shrinking Careers

The short answer to the question of imminent financial disaster is that no woman in this study was living on welfare when I called for an update. As a matter of fact, the median income for this group was $66,615, compared to the median family income in Massachusetts of $68,701.[18] Only three women were unemployed, two just in the previous several months—they had worked at their present jobs for over a decade when their place of employment closed or their division was phased out. But they were hopeful about finding employment rather quickly, though one woman was still without a job after two years of searching in the floundering technology market. To get by, she refinanced her house several times. A fourth was living off interest from her trust fund on a motherhood hiatus from employment. A few others were also laid off at early points, but they had found other employment in their area of expertise within six months. Overall, stable employment was a fixture in these women's lives.

Having a home to call one's own is a goal women attained. The good jobs already placed them solidly in the middle class and had given many the opportunity to purchase homes at the time of the first interview. Nearly half (48 percent) owned property, a major symbol of family stability, when I first spoke with them. Since that time an additional ten women had become first-time home or condo owners, including three who bought for the first time with spouses. Ten women without partners sold their first homes and bought larger ones. Real estate, a major asset, could be parlayed into a larger investment. Not only providing economic stability, these houses provided the social stability of a community. By placing their families in neighborhoods where their children would make school friends and they would become part of a broader community life, they secured middle-class citizenship for their kids as they displayed their ability to be good providers as moms. Most women tried to find new housing in their town, often in the same school district; those who moved farther did so before their children were in the first grade, usually moving to the suburbs for better public schools.[19] Women with multifamily homes were most likely to remain in their original housing, as rents in the Boston area had increased significantly, providing an important source of income (which was often used for expensive extracurricular activities for their children). In general, housing provided middle-class status through both the income it produced and the social ties with other middle-class families it fostered.[20] Membership in the middle class took precedence over traditional family structure as more of the suburbs filled with divorced families and other variations.

Home ownership is all-important. Not only does it ensure middle-class membership for their children, but also it shelters these women's future from the pinch of having only one paycheck, no matter how substantial. However, for the present time, women continue to worry about money despite stable employment. Their paycheck, combined with other sources of income, covered their expenses but often did not stretch into the future. When asked about money, women shrugged off the worries of paying college tuition by projecting the hope that their children would find scholarship money or go to state schools. Boston and the surrounding communities had become among the most expensive areas in the country, and living there had taken a toll on their ability to save—one woman who had a substantial paycheck said she felt "fragile."[21] Because so many had bought property before the housing market exploded, their mortgages were small and their potential profit (and bargaining power) is increasing.[22] These homes are the saving grace for living on one paycheck in eastern Massachusetts.

The majority of women continued to work in the same or related occupations as they had at the time of the first interviews, especially those who worked in the helping professions (making minor changes to increase their clientele or moving into institutional settings). Half had changed jobs and had different employers, using their degrees and skills in new ways (such as moving from a clinical social work position to a professorship), often increasing their hours of employment as their children moved to elementary and middle schools. Other women found new ways to earn a living (from receptionist to police officer, from consultant to financial officer in a private college), but the poorest women in this study, especially those employed in child care, largely continued to work in the same positions.

Often women found ways to carve up the week's schedule differently to give them a few longer days in order to shorten the other days so that they would be available for afternoon and evening activities with children. Annette had left her managerial position in a technology firm when her son was young, transitioning to a small consulting firm. Recently, she reported choosing to work part time at a new job in technology, noting, "It's such a relief to have time to structure on my own!" Annette is not alone in the group of women who continued to downshift their careers, though only a few women were working less than full time when I called for an update. The rest of the women tried to find niches, such as Joy described, to be available in the evenings, with the possibility of working after children were in bed. Theresa, for example, left her very lucrative corporate career for a job within the school system as director of technology. She took a major pay cut but enjoyed not having to constantly travel, which meant she could be around for her children. Many women left large organizations and became their own bosses (in consulting and law in particular). They could better control the hours they worked. Overall, they left the fast track of organizational life for scaled-back but satisfying employment.

A few women dramatically accelerated their careers, exploding their paycheck and climbing the organizational ladder. Some did so through education. While employed at other jobs, two women who held advanced degrees had gone back to school in the evenings in order to completely change their employ-ment (to earn an MBA in order to broaden career mobility in engineering and to transition from a financial analyst to a massage therapist). Two women had also completed four-year college degrees and another the police academy, which gave them larger paychecks (and allowed at least one woman who had been piecing together employment to finally land a single adequate job). Other women took on more at their jobs as their children became heavily involved in school. Naomi, for example, a real estate broker, increased her work commitment to seventy hours a week, with some weekends. When I spoke with Naomi last, she was a property manager with another firm, but she took her lead from other women in the organ-ization to jump at this career change, doubling her paycheck. Valerie took con-trol of her employment as well as taking a new step in her career—she expanded her own business, increasing her paycheck and diversifying the kind of work she was taking on. When I spoke with her over the phone, her small business had recently won a major government contract, a feat that will keep her employed for several years. Even though she had married, Valerie was still the main breadwinner.

Because most of the women had completed educational and career goals before having children, I was not surprised to hear that employment had not drastically changed. Work remained an important part of their identity, though women continued to downshift and transition in the ways I observed in chapter 8. While I was cheered to hear that several women who had just been getting by at the time of the earlier interview had now completed their educations and found good jobs, the fact the most women's employment was relatively stable in the intervening years is reassuring—it shows that educated women can make it financ-ially on their own. However, I did find it disconcerting that home ownership, which is the security blanket for many of older women, was simply out of reach for the younger women. To be fair, with the rising cost of living and raising a child today, doing what these women do is becoming more costly and therefore more difficult. For this generation of single mothers, though they might not be able to afford luxuries or have college funds for their children, the future looks stable. In short, single motherhood did not become a career death sentence, though it definitely entailed rethinking time commitments and reinventing themselves.

## Empty Nest: Life after Hard-Won Children

When I asked women over the phone about major life changes since we last spoke, many of them told me of their anticipation for life after children. By the time I called them for the update, women had begun to think about their lives once hard-won children left home, heading for college. Preparation for the empty nest was under way—these women again had become "thinkers," contem-plating their next major life transition. A smaller group had already watched their children leave for college and had their post-child life already in progress. As they began to think about what they wanted to do with the rest of their lives, some talked about renewing old friendships or finding new ones; others considered developing new interests, while still others talked about maybe finding a partner as intensive child rearing came to a close.

Those women with children completing middle school or in their early high school years are in a new stage where they have a taste of life without their child. As teenagers become more independent and have their own social lives that often include a Friday night dance or a sports competition, a Saturday night movie or sleepover at a friend's, mothers ask, "What will it be like without my child?" As Erika told me:

> First it was unnerving. Then I sat down, had a glass of wine, and listened to some good music that I selected, and I thought, "This is actually nice." But I knew that she would be home at the end of the weekend. As much as I did miss her, I knew that this next stage would be both of us exploring and becoming more independent. I have started to date in the last year and I have realized that even at my age I can do this and it is fun. Would I like a companion? You bet. I also want my daughter to leave for college and not worry about me. So, I am beginning to think about all the things I want to do—creative things and more—that I have put on hold.

Time for themselves is either lost or transformed when women become mothers. That time can now can be recaptured. Women reclaim hobbies or develop long-standing interests once the intensive early years of motherhood start becoming a distant memory. In the present, many dabbled with independent lives and their thoughts turned to how they would occupy themselves after the nest emptied, again finding time for themselves. They looked ahead even further to retirement, confronting a question mark as to how they would fund their post-employment years.

Among the women with a middle schooler at the time of the first interview, Colleen provides one of the most dramatic examples of a post-child life. When her daughter was in high school and her property was worth double what she had originally paid, Colleen sold the Victorian home that had housed her bed-and-breakfast. She bought a smaller home in the neighborhood, mortgage free, using the real estate profit to support her transition back into a full-time career as an artist. When her daughter entered college on a scholarship, Colleen made a big move, deciding to start a bed-and-breakfast again—this time in Africa. When I spoke to her on the phone, she was preparing for her international move, still planning on spending winters in Massachusetts.

Other women spoke of less definitive and daring plans for their empty nest. The words of one woman resonated in the group as a whole, saying, "I really need to figure out life separate from having a partner." Many women still hoped to find a companion, and "finding a relationship" was still on their agenda. More broadly, women spoke of wanting to travel, explore old hobbies and new interests, and invest more time in friends. As another woman said, "We are lucky if we get to use all the potential we are born with. I'm trying to tap into some of the things I have let lay dormant. I don't want to die not having tried those." She continued, "We all have dreams at different stages in our lives." The dream of these women to have and raise a child is coming to a close—they believe they must reinvent themselves one more time, finding a new dream to put at center stage.

## Reflecting Back

These women's stories had changed much, much more than I ever expected. Hearing the new ways women explained their lives and choices today made them alive for me once again, not simply subjects with paper transcripts. It is no secret that life does not always turn out as planned, and in many ways, this reality is what characterizes our human existence. I realized that it was in the telling and retelling of their stories that each woman recasts her humanity. That is to say, their own rewriting of their master plan, especially their agenda to resequence children and marriage, shows the very inconsistencies and changes that bring them once again to life. How they have adapted and integrated, making sense of less than tidy situations, is what I find most compelling. Humanness is best captured by life's vicissitudes and the way in which one navigates one's path through them. It is the humanity of these women's stories that I hope that I have conveyed not only in this epilogue, but also in the book as a whole. The women you have met here are not simply quotes and trends, but part of the process of making unexpected and complicated choices as women, of which it is my job to make sense and fit into a larger picture.

# Appendix 1

---

## DEMOGRAPHIC APPENDIX: FEATURED WOMEN

Below are short summaries of women featured in the book. This appendix is meant to connect featured women with basic demographic information, details too cumbersome to include in the body of the book. All women have been given pseudonyms, and I have changed certain details for some women to protect their identity, such as sex of child, exact occupation, and community of residence. However, income, level of education, race, age, and routes to motherhood are unchanged. All information is consistent with that given at the time of the first interview, with the exception of income, which is approximated here to correspond to 2004–2005 dollars. Social class is complicated to assess. Following Ellwood and Jencks (2001), I have taken into account both education and income as I assigned each woman to a social class. The page numbers that follow the description of each woman are a good tool with which to trace the women featured in the book.

**Abby Pratt-Evans**, a white 38-year-old woman, has one child, age 2, whom she gave birth to using anonymous donor sperm. Middle-class, Abby has two master's degrees, works as a teacher, and makes $60,000 a year. She owns her own condo, and her mother provided child care for Abby's son, who has recently begun to transition into family day care. (6, 8, 14, 57–60, 65, 69, 71, 162, 171, 178, 206–7, 215, 237n1 (Ch. 4))

**Althea Williams**, an African American 40-year-old woman, has one child, age 3, whom she conceived with a known donor who lives abroad. Middle-class, Althea works as a professor and makes $85,000 a year. She lives in a multifamily home that she owns and rents out two units, bringing in an additional $34,000 a year. (16–17, 44, 78–79, 205, 206, 215–16)

**Angie Dasilva**, a white 46-year-old woman, has one child, age 3, whom she conceived with a known donor, who is a parenting partner. Middle-class and with several advanced degrees, she works as a self-employed consultant, making $39,000 a year while receiving an additional $60,000 a year from her trust fund. She owns her condo. (148–49, 150, 151, 216, 248n9 (Ch. 7))

**Annette Barker**, a white 42-year-old woman, has one child, age 3, whom she gave birth to using a known donor, who became involved with the child. Upper-middle-class, Annette works as a manager in a technology firm and makes $100,000 working four days a week. She has a small trust fund and owns her condo. (7–8, 33–34, 46, 81–83, 156, 162–63, 178, 205, 211, 216)

**Barbara Graham**, an African American 45-year-old woman, has one African American child, age 5, whom she conceived using an anonymous donor. Middle-class, holding several degrees, Barbara works as a professional in a university, making $78,000 a year. She owns a two-family home. Her mother, whom she considers a parenting partner, occupies the other apartment. A lesbian woman, Barbara also has a steady romantic partner. (18, 152–53, 216)

**Beth Marshall**, a white 41-year-old woman, has one child, age 2, whom she adopted through the Department of Social Services as an infant, rare for a white baby. Middle-class, she works as the director of a nonprofit organization, making $65,000 a year, adding to her paycheck with a yearly $10,000 gift from her parents. She has a master's degree and owns her condo. (172, 216)

**Brandy Heines**, an African American 26-year-old woman, has one child, age 3. Working-class and with a high school degree, she works as a child care worker in a day care center and makes $25,000 a year. She receives two days of free child care for her daughter at the center where she works, and her mother helps with child care two days a week. She rents her apartment. (95–96, 164, 206, 216, 242n9, 242n12)

**Cara DeSouza**, a white 32-year-old woman, has one biracial child, age 3, the result of a one-time encounter. Lower-middle-class, Cara, who has a two-year associate's degree, owns a salon and makes $80,000 a year. She rents her home and her parents help her with child care. (91–92, 216)

**Caroline Barton**, a white 46-year-old woman, adopted two sibling sets. At the time of the interview, they were ages 18 and 19 and ages 4, 7, and 8. Middle-class, she works as a high-level administrator employed by the state, making $60,000 a year while completing a doctoral degree. She receives approximately $10,000 a year in financial assistance for the younger sibling group from a government agency to pay for the special services her children need. (121–23, 216)

**Charlotte Alvord**, a white 48-year-old woman, has one child, age 5, whom she adopted from Romania. Middle-class, Charlotte works as a professor, making $70,000 a year, and lives in campus housing. (10, 11, 183–84, 207–8, 217)

**Claudia D'Angelo**, a white 52-year-old woman, has one son, age 7, whom she adopted from Russia. Middle-class, Claudia works as a clinical psychologist and makes $50,000; she receives additional yearly money from her mother. She owns a multi-family home, renting out two apartments. She has a long-term romantic partner, Carl. (xii–xiv, 3, 5–6, 8–9, 11–12, 20, 24, 25, 48–49, 110–12, 145, 146, 158, 162, 173, 180, 203, 217)

**Colleen O'Neil**, a white 53-year-old woman, has one child, age 13, the result of a planned pregnancy with her then-boyfriend. Middle-class, Colleen works as an artist and runs a bed-and-breakfast, bringing in $55,000 a year from the latter. A small trust fund left by her father, who lived with her until his death, adds $10,000 a year, replacing his Social Security check, which used to add to her family income. She owns her own home. (90, 92, 93–94, 168, 213, 217, 242n10)

**Corina Joseph**, a white 44-year-old woman, has one child, age 3½, whom she gave birth to using an anonymous donor. Middle-class, Corina, who holds a series of degrees, works on contract as a software developer and made $40,000 a year at the time of her interview, an amount that can vary drastically. She owns her own home and usually rents out two rooms. (70–72, 217)

**Crystal Stevens**, an African American 28-year-old woman, has one child, age 3½, the result of chancing pregnancy with her then-boyfriend. Working-class, she works as a secretary, making $20,000, while finishing up her associate's degree. She rents her apartment. (93, 217)

**Darlene Caroff**, a white 47-year-old woman, has one child, age 23, the result of a chanced pregnancy. Working-class with a high school diploma, she works a secretary, making $50,000 a year. She rents her apartment. (101–2, 217, 242n10)

**Deborah Toland**, a white 44-year-old bisexual woman, has one child, age 9, whom she gave birth to using a known donor, who has escalated his involvement. Lower-middle-class, Deborah, who has a bachelor's in education, works as a child care worker in a day care center and makes $25,000 a year. She owns a two-family home and rents the other unit, bringing in $12,000 a year. (72–73, 75, 217, 240n28)

**Ellen Hammond**, a white 31-year-old woman, has a daughter, age 2, the result of what she terms an unplanned pregnancy with her boyfriend, Gavin, who remains sporadically involved. Middle-class, Ellen works as a financial analyst and makes $105,000 a year. She lives in and rents out rooms in the house her mother owns. (12, 48, 86–88, 89, 92, 96, 102, 156, 159, 162, 169, 178, 180, 206, 217)

**Elyce Fischer**, a white 37-year-old lesbian, has one child, age 4, whom she conceived using a known donor. Middle-class, Elyce was working as a doctor until her daughter was born, making $48,000 a year. As she transitions to a new career, her parents are supporting her financially. She owns her own home. (41, 217–18)

**Erika Bailey**, a white 49-year-old woman, has one child, age 4½, whom she adopted from China. Middle-class, she works as a director of communications, making $83,000 a year. She owns a two-family house, the rent from the other unit adding $15,000 to her income. (186, 213, 218)

**Evelyn Martinez**, a 28-year-old Hispanic woman, has one child, age 4, the result of what she terms an unintended pregnancy. She is finishing an associate's degree as well as applying for a bachelor's degree program. Working-class, she does part-time work as a personal trainer, making $16,000 a year. She rents her apartment. (49, 146, 218)

**Fran Tobin**, a white 36-year-old-woman, has an 18-month-old baby, whom she gave birth to using anonymous donor sperm. Upper-middle-class, she owns her own home and relies on her mother to take care of her child, allowing her to build up her client base. As a self-employed consultant, she made $200,000 in 2004, an amount that can vary. (33, 163, 218)

**Gina Schecter**, a white 51-year-old woman, has a biracial (white and black) daughter, age 7, whom she adopted privately as an infant. Middle-class, Gina works as a manager and makes $58,000 a year. She rents an apartment. (21–24, 28, 30, 31–32, 119–21, 123–24, 125–26, 126–27, 130, 131, 180, 208, 218)

**Heather Johnson**, a white 43-year-old woman, has one child, age 10, whom she gave birth to using a known donor. Working-class, Heather works as a secretary and makes $17,000 a year. She rents a house and has a foster child in her home, adding to her income. (xviii, 80–81, 218)

**Hillary Doyle**, a white 38-year-old woman, has two sons, a newborn and one age 5½, both conceived using the same known donor. Middle-class and holding several advanced degrees, she works as a nurse four days a week, making $55,000 a year. She rents her apartment, and her parents are willing to help if she needs financial assistance. (181, 185, 187, 205–6, 218, 254n15)

**Janica Louis**, an African American 50-year-old woman, has two African American children, ages 14 and 16, whom she adopted domestically via the Department of Social Services. Middle-class, Janica works as a school administrator, earning $94,000 a year. Janica's mother, a parenting partner, lives in the home that Janica owns. Janica's sister, who bought the multi-family house with Janica, lives in the apartment below. (17, 34, 115–17, 124–25, 150–51, 152, 155–56, 167, 207, 218, 245nn19–20, 248n9 (Ch. 7))

**Jasmine Duarte**, a 27-year-old woman of Caribbean descent, has one child, age 3, the result of what she calls an unintended pregnancy with her then-boyfriend.

Working-class, Jasmine works as a secretary, cocktail waitress, and housekeeper, making a total of $18,000 a year. She rents her apartment, is finishing up her associate's degree, and is applying to a B.A. program. (159–60, 162, 164, 218–19)

**Jennifer Sanders**, a white 42-year-old woman, has a 10-month-old baby, whom she gave birth to using a known donor. Upper-middle-class, she works as a therapist and makes $90,000 a year. She owns her own condo. The second time I talked to Jennifer in my first round of interviews, Jennifer was about to be married. (76–77, 78, 133, 143–44, 157, 171, 204–5, 219)

**Joy McFadden**, a white 47-year-old woman, has two children, ages 7 and 11, to whom she gave birth using anonymous donor sperm. Upper-middle-class, Joy works as a physician, makes $185,000 a year, and owns her own house. (ix–xii, 3, 5–6, 8, 11–12, 20, 24, 25, 27, 31, 144–45, 158, 162, 172, 186, 200, 204, 211, 219, 250n20, 253n3 (Epilogue))

**Kerry Brennan**, a white 43-year-old lesbian woman, has one child, age 4, whom she gave birth to using an anonymous donor. Middle-class, Kerry works as a film producer and makes $75,000 a year, which is supplemented by the $15,000 a year she receives from the rental unit in the two-family home she owns. She also has a roommate with whom she barters child care for rent. (62–63, 169–70, 201, 219)

**Leigh Newell**, a white 49-year-old woman, has one child, age 4, whom she adopted from China. Middle-class, Leigh transitioned from working as a journalist to working as an editor, making $75,000 a year. Her child is in family day care, and she owns her own home. (8, 219)

**Lily Baker**, a white 40-year-old woman, has a 1-year-old child, whom she gave birth to using anonymous donor sperm. Middle-class, Lily works as a teacher and makes $54,000 a year, while tutoring brings in another $12,000. She splits her rent with a roommate. (9–10, 11, 25, 27–28, 32, 49, 219)

**Lori-Ann Stuart**, a white 41-year-old lesbian, has one child, age 4, whom she conceived using a known donor. Middle-class, Lori-Ann is a school administrator and makes $55,000 a year. She rents an apartment, which she shares with a roommate. She relies on a group of friends to watch her child on the days she works nonstandard hours. (37–39, 40, 41, 43, 45, 46, 47–48, 74–75, 159, 162, 185, 205, 219)

**Maeve Stanton**, a white 30-year-old woman, has two children, ages 6 months and 8 years. The younger child, African American, was adopted domestically through a private agency, while the older son was conceived while she was changing birth control pills. The older son's father has been a sporadic visitor for the last few years. On the edge of middle-class, Maeve works mainly as a freelance writer but also teaches evening college classes, earning a combined income of $30,000 a year. She is gambling on selling her first novel to allow her to buy a home. (13–14, 90, 92, 98, 100–101, 102, 154–55, 219)

**Marli Simmons**, a white bisexual 46-year-old woman, has one child, age 3, whom she adopted from China. Middle-class, she works as a professor, making $60,000 a year with an additional $10,000 gift from her mother. She rents her home. (107–8, 112–13, 114, 127–28, 129–30, 219–20, 244nn13–14, 244n16, 245n20)

**Mary Conners**, a white 49-year-old woman, has one child, age 13, the result of chancing pregnancy with her then-boyfriend, who serves as a parenting partner even though the romance ended. Middle-class, Mary works as a teacher and makes $55,000 a year. She owns her own home, in which she periodically rents rooms. (99–100, 153–54, 156, 220, 242n14)

**Melissa Manning**, a white 40-year-old woman, has twins, age 4, whom she gave birth to using an anonymous donor. Middle-class, Melissa works as a clinical social worker with a private practice and makes $65,000 a year, supplemented by a trust fund that yields $20,000 annually. She owns her own home. (64, 66, 69, 181–82, 188, 220)

**Nadine Margolis**, a white 39-year-old woman, has twins, age 2, whom she conceived using an anonymous donor. Middle-class, Nadine works as an engineer and makes $100,000 a year. She rents her home, hoping to buy in the neighborhood. (25–26, 30–31, 43, 64–65, 66, 69, 173, 174, 174–75, 186, 220)

**Naomi Henderson**, a white 33-year-old woman, has one child, age 1, the result of a chanced pregnancy with a boyfriend who fathered a child with another woman at the same time. Middle-class, she works as a property manager, making $70,000 a year. She rents her home. (15, 96–97, 206, 220)

**Nicole Shiff**, a white 45-year-old woman, has two biracial (Native American and white) children, ages 12 and 15, whom she adopted out of foster care at ages $6\frac{1}{2}$ and 8. Middle-class, Nicole works as a self-employed consultant and makes between $60,000 and $120,000 a year. She owns her own house. (10, 11, 220)

**Patricia Sullivan**, a white 45-year-old woman, has one African American child, age 3, whom she adopted through a private agency. Middle-class, she works as a nurse, making $50,000 a year. A former lover occasionally helps her out financially. She rents her apartment and sublets out a room. Her roommate has a special relationship with the child. (114, 115–16, 117, 128–29, 163, 166, 168–69, 220)

**Penny Hawkins**, a white 39-year-old woman, has a $1\frac{1}{2}$-year-old child, whom she adopted from Romania after her infant conceived using an anonymous donor died. Middle-class, Penny works as an editor and makes $57,000 a year. Her widowed mother moved into the home Penny owns to help care for her child. (15, 220)

**Rebecca Thompson**, a white 45-year-old woman, has a 4-year-old child, whom she adopted out of China as an infant. Middle-class, Rebecca works as a lawyer and makes $130,000 a year. She owns her own house and runs a small bed-and-breakfast out of her house, which pays for the property taxes. (15, 104–5, 106, 107, 109–10, 112, 131, 163–64, 165, 184, 187–88, 220)

**Rosalie Rodriguez**, a 22-year-old Hispanic woman, has a 9-month-old baby, the result of what she terms an unintended pregnancy. She is a college senior and does part-time office work, making $15,000 a year. She rents her apartment. Upon graduation, she hopes to improve her income. (34–35, 42, 201, 221)

**Sienna Martin**, a white 50-year-old woman, has one child, age 3, whom she adopted from China. Middle-class, she works as a literary agent, making $45,000 a year, supplemented by $8,000 from a small trust fund. She owns her own home, which she shares with her live-in lover, who is not a parenting partner. (145–46, 200–201, 221, 247n2, 254n5)

**Sophie Taylor**, a white 39-year-old woman, has one child, age 1, whom she gave birth to using an anonymous donor. Middle-class, Sophie works as a clinical social worker and makes $58,000 a year. She owns her own home. (40, 41, 45, 221)

**Susan Jaffe**, a white 48-year-old woman, has one child, age 9, whom she conceived using an anonymous donor. Middle-class, Susan works as an occupational therapist and makes $65,000 a year, supplemented by the $5,000 she makes from outside clients. She rents an apartment. (4, 5, 19–20, 66–67, 68–69, 187, 221, 238n12)

**Theresa Stoppard**, a white 42-year-old woman, has one child, age 1½, whom she gave birth to using an anonymous donor. Upper-middle-class, Theresa works as a corporate sales vice president and makes $110,000 a year, with a $25,000 bonus. She also receives $10,000 from rental property. She owns her own home, and her mother, who could no longer live alone, has recently moved in with her. She leaves her child with paid help in her home, not using her mother for child care. (70, 211, 221)

**Trish Maloney**, a white 48-year-old woman, has one child, age 11. A gay woman, she gave birth using a known donor, who is a contracted co-parent to the child with his male partner. Middle-class by virtue of her master's degree, Trish works full time as a social worker, making $20,000 a year. She rents her apartment in a building that she loves. (15–16, 147–48, 150, 151–52, 221, 248n9 (Ch. 7), 253n3 (Part III))

**Valerie Newman**, a white 38-year-old woman, has one mixed-race (white and Hispanic) child, age 1, the result of a passionate affair. Middle-class, Valerie works as a self-employed consultant and makes $100,000 a year. Her ex-boyfriend gives her regular financial gifts. She owns her own home. (166, 221)

**Veronica Baher**, a white 42-year-old lesbian, has one child, age 5, whom she adopted from Central America. Middle-class, Veronica works as a social worker and makes $30,000 a year, which is supplemented by a gift of $10,000 a year from her parents. She owns her home. (18, 144, 221)

# Appendix 2

## METHODS AND SAMPLING

This study was triggered by a small but intriguing advertisement in a Brookline, Massachusetts, community newspaper.

The headline read "SINGLE ♡ ISSUES." It went on:

> **Is single motherhood for me?** 9 sessions
> on decision-making for women whose biological
> clock is ticking. Explore single parenting options
> vs. childfree living. Call Jane Smith at . . .

The ad piqued my curiosity. As a family sociologist, I had been following the data on the rise in single motherhood. Ever since the famous incident of then vice president Dan Quayle attacking the fictional TV sitcom character Murphy Brown for becoming a single mother and hence a bad role model, I had been keeping track of the mismatch between media portrayals and demographic reports on single mothers. I immediately dialed Jane Smith, told her I was a social scientist, and asked if I could observe her group. I explained that I had a child through marriage, but I was interested in finding out more about older women who were considering becoming or who had become single mothers. She recommended I attend a meeting of the local chapter of Single Mothers by Choice, which met once a month in a neighboring town.

I entered the building feeling the same sort of stage fright that overtakes my body each semester as I begin teaching a new group of students. Who would I find attending this meeting? Would they kick me out because I had a child and a husband? Would they grant me permission to attend their monthly sessions? And how did they manage to raise a family and simultaneously hold down a job when two-earner couples struggled with the challenges of both?

I knew that this group might be able to answer some of the questions I had about the process that led women to become single mothers. The data I read told me only about outcomes; they didn't tell me how women came to their decision to become a single mom. What did it mean to them to make this choice?

The meeting was just starting as I entered the room. This first meeting consisted of self-described "thinkers"—women who were trying to decide whether or not single motherhood was for them. They were meeting to discuss questions that the women who would attend the later meeting had already faced. The second of that afternoon's meetings featured a panel discussion by experts and experienced single moms and included a mix of women in different stages of becoming mothers. Some women were trying various routes to motherhood; others were pregnant or in an adoption queue. Finally, there were the women who had children ranging from newborns to age twelve. The older ones played outside but joined in for the potluck dinner.

The women seemed a bit hostile when my assistant and I were introduced. We were not single mothers, and we told them so. They wanted assurances that we were not right-wing zealots or nosy journalists who might do them harm, intentionally or not. They wanted to know more than just my professional credentials and past publications; they wanted to know which side of the contested debates about family I supported. I suppose that my being a professor of women's studies and a sociologist helped a bit, but their concerns were more personal. Could I capture their world accurately? Would I?

I left understanding that these women were different from me in more ways than I had anticipated. Most important was that I had not expected to find that these women made becoming a parent the primary focus of their lives. At the moment, this was what seemed to define these women in a way that I could not fathom for myself, as I saw parenthood as one of a number of identities I had, something that was an outgrowth of a relationship with another adult, not separate from one. I needed to understand why and how they placed motherhood at the center of their lives.

The organization was interesting from a social science perspective because it operated as a focus group at each meeting. At least part of each afternoon meeting was spent discussing topics the women put together. For instance, a newly pregnant woman asked a lot of questions of the other mothers about their experiences with child care. Often my field notes were about topics common to all mothers. But impromptu panel discussions—where several women would volunteer on the spot to talk about their concerns—demonstrated unique issues they faced because of the route to motherhood. When did other women start to date again? a pregnant woman asked. Would a Big Brother program provide male role models for her children? another new mother wondered.

Ultimately, this local organization provided a wealth of information that we could turn into researchable questions for in-depth interviews.

## The Study

This is an in-depth, audiotaped, interview study of sixty-five single mothers who were over the age of twenty when they had their first child and were economically self-sufficient at the time of the interview.[1] Initially, I was interested in the decision-making processes that led to older women becoming single mothers and whether or not fathers were in fact becoming bystanders to family life. I was also interested in extending my prior research on the relationship between work and family to look at how women without partners manage to combine both.[2] Therefore, women were eligible for inclusion in the sample if they were unmarried and not living with either the father of their child or a romantic partner at the time of birth or adoption *and* at the time of the first interview. I wanted to avoid women who were cohabiting with someone who was defined both as a romantic partner and as a parenting partner.

National reports of out-of-wedlock births, written primarily by demographers, focus on birth as the outcome of pregnancy.[3] It is not possible from these reports to learn about the process that led to pregnancy. It is my hunch that the vast majority of women become pregnant "accidentally"—a term that misdirects our attention to intent instead of birth control use or misuse. I wanted to include in this study women who had children through various routes to motherhood in order to look at the father's involvement after birth. Initially, I thought that women who become pregnant by anonymous donors would provide an interesting and extreme contrast, since the possibility for father involvement in daily life would be nonexistent. There are no national data on the number of women who become pregnant using anonymous donor sperm or known donor sperm.[4] The data on single mothers who adopt are also problematic.

Grounded theory initially informed my choice of sampling frame.[5] That is, I wanted to compare women who had the possibility for father involvement (e.g., they became accidentally pregnant) with women who did not (e.g., they were artificially inseminated using anonymous donor sperm). As I began the interviews, I discovered that the use of known donors was another route to motherhood, where the father of the child fit neither of my original categories. I later decided that I was missing a fourth route to motherhood: adoption. I struggled with how it compared to the other three possibilities and went back to do more interviews to fill in gaps provided by adoptive mothers. There are also no national data on the numbers of single women who adopt domestically or internationally.

Ultimately, I designed a sample that targeted women on the basis of known and unknown fathers.[6] Children of known fathers were either conceived through men recruited by the mother to be donors (biological fathers but not social fathers), or they were conceived within short-term or long-term relationships ("accidentally"). Children with unknown fathers were conceived through anonymous donor insemination or were adopted. Therefore, this is not a randomly drawn sample, but instead is meant to capture the less visible (and often secretive) ways that women become mothers in order to tease out various properties of social and sociological concepts as well as the conditions and limits of their applicability. Women were recruited through social networks. To avoid the likelihood of drawing upon insular social networks, no more than three women are known to each other.

I developed analytical constructs for each of the four categories. Once consistent patterns emerged from the interview narratives, I defined a category as analytically saturated. In the main text I discuss all four paths to motherhood. The Demographic Appendix gives short summary backgrounds only on each woman quoted in the book, her child(ren), and the route that led to motherhood. I arrived at this point with a sample that included thirteen women who became pregnant through the use of known donors, fifteen women who used anonymous donor sperm to have a child, seventeen women who became pregnant by chancing pregnancy, and twenty-two women who adopted.[7]

I monitored race, seeking to include women of different races in all categories. The majority of women who became pregnant using either anonymous donors or known donors were white, though two women were African or Caribbean American. The majority of women who adopted were white, though two women who adopted were black and three women who adopted were Hispanic (or part Hispanic). While I do not have national data on single mothers' race and their particular routes to motherhood, reading the anonymous donor Web sites leads me to the conclusion that there are few donors of color. Black middle-class women who adopted are also difficult to find, and it may be the case that they are more likely to adopt children informally. I decided to limit my search to women who legally adopted children as a parameter. However, I did call several private agencies, and they told me that they had few clients who were single African American women, and almost none of those sought to adopt outside of the United States. The public agencies would not answer my question about the race of single mothers adopting. The women who chanced pregnancy include five women of color. Certainly more research needs to be done on single mothers of color.

I also asked about sexual identity, though it was not a sampling criterion. During the first round of interviews there were seven women who self-identified as either lesbian or bisexual. Most had become pregnant using known and anonymous donors; two had had intercourse to become pregnant. They also adopted domestically and internationally. I deliberately decided during the fall of 2004 that I wanted to increase this group to eleven so that I could confidently include material that reflected their experience as single lesbian or bisexual women. Four of the eleven lesbian or bisexual women were Hispanic or African American.

The sixty-five interviews include women from twenty-one different communities in eastern Massachusetts conducted between 1995 and 2004 by a former graduate student, Faith I. T. Ferguson, or myself.[8] I sought to include women of different races and sexual identities even though neither was a major focus of how I conceptualized this study. While the majority of women in the study are white, 46 percent of the families are either transracial or minority. The majority of women are heterosexual; eleven are lesbian or bisexual single mothers. The majority of women had children between the ages of two and seven, though a quarter had children over eight at the time of the first interview.

Women in this study hold jobs as varied as lawyers and waitresses. While the majority of women in this study were salaried or contract employees on consulting or technical projects, a smaller group who worked in the lower-paid service sector earned hourly wages, and some even pieced together employment through two jobs. All the women in this study were employed and not collecting welfare at the time of the first interview and at the time of the update, though a few were in transition between jobs at either point.[9] In addition to wages, the majority of women in this study had a nonwage source of income, usually rental property, roommates, assistance from extended family, or child support. At the time of the first interview, 65 percent of the women (forty-two) held at least one advanced degree beyond a B.A., 22 percent (fourteen) held an associate's or bachelor's degree, and the remaining 14 percent of the women (nine) had completed at least high school, often with some college.

All the women in this study describe themselves as middle-class—even those with incomes under $20,000 and those with six-figure incomes. Income, education, and occupation do not capture the widespread belief expressed in the United States that everybody but the very poorest and the most wealthy is entitled to claim membership in the middle class. Despite the growing discrepancies between the richest and the poorest, there is a continued belief that everyone who is self-supporting is bound together in the "middle class." Because these women are neither the poorest (collecting welfare) nor the richest, they are using a cultural construction of "middle class," regardless of the traditional sociological markers mentioned above. A middle-class lifestyle provides for a future, not simply coping or hanging on financially from paycheck to paycheck. Even those women who have the least income in this study aspire to be part of the middle class and are proud that they are earning a living. Those women with the least income are "bettering themselves" through present enrollment in educational institutions and look forward to a future that is more financially secure. Between the first interview and the epilogue some women's incomes increased, while the change of careers led some women's incomes to decline. Most remained the same, increasing with inflation. I have provided incomes for the first round of interviews in 2004–2005 dollars in the demographic appendix for those women who appear in the book. Overall, the median income of the group was about the same as the median income for all families in Massachusetts at the the time of both the first interview and the epilogue. By the time of the updated interviews, their incomes ranged from under $20,000 per year to $210,000. The median income from wages at the time of the epilogue was $66,615, which approximates the median income for all families in Massachusetts in 2004.[10] I remind the reader that this does not include nonwage income.

In order to find women to interview, I "talked up" this study. That is, I mentioned it to everyone I came in contact with, hoping they would provide me with a lead to a single mother. For instance, when the study began, I moved into a new home and started a room-by-room renovation. I happily enjoyed the company of a steady stream of people in the trades working in my house, interrupting them when I need a break from my work and bringing my study up in the course of the conversation. I tested out parts of what I was writing up on people working in my house. I found their insights to be as useful as the insights my academic friends offered. Similarly, every time I took a cab, I talked to cab drivers about my study, and I mentioned it to the owners of the neighborhood stores I frequented, from the hairdresser to the dry cleaner. Every place I went, including professional appointments with lawyers, doctors, and accountants, I made sure to include my study in the conversation. I told people, "I am doing research," and they loved to ask, "What about?"—a terrific conversation opener. Just about everyone knows someone who is a single mother, since a third of all births today are to single mothers. These strangers provided lots of names. My daughter's several day care settings and after-school programs became additional sources of people to tap for other networks of single mothers.

When they told me about a woman they knew (in a few cases, they were relatives of a mother or child), I would ask them if they would ask the single mom they knew if I could contact her. If the contact was someone whom I had a momentary encounter with and we were swapping our stories about work (such as with a cab driver), I would give them my business card. I relied upon those who knew the single moms to broker an initial phone call because, as a total stranger, I needed entry and a good recommendation in order to ensure that the woman on the other end of the phone would not hang up on me. This way of gathering single mothers to interview made sense to me because often the informant told me information about the single mom that I couldn't initially ask on the phone but needed to know in order to understand whether or not she fit the parameters of my study. The informants knew intimate details that allowed me to decide if I should ask that person to speak with his or her friend about a possible interview. Further, the informant could say to the friend or relative, "I know her and she's nice or okay," or "I like what she has to say and she is looking for you to help her."

Once I had the name of a person who agreed to a phone conversation, I had to "sell" the study and myself. I told the women I called that economically self-sufficient single mothers are given little attention in the media or policy discussions, leaving both professionals and the wider population to believe that all single mothers are living at taxpayer expense. I hoped to counter such stereotypes. But, even more than countering stereotypes, I wanted to know how they had made the decision to become single moms and how they were managing to raise children and be employed. In addition, the graduate student I worked with and I both used our own status as mothers of young children instrumentally, to establish rapport before beginning the interviews.[11] Like the mothers we studied, we spent much of our free time in middle-class child-oriented environments (from day care centers to after-school programs to parks and enrichment and athletic programs). It is these commonalities that enabled us to swap information with these mothers, minimizing the traditional power differential between researcher and subject and emphasizing instead our shared status as working mothers.[12]

It also took me longer to have a baby than to receive my Ph.D. I knew the regimen that women who went through fertility treatments or insemination experienced and had shared the emotional roller coaster of becoming pregnant through medical intervention. This gave me familiarity with what to ask but also gave me a way to have a shared conversation. The women I connected with least on a personal level were the women who chanced pregnancy; my connection to these women was usually around other issues surrounding child rearing or work/family balance. All women were asked to explain the hard decisions of single motherhood without a life partner, an experience I did not share.

The interviews were very open-ended. Data were collected on topics ranging from their initial decision to parent (i.e., reproductive histories, relationships with friends, and lovers in the past and present, views on mothering) to present decisions on how they integrated employment, child rearing, and family life. Their assessment of how their children understood their family arrangements (including household kin and fictive kin) and what they perceived they needed to do to provide for their children emotionally, socially, and economically constituted the core in-depth questions. In addition, there was a set of standard demographic questions. The vast majority of women preferred to be interviewed in their homes; a few women preferred their workplace or my office.

The interviews were hand-coded using both descriptive and analytical codes, which were changed, added, or deleted as I worked with the transcripts. Computer-assisted searches were used only for simple counts (i.e., number of donor contracts, wills, prior marriages, or living with someone).

I asked if they wanted copies of the transcripts of their interviews. Those who wanted copies told me that they were interested in using the transcript as a record to share with their child about their decisions when their child was older. A few women e-mailed me years later to ask for copies because they wanted to understand what they had been thinking when I first interviewed them. Others whom I called for an update in January 2005 asked at that time if I could send them an e-mail attachment with the transcript of their original interview. Women asked for copies of published articles from the study; a few have volunteered to read drafts of the eventual book manuscript. I have stayed in touch, sending holiday cards yearly.

I interviewed a small group of women a second time because, as I wrote, I wanted more detail on certain topics. These interviews gave me the idea that in 2005 I would call back all the women interviewed at least four years earlier for an update on their lives. These phone interviews lasted between thirty minutes and an hour. I wanted to know how their lives had changed. The surprises are in the epilogue.

# NOTES

## Introduction

1. See U.S. Census Bureau 2005: 5, figure 1. This statistic reflects unmarried mothers, not differentiating between those cohabiting with a partner and those living alone. Among U.S. births outside of marriage, about 40 percent are to cohabiting couples (Seltzer 2004: 924). My study deliberately includes only women who were not living with a romantic partner at the time of the birth or adoption of the child *or* at the time of the first interview. However, the term *single* is problematic and will be explored in Chapter 7. Because cohabiting couples make up a significant portion of out-of-wedlock births, it is important to differentiate these women from those who choose cohabitation with children as an alternative to marriage.

2. Data on the age demographics of total unwed mothers from *National Vital Statistics Report*, written by Hamilton, Martin, and Sutton 2003: 4, Table C.

3. The proportion of unmarried women over the age of thirty who gave birth has increased from 8 percent in 1970 to 16 percent in 1993 (Ventura et al. 1995: 11) but has remained at 12 percent for the last three U.S. Census Bureau reports on the fertility of American women. For more on 2004 demographic data, including labor force participation, see U.S. Census Bureau 2005.

4. At the time of the first interview, 22 percent of the women (n = 14) held an associate's or bachelor's degree, and 65 percent (n = 42) held at least one advanced degree as well. The remaining 14 percent of the women (n = 9) had completed at least high school, often with some college. Education is the enabler for income and self-sufficiency, as much of a determinant of social class as the dollar amount of women's paychecks (Ellwood and Jencks 2001). Additional sources of income outside of employment will be discussed in Chapter 8.

5. I called back all the women I had interviewed at least four years earlier. See Appendix 2.

6. See Hewlett 2002 for older professional women and Edin and Kefalas 2005 for young low-income women.

# Chapter 1

1. The marital agreement asks men to share their wages with women in exchange for domestic service (food, sex, children, etc.). Historically there has been substantial variation in how stable this exchange has been.

2. Marriage once joined families in economic and political alliances. Often love occurred outside of marriage. Love as the basis for marriage is a modern invention and far from universal. Coontz (2005) argues that it is love as the basis for marriage that has made this institution fragile. The expectations for marriage as personal fulfillment were very low throughout history; love was a threat to a properly ordered marriage.

3. Economist Claudia Golden (2004) discusses the changing expectations of different cohorts of women since the turn of the century who faced different sets of constraints when negotiating their future employment and family. The women in my study are members of the two youngest cohorts that Golden describes, and they share the broader points she outlines. Careers came before family for the women born into the latter part of the baby boom generation. They postponed family life. But the youngest women in my study, who finished college after the mid-1980s, did not face the same singular career focus, having more employment and higher education opportunities. They see career and family as possible to have simultaneously even at the start of a career. Therefore, in my study they have their children at younger ages.

4. I thank Anita Garey for finding an early use of the term "compulsory motherhood." Feminist activist F. W. Stella Browne advocated in 1917 that birth control in Britain should be legalized, arguing that if motherhood is compulsory—a fundamental part of being a women— then women would be better mothers if they had control over its timing. Therefore, legalization of birth control by the government would protect and advance the mother's maternal love. More recently, feminist sociologist Arlene Stein (1997: 132) also uses the term compulsory motherhood when she describes the place of motherhood in early second-wave feminism. While these early feminists advance women's ability to compete with men on equal footing in order to counter male domination, there never was an explicit motherhood moratorium.

5. Adrienne Rich (1980) introduced the concept of "compulsory heterosexuality" in her writings. Rich argues that heterosexuality is social reinforced as the only "natural" inclination of all individuals. Heterosexuality establishes a social order that supports male privilege. My use of the term *compulsory* in the context of motherhood presumes a particular social authority in which women's compliance reinforces a particular gendered power structure.

6. Motherhood is now readily available to gay women. However, the way in which the rupture of compulsory motherhood and lesbian identity, very present in past generations, influences the current hold of compulsory motherhood on younger lesbian women is unclear.

7. Canadian sociologist Charlene Miall (1994: 403) finds that motherhood and fatherhood are not experienced the same way. Both men and women overwhelmingly believe that women want children more than men and they experience biological and social pressures to reproduce that men do not. As a result, these women and men experience infertility differently. The pain of infertility exposes the assumptions of compulsory motherhood (see especially Miall 1986; Sandelowski 1990).

8. See Zelizer 1985.

9. I use the terms *dad* and *father* in specific ways in the book in order to differentiate the biological function of fatherhood from the social one. I use the term *father* to refer to a genetic contributor to a child. A father may contribute gametes to a specific woman (through intercourse or artificial insemination), or he may donate his gametes to a sperm bank for use by unknown women. Some families use the term *donor* instead of *father*. *Dad* implies a social relationship to a child. These are not simply linguistic terms but ways in which men are distant and

unavailable or physically and emotionally involved in the lives of these children. I am not using a parallel set of terms to refer to mothers in this book, terming all the women in this sample as "mothers," defined through their social parenthood. In the case of adoption I designate birth fathers or mothers.

10. Garey 1999.

11. The majority of women in this study were raised in married, two-parent households, despite the rising divorce statistics of the 1970s and 1980s.

12. For a history of second-wave feminism and the women in the workplace, see Rosen 2001, in which she details the changes in social policy regarding women's rights within the family and employment opportunities. Particularly relevant to the context of this study, Rosen chronicles in President Kennedy's 1961 creation of the first Commission on the Status of Women, the 1964 Civil Rights Act, including Title VII, and the 1971 Title IX. By 1972, much of the critical legislation, particularly that pertaining to business and educational institutions that received federal funding, was in place for women's entry into the workplace.

13. See Hochschild 1989.

14. We once assumed, perhaps naively, that when women became a permanent part of the paid labor force, their husbands would begin to share equally in housework and child care (Hertz 1986). As we now know from over three decades of research on work and family among two-income couples, the division of labor between spouses is not equally shared. Further, the clash between work and family life has become an increasing concern as academics expose the ways American families experience a shortage of time. See especially Shor 1991; Hochschild 1997; Moen 2003; Jacobs and Gerson 2004; Milkie et al. 2004.

15. This reflects a general trend of women looking to the paid labor force for economic stability and social status, an increasing emphasis that results from an interplay of several factors. As Kathleen Gerson (1998: 12) noted, "In addition to the pull of job opportunities, factors such as divorce, declining male wages, the general devaluation of homemaking . . . have pushed most women to build their lives around paid work."

16. Sociologists have had a long-standing interest in studying love and marriage. As much as most of us believe in "falling in love," sociologist William J. Goode (1959) debunked the myth that there is free choice in love, arguing instead that it is controlled through various processes that maintain the social order. Other social psychologists focused on trying to capture the elusive idea of love by looking for ways to quantify mate selection (see especially Winch 1954). More recently, demographer Andrew Cherlin (2004) provided a summary of marriage's major changes that exposes the historical dimensions of changes in what individuals sought in marriage. The companionate model of the mid-twentieth century, based upon mutual affection and shared interests, gave way to a more "individualized model" rooted in self-realization and personal satisfaction. This is a harder goal to achieve in the context of marriage, which embeds the individual in obligation and responsibility to a partner and possibly children.

17. Women, whether heterosexual or lesbian, wanted ideally to parent with partners. Cohabitation was sometimes a way station for heterosexual couples. That is, living together was a preliminary step toward the simultaneous commitment of marriage and children. These women might have settled for cohabitation, compromising on their wish for marriage, if their partners had agreed to have children. Other heterosexual women in this study were cohabiting with partners who already had children and, as a lifestyle choice, might have remained permanently in such relationships, with the partner's children as a part of their own lives, if they had not changed their minds about having children of their own; they, too, might have agreed to have children with these partners without marriage. Lesbian couples could not marry until spring 2004 in Massachusetts, and thus their commitment to a marriage-type relationship is established through cohabitation and a recognized long-term commitment (including commitment ceremonies). My sample (which excluded women who were cohabiting at the time their

child arrived) may account for more talk emphasizing marriage than might otherwise exist in the general population. But, with only a few exceptions, these women saw cohabitation with children as settling for a lesser kind of commitment than they believed they would have with a legal marital relationship. However, women who had been in a relationship prior to becoming single moms report that their disagreement with partners was not about a marriage license but about parenthood.

18. Marriage still has a social and legal backing that other relationships (e.g., cohabitation and civil unions) do not. But cultural conformity would no longer propel individuals into marriage as a natural path. Cherlin (2004: 858) predicts that marriage will always remain, though as it becomes rarer its value will be as a symbol of personal achievement and prestige, rather than as essential for the early functions it once provided. The women I studied were surprised that either they were not asked by anyone to marry them ("chosen," as one woman put it) or they did not feel compelled to marry a man who was not Mr. Right. The concept of "Mr. Right" represents the right to presume individual self-fulfillment as essential to equal partnerships. This is a shift in the meaning of marriage (Hackstaff 2000).

19. The median age at marriage was twenty-seven for men and twenty-five for women in 2000 (U.S. Census Bureau 2003).

20. In 1960, there were just over 400,000 cohabiting couples. Today, nearly 4.6 million heterosexual couples cohabit. (See Seltzer 2004, which compiles the work of several scholars on this topic, detailed by education, social class, and race.) In 1999, a third of cohabiting couples in the United States lived with children under fifteen, an increase from just over a quarter in 1980 (census data cited in Seltzer 2004). See also Sassler 2004 for an in-depth ethnographic examination of how cohabiting relationships develop into unions.

21. I focus on the changing social climate, specifically from the 1950s on. When I refer to earlier generations, I am discussing the mothers of the women in this study, who were born from approximately the 1930s on.

22. For a rich account of the legal precedent that shaped today's family law in regards to the rights of unwed mothers and fathers, see Shanley 2001, in particular chapter 2. She argues that legal precedent of married couples is unsatisfactory in resolving custodial disputes of unwed parents. Overall, Shanley presents a comprehensive picture of the transition between common law and legal precedents as the determinant of legal custody of children, a shift in familial authority and obligation. Despite this transition, child custody and support still remain gendered issues. See also Dowd 1997: 89–92.

23. This is a shorthand version of the insightful arguments made in Shanley 2001. See especially chapter 2 for the historical legal cases that set the stage for a gradual shifting of parental rights.

24. For a comparative history of illegitimacy, see Laslett, Oosterveen, and Smith 1980. For a more specific historical account of the ways in which illegitimacy has varied in the United States according to race and social class of the women and children involved, see Kunzel 1995. Other social histories discuss how different cultures in various historical periods dealt with out-of-wedlock births. For instance, scattered throughout social histories, such as the ambitious Burguiere et al. 1996, are occasional glimpses of that type of information. Basically, they occurred in discussions of inheritance and the distribution of land, for instance in ancient Athens.

25. The stigma of single motherhood has not been erased for poor mothers who remain dependent upon the state (Hays 2003). Self-sufficiency as part of the American dream continues to define who is stigmatized as a single mother and who is not. With the rise of women's employment in general and proof that women could hold a job and be mothers, those without a paycheck continue to be criticized for their choices and thought of as morally lacking. The single mothers in this study escaped that stigma because they are economically not a burden to the state.

26. The famous scarlet letter worn by Hester Prynne in Hawthorne's seventeenth-century New England represents the town officials' attempt to publicly shame and scorn her for immoral behavior; the community's tolerance for immoral acts ends with adultery and the resulting birth of Pearl. More recently, sociologist Laurel Richardson (1985) studied single women who have long-term relationships with married men. They are usually undetected, because their relationships are kept secret while the women appear autonomous and independent. While I did not seek single mothers who had their children with married men, I do have three women who did so in this study. They wanted children, not long-term lovers. They selected these men to father their child knowing they lived far away and could neither be involved in their lives nor be taxed with child support. These women did not shake tightly knit community norms about intimacy with married individuals.

27. See Hunter 1991.

28. The Comprehensive Child Development Act of 1971 passed both houses of Congress. President Nixon vetoed this legislation as "the most radical act of the 93rd Congress," (Rosen 2001: 90–91). claiming that the government's support of day care was a tacit endorsement of a Soviet model of communal child rearing. Imagine what a difference the passage of this act would have made to women in 2005!

29. See Hays 1996 and Blair-Loy 2003 for arguments about how women are expected to devote more time to mothering as their careers intensify. Unable to meet expectations at work and home, some women who, because of their husband's income, can financially afford to drop out of the labor force do so, while others resist by not having children.

30. Although African American middle-class families are disappointed when their daughters do not find husbands to marry, they are also aware that the pool of eligible African American men who are educated and hold good-paying professional jobs like theirs is small.

31. Arlene Stein (1997: 125) coined this phrase for lesbian baby boomers. For a longer argument about lesbians on the forefront of social change, see her book.

32. The feelings women articulate as they choose motherhood over marriage are akin to those of the working class as studied by Rubin (1994). Rubin exposes the deeply held beliefs that shape men's and women's lives as they make decisions abut how they will live, in particular how their family should be. These beliefs often surface only when things fall apart or people feel deprived of something they thought was a given. In my study, the deep longing for motherhood surfaces for these women only when the package of married motherhood falls apart. While in Rubin's study the given among the working-class people she studied was the right to a family wage and a wife at home, for the women in my study the given was that marriage and mother-hood were intertwined and taken for granted, until both seemed to be slipping out of their grasp. Just as Rubin's families could not afford for the wives to stay at home, these women cannot afford to hold out for marriage.

33. David Blankenhorn (1995), founder and president of the Institute for American Values, blames women for the phenomenon of fathers becoming increasingly superfluous to family life. He urges Americans to value fatherhood once again.

34. Women hesitate for good reason. As social scientist Alan Wolfe (1998: 102–4) points out, the middle class views single-parent families as "not as good" as two-parent families. Wolfe's own data are in accordance with national polls on what people think about individual choices in family life. Further, he also provides evidence that Boston is more likely to be sympathetic to nontraditional families (single-parent families and gay marriage).

35. Journalist Melissa Ludtke's (1997) comparative study of single mothers finds that regardless of income or age, single motherhood is rarely a woman's first-choice way to parent.

36. What motivates women (or anyone for that matter) to have children is a complex question, one that I do not attempt to answer in this book. For a philosophical perspective, see Alpern 1992a, 1992b. I use this idea of "mother hunger" because it was frequently brought up

in my interviews as an internal explanation for the desire for children, but I remind the reader that this group of women, those that pursued motherhood and succeeded in having children, are predisposed to this explanation. Other women decide not to pursue motherhood, but these women are not in this sample. A comparison would be necessary to answer the question of where baby hunger comes from.

## Chapter 2

1. Newman (1999: 90–94) explores the downward mobility of managers in the context of liminality as an unexpected phase of identity change when people are "betwixt and between" the vision of who they expected to be as employees and the loss of this identity.

2. A revealing account of this is provided by Arlene Skolnick (2003), who discussed the liminal period in her life as she was caught between the generation of women who wanted careers independent of husbands and those who expected to complement their husbands' careers. She illustrates how her life represents a shifting ground as the individual confronts changing social norms.

3. Even among the group of women who chanced pregnancy, all of them had to make an active decision to keep the pregnancy. This decision to give birth, not unlike that of women who used donor-assisted routes, was made and remade.

4. Orthodox Jewish clergy have even begun to give support to artificial insemination for single women, interpreting Jewish law as amenable to the creation of these families, no longer believing their creation violates the prohibition against sex outside of marriage (Furstenburg 2005). For more on the controversies surrounding reproductive technologies and Jewish law, see Kahn 2000.

5. These defining moments are what Bennis and Thomas (2002: chap. 4) describe as "crucible events," "the process of meaning-making" that pushes these women to transform their lives.

6. Endometriosis was once called "the career women's disease" because women who sought diagnosis were usually over thirty and childless.

7. The term *marriage* is used here as a stand-in for long-term monogamous partnerships, whether heterosexual or homosexual.

## Chapter 3

1. The rights of fathers in adoption cases in recent years, such as that of Baby Richard and Baby Jessica, established that birth fathers had rights to children of whom they had no prior knowledge. See Shanley 2001: chap. 2. The cases of unwed parents, the birth fathers' rights movement, changing divorce practices that encourage joint custody, open adoption, and known donors suing for custody have given men increasing legal precedent to claim children. Women who choose to have children outside the traditional family are more conscious of the implications this trend and future victories would have on paternity claims in their individual situations.

2. Massachusetts is one of a handful of states in which it is cheaper to try to become pregnant than to adopt because of existing medical insurance coverage available for fertility treatment, including all the latest artificial reproduction technologies. Women are only required to purchase gametes in this process (if not already available by way of a known donor), which makes it considerably less expensive than the adoption procedure.

3. This speculation is often based upon media stories of adopted children who search for genetic parents with the idea that these meetings are breakthrough moments that will answer questions of identity. Questions of identity have also been raised for families formed through

anonymous donor sperm. As more women discuss having anonymous donors on public forums such as Web sites, making links to genetic identity is brought into reach.

4. See Maine 1986 for a parallel argument discussing a similar transition in ancient societies from familiar to contractual. See also Burguiere et al. 1996, which focuses on this transformation from a global historical perspective.

5. Weston (1991) coined this term to describe families that comprise individuals who are not always tied through traditional blood relations.

6. See Goffman 1963 on stigma.

7. Agigian 2004 discusses how lesbians are transforming the means of reproduction through the use of artificial insemination even as they (along with heterosexual single women) have been co-opted as a new market for the use of new reproductive technologies. In 1993 the first U.S. birth from intracytoplasmic sperm injection (ICSI) (in which a single sperm in injected into an egg with a needle) was reported, allowing men with low sperm counts to father children. This procedure dramatically changed the couple's needs for sperm donors. Lesbians who use sperm banks, Agigian argues, are likely to be middle- and upper-middle-class white women.

8. Ehrensaft (2005) uses the term "birth other" to refer to the use of another person who is not a sexual partner who helps create the child. Regardless of martial status or sexual identity, the "birth other" encompasses any individual who provides sperm, eggs, a womb, or any combination of gestational or genetic aid.

9. This is also apparent with gay couples who form families. Those who can afford to do so and live in certain states usually have extensive legal documentation to protect their family, including second-parent adoption papers (second parents are not automatically given parental rights). Their alternative family structures make them vulnerable to attack. Single mothers are likewise vulnerable; however, single gay mothers are doubly at risk, having twice rebelled against the patriarchal establishment.

10. In the group of donors, there are two exceptions to this statement, which will be explored in depth in chapter 8. The contract is also used to write men into family in new ways.

11. Individual countries determine eligibility for adoption and may decide to exclude individuals on the basis of marital status and sexual identity. Today, numerous countries treat single women as equivalent to couples in the adoption process, uninterested in the politics of family surrounding nonmarital motherhood in the United States. International adoption has increased dramatically in past years, spurred by the idea of saving children. Altruism is an appealing antidote to the idea of parenthood, especially single parenthood, as selfish. The effect on domestic adoption policies of other countries' broadening their adoption markets to single mothers is unknown. In general, single mothers have low priority in the adoption hierarchy, with preference given to two-parent heterosexual families, as discussed in chapter 6 (ironically, it is in gay women's favor to be uncoupled, as being single is less of a sin in adoption than being gay).

12. Garey and Townsend's 1996 article focuses on the problem of importing child custody laws to a setting such as a village in Botswana. The social norms that govern these villages differ from the "traditional law." This makes who is financially responsible for children problematic.

13. In any society with a matrilineal descent system (inheritance of position and property is from mother's brother to sister's son), the mother's brother tends to have authority over a woman's children; the father is an affectionate but nonauthoritative person. These matrilineal systems are all over the world. One of the classic descriptions of this system is of the Trobriand Islanders in Malinowski 1926.

14. See Weger 1997 for an extensive argument about opening up sealed birth records.

15. See Fischer 1982 and Wellman 1999 for important literature on support networks, including friends and kin.

16. See Hertz and Ferguson 1998 on the importance of good friends and close kin as part of the "repertory family" that mothers emphasize.

## Introduction to Part II

1. *Hegemony* refers to the pervasive but often unnoticed presence of ideology in everyday life. See especially Lyotard 1984. Master narratives are part of this framework but far more consciously recognized. According to Romero and Stewart (1999: xiv), master narratives "gain strength from repetition and mirroring; they accumulate familiarity and clarity while blurring and erasing plot elements that don't fit."

2. I am grateful to Jane Hood for her insightful commentary (2002) on how these donor assisted families are shaped by the family master narrative. Her commentary prompted this theoretical framing.

3. The exception is states that allow second-parent adoptions by same-sex parents.

## Chapter 4

1. Abby had over fifty profiles from the donor bank. One donor was African American and one donor was Asian (Korean). All the rest were white, but of varying ethnicities. As a white woman, Abby had many choices. Abby, like the other white women, selected a donor who was white. The two black women in this study, one Caribbean American and African American and the other African American, also wished to find an anonymous donor who shared their race. At the time these women searched for available anonymous donors through a major sperm bank, they could find only three and four donors of color, respectively. Nonetheless, both women selected donors who listed their race as mixed but predominately black. The pool of anonymous donors of color is limited. Even though the sperm banks refused to give me any information on the race of available donors, the Web sites for these banks list preliminary information on sperm donors by race. These Web sites have been redesigned several times since I started to check them once a month. The available donors the Web sites display are disproportionately Caucasian (though the number of donors from a particular ethnic background may limit a woman's options). Only a few donors are listed as black, Hispanic, or "mixed." Under the heading "Asian" the number of donors increases, but different Asian ethnicities (e.g., Korean, Chinese) are limited.

2. See in particular Hood 2002; her comments on donor-assisted families aided my thinking and revisions.

3. This is a summary of Cooley's (1983: 184) principal elements that comprise the "looking-glass self."

4. I am summarizing Strauss 1959: 33–34.

5. Strauss 1959: 37.

6. This woman hoped the known donor would want to become a family once the yet-to-be child was born. However, even this woman had a contract saying he had no financial obligation to the child.

7. This can be likened to the transformation ill individuals experience, which, according to Charmaz's (1995) argument, objectifies their bodies less and allows them to admit cues from their bodies about their illness. Once the illness is acknowledged, they gain control over their lives as they learn how to protect their bodies. When women craft these birth stories about fathers residing in another place, they may master a presentation of conception for the child but mask the acceptance of a man who will never be present in the child's life.

8. This point is derived from Cooley's (1983) theorizing about the "looking-glass self."

9. Strauss 1959 noted this about the self.

10. It is ironic that anonymity of gamete donors remains the norm in the United States at the same time that more and more states open up adoption records as a moral obligation to the adopted.

11. This is a shorthand version of the insights in Mead 1934 on identity formation.

12. Charlene Miall (1986, 1987, 1989) has done important work on social stigma among childless couples and among adoptive parents. E-mail correspondence with her helped to clarify my thinking concerning the possible roots of "half-adopted" children. In preliminary work with married women who used anonymous donor insemination, the women were encouraged during counseling provided as part of the process they underwent "to think of the donor sperm as part of the adoption spectrum—that is, donor ova or sperm were just adoption one step removed. They were all married and they talked at length about the intimations of adultery that had arisen after conception took place using ADI." Susan most likely borrowed this term and way of conceptualizing a sperm donor from the helping professionals whose workshops she attended.

13. See especially Weger 1997 and March 2000 on adoption. These scholars analyze the importance of birth families to adoptees. March argues that "this exclusion reaffirms their sense of having no bodily self-reference." Both authors primarily discuss searching (though there are exceptions) for birth mothers and the relief and realizations that result from their reunions.

14. Strauss put it this way: "The naming of an object provides a directive for action, as if the object were forthrightly to announce, 'You say I am this, then act in the appropriate way toward me.' Conversely, if the actor feels he does not know what the object is, then with regard to it his action is blocked" (1959: 22).

15. Certain sperm banks, though not compelled by anything but the market, have begun to give clients more information about the donor, including a baby photo, an audiotape, and various psychological tests they have administered. Only the women interviewed most recently had these pieces of information. Further, until recently donors checked either yes or no to having contact with the child at the age of eighteen years or older. There is also a new "openness policy" that some banks have instituted. This policy states that at age eighteen the child of a recipient may request additional information about the donor. The bank will maintain records on the donors and recipients. The bank will make a "responsible effort" to supply information from their records or to contact the donor. As one of the major banks writes on its Web site: "We are obligated by mutual agreements to maintain the anonymity and privacy of both the donor and recipient. The only exception to this would be by mutual consent of the involved individuals." This new statement gives women a faint possibility that the donor they used might be amenable to meeting their child. It is far from the guarantee that women I spoke with believe it to be.

16. Whether children conceived through anonymous donor fathers experience these absent men as missing pieces of their identities similar to adopted children remains a question this study cannot answer. See Ehrensaft 2005 for clinical insights on two-parent families created through donor assistance and surrogacy. See also Orenstein 1995 for an account of adult children conceived through donors. The publication of this story coincided with Father's Day.

17. States rarely regulate sperm banks, with the exception of California and New York. Sperm banks arose in the 1980s as a way to provide health-screened sperm in order to reduce the rates of reproduction-related HIV transmission and other sexually transmitted diseases. A system that screens donors is safer than either the older practice of private doctors providing fresh sperm from local medical students or a "one-night sexual encounter." Further, the commercialization of sperm banks has created an industry that produces particular knowledge claims about the donor beyond medical information. For instance, the California Cryobank

also requires that donors have particular post-high-school educations, a claim that establishes these donors as not "regular Joes." Sperm banks sort semen along a particular set of masculine ideals (Schmidt and Moore 1998), and the same can be claimed about a particular feminine ideal for egg donors. An interesting example of this is the Repository for Germinal Choice, dubbed the "Nobel prize sperm bank"—though this bank turned out not to have many Nobel prize winners on its roster (Plotz 2005). This "genius bank," which received much media attention, represented a kind of genetic engineering that smacked of choosing super-intelligent babies, which was more upsetting to the public than either the information offered on donor profiles or the fact that men can choose to never meet the children that result from their sperm.

18. The right to privacy of sperm donors was recently challenged. Parents Diane and Ronald Johnson sued Cryobank to depose an anonymous sperm donor after their child was diagnosed with an inherited kidney disease. Cryobank invoked the donor's right to privacy and confidentiality, but the court ruled for the Johnsons. However, even though the court ordered donor number 276 to appear for a deposition to learn the facts of what he had disclosed to the Cryobank regarding his medical history and to obtain all his medical records, the order maintained his anonymity by not releasing his name, and his deposition was attended only by the parties' counsel (*Johnson v. Superior Court of Los Angeles*, decided May 18, 2000).

19. Canada, Britain, the Netherlands, Switzerland, Sweden, and New Zealand ban individuals from donating their gametes without agreeing to reveal themselves to the child. These countries have established donor registries. At age eighteen a child born using donated gametes can go to the registry, look up the individual, and locate the person. These are recent developments. For instance, Britain's ban went into effect in April 2005, and it is not retroactive, which means that the first time children will be able to look up their genetic donors will be in 2023. The British government carried out a two-year public consultation with findings presented at the Human Fertility and Embryonic Authority annual conference on what information a child has a right to know (BBC News, January 21, 2004).

In the United States, privacy of the donor prevails. Donors are not considered a "rights issue" of children. In the United States, among the large sperm banks few donors volunteer to reveal their identities. With one exception, women in this study would have preferred such donors but their gametes are hard to come by. Ultimately, all the women I interviewed decided to purchase gametes without a consent to identity release after being unable to secure sperm from the short supply of those donors who consented. Privacy of the donor is weighed against the child's rights to know their genetic lineage.

20. While the vast majority of women trusted the health screening process and the medical histories provided by the donors they selected as accurate and of no present concern, two women had genetic family histories they wished to avoid. Since there were no genetic tests to rule out potential donors who might also be carriers, the women deliberately selected donors who were ethnically far from their own backgrounds (e.g., a Jewish woman selected a Nordic donor for this reason). Her explanation was that this donor was less likely to have this problem in his gene pool.

21. The idea of "clean genes" is fascinating because it points to the fantasies that lie behind the women's attempt at genetic selection from paper profiles of men. They are seeking perfection and flawlessness from a donor that they might not choose to pursue in a lover. Ultimately, the donor profiles are also flawed, and women have to choose between which flaws they are willing to accept.

22. While watching the *Oprah* show on June 1, 2003, Raechel McGhee learned about the ability to post messages for donors on a Web site. The anonymous donor, also hearing about this Web site, checked to see if his number was listed and after a second look found Raechel's note. He posted back, and the rest is history: this happily-ever-after story ends with the mom and two kids, both his, flying to Los Angeles for a week to become a "real" family (Leahy 2005).

It is a true story that raise hopes among single mothers—more of meeting the donor to answer lingering questions of identity than of turning gametes into dads, which is a media tale reinforcing the importance of two biological parents. But it raises troubling questions about why the United States does not have a national registry and how commercial Web sites broker these families' relationships.

23. Stein 2005 reports that a fifteen-year-old boy used his own DNA sample and the Internet to locate his anonymous donor. Using a database not intended for finding an anonymous donor has raised new questions about privacy issues. As more government agencies have access to DNA samples, this exceptional case might prove to lead to the inability of donors to remain anonymous. More interesting, the boy refused comment on how the anonymous donor responded to this child's discovery.

24. Without the development of sperm banks and the Internet this would not be possible. Sperm banks give numbers to each donor. Through Web sites created in the last few years women are registering their donor's number. They hope for a match in order to meet these genetic relatives. For instance, the California Cryobank recently created a sibling registry as part of its Web site because women were asking for help in locating genetic siblings. This Web page acknowledges a new basis for kinship: "We are committed to helping our clients build families . . . for those clients and their children who are interested in extending their 'family circle.'" While I do not know how many individuals are posting on the Cryobank Web site, the Yahoo search engine also hosts a registry with over five thousand entries from mothers, kids, *and* donors. I suspect that what I have captured in this section is the core of a new potential for kin relationships between genetic-based siblings born to different mothers.

While researching the children produced through the "Nobel prize sperm bank," Plotz (2005) stumbled across another interesting example of yearning to connect. In his journalistic pursuit to find out if any geniuses were in fact produced, the main reason his sources (donors, mothers, and children) responded to a series of his articles is that they hoped he would facilitate contact with one another in order to dispel the anonymity. Locating genetic half siblings is as important to these families as the donor himself.

25. The number of children sired by a particular donor, a figure supplied by the sperm bank, is not exact, as it is based on the voluntary self-reports of women who used donor sperm. Even though women view this number as factual, there is no way to verify this information.

26. Interestingly, in the few cases of twins in this study the issue of searching for other paternal kin was less likely to be raised. Having a fraternal twin who shares physical traits provides satisfactory self-directives because the self of the "missing" paternal side can be authenticated through one's twin. This is not to suggest that twins or genetic siblings (when a woman uses the same donor for a second child) replace the father's affirmation of self, but physical resemblance to a twin may more readily facilitate the internalization process of self that Mead (1934) discusses.

27. This is the best description of the facets that make up fatherhood (dads), described historically by family sociologist Ralph Larossa (1997).

28. When known donors escalate their involvement, there is often the opportunity for paternal kin to become involved with the child. In Deborah's case, her daughter visits once a year with her paternal grandmother and aunt. It is the known donor who brokers these relationships with his kin, made possible by the open nature of his contract with Deborah.

29. See especially Ambert 1989 and Stacey 1990.

30. See Weston 1991 and Weeks, Heaphy, and Donovan 2001 on families of choice.

31. As Margaret Mead and other anthropologists found, genetics do not determine the binding relationship of social relations, nor do they necessarily establish who has authority over children within the family. See also Furstenberg 1995 for a discussion of the importance of daddies who are not biological kin among inner-city African American families.

32. Women who became pregnant with known donors in the study are just as likely to be artificially inseminated as they are to have sexual intercourse. The hegemony of fatherhood that rests on sexual penetration is not the basis for determining the child's future relationship with the donor or how the mother will set boundaries regarding the child's relationship with that man. However, the sexual tie between the mother and the known donor creates a permanent intimacy that does not exist with and was not expressed by women who artificially inseminated.

33. Strauss is quoting Kenneth Burke (1945: xix), "It is in the areas of ambiguity that transformations take place. . . . without such areas transformations would be impossible" (in Strauss 1959: 26).

34. Hochschild 2001 discusses how eavesdropping is a tool that children use to pick up information about their parents' views on those individuals who care for them.

35. Whether an anonymous donor is important or ignored might also vary for lesbian couples (Ehrensaft 2000). The social significance of a second parent who is not genetically related confounds the social construction of self and is beyond the purview of this book.

36. See Hood 2002: 35, where the broadening of kinship systems to include gamete donors and donors' other gamete offspring is dubbed "kin claiming."

## Chapter 5

1. No women in this study were lured to motherhood by a man's flattery. Edin and Kefalas (2005: 31) argue that in the case of young poor women, it is the men who often initiate the idea of pregnancy—it is flattering to a woman for a man to tell her that he would like to have a child by her. The authors note that this statement is more a reflection of creating a "significant long-lasting bond through the child" to the mother and less of "a promise of life-long commitment." See also LeBlanc 2003, which poignantly captures how these ties of parenthood extend into the prison system.

2. There are women in this study who became pregnant and had an abortion specifically because they did not want that particular man to be in their life in any permanent way. These women, who eventually chose a different route to motherhood, foresaw an inevitable entanglement with these men, and wished to avoid it.

3. The largest group of women who became out-of-wedlock mothers in the United States is typically lumped together under the heading of "accidental" pregnancies. This label is a misnomer. It implies that a woman's pregnancy happens by chance. But becoming pregnant, carrying a child to term, and keeping a child are, today, separate decisions. Each decision heightens a woman's insight on how to weigh moral, religious, and political issues, ranging from individual views on abortion to single motherhood. In fact, several women suggested that the availability of legal abortion compelled them to defend their choice to continue the pregnancy.

4. Luker (1995: 70) discusses a variation of what women told me in these interviews. Luker explores conceptually the idea that some women become pregnant as a way to test a man's commitment to the relationship. In regard to this study, Luker's point describes the exception, not the rule, for these single women.

5. None of the lowest-paid women in this study, earning from $17,000 to $22,000 a year in the late 1990s, was collecting welfare payments at the time of the interview, an intentional exclusion in this sample. However, a few women periodically had used government supplements, such as day care vouchers and welfare, in lieu of maternity leave briefly after the birth of their child. Notably in this group, despite the presence of lower-paid women, all had their children in solidly middle-class settings, such as day care in particular communities and schools in particular districts. This was an intentional calculation on the part of these mothers, who, regardless of income, sought middle-class citizenship for their children outside the home.

6. These women are prioritizing what Townsend (2002) calls "emotional closeness," a "facet of fatherhood."

7. Zelizer 1985 discusses the ways in which the value of children has historically changed. In many ways, fatherhood has been likewise transformed. Fatherhood appears to be a sentimental commodity, which the courts cannot give. Courts can only assign a financial contribution to fathers, not an emotional one.

8. Exchange of money between parents becomes an acknowledgment of a past intimacy that created a child. Simmel 1978 argued that money is a means to understand the most profound of human relations. I argue that children that are the product of only intimacy are entangled in the process by which money is used to place a value on the parent-child relationship. This process also occurs in cases of divorce. See Millman 1991 for how people argue about the worth of children in the courtroom.

9. According to Edin and Kefalas (2005), it is not uncommon for unwed fathers to be at the birth of their child. They argue that the birth is a "magical moment" and often the fathers of these children vow to mend their ways at that point, sometimes reconnecting with the mothers briefly. Edin and Kefalas also cite surveys by McLanahan et al. (2003) that show that in seven of ten cases, unmarried fathers do come to the hospital and sometimes are even there for the delivery itself. Brandy's experience of having the father at the hospital (though not in the delivery room) is not unlike that of other women chancing pregnancy. However, her feeling that he had a right to be there is symptomatic of the generally held belief that fathers who are part of a chanced pregnancy have claims to children regardless of the circumstances of conception.

10. In the two cases (Colleen and Darlene) women pursued a paternal relationship for their child but the men refused any contact, opting only to pay consistent child support; their kin followed suit, rejecting a relationship with the child also.

11. This group has seven involved dads, while there are eight with a minimal presence in their child's life. Three out of the eighteen have disappeared completely.

12. Brandy, mentioned earlier, named her daughter after the father, making a nod to his paternity in the daughter's first name, though the child was given Brandy's last name.

13. Edin and Kefalas (2005: 60–62) find among the poor women in their sample that "giving a child the father's last name is one of the most reliable barometers of the state of the couple's relationship just after a child's birth." Failing to give the child the father's last name is a signal that she will give him no role in the child's life. Children are an accomplishment of which poor men are proud, as it is one of the few things that a man can point to as something he did. In my sample there is no correlation between whether the child carries the father's name and his involvement either directly after the birth or years later. However, I remind the reader that I deliberately pulled a sample of women who were not living with a partner at the time of the child's birth.

14. Mary's thoughts on the importance of a father were a combination of what she believed a man and a second parent would bring. Her belief is not uncommon for the women in this study, and it will be examined analytically in Chapter 9.

15. See Waller 2002: 87, which also discusses mothers as gatekeepers among unmarried parents.

16. Paternal kin are in contrast with maternal kin in terms of the financial support of these women and their children. While sometimes gifts were made, there was no financial obligation or expectation for paternal kin.

## Chapter 6

1. Shanley 2001: 14–15.
2. Shanley (2001: 15) coined this phrase.

3. See Zelizer 1985 for a fascinating historical examination of the transformation of children's worth. In earlier times children's labor, needed to work farmland, made adolescent boys desirable adoptees. As the U.S. economy changed, children become economically worthless and emotionally priceless. White baby girls became the most desirable adoptees.

4. Simon and Altstein's (2000) twenty-year study (1972–92) on transracial adoption in the Midwest (nonwhite children raised in white families) supports the findings from other empirical studies analyzed by Elizabeth Bartholet (1999). Simon and Altstein quote Bartholet as further evidence of their own findings: "transracial adoptees do as well on measures of psychological and social adjustment as adoptive nonwhite children raised inracially [same race children] in relatively similar socio-economic circumstances" (p. 78). Like many of the single mothers in this book, only a minority of the families interviewed in the Simon and Altstein study initially considered adopting a nonwhite child. Yet learning that healthy white infants were scarce, the majority in the Simon and Altstein study eventually decided to adopt a nonwhite infant. Despite the families' initial reservations, in the 1991 follow-up interviews the Simon and Altstein study asked these families "with the knowledge of hindsight if [they] would adopt transracially again," and 92 percent of the parents answered yes (p. 64).

5. Presently five states will not allow gay couples to adopt, but in some of these cases, they may become foster parents.

6. In 2005 the average time to adopt a child from Russia is five months and from China ten to twelve months from the time the U.S. adoption agency submits the required paperwork. While these adoptions are costly, older infants and toddlers are available if the adopting parents fit the criteria/requirements set by the adopting country including age of the parents, marital status, income, and sexual identity. Only the two women of color who were matched to children of color and two social workers with connections (one adopted a white infant and another an American-born Vietnamese infant) adopted infants through the state adoption system. Women who adopted healthy children domestically through either a public or private agency faced the longest time frames—often a minimum of two years, and usually at least one match did not work out. Women who adopted internationally were guaranteed that a child would be available and theirs; women who adopted domestically did not feel they had similar assurances. They also had more extensive bureaucratic hurdles to face, such as legal obstacles from problems living in one state and adopting from another state, and the length of time during which a birth mother could reclaim a child varied from state to state. Finally, international children were adopted before leaving the child's birth country. In the United States, finalizing the adoption was another protracted process.

7. Adoption costs vary. The least costly are domestic public agencies, in this study costing one-tenth of private adoptions. Domestic private agencies and international agencies have a similar range, from $4,000 to over $30,000. For the international country costs at this time, see www.travel.state.gov/family/adoption. Women in this study who adopted internationally usually paid more than women who adopted through private domestic agencies, but not always. In most states, the cost of using fertility clinics would rival the costs of adoption; however, in Massachusetts fertility treatments were covered through medical insurance.

8. However, some mothers who adopted older children had limited contact with the birth mother.

9. Of the adoptive mothers, all but five are white. I would have preferred more respondents of other races in this segment of the study. I had difficulty finding women of color who had adopted. It may be that informal adoption, where members of the same racial community raise both kin and nonkin without the intervention of social services and the legal system, is a common route to raising children among nonwhite single women. Since this route to motherhood raised other questions outside the purview of this study I did not try to find single women who were raising children they did not legally adopt.

10. In the time period during which the women in this study adopted, the leading countries from which children were adopted were China, Russia, South Korea, Guatemala, and Romania. All but Romania remain in the top five countries of origin for international adoptions in 2005. (See the U.S. Department of State Web site, http://www.travel.state.gov/family/ adoption_resources_02.html, for current statistics on adoption by country.) The total of immigrant visas issued to orphans from all countries increased from 7,093 in 1990 to 22,728 in 2005, the last year for which figures were available.

11. Another adoptive mother who is Cuban American recalled fondly her grandmother's cooking and the delightful summer vacations spent visiting. She decided to adopt from Central America to reinforce and affirm her Hispanic identity. Even though she can pass as white herself, she reclaims this part of her identity through adopting a child from Central America. She hopes to learn more Spanish. The recipes her grandmother once cooked she now prepares for holiday community events. From the menu of identities she carries she selected this one as most salient when deciding upon a child to adopt. (See Waters 1990 for an argument about how ethnic identity among immigrants of European descent plays out.)

12. The majority of women are not aware that their U.S. citizenship advantages them in the adoption market.

13. Her mother helped offset the $25,000 cost for a Chinese international adoption. Without this help Marli would not have had as many options for children available to her.

14. At the time Marli adopted, China did not ask about sexual identity, even though the home study required in Massachusetts might have, depending on the agency. This has changed. The China government specifically states that "adoption applications by homosexuals are not acceptable," based on April 2003 updates. (See http://www.travel.state.gov/ family/adoption_resources_02.html.)

15. Even though the Hague Convention supports giving preference to local adoption over international adoption, this document offers contradictory prescriptions for adoption. That is, the codes offer a narrow definition of adoption that actually encourages social workers and lawyers to overlook local adoption placements in favor of wealthier, international nuclear homes (Johnson 2002).

16. United States backing of rightist forces created the circumstances that put children at risk for becoming orphans or impoverished; this was Marli's concern. She was comfortable adopting from China because that country's own internal policies were what led to so many orphaned and abandoned children becoming available for adoption. However, in the last fifty years Americans have adopted children from all over the world, sometimes creating transracial U.S. families. For instance, in the early 1950s, children were adopted from Korea as a result of the Korean conflict. Most of these children were biracial and fathered by U.S. military personnel before and after the war. "Operation Baby Lift" from Vietnam in 1975 brought several thousand children to the United States and other countries. The lack of adequate documentation about the children, who were all placed in adoptive homes, resulted in lawsuits by Vietnamese birth parents and other relatives who came to reclaim their children.

17. Numerous journalists, including Tama Janowitz (1988) and Karin Evans (2000), have written accounts of their adoption of Chinese daughters. In addition, a 1993 cover story in the *New York Times Magazine* (Porter 1993) is one of the earliest journalistic accounts to discuss the consequences of China's one-child-per-family policy leading to the newest Chinese export. The cover photograph is a poignant image of a healthy baby girl with a gaze that seemingly invites the reader to reach out, hold her, and offer her a better home. By the mid-1980s the number of South Korean babies adopted by foreigners had sharply declined, and South American adoptions also were declining due to local legal entanglements. Beginning in late 1991 China modified its adoption regulations to be more friendly to middle-aged, single foreigners not of Chinese descent (Porter 1993: 26).

18. Kay Johnson (2002) argues that China has not only a limited history of adoption, preferring biological offspring, but also restrictive laws that contribute to the lack of local adoptive families. She suggests that if the restrictions on parental age and the number of children were eased that local families would be willing to adopt abandoned children.

19. See Patricia J. Williams (2004) for her personal memoir of how the dynamics of race (including skin color) and social class played out in her life and her extended family's. The "paper bag test" is shorthand for the shade of one's skin, differentiating darker- from lighter-skinned African Americans. Light-skinned children were more socially advantaged in that they were thought to have the potential to fit into the middle class. Skin color as part of creating an "as if" family was also raised by the social worker when Janica adopted her first daughter. The sense of privilege accorded lighter-skinned African Americans dates back to slavery. Janica monitored the hurtful treatment of her two daughters—one lighter-skinned than the other—and noticed the differences in the remarks made about them by school officials and others in positions of power. She was sensitive to this, as it harkened back to her own childhood and how her sister, the fairer-skinned child, was always the chosen one. She does not want this replicated in her daughters' lives.

20. Just as Marli decided to omit reference to her sexual identity when answering the questions of the social worker, Janica, too, decided it was easier to follow the agency guidelines and remove her lover's belongings than have a live-in boyfriend be an issue in her younger daughter's adoption.

21. However, in cases where heterosexual couples have a known donor of either sex, the genetic parent is separate from the social parent. And in cases where lesbian couples have a donor, the donor is the opposite sex parent. Same-sex couples need to be studied further, as their dynamics may unfold differently.

22. A few other adoptive mothers sent photos and written updates through agencies or attorneys to the birth mothers for a while, but these women were not in direct contact with the birth mother. By the time I interviewed them, this connection to the birth mothers had petered out.

23. See Melosh 2002 for an excellent history of adoption from the early twentieth century to today. She discusses the cultural norms and social science debates and their changes over time. Weger (1997), using in-depth interviews, discusses the adoption reform movement and adoptees' search to reunite with their families of birth. She advocates opening closed adoption records, which is a topic of debate in the sociological literature, in social policy circles, and in the popular press. Pertman (2000: 17, 24) also makes a case that open adoptions are best for all members involved in an adoption: birth parents, adoptee, and adoptive parents. He asserts that although the adoption process is difficult and "must balance the rights and needs of vulnerable people," ultimately, greater openness in the adoption process leads to greater rootedness and security of self-identity for all individuals involved. These three books combined demonstrate how the norms and social practices surrounding adoption have changed. Yet debates about the rights of adoptive children to birth records continue, and as transracial adoption increases in frequency, the laws and social policies of other countries become another layer as children are transported across national boundaries.

24. The Minnesota/Texas Adoption Research Project has followed 190 adoptive families and almost as many birth parents for more than fifteen years. Grotevant and McRoy (1998) have a large study of over seven hundred people involved in open adoptions. The study finds that adopters in full-disclosure adoptions were less likely than others to fear birth parents reclaiming children. It also found that most adopters were satisfied with the degree of contact with birth parents. Interestingly, it was birth mothers who were most negative about future meetings with their birth children.

25. Rob Geen (2003) in "Who Will Adopt the Foster Care Children Left Behind?" examines the characteristics of parents who have adopted children from the foster care system

and those of children who are waiting for permanent homes. Of the 47,000 children adopted in 1999, foster parents adopted 56 percent, relatives adopted 20 percent, and adults with whom they had no prior relationship adopted 24 percent.

26. Fogg-Davis (2002: 5) describes this process as "a racial navigation, which is a metaphor for mediating the personal and political meaning of race." She discusses how this concept is both a coping mechanism for living in a racially segregated society and a tool for eliminating racial barriers in public and private lives.

27. Race and social class are heavily influenced by the women's own life experiences and geopolitical location. Women were quick to tell me that their ability to create transracial families in Boston and their perception of how transracial families could be constructed would be different from their ability to do so in other parts of their country where there were fewer transracial families. For a longer discussion of the politics of location and their influence on experience and cultural awareness, see Rich 2001.

28. According to Kim 2003, adoptive white families of Chinese babies celebrate Chinese holidays with traditional festivities often learned through the local Chinese community. The article focuses on ways that white adoptive families create extended families through the local Chinese community by participating in language schools, shopping in Chinese stores, etc. They are attempting to create "extended Chinese families" through involvement with the Chinese community. Some families have located day care providers who are Chinese, and they become surrogate aunts.

29. See Kibria 2002, which discusses Korean and Chinese second-generation immigrants and the ways in which they retain and reject their ethnic identity.

30. See Hertz and Ferguson 1996; Uttal 2002.

## Conclusion to Part II

1. For instance, one mother in the study reported that her three-year-old daughter asked if she knew how her classmate had two moms. The mother recounting this story said that she did, and her child responded, "I understand how one mom can have two babies, but how can two moms have one baby?" Having gay or lesbian parents is difficult to explain and not simply taken as a matter of fact.

## Introduction to Part III

1. I refer here to issues surrounding child care, health care, after-school programs, and parental leave, as well as the implicit assumptions made by the workplace conflict with families.

2. See Gornick and Meyers 2003 for an examination of how the United States fares in comparison to other industrialized countries, exploring the way in which American child care is considered a private concern. Also see Williams and Cooper 2004 on a new legal trend of caregivers suing the workplace on the basis of discrimination, an extension of the tension between work and family.

3. This type of quilting was exhibited in the Museum of Fine Arts, Boston, in 2005 as part of "The Quilts of Gee's Bend," a display of work from an intergenerational African American collective in Alabama, formerly an outgrowth of the Pettway Plantation. "Symbolically, the name 'housetop' reflects the shared roles of home and quilt as providers of both physical protection and emotional belonging" (quoted from the Boston exhibition). The original exhibition was organized by the Museum of Fine Arts, Houston, and the Tinwood Alliance, Atlanta.

## Chapter 7

1. Women's placement in these categories reflects how they described their life in the first round of interviews, but, in a testament to changing intimacies, a group of women had already shifted categories, sometimes more than once. Women with older children had often experienced more variation of their family lives, adding a lover or gaining a parental figure. Mindful of the possible transitions, I provide examples of both women at a fixed point in their own narratives. To illustrate these four variations, I use snapshots of their lives, though it is clear that many transition to other categories.

2. I discovered Sienna's cohabiting situation not in the first interview but when I encountered her unexpectedly in the grocery store. It was only in a second interview that resulted from this chance meeting that I learned of her lover's move into her home. Because she was not cohabiting with a man who was also the father of her child at the time of the first interview, I still include her in the sample. However, I later discovered that living together can end as suddenly as it begins: at the time of the final interview, this man had disappeared from her life, never having occupied the place of a dad (which she made a point of telling me).

3. In this case, the biological father was listed on the birth certificate. He was technically not a legal parent. However, their wills specified that the two dads would become the child's guardians if the mom died. Naming these men on legal documents (birth certificates, wills, and contracts) is not done by women who have known donors with limited paternal obligations, if any, to their child.

4. Fourteen women in this study had some form of intergenerational caregiving, ranging from taking the child one night a week while the mother worked to living in close proximity, either in the same apartment or in the apartment downstairs. Not all of these intergenerational caregiving arrangements were co-parenting arrangements, as described in this section. More likely, grandparents were part of a social network, providing child care. While kin (grandmothers) can be an important support in child rearing, the difference between kin as part of social networks and as parenting partner is somewhat blurred—I use joint decision making as the deciding factor, not simply time spent with the child. While both women whose multigenerational caregiving partnerships featured in this chapter are African American, my intent in selecting them for this chapter is illustrative simply of the themes, not linked to race or social class in any way. Both these women were born into middle- to upper-middle-class families, excluding them from the intergenerational model often seen in poor families. Of the fourteen women in this study who used intergenerational caregiving in some form, only four are African American or Caribbean American, while the others are white.

5. Single mothers, Nelson (2006) finds, carve out a motherhood niche in which they direct their children's behavior, which lets both the children and the other significant adults in their lives know that they are in charge.

6. Burton (1990) described poor teenagers who have children that they turn over to their mothers to raise, a system that has been in place for several generations. This kind of intergenerational parenting is a second chance for grandmothers who had relinquished their children to their own mother to parent their grandchildren as their own. This model is not one of co-parenting and not what is being described in this section.

7. Divorced parents with joint custody also have adult time and children's time, similar to women in this category. In a way, divorced families become a kind of transactional family, but after giving the traditional model a try. The contract in these families comes after the breakup and is the result of legal intervention, which specifies the rights and obligations of parents to their child.

8. After the case of Baby M in New Jersey (decided in 1987, appealed in 1988), contracts prior to the birth of a child came into question under the jurisdiction of state law. In

Massachusetts, the 1998 Supreme Judicial Court case *R.R. v. M.H.* regarding surrogacy dictated that contracts made prior to the birth of a child are unenforceable. There is no legal precedent at this time regarding contracts for co-parenting. How the surrogacy ruling could be applicable, if at all, to other parenting arrangement is unclear.

9. Angie's child was three years old at the time of the first interview and eleven years old at the time of the last interview. Trish's daughter was eleven years old at the time of the last interview. Janica's two children were fourteen and sixteen years old during the last interview.

10. This balancing act of romance and motherhood is one performed by many divorced women. Social scientists have been focused on studying these women and their children during divorce and remarriage, ignoring for the most part the gray area in between. Where dating and child rearing overlap needs attention because the process by which men are accepted into newly formed families is unclear. Nelson (2006) explores single mothers and their shifting household arrangements, arguing that women work at keeping families "in motion."

## Chapter 8

1. I am more interested in this book in the various ways that mothers manage work and family than in a systematic look at mothers' social networks. The bulk of the detailed information I gathered primarily recorded child care arrangements, the crucial nexus that women must navigate as single mothers. See Hansen (2005), whose case studies of broader social network reveal that, despite socioeconomic differences, the desire to help raise children obligates kin. Hansen dispels the myth that only poor families rely upon others (including nonkin).

2. See Moen 2003, which argues that this is an outmoded model of work culture that does not meet the needs of today's employees.

3. Taking in boarders to supplement income was historically a tactic used by widows. While it is not new, it has been reinvented by these single mothers.

4. See Hertz 1999.

5. Jacobs and Gerson (2004) find that overworked Americans are concentrated among professionals and managers whose workweek hours have increased. The single mothers in this study who work in these sectors experience this same time squeeze; the pressure is heightened by their single-parent status. Jacobs and Gerson also find that there is a smaller, less affluent group of Americans who work overtime or more than one job and experience similar time pressures. A few women in this study fall into this latter group. In short, the time squeeze these women experience is as much about their professional location as it is about their single status.

6. See especially Williams 2001 and Moen 2003.

7. See Blair-Loy 2003 and Stone and Lovejoy 2004 on the reasons professional married women disrupt their careers. It is not that they want to return to a traditional family lifestyle; hostile work environments and other work-related factors are the primary reason. However, these women are elites in that they can financially afford to do so because they have husbands with large enough salaries of their own.

8. See especially Sered and Fernandopulle 2005, who offer a disturbing picture of uninsured American workers.

9. The vast majority of women in this study have pursued traditional career mobility for many years (see Hertz 1986 on the distinction between careers and jobs). Eighty-five percent of them have careers (though not all offer clear ladders for advancement, such as jobs in the helping professions, e.g. social work and education). The other 15 percent of the women fall into a second category, having always held jobs with little mobility and less flexibility (often doing secretarial, child care, or low-end service work). Since the women in this group, generally

having only a high school diploma, tend to work in occupations that pay an hourly wage, for the sake of distinction I label this group "hourly wage women."

10. Most chilling are the challenges faced by single mothers with less education. They are most likely to work a nonstandard work schedule and receive the lowest pay (Presser 2003). Working during nonstandard hours means that child care is difficult to arrange. Without the option of nighttime center-based care, women rely on neighbors and kin. Since these women are most likely to encounter a misfit between child care arrangements and work schedule, the work/family tension is all the more heightened.

11. Presser 2003.

12. For the hourly wage women in this study who piece together employment to support their family, being a good provider is often their first priority, and they delegate nurturance to trusted family members (Collins 1990; Segura 1994). This arrangement allows them to continue to work the long hours each week necessary to provide a semblance of a middle-class lifestyle. These women are borrowing an intergenerational model of child rearing from poorer women, without the assumption that grandparents are obligated to raise their children (Burton 1990; Stack 1974).

13. It remains unclear whether or not the same level of gift giving exists for the two-parent family. However, most of the women did tell me that their parents' generosity extended to other siblings or grandkids in their natal families, regardless of single parenthood status.

14. Wellman (1990) reviews the importance of immediate kin in what he calls the "core of personal community networks." Interestingly, one of the ways in which grandparents in this study maintain intensive relations with their daughters and grandchildren is through financial gifts, even more so than regular contact. Intergenerational financial support is a middle-class way of connecting with immediate kin.

15. These seventeen women are those who received strictly monetary additions to their income from parents or trusts. These gifts are usually used to cover the cost of child care. This does not include gifts from parents that went directly to the purchase of a house or the cost of adoption (friends' contributions were also sometimes instrumental in the latter). A few other women received onetime inheritances from relatives.

16. Hertz and Ferguson 1998.

17. Living with only kin, not even including extended kin, characterizes the idealized family. However, among other families in America, such as poor or immigrant families. these households are more fluid, comprising kin, extended kin, and even other families. See especially Kibria 1995 on Vietnamese immigrant families and Menjivar 1995 on other recent immigrants to California.

18. Proximity increases the likelihood that kin care for children (Hogan, Hao, and Parish 1990; Roschelle 1997). Fourteen women had kin, usually the maternal grandmother but sometimes the grandfather, who cared for the child during some of the baby and toddler years. The majority cared for the grandchild five days a week, with a nursery school supplement. But in a few cases grandparents took the child one or two days a week, with day care arrangements on the other days. Distinct from the parenting partners discussed in chapter 7, these grandparents do not have parental say in any way that is comparable to parents. They only provide child care, helping out while Mom works.

19. See Wrigley 1995, Macdonald 1998, and Hondageu-Sotelo 2001, which point out the social class and cultural conflicts between career mothers and those they hire to care for their children. While Wrigley emphasizes power differential in social class and citizenship status between employer and employees, which creates a clash of expectations, Macdonald and Hondageu-Sotelo focus on the symbolic ways in which nannies are expected to replace the mother, only to fade into the shadows upon her return. In all these studies, employers expect

carework to be both invisible and seamless, detectable only when careworkers are deficient, as defined by the employer.

20. Joy's phrase "only one pair of hands" is borrowed for the title of Hertz and Ferguson 1998.

21. From the perspective of the family day care provider, their work is an extension of their roles as women and mothers (see especially Fitz Gibbon 2001). They walk a fine line between being part of the market and part of the family, the difference being that between a job and a labor of love (Nelson 1990).

22. Cameron Macdonald (1998) coined this concept as one type of relationship women develop with nannies. These nannies are expected to act as extensions of the mom, who dictates every aspect of child care.

23. A testament to this unique relationship between single mothers and their child care providers is that few change providers. They prefer continuity of care, choosing to maintain relationships. For this reason, the vast majority of women who place their children in paid child care situations have their children in family care settings.

24. See Fitz Gibbon 2001, who argues that middle-class women often take advantage of the child care provider by not treating her as a serious paid person who is providing an important service to families. Macdonald (1998) also demonstrates how the nannies she studied are hardly treated as paid professionals. Instead, mothers guard their status as the child's mom by trying to dictate how the provider should do her job. The single mothers in this study tried instead to develop partnerships with their caregivers. They more readily admit that they are dependent on the people who care for their children.

## Chapter 9

1. See McLanahan and Sandefurt 1994, where it is argued that economic disadvantage may be partly responsible. Blankenhorn (1995: 45) reinforces that children of single mothers are at risk for not turning out as successful adults.

2. DeParle 2004. I read this article as a pitch for helping men make a new start as the Welfare Reform Act of 1996 was revisited. Kevion, a reformed ex-con, has become a responsible dad caring for his son despite the lack of social supports for his new model behavior as dad.

3. See especially Stacey 2000 for her critique of conservative views on the need for dads in families.

4. See Blankenhorn 1995 for an exaggerated but important conservative position on the politics of fathers; see Daniels 2000 for articles on both sides; see the final chapter of Townsend 2002 for an excellent and concise review of the literature on fatherhood; see Pleck 1997 for an examination of fatherhood and child development.

5. Townsend 2002 argues that fatherhood is embedded in a broader masculine script about what it means to be a man. There are four facets to fatherhood, he observes, including the idea that men endow children with opportunities and character. Townsend writes of "the continuing salience of paternal influence toward achievement, physical activity and competition" (p. 72). However, he does not say that only fathers or men bring this to families (and that women do not)—just that these expectations of fathers toward their children continue even if fathers today try to instill them without the authoritative voice their own fathers brought to family.

6. See especially Hansen 2005, which provides an in-depth look at men's involvement in child care in four families. She argues that men do provide both practical and emotional care of children, but rarely are nonkin included as part of each family's child care system. Female friends, though almost all are also mothers, are included in the construction of the cases

she compared. I am emphasizing the involvement of men who are not relatives, even though I mention male kin, in the lives of these children. Caregiving is only one of numerous ways that men might be involved in these children's lives.

7. See Blankenhorn 1995 for an extreme view on the crisis of a "fatherless America." While his arguments are provocative, Blankenhorn lays the fault at the feet of women, overestimating their intent to exclude men.

8. The single poor rural women that Nelson (2005) studied are willing to excuse men who do not do their share of practical tasks, giving as a "strategic explanation" that love overrides inequality in practical arrangements. This too might seem like a contradiction, but they are getting something emotional that is more important. Similarly, it is not that the women I studied need men to take their children to the ballpark; it is that there is something hard to pin down that the presence of men represents in children's lives.

9. The messages are everywhere in popular culture, but mostly the women give examples from TV and from schools and other institutional settings. It is impossible for a child to escape messages of gender stereotypes.

10. In William Goode's (1982) classic article titled "Why Men Resist," women seek out the power and privilege of men primarily in the labor force, where they are direct competitors, preferring to ignore that masculine power and privilege is inextricably linked to violence in its extreme form. To further complicate matters, men see themselves in coalition with wives, mothers, and daughters. They do not see themselves as dominating women; rather, Goode argues, they are protecting their women from other men. To take this a step further, social historian William H. Chafe (1977) argues that what keeps women segregated from each other is their ties to men of their same privilege, never having been united in a ghettoized existence. In this study, the tension with male privilege and women's continued ambivalence about the place of men in their children's lives are a result of this dynamic.

11. Barbara J. Risman and Kristen Myers (1997) interviewed children raised in self-identified feminist households as part of their broader study and found that children adopted their parents' egalitarian views, but outside the family they have to negotiate inconsistencies between what they learn at home (their ideological beliefs) and what they experience with their peers. These children develop an interesting rationalization of this disparity, explaining that while women and men are similar and equal, girls and boys are not. While I did not interview the children, mothers in this study can be seen as similarly rationalizing their mediation between what they teach at home and the lived experiences they expose their children to in the broader settings in which they place their children.

12. For a more in-depth discussion of the interplay between gendered socialization and sex difference in the creation of a sexist society, see Epstein 1988.

13. Mothers' conflation of gender and sexual identity as they raise their sons needs to be further explored and was not a part of this particular study. Some mothers' comments appear to express acceptance of the idea that masculinity and by extension male sexuality can only be learned from men. Therefore, single mothers must provide their sons with men lest they fail to provide adequate instruction in traditional masculinity and sexuality. For whatever reasons, it remains more problematic for boys to display traditionally feminine gender expressions such as crying in public than for girls to pick fistfights. The empirical indicator of broader gender expression begins even early: baby girls are easily dressed in blue, whereas boys are rarely swaddled in pink. From birth on, dominant culture remains more accepting of fluid expression of gender by girls than by boys. Mothers in this study are rarely exceptions.

14. See Lareau 2003: 275–78 for an excellent synopsis of the work of Pierre Bourdieu on social and cultural capital and their importance for social class. Her research explores how mothers groom children through their enrichment activities, further ensuring their children's class position.

15. The visibility that men experience as "token" teachers or nurses helps them in the workplace and, in our case, makes them attractive to mothers as leaders in children's daily lives. See Williams 1995, which finds that women experience a glass ceiling when entering a male-dominated occupation, while men often experience an escalator of opportunity, rising easily to the top in traditionally female fields of employment.

16. Fortunately, the self-selection of men into these female-dominated occupations may reinforce those men's nurturing abilities, making them especially appealing for women seeking to involve men in their children's lives. It is unknown whether heterosexual two-parent families are similarly requesting the male teacher for the children and whether the parents of sons and daughters are equally drawn to these male-led classrooms. As schools become less feminized, further research would shed light upon this shift.

17. Founded in 1904, the Big Brother/Big Sister programs targeted "at-risk youth," who often came through the courts and were poor children lacking appropriate parental models. This mentoring program has expanded beyond charities and court arrangements and is readily accessible to all those who apply. However, the demand means that receiving a Big Brother or Big Sister placement can take as long as a year or more.

18. "Big brothers" can remain part of these families for longer than the initial terms of the arrangement, while some children have had multiple "big brothers." These special friends and mentors, originally designated for at-risk children, have become acceptable and prevalent for middle-class children. Women report that these men develop important relationships to their children, maintained by frequent contact, a host of activities, and phone calls as children grow older. The strength of these ties between child and "big brother" often endures as the "big brothers" marry and have children of their own or even move from the area. These men are voluntarily choosing to engage in a quasi-familial relationship that is based purely on an emotional tie and which does not obligate them to the child in other ways (such as financial). These kinds of voluntary associations are important examples of ways families can incorporate other adults into everyday life.

19. Friendship is an understudied topic, even more so for adult friendships between men and women. For an eclectic look at friendship within community, see Lopata and Maines 1990 as well as Rubin 1986. See Lopata and Maines also for a summary of the early literature on friendship from a historical and theoretical perspective, focusing mainly on the symbolic interactionist and social psychological frameworks. Early community studies as well as the literature on utopian communities all include interesting material about friendship throughout the life cycle.

20. As discussed in chapter 2, when women debated whether to use a known or anonymous donor, the vast majority asked their male friends—relationships formed at various points in their lives and maintained—to be donors. The complicated piece of why many of the women rejected the men was that the men would not concede control. While women welcomed these men in their lives, they refused to allow the men to parent with them. Those women who did decide to make these close friends known donors may have become watchful over the relationship between the donor and child, but nonetheless, the donor was an uncle figure to the child and frequent visitor to the family, with the child understanding the genetic importance of this man.

21. Women are trying to avoid the inverse of what Lynn Davidman calls "motherloss." "Since the mother is seen by both her male and female children as the exemplar of womanhood, both male and female respondents felt that her loss shaped them into adults that lacked clarity about some aspect of their gender roles. . . . As the emotional center of her family, the maternal figure is seen as a model as well as a ready source about interpersonal, and in particular intimate, relationships" (Davidman 2000: 103). Even though her study is about the construction

of gender following the death of mothers, she is particularly interested in biological disruption in the lives of her respondents. Children in my study do not experience this kind of loss.

## Conclusion to Part III

1. DeVault (1991) argues that dinnertime is a good empirical indicator of visibility. Having dinner on the table is invoked as a symbol of being a good mother, but the meal entails not just the work of the preparing food but also invisible labor of all kinds. The mother must consciously orchestrate dinnertime, including food, conversation, and the overall experience.

2. Hertz 1986.

3. This is not the case for the few women who have parenting partners (as described in chapter 7). For these women, decisions about children are negotiated. For example, Trish has a weekly meeting with her child's two fathers to discuss weekly happenings and major decisions.

4. See Carrington 1999 for another example of how a culturally assaulted group portrays themselves using ideals to avoid further critique. His study of gay and lesbian families demonstrates how people are willing to go so far as to perpetuate myths such as an egalitarian division of labor in order to protect the image of group.

## Chapter 10

1. One of the most popular Web sites for pursuing contact with donors and donor siblings is www.donorsiblingregistry.com. As of December 2005, there were 6,604 people listed in the donor sibling registry, which has facilitated matches to more than 1,230 half siblings. Both of those figures are growing rapidly.

2. Not only coming from the families of single mothers by choice, the mother-child core is part of a long transition created initially from divorce in the U.S.

## Epilogue

1. Out of the sixty-five women in the sample, eight had been interviewed for the first time within the last three years. Because their interviews were so recent, they are not included in this epilogue. I tried to reach the remaining fifty-seven women in the winter of 2005 for a phone update and succeeded in speaking with forty-three of them (75 percent). Phone interviews lasted approximately an hour, and I took handwritten notes on a series of prepared questions.

2. Of the ten women who married or had a civil union, only three had more children with this new partner, and a fourth married the father of her first child.

3. Joy was one of ten women (15 percent) who had more than one child at the time of the first interview. Unlike Joy, most of this group had either adopted a sibling group or had birthed twins.

4. Ten women had more children; seven women had these children as single moms, through either adoption or donor-assisted insemination, including the use of donor eggs. The number of women having more children is likely to increase in the future, since the youngest should follow older women in having second children, particularly since the youngest women did not wait until the last minute to have their first child.

5. This is Sienna, also mentioned in chapter 7 as living a split life when she adopted her first daughter. Her boyfriend, who made clear he had no interest in becoming the child's dad, left when Sienna's first daughter was a toddler.

6. According to Jane Mattes, the founder of the Single Mothers by Choice (SMC) organization, established in 1981, having a second child as a single mother is "at the forefront of discussion on the SMC Web site in the past few years." She believes this to be a result of single mothers by choice becoming more "normalized." One of the forums on her Web site that discusses trying for a second child (the process is dubbed "T42") is very active. She reports, "Many women prefer to use the same route to motherhood the second time around and, if possible, even the same donor" (personal communication, September 9, 2005).

7. When discussing the intensity of the mother-child dyad, I am not judging the quality of this relationship between parent and child; rather, I am commenting upon how often women see additional family members as expanding the possibility of interactions. It is unclear whether the "dilution solution" is a rationalization for women's decisions or motivation for the decision itself. Regardless, size of family seems to matter.

8. By 2005, a total of thirty-two women had added an additional family member, either a partner or another child or both.

9. Simmel (1950) theorizes that the triad is the simplest structure in which the processes of group life are experienced and rehearsed for other forms of association.

10. See Gerstel and Zussman's 1999 insightful dialog about how their dyadic relationship changed when they became parents.

11. Thirty-two women (49 percent of the original sixty-five) had more than two members in their family. This includes additional children and parenting partners at the time of the first interview and second children and new partners (joined through marriage or civil union) at the time of the update. This figure could be higher given that the fifteen women I was unable to reach for an update could have added a second child or married. Further, this number leaves aside the women who by the time of the update were cohabiting, as well as the smaller group who had lived with a partner in the intervening years but since broken up by the time I talked with them.

12. The "economies of scale" in family formation, as Schnaiberg (1972) termed part of the decision couples make in adding additional numbers of children to their family, are about a calculation in cost and time of raising more children. The addition of a second child may be marginal for couples but is quite different for single mothers.

13. Seven women reported living with a partner, either full time or part of each week. But these women were careful not to lead their children to expect this person to become a second parent.

14. A few other women who had shorter relationships that did not work told me their children helped sabotage the romance. These children wanted a dad at younger ages but then as they grew older and their mom found romance, a man was competition for their mother's affection and time.

15. Hillary and her sons are the only family created using a known donor who have no contact with this man.

16. Questions about dads bubble up at different development ages. This needs to be studied further, but the following appears to be the preliminary pattern. Children in preschool and early grade school ask very concrete questions about absent fathers, as they are constantly confronted with the dilemma of drawing their families in school units on family. Mothers' responses vary, but all say, "You have a father somewhere" (some use the word *donor*), an answer that children parrot in the classroom. When older grade-school children push further, mothers often turn it on themselves, telling their children that maybe they would find one in the future, but it would have to be "a man that is good enough." Sometimes the children take on the search themselves, offering up everyone from the postman to the bus driver to the real estate agent. For children in middle school, the father issue generally fades and children's questions to their mother largely cease, though I imagine they still contemplate the question.

17. Only one woman reported that the lack of a dad was a major issue for her child—her son was embarrassed and refused to invite friends home, deeply hurting his mother. However, for the majority, the alternative nature of their family structure soon faded into the background.

18. The first figure given is the median income of the women in the update interview and those interviewed in the last four years (a total of fifty-two women). Their incomes ranged from under $20,000 to over $200,000, reflecting both varied occupations and number of days/hours employed. Some women whose salaries are given in the demographic appendix had their income change (increase or decrease) in the intervening years, notably due to career changes. The Massachusetts figure is from the U.S. Census Web site, "State Median Income by Family Size" (2004), using data from the 2004 American Community Survey (www.census.gov/hhes/www/income/medincsizeandstate.html).

19. Only five women had moved out of state; four of these had gotten married.

20. Education is also an important part of their children's middle-class citizenship, with private school not essential given the excellent public school systems in eastern Massachusetts. With only two exceptions, women placed their children in the public school system. As already noted, some made local moves to guarantee their children a place in relatively better schools.

21. Single middle-class mothers have not experienced the downward mobility described by Newman (1999) because they have fewer children than their parents. They talk of being able to afford the same experiences for their child as they had in childhood because they only have to pay for them once (or twice). Further, these women's foothold in the real estate market, perhaps unique to the economics of the present period, guards them from a significant downward slide. Both having fewer children and profitable home ownership keep these women and their children in the middle class. Intergenerational downward mobility is difficult to measure among these women, but it is something they fear, given dwindling savings and only one paycheck.

22. The youngest women in this study missed the opportunity to buy a home and are likely to experience a very different financial reality than their older counterparts. They pay the equivalent (if not more) of the older women's mortgage payment in monthly rent. It is clear even from this study that salary increases have not keep up with the exploding real estate market.

## Appendix 2

1. I have conducted a few second-round interviews with women I interviewed in the early part of the study to learn something about how their lives have changed since the first interview. I planned on contacting the women for an additional phone interview in the future so that I have longitudinal data on their lives and changes on the key topics. I also hoped that this would have given me more systematic information on how the images of fathers change over years and whether the dream of finding a partner who also becomes a co-parent materializes.

2. See Hertz 1986; Hertz and Charlton 1989; Hertz 1997.

3. See, for example, U.S. DHHS 1995.

4. There are no national data or small qualitative studies that include women who did not achieve pregnancies through donors. Reproductive histories should include these questions.

5. Glaser and Strauss 1967; Charmaz 2000.

6. Faith I. T. Ferguson, then a graduate student, and I discussed how to refine the sampling frame as we conducted the early interviews. I thank her for her involvement with this stage of the research. Faith conducted twenty-two of the interviews that became part of my sample.

7. These totals include the two women who successfully used two different routes to motherhood. They are counted in both categories because they told two different stories about their experiences with each route.

8. Redefining the initial questions that led to this study, I continued to interview additional single mothers through the year 2000. I returned to a few of the single mothers I had initially interviewed both for more details about their relationship histories and for an update on their children, employment, and relationships. To complete the interviews, I again interviewed a small group in 2003–2004. The stories of the first women and the later women I interviewed have not changed much. I note in the book when there are differences.

9. A few women did receive day care vouchers for their children. A larger group, regardless of income, either had no health insurance for themselves and their children or they had state-provided insurance for their children and none for themselves. This includes self-employed women who were contract workers or had private practices.

10. Median income for Massachusetts is $68,701, from the U.S. Census Web site "State Median Income by Family Size" (2004), using data from the 2004 American Community Survey.

11. Hertz 1995.

12. Reinharz 1992; DeVault 1996.

# REFERENCES

Agigian, Amy. 2004. *Baby Steps: How Lesbian Alternative Insemination Is Changing the World.* Middletown, CT: Wesleyan University Press.

Alpern, Kenneth D. 1992a. "Why Have Children? Meaning and Significance." Pp. 129–31 in *Ethics of Reproductive Technology,* edited by Kenneth Alpern. New York: Oxford University Press.

——. 1992b. "Genetic Puzzles and Stork Stories: On the Meaning and Significance." Pp. 147–69 in *Ethics of Reproductive Technology,* edited by Kenneth Alpern. New York: Oxford University Press.

Ambert, Anne-Marie. 1989. *Ex-Spouses and New Spouses: A Study of Relationships.* Greenwich, CT: JAI Press.

Bartholet, Elizabeth. 1999. *Nobody's Children: Abuse and Neglect, Foster Drift and the Adoption Alternative.* Boston: Beacon Press.

Bennis, Warren G., and Robert J. Thomas. 2002. *Geeks and Geezers: How Era, Values, and Defining Moments Shape Leaders.* Cambridge, MA: Harvard Business School Press.

Blair-Loy, Mary. 2003. *Competing Devotions: Career and Family Among Women Executives.* Cambridge, MA: Harvard University Press.

Blankenhorn, David. 1995. *Fatherless America: Confronting Our Most Urgent Social Problem.* New York: Basic Books.

Browne, F. W. Stella. 1917. "Women and Birth Control." In *Population and Birth-Control: A Symposium,* edited by Eden and Cedar Paul. New York: Critic and Guide. Available at http://homepages.primex.co.uk/~lesleyah/steltxts.html

Burawoy, Michael. 1979. *Manufacturing Consent: Changes in the Labor Process Under Monopoly Capitalism.* Chicago: University of Chicago Press.

Burguiere, André, Christiane Klapisch-Zuber, Martine Segalen, and Françoise Zonabend, editors. 1996. *A History of the Family,* 2 vols. Cambridge, MA: Belknap Press of Harvard University Press.

Burke, Kenneth. 1945. *A Grammar of Motives.* New York: Prentice Hall.

Burton, Linda. 1990. "Teenage Childbearing as an Alternative Life-Course Strategy in Multigenerational Black Families." *Human Nature* 1, 2: 123–43.

Carrington, Christopher. 1999. *No Place Like Home: Relationships and Family Life Among Lesbians and Gay Men*. Chicago: University of Chicago Press.

Chafe, William H. 1977. *Women and Equality: Changing Patterns in American Culture*. New York: Oxford University Press.

Charmaz, Kathy. 1995. "The Body, Identity, and Self: Adapting to Impairment." *Sociological Quarterly* 36: 657–80.

———. 2000. "Grounded Theory: Objectivist and Constructivist Methods." Pp. 509–35 in *Handbook of Qualitative Research*, 2nd ed., edited by Norman K. Denzin and Yvonna S. Lincoln. Thousand Oaks, CA: Sage Publications.

Cherlin, Andrew J. 2004. "The Deinstitutionalization of American Marriage." *Journal of Marriage and Family* 66, 4: 848–61.

Collins, Patricia Hill. 1990. *Black Feminist Thought: Knowledge, Consciousness and the Politics of Empowerment*. New York: Unwin Hyman/Routledge.

Cooley, Charles Horton. 1983 [1902]. *Human Nature and the Social Order*. New Brunswick, NJ: Transaction.

Coontz, Stephanie. 2005. *Marriage: A History*. New York: Viking.

Daniels, Cynthia R., editor. 2000. *Lost Fathers: The Politics of Fatherlessness in America*. London: Palgrave Macmillan.

Davidman, Lynn. 2000. *Motherloss*. Berkeley: University of California Press.

DeParle, Jason. 2004. "Raising Kevion." *New York Times Magazine*, August 22.

DeVault, Marjorie L. 1991. *Feeding the Family: The Social Organization of Caring as Gendered Work*. Chicago: University of Chicago Press.

———. 1996. "Talking Back to Sociology: Distinctive Contributions of Feminist Methodology." *Annual Review of Sociology* 22: 29–50.

Dowd, Nancy E. 1997. *In Defense of Single Parent Families*. New York: New York University Press.

Edin, Kathryn, and Maria Kefalas. 2005. *Promises I Can Keep: Why Poor Women Put Motherhood Before Marriage*. Berkeley: University of California Press.

Ehrensaft, Diane. 2000. "Alternatives to the Stork: Fatherhood Fantasies in Sperm Donor Families." *Studies in Gender and Sexuality* 1, 4: 371–97.

———. 2005. *Mommies, Daddies, Donors, Surrogates: Answering Tough Questions and Building Strong Families*. New York: Guilford Press.

Ellwood, David T., and Christopher Jencks. 2001. "The Spread of Single-Parent Families in the United States Since 1960." Cambridge, MA: John F. Kennedy School of Government, Harvard University.

Epstein, Cynthia Fuchs. 1988. *Deceptive Distinctions: Sex, Gender, and the Social Order*. New Haven: Yale University Press.

Evans, Karin. 2000. *The Lost Daughters of China*. New York: Penguin Putman.

Fischer, Claude S. 1982. *To Dwell Among Friends: Personal Networks in Town and City*. Chicago: University of Chicago Press.

Fitz Gibbon, Heather M. 2001. "From Baby-sitters to Childcare Providers: The Development of a Feminist Consciousness in Family Daycare Workers. Pp. 270–90 in *Working Families: The Transformation of the American Home*, edited by Rosanna Hertz and Nancy L. Marshall. Berkeley: University of California Press.

Fogg-Davis, Hawley. 2002. *The Ethics of Tranracial Adoption*. New York: Cornell University Press.

Furstenberg, Frank F., Jr., and J. Brooks-Gunn. 1995. "Fathering in the Inner City: Paternal Participation and Public Policy." Pp. 119–47 in *Fatherhood: Contemporary Theory, Research and Social Policy*, edited by W. Marsiglio. Thousand Oaks, CA: Sage Publications.

Furstenberg, Rochelle. 2005. "Family Matters: Israeli Single Orthodox Mothers." *Hadassah Magazine*, March, 12–19.

Garey, Anita Ilta. 1999. *Weaving Work and Motherhood*. Philadelphia: Temple University Press.

Garey, Anita Ilta, and Nicholas W. Townsend. 1996. "Kinship, Courtship, and Child Maintenance Law in Botswana." *Journal of Family and Economic Issues* 17, 2: 189–202.

Geen, Rob. 2003. "Who Will Adopt the Foster Care Children Left Behind?" Urban Institute. Available at http://www.urban.org/publications/310809.html.

Gerson, Kathleen. 1998. "Gender and the Future of the Family: Implications for the Post-industrial Workplace." Pp. 11–21 in *Challenges for Work and Family in the Twenty-First Century*, edited by Dana Vannoy and Paula J. Dubeck. New York: Aldine de Gruyter.

Gerstel, Naomi, and Robert J. Zussman. 1999. "A Conversation About Parenting." Pp. 61–68 in *Qualitative Sociology in Everyday Life*, edited by Barry Glassner and Rosanna Hertz. Thousand Oaks, CA: Sage Publications.

Gilman, Charlotte Perkins. 1979 [1915]. *Herland: A Lost Feminist Utopian Novel*. New York: Pantheon.

Glaser, Barney G., and Anselm L. Strauss. 1967. *The Discovery of Grounded Theory*. Chicago: Aldine.

Goffman, Erving. 1963. *Stigma: Notes on the Management of Spoiled Identity*. New York: Simon and Schuster.

Golden, Claudia. 2004. "The Long Road to the Fast Track: Career and Family." *Annals of the American Academy of Political and Social Sciences* 596: 20–35.

Goldman, Emma. 1969 [1906]. "The Tragedy of Woman's Emancipation." In *Anarchism and Other Essays*. New York: Dover.

Goode, William J. 1959. "The Theoretical Importance of Love." *American Sociological Review* 24: 38–47.

——. 1982. "Why Men Resist." Pp. 131–50 in *Rethinking the Family: Some Feminist Questions*, edited by Barrie Thorne and Marilyn Yalom. Boston: Northeastern University Press.

Gornick, Janet C., and Marcia K. Meyers. 2003. *Families That Work: Policies for Reconciling Parenthood and Employment*. New York: Russell Sage Foundation.

Grotevant, Harold D., and Ruth G. McRoy. 1998. *Openness and Adoption: Exploring Family Connections*. Thousand Oaks, CA: Sage Publications.

Hackstaff, Karla B. 2000. *Marriage in a Culture of Divorce*. Philadelphia: Temple University Press.

Hamilton, Brady E., Joyce A. Martin, and Paul D. Sutton. 2003. "Births: Preliminary Data for 2002." *National Vital Statistics Report* 51, 11: 1–20.

Hansen, Karen V. 2005. *Not-So-Nuclear Families: Class, Gender and Networks of Care*. New Brunswick, NJ: Rutgers University Press.

Hays, Sharon. 1996. *The Cultural Contradictions of Motherhood*. New Haven: Yale University Press.

——. 2003. *Flat Broke with Children: Women in the Age of Welfare Reform*. New York: Oxford University Press.

Hertz, Rosanna. 1986. *More Equal than Others: Women and Men in Dual-Career Marriages*. Berkeley: University of California Press.

——. 1995. "Separate but Simultaneous Interviewing of Husbands and Wives: Making Sense of Their Stories." *Qualitative Inquiry* 1, 4: 429–51.

——. 1997. "A Typology of Approaches to Childcare: The Centerpiece of Organizing Family Life for Dual-Earner Couples." *Journal of Family Issues* 18, 4: 355–85.

——. 1999. "Working to Place Family at the Center of Life: Dual-Earner and Single-Parent Strategies." *Annals of the American Academy of Political and Social Sciences* 562: 16–31.

——. 2002. "The Father as an Idea: A Challenge to Kinship Boundaries by Single Mothers." *Symbolic Interaction* 25, 1: 1–31.

Hertz, Rosanna, and Joy Charlton. 1989. "Making Family Under a Shiftwork Schedule: Air Force Security Guards and Their Wives." *Social Problems* 36, 5: 491–507.

Hertz, Rosanna, and Faith I. T. Ferguson. 1996. "Childcare Choices and Constraints in the United States: Social Class, Race and the Influence of Family Views." *Journal of Comparative Family Studies* 27, 2: 249–80.

——. 1998. "Only One Pair of Hands: Ways That Single Mothers Stretch Work and Family Resources." *Community, Work and Family* 1, 1: 13–37.

Hewlett, Sylvia Ann. 2002. *Creating a Life: Professional Women and the Quest for Children*. New York: Talk Miramax Books.

Hochschild, Arlie Russell. 1997. *The Time Bind: When Work Becomes Home and Home Becomes Work*. New York: Metropolitan Books.

——. 2001. "Eavesdropping Children, Adult Deals, and Cultures of Care." Pp. 340–53 in *Working Families: A Transformation of the American Home*, edited by Rosanna Hertz and Nancy L. Marshall. Berkeley: University of California Press.

Hochschild, Arlie Russell, with Anne Machung. 1989. *The Second Shift: Working Parents and the Revolution at Home*. New York: Viking.

Hogan, Dennis P., Ling-Zin Hao, and William L. Parish. 1990. "Race, Kin Networks and Assistance to Mother-Headed Families." *Social Forces* 68: 797–812.

Hondageu-Sotelo, Pierrette. 2001. *Doméstica: Immigrant Workers Cleaning and Caring in the Shadows of Affluence*. Berkeley: University of California Press.

Hood, Jane C. 2002. "The Power of Gametes Versus the Tyranny of Master Narratives: Commentary." *Symbolic Interaction* 25, 1: 33–39.

Hunter, James Davison. 1991. *Cultural Wars: The Struggle to Define America*. New York: Basic Books.

Jacobs, Jerry A., and Kathleen Gerson. 2004. *The Time Divide*. Cambridge, MA: Harvard University Press.

Janowitz, Tama. 1988. "Bringing Home Baby." Pp. 92–100 in *Wanting a Child*, edited by Jill Bialosky and Helen Schulman. New York: Farrar, Straus and Giroux.

Johnson, Kay. 2002. "Politics of International and Domestic Adoption in China." *Law and Society* 36, 2: 379–96.

Kahn, Susan Martha. 2000. *Reproducing Jews: A Cultural Account of Assisted Conception in Israel (Body, Commodity, Text)*. Durham, NC: Duke University Press.

Keillor, Garrison. 1995. *Lake Wobegon Days*. New York: Penguin Books.

Kibria, Nazli. 1995. *Family Tightrope*. Princeton, NJ: Princeton University Press.

——. 2002. *Becoming Asian-American: Second Generation Korean and American Identities*. Baltimore: John Hopkins University Press.

Kim, Queena Sook. 2003. "Adopters of Chinese Also Adopt Culture." *Wall Street Journal*, June 11.

Kunzel, Regina. 1995. *Fallen Women, Problem Girls: Unmarried Mothers and the Professionalization of Social Work, 1890–1945*. New Haven: Yale University Press.

Lareau, Annette. 2003. *Unequal Childhoods: Class, Race, and Family Life*. Berkeley: University of California Press.

Larossa, Ralph. 1997. *The Modernization of Fatherhood: The Social and Political History*. Chicago: University of Chicago Press.

Laslett, Peter, Karla Oosterveen, and Richard M. Smith. 1980. *Bastardy and Its Comparative History: Studies in the History of Illegitimacy and Marital Nonconformism in Britain, France, Germany, Sweden, North America, Jamaica, and Japan*. Cambridge, MA: Harvard University Press.

Leahy, Michael. 2005. "Family Vacation." *Washington Post Sunday Magazine*, June 19.

LeBlanc, Adrian. 2003. *Random Family: Love, Drugs, Trouble and Coming of Age in the Bronx.* New York: Scribner.

Lopata, Helena Znaniecka, and David R. Maines, editors. 1990. *Friendship in Context.* Greenwich, CT: JAI Press.

Ludtke, Melissa. 1997. *On Our Own.* New York: Random House.

Luker, Kristen. 1995. *Dubious Conceptions: The Myth of Teenage Pregnancy.* Cambridge, MA: Harvard University Press.

Lyotard, Jean-François. 1984 [1979]. *The Postmodern Condition: A Report on Knowledge.* Translated by Geoff Bennington and Brian Massumi. Volume 10 of Theory and History of Literature. Minneapolis: University of Minnesota Press.

Macdonald, Cameron. 1998. "Manufacturing Motherhood: The Shadow Work of Nannies or Au Pairs." *Qualitative Sociology* 21, 1: 25–53.

Maine, Sir Henry. 1986. *Ancient Law.* New York: Dorset Press.

Malinowski, Bronislaw. 1926. *Crime and Custom in Savage Society.* Boston: Rowman and Littlefield.

March, Karen. 2000. "Who Do I Look Like?: Gaining a Sense of Self-Authenticity Through the Physical Reflections of Others." *Symbolic Interaction* 23: 359–74.

Mattes, Jane. 1994. *Single Mothers by Choice: A Guidebook for Single Women Who Are Considering or Have Chosen Motherhood.* New York: Random House.

McLanahan, Sara, Irwin Garfinkel, Nancy Reichman, Julian Teitler, Marcia Carlson, and Christina Norland Audigier. 2003. *The Fragile Families and Child Well-being: Baseline National Report.* Princeton, NJ: Center for Research on Child Well-being, Princeton University.

McLanahan, Sarah, and Gary Sandefur. 1994. *Growing Up with a Single Parent: What Helps, What Hurts.* Cambridge, MA: Harvard University Press.

Mead, George Herbert. 1934. *Mind, Self and Society.* Chicago: University of Chicago Press.

Melosh, Barbara. 2002. *Strangers and Kin: The American Way of Adoption.* Cambridge, MA: Harvard University Press.

Menjivar, Cecilia. 1995. "Kinship Networks Among Immigrants: Lessons from Qualitative Comparative Work." *International Journal of Comparative Sociology* 36, 3–4: 219–314.

Miall, Charlene. 1986. "The Stigma of Involuntary Childlessness." *Social Problems* 33: 268–82.

———. 1987. "The Stigma of Adoptive Parent Status: Perceptions of Community Attitudes Toward Adoption and the Experience of Informal Sanctioning." *Family Relations* 36: 34–39.

———. 1989. "Authenticity and the Disclosure of the Information Preserve: The Case of Adoptive Parenthood." *Qualitative Sociology* 12: 279–302.

———. 1994. "Community Constructs of Involuntary Childlessness: Sympathy, Stigma, and Social Support." *Canadian Review of Sociology and Anthropology* 31, 4: 392–421.

Milkie, Melissa A., Marybeth J. Mattingly, Kei Nomaguchi, Suzanne M. Bianchi, and John P. Robinson. 2004. "The Time Squeeze: Parental Statuses and Feelings About Time with Children." *Journal of Marriage and Family* 66: 739–61.

Millman, Marcia. 1991. *Warm Hearts and Cold Cash: The Intimate Dynamics of Families and Money.* New York: Free Press.

Moen, Phyllis, editor. 2003. *It's About Time: Couples and Careers.* Ithaca: Cornell University Press.

Nelson, Margaret K. 1990. *Negotiating Care: The Experience of Family Day Care Providers.* Philadelphia: Temple University Press.

———. 2005. *The Social Economy of Single Motherhood: Raising Children in Rural America.* New York: Routledge.

———. 2006. "Single Mothers 'Do' Family." *Journal of Marriage and the Family*. In press.

Newman, Katherine S. 1999. *Falling from Grace: Downward Mobility in the Age of Affluence*. Berkeley: University of California Press.

Newman, Leslea. 1989. *Heather Has Two Mommies*. Los Angeles, CA: Alyson Publications.

Orenstein, Peggy. 1995. "Looking for a Donor to Call Dad." *New York Times Magazine*, June 18.

Pertman, Adam. 2000. *Adoption Nation*. New York: Basic Books.

Pleck, Joseph H. 1997. "Parental Involvement: Levels, Sources, and Consequences." Pp. 66–103 in *The Role of the Father in Child Development*, 3rd edition, edited by M. E. Lamb. New York: Wiley.

Plotz, David. 2005. *Genius Factory: The Curious History of the Nobel Prize Sperm Bank*. New York: Random House.

Porter, Bruce. 1993. "China's Market in Orphan Girls." *New York Times Magazine*, April 11.

Presser, Harriet B. 2003. *Working in a 24/7 Economy: Challenges for American Families*. New York: Russell Sage Foundation.

Quindlen, Anna. 2005. "The Good Enough Mother." *Newsweek*, February 21.

Reinharz, Shulamit, with Lynn Davidman. 1992. *Feminist Methods in Social Research*. New York: Oxford University Press.

Rich, Adrienne. 1980. "Compulsory Heterosexuality and Lesbian Existence." *Signs* 5: 621–61.

———. 2001. "Notes Toward a Politics of Location." Pp. 62–82 in *Arts of the Possible*. New York: W. W. Norton.

Richardson, Laurel. 1985. *The New Other Woman: Contemporary Single Women in Affairs with Married Men*. New York: Free Press.

Risman, Barbara J., and Kristen Myers. 1997. "As the Twig Is Bent: Children Reared in Feminist Households." *Qualitative Sociology* 20, 2: 229–52.

Robbins, Tom. 1990 [1971]. *Another Roadside Attraction*. New York: Bantam Books.

Romero, Mary, and Abigail J. Stewart, eds. 1999. *Women's Untold Stories: Breaking Silence, Talking Back, and Voicing Complexity*. New York: Routledge.

Roschelle, Anne R. 1997. *No More Kin: Exploring Race, Class, and Gender in Family Networks*. Thousand Oaks, CA: Sage Publications.

Rosen, Ruth. 2001. *The World Split Open: How the Modern Women's Movement Changed America*. New York: Penguin Books.

Rubin, Lillian Breslow. 1986. *Just Friends: The Role of Friendship in Our Lives*. New York: Harper Perennial.

———. 1994. *Families on the Faultline: America's Working Class Speaks About the Family, the Economy, Race, and Ethnicity*. New York: HarperCollins.

Sandelowski, Margarete. 1990. "Fault Lines: Infertility and Imperiled Sisterhood." *Feminist Studies* 16: 31–51.

Sassler, Sharon. 2004. "The Process of Entering into Cohabiting Unions." *Journal of Marriage and Family* 66, 2: 491–505.

Schmidt, Matthew, and Lisa Jean Moore. 1998. "Constructing a 'Good Catch,' Picking a Winner: the Development of Techno-Semen and the Deconstruction of the Monolithic Male," pp. 21–39 in *Syborg Babies: From Techno-Sex to Techno-Tots*, edited by Robbie Davis-Floyd and Joseph Dumit. New York and London: Routledge.

Schnaiberg, Allan. 1972. "The Concept and Measurement of Child Dependency: An Approach to Family Formation Analysis." *Population Studies* 27, 1: 69–84.

Schor, Juliet. 1991. *The Overworked American: The Unexpected Decline of Leisure*. New York: Basic Books.

Segura, Denise A. 1994. "Working at Motherhood: Chicano and Mexican Immigrant Mothers and Employment." Pp. 211–33 in *Mothering: Ideology, Experience and Agency*, edited by Evelyn Nakano Glenn, Grace Chang, and Linda Forcey. New York: Routledge.

Seltzer, Judith A. 2004. "Cohabitation in the United States and Britain: Demography, Kinship, and the Future." *Journal of Marriage and Family* 66, 4: 921–28.

Sered, Susan Starr, and Rushka Fernandopulle. 2005. *Uninsured in America: Life and Death in the Land of Opportunity*. Berkeley: University of California Press.

Shanley, Mary Lyndon. 2001. *Making Babies, Making Families*. Boston, MA: Beacon Press.

Simmel, Georg. 1950 [1908]. "On the Significance of Numbers for Social Life." Pp. 87–104 in *The Sociology of Georg Simmel*, translated and edited with an introduction by Kurt H. Wolff. Glencoe, IL: Free Press.

——. 1978. *The Philosophy of Money*. Translated by Tom Bottomore and David Frisby. Boston: Routledge & Kegan Paul.

Simon, Rita J., and Howard Altstein. 2000. *Adoption Across Borders: Serving the Children in Transracial and Intercountry Adoptions*. Lanham, MD: Rowman and Littlefield.

Skolnick, Arlene. 2003. "Confessions of an Accidental Sociologist." Pp. 115–26 in *Our Studies, Ourselves*, edited by Barry Glassner and Rosanna Hertz. New York: Oxford University Press.

Stacey, Judith. 1990. *Brave New Families*. New York: Basic Books.

——. 2000. "DaDa-ism in the 90s: Getting Past Baby-Talk About Fatherlessness." Pp. 51–84 in *Lost Fathers: The Politics of Fatherlessness in America*, edited by Cynthia R. Daniels. London: Palgrave Macmillan.

Stack, Carol B. 1974. *All Our Kin: Strategies for Survival in a Black Community*. New York: Harper and Row.

Stein, Arlene. 1997. *Sex and Sensibilities: Stories of a Lesbian Generation*. Berkeley: University of California Press.

Stein, Rob. 2005. "Found on the Web, with DNA: A Boy's Father." *Washington Post*, November 13.

Stone, Pamela, and Meg Lovejoy. 2004. "Fast-tracked Women and the Choice to Stay Home." In "Mommies and Daddies on the Fast Track: Success of Parents in Demanding Professions," edited by Jerry A. Jacobs and Janice Fanning Madden: *Annals of the American Academy of Political and Social Science* 596: 62–83.

Strauss, Anselm L. 1959. *Mirrors and Masks: The Search for Identity*. Glencoe, IL: Free Press.

Townsend, Nicholas W. 2002. *The Package Deal Dad: Marriage, Work and Fatherhood in Men's Lives*. Philadelphia: Temple University Press.

Turner, Victor. 1967. *Ritual Process*. Chicago: Aldine.

U.S. Census Bureau. 2003. "Estimated Median Age at First Marriage, by Sex: 1890 to Present." Available at www.census.gov/population/socdemo/hh-fam/tabMS-2.pdf.

——. 2005. "Fertility of American Women: June 2004." Current Population Reports P20-555. Washington, DC: U.S. Department of Commerce, Economics and Statistics Administration, U.S. Census Bureau.

U.S. Department of Health and Human Services. 1995. *Report to Congress on Out-of-Wedlock Childbearing*. Publication number PHS 95-1257. Hyattsville, MD: U.S. Government Printing Office.

Uttal, Lynet. 2002. *Making Care Work: Employed Mothers in the New Childcare Market*. New Brunswick, NJ: Rutgers University Press.

Van Gennep, Arnold. 1960. *Rites of Passage*. Chicago: University of Chicago Press.

Ventura, Stephanie J., Christine A. Bachrach, Laura Hill, Kelleen Kaye, Pamela Holcomb, and Elisa Koff. 1995. "The Demography of Out-of-Wedlock Childbearing." Pp. 1–133 in *Report to Congress on Out-of-Wedlock Childbearing*. Publication number PHS 95-1257. Hyattsville, MD: U.S. Government Printing Office.

Walker, Karen. 1995. "Always There for Me": Friendship Patterns and Expectations Among Middle- and Working-Class Men and Women." *Sociological Forum* 10, 2: 273–96.

Waller, Maureen R. 2002. *My Baby's Father: Unmarried Parents and Parental Responsibility.* Ithaca: Cornell University Press.

Waters, Mary. 1990. *Ethnic Options: Choosing Ethnic Identities in America.* Berkeley: University of California Press.

Weeks, Jeffrey, Brian Heaphy, and Catherine Donovan. 2001. *Same Sex Intimacies: Families of Choice and Other Experiments.* London: Routledge.

Weger, Katarina. 1997. *Adoption, Identity, and Kinship: The Debate over Sealed Birth Records.* New Haven: Yale University Press.

———. 1998. "Adoption and Kinships." Pp. 41–51 in *Families in the U.S.: Kinship and Domestic Politics*, edited by Karen V. Hansen and Anita Ilta Garey. Philadelphia: Temple University Press.

Wellman, Barry. 1990. "The Place of Kin Folk in Personal Community Networks." *Marriage and Family Review* 15, 1–2: 195–228.

———. 1999. "The Network Community: An Introduction." Pp. 1–47 in *Networks in the Global Village: Life in Contemporary Villages*, edited by Barry Wellman. Boulder, CO: Westview.

Weston, Kath. 1991. *Families We Choose: Lesbian.* New York: Columbia University Press.

Williams, Christine L. 1995. *Still a Man's World: Men Who Do Women's Work.* Berkeley: University of California Press.

Williams, Joan C. 2001. *Unbending Gender: Why Family and Work Conflicts and What to Do About It.* New York: Oxford University Press.

Williams, Joan C., and Holly Cohen Cooper. 2004. "The Public Policy of Motherhood." *Journal of Social Issues* 60, 4: 849–65.

Williams, Patricia J. 2004. *Open House: Of Family, Friends, Food, Piano Lessons and the Search for a Room of My Own.* New York: Farrar, Straus, and Giroux.

Winch, Robert F. 1954. "The Theory of Complementary Needs in Mate Selection: An Analytic and Descriptive Study." *American Sociological Review* 19: 341–49.

Wolfe, Alan. 1998. *One Nation, After All.* New York: Viking Penguin.

Wrigley, Julia. 1995. *Other People's Children.* New York, Basic Books.

Zelizer, Viviana A. 1985. *Pricing the Priceless Child: The Changing Social Value of Children.* New York: Basic Books.

# INDEX